MW00780320

The Coast Guard
at War

The Coast Guard at War

Vietnam, 1965–1975

Alex Larzelere

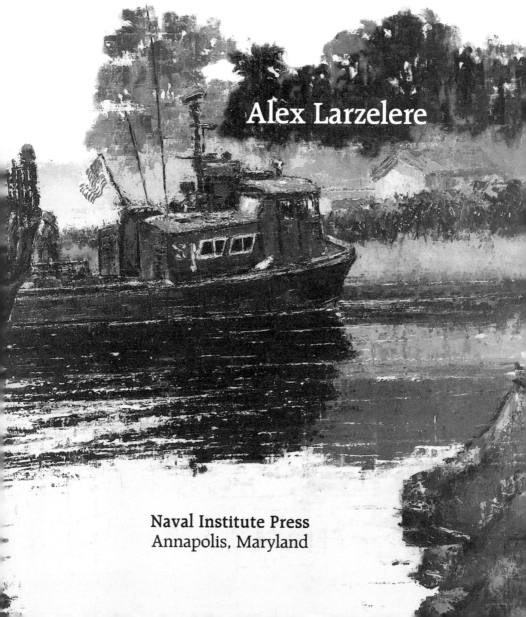

Naval Institute Press
Annapolis, Maryland

Library of Congress Cataloging-in-Publication Data

Larzelere, Alex, 1936–
    The Coast Guard at war : Vietnam, 1965–1975 / Alex Larzelere.
       p.   cm.
    Includes bibliographical references and index.
    ISBN 1-55750-529-2 (alk. paper)
    1. Vietnamese Conflict, 1961–1975—Naval operations, American.
2. United States. Coast Guard—History—Vietnamese Conflict,
1961–1975.   I. Title.
    DS558.7.L37   1997
    959.704'345—dc20   96-32130

Printed in the United States of America on acid-free paper ∞

04 03 02 01 00 99 98   9 8 7 6 5 4 3 2

All photographs are from the files of the U.S. Coast Guard Historian.

Frontispiece: USCGC Point Banks *(WPB 82327) and a Navy Swift boat enter a canal in the Mekong delta on a SEA LORDS mission.*

*To all Coast Guardsmen who served in Vietnam
and the families who waited for them*

Contents

Illustrations

Maps

Photographs

Foreword

Of the hundreds of books written about the Vietnam War, this study is the first to address the Coast Guard's significant role in the conflict. The author makes a valuable contribution to the history of the war by documenting the participation of the nation's smallest armed force. The extent of Coast Guard operations in Vietnam is largely unknown to the general public. Cutters and patrol boats conducted coastal interdiction operations with the Navy, port security and explosive loading detachments served with the Army, and Coast Guard helicopter pilots flew combat rescue missions with the Air Force. Coast Guard units and personnel supported merchant vessel operations and provided and maintained navigation support for U.S. shipping. They built and manned a chain of electronic navigation stations in Vietnam and Thailand that provided highly accurate positioning data to support U.S. air operations.

As a young lieutenant, the author commanded two patrol boats with the first Coast Guard units deployed to Vietnam; his writing reflects the emotion and immediacy of someone who was there. His depictions of actions and events are based on personal experiences, exhaustive research, and scores of interviews with Coast Guardsmen who served in Vietnam. Personal interviews give the writing a sense of reality and drama. The book is fast-paced and highly readable, with combat actions narrated in vivid detail.

While the book will appeal to the audience with interest in the Coast Guard, the Vietnam War, and military operations in general, it is important, as well, as a scholarly work. Carefully researched and thoroughly documented, it will serve as a valuable reference for serious historians of the future.

The Honorable Brent Scowcroft

Preface

Countless waves have washed the shores of Vietnam since Americans fought and died in that far-off land. The world has changed. Old wounds have healed. New wounds have opened. And, for many, memories of America's longest war have been relegated to a few pages in a history book. But, for those who were there, the memory will never fade. This book was written for the Coast Guardsmen who served in Vietnam. What they did—and how they did it—should not be forgotten.

I first saw Vietnam from the bridge of an 82-foot Coast Guard cutter on 29 July 1965. Our division of nine patrol boats had pounded into 15-foot seas for five days after leaving Subic Bay in the Philippines. The mountainous heights of Con Son Island, rising out of the stormy sea, were a welcome sight.

After anchoring in a sheltered cove, we saw our first Vietnamese: curious, dark-eyed children came to the sandy shore to stare and giggle at the strange-looking foreigners.

In the year that followed, I commanded *Point Comfort* and then *Point Banks*, completing my Vietnam duty as operations officer for Coast Guard Division 11. I sailed thousands of miles, in all kinds of weather, patrolling the Vietnamese coast and islands in the Gulf of Thailand. The cutters I commanded engaged in combat operations, exchanging fire with the Viet Cong. We routinely provided illumination and gunfire support for U.S. and South Vietnamese units under attack. We boarded every junk we could, checking for arms and munitions being smuggled to the Viet Cong.

A year after returning to the United States, I was selected to attend the Naval War College. As a student, I had an opportunity to study the causes and consequences of the ongoing war. Ten years later, I was again given an opportunity to analyze the conflict as a student at the National War College.

To write this book, I relied heavily on records and material held by the Coast Guard historian and the Navy historical center. In conducting my research, I inventoried and cataloged the contents of thirty-five file boxes of Vietnam material stored at Coast Guard headquarters. Ten file boxes of Coast Guard Vietnam material at the Navy historical center—correspondence, communications, and unit diaries—had not yet been declassified. I gained access to these records under the Freedom of Information Act.

While Coast Guard and Navy historical records were excellent and provided an abundance of data to document events, they lacked a sense of what it was like to be in Vietnam. My personal experience was limited to one geographical area, one operation, and one time span. To understand and appreciate what really happened in other areas and at other times, I knew I had to talk to the people who were there. I had to hear what it was like from the men who were on-scene, doing the jobs and facing the dangers. To accomplish this, I selected seventy-five individuals—officers and enlisted men—to interview. They told me about their experiences in tape-recorded, hour-long conversations.

Narratives, describing combat actions and operations, are representative of the types of events that occurred throughout the ten years the Coast Guard was in Vietnam. Unfortunately, I could not include all the significant actions and operations Coast Guardsmen were involved in; that would have been impossible. I placed a heavy emphasis on the initial deployments of Coast Guard units and the withdrawal from Vietnam; these transitional phases of the Coast Guard had the greatest historical significance. In no way was this emphasis intended to diminish the importance of the service's operations in the interim.

In expressing appreciation for assistance with the book, I first extend my gratitude to the Coast Guard Vietnam veterans I interviewed. They were all willing and enthusiastic, and my discussions with them were informative and candid. While they could not always remember exact dates or names of places—those details were contained in record materials—their recollections of events were excellent and their recall improved as interviews progressed. Many of the men I interviewed sent me personal records and files to help with my research. This book could not have been written without their cooperation.

I am grateful to Dr. Robert M. Browning, Coast Guard historian, and his assistant, Mr. Scott Price, for their help. They gave me unlimited access to Coast Guard Vietnam materials. At the Navy historical center, Mr. Bernard Cavalcante, Mrs. Kathy Lloyd, and Ms. Gina Akers assisted and encouraged me during my numerous visits to the center. Two fellow writers, Ms. Brie Combs and Mr. John Grady, read my work while in progress; their critical comments were invaluable and greatly appreciated. And, I of course thank the most important person—my wife, Sallie. Her patient confidence and encouragement over the past three years gave me the inspiration to complete the project.

Chronology

1965

16 February	South Vietnamese Air Force sinks North Vietnamese coastal freighter at Vung Ro Bay, South Vietnam. South Vietnamese troops find a hundred tons of arms and ammunition in caches ashore.
16 April	Navy Secretary Nitze asks Treasury Secretary Fowler about the availability of Coast Guard coastal patrol boats.
29 April	Defense Secretary McNamara and Treasury Secretary Fowler send joint memorandum to President Johnson, who initials approval, committing Coast Guard to service in Vietnam under operational control of U.S. Navy.
27 May	Coast Guard commissions Squadron One at Coast Guard Base Government Island, Alameda, Calif.
12 June	Squadron One reports to commander, Seventh Fleet for duty with Vietnam Patrol Force.
17 June	First 82-foot cutters arrive at Subic Bay, the Philippines.
10 July	Squadron One divides into Division 11 and Division 12.
20 July	Eight cutters of Division 12 arrive at Danang, Vietnam.
24 July	USCGC *Point Orient* exchanges fire with Viet Cong ashore. First cutter in combat since World War II.
30 July	Navy activates Coastal Surveillance Force Task Force, CTF 115 (Market Time).
1 August	Nine cutters of Division 11 arrive at An Thoi, Vietnam. Surveillance patrols commence in Gulf of Thailand.
4 August	U.S. Military Assistance Command Vietnam requests Coast Guard to conduct port security survey of South Vietnamese ports.

19 September	USCGC *Point Glover* and USCGC *Point Marone* engage hostile junks in separate night actions.
29 October	Navy requests nine additional cutters for coastal patrols.
15 November	Naval advisory group assigns commander, Coast Guard Squadron One, additional duty as senior naval advisor to Vietnamese Navy's fourth coastal zone commander.
12 December	Coast Guard commissions Division 13 at Subic Bay.
13 December	Department of Defense requests Coast Guard to construct long-range electronic navigation stations (LORAN-C) to provide accurate navigation for air strikes over North and South Vietnam.
15 December	Coast Guard assigns captain to naval advisory group in Saigon to command Squadron One and serve as Coast Guard advisor.

1966

17 February	U.S. Military Assistance Command Vietnam requests two Coast Guard explosive loading detachments for deployment to Vietnam.
22 February	Nine cutters of Division 13 arrive at Cat Lo, Vietnam, and commence surveillance operations along coast and in Delta.
1 April	Navy establishes Naval Forces Vietnam to replace naval advisory group.
22 April	First Coast Guard buoy tender, USCGC *Planetree,* deploys to Vietnam to set tanker moorings along South Vietnam's coast.
10 May	USCGC *Point Grey* engages and forces North Vietnamese infiltration trawler aground on Ca Mau peninsula.
3 June	Two Coast Guard explosive loading detachments arrive at Saigon to serve as advisors to U.S. Army Vietnam.
21 June	USCGC *Point League* detects, engages, and forces North Vietnamese arms trawler aground south of Co Chien river.

8 August	Coast Guard's Southeast Asia LORAN-C stations begin transmitting.
11 August	U.S. Air Force jets attack USCGC *Point Welcome* patrolling near DMZ. First Coast Guardsmen are killed in action.
15 October	Coast Guard Port Security and Waterways Detail arrives to assist U.S. Army's 1st Logistical Command.
28 October	Operation Tight Reign LORAN-C chain is fully operational.
3 December	Coast Guard marine inspector arrives in Vietnam to serve as shipping advisor to Navy's Military Sea Transportation Service.
18 December	Coast Guard aids to navigation team arrives in Vietnam to assess navigation requirements.

1967

1 January	USCGC *Point Gammon* and two USN Swift boats destroy North Vietnamese trawler off Ca Mau peninsula, south of Bassac river.
11 January	Coast Guard establishes Coast Guard Activities Vietnam.
14 February	Navy requests five Coast Guard high-endurance cutters for Market Time patrols.
14 March	USCGC *Point Ellis* and Navy units engage and destroy North Vietnamese trawler at Cape Batangan, south of Danang.
31 March	Coast Guard signs memorandum of agreement with Air Force for exchange of pilots. Coast Guard pilots are trained to fly rescue missions behind enemy lines with Air Force's Jolly Green Giants.
24 April	Coast Guard establishes Squadron Three at Pearl Harbor, Hawaii.
4 May	Squadron Three, with five 311-foot high-endurance cutters, reports to commander Seventh Fleet for duty.
10 May	Squadron Three arrives at Subic Bay and is designated Task Unit 70.8.6.

15 May	Squadron Three cutters commence Market Time patrols off Vietnam.
15 July	USCGC *Point Orient* engages and destroys trawler off Chu Lai.
27 August	U.S. Navy requests Coast Guard to install and maintain aids to navigation until South Vietnam can assume responsibility.
31 August	Naval Support Activity Da Nang requests explosive loading detachment.
1 October	Navy destroyers and Coast Guard high-endurance cutters combine to form Task Unit 70.8.5. Navy designates commander Coast Guard Squadron Three as task unit commander.

1968

31 January	North Vietnamese and Viet Cong launch Tet offensive, attacking cities and towns throughout South Vietnam.
1 March	USCGC *Androscoggin,* USCGC *Point Welcome,* USCGC *Point Grey,* and two USN Swifts destroy trawler bringing arms to support North Vietnam's Tet offensive. USCGC *Winona* destroys arms trawler off Ca Mau peninsula.
3 April	Coast Guard pilots report for duty with Air Force's 37th aero rescue and recovery squadron (ARRS), Danang.
1 July	Coast Guard establishes merchant marine detail at U.S. Embassy, Saigon.

1969

3 February	Vietnamese Navy crews begin reporting aboard 82-foot cutters for training.
16 May	First cutters, USCGC *Point Garnet* and USCGC *Point League,* are turned over to Vietnamese Navy at ceremony in Saigon. USN destroyers withdraw from Market Time. Squadron Three's five high-endurance cutters remain on patrol.

1 June	Coast Guard accelerates transfer of 82-foot cutters to South Vietnamese Navy.
5 June	Coast Guard Division 11 is disestablished. South Vietnamese Navy takes over operations in Gulf of Thailand. Cutters are transferred to Division 13.

1970

10 March	Coast Guard and Navy sign joint letter of agreement for turnover of high-endurance cutters to South Vietnamese Navy.
16 March	Division 12 turns over its last 82-foot cutter to Vietnamese Navy and is disestablished.
22 May	Army transfers Coast Guard Port Security and Waterway Detail from 1st Logistical Command to headquarters, U.S. Army Vietnam.
2 July	Coast Guard reduces Squadron Three to four high-endurance cutters.
15 August	Coast Guard transfers last two 82-foot cutters, USCGC *Point Marone* and USCGC *Point Cypress,* to the Vietnamese Navy and disestablishes Division 13. Coast Guard Activities Vietnam and Squadron One disestablished. A new unit, Senior Coast Guard Officer Vietnam, is created to manage remaining Coast Guard activities in Vietnam.
21 November	USCGC *Rush,* USCGC *Sherman,* and USS *Endurance* destroy North Vietnamese infiltration trawler off Ca Mau peninsula.

1971

1 January	Coast Guard turns over USCGC *Yakutat* and USCGC *Bering Strait* to Vietnamese Navy in Saigon, reducing Squadron Three to two cutters.
11 April	USCGC *Rush,* USCGC *Morgenthau,* and USS *Antelope* engage and sink 150-foot North Vietnamese infiltration trawler off Ganh Hao river.
21 December	Coast Guard turns over USCGC *Castle Rock* and USCGC *Cook Inlet* to Vietnamese Navy.

1972

31 January   Coast Guard disestablishes Squadron Three.

5 May   Buoy tender *Basswood* completes final aids to navigation deployment and departs Vietnam.

9 May   Coast Guard transfers an additional three 311-foot high-endurance cutters to U.S. Navy at Guam for delivery to Vietnamese Navy.

1 November   Coast Guard disestablishes last explosive loading detachment, completing turnover of explosive handling operations to Vietnamese Army Ordnance Command.

30 November   Air Force transfers 37th ARRS helicopters and personnel from Vietnam to Thailand for duty with 40th ARRS at Nakhon Phanom.

1973

22 January   Coast Guard disestablishes LORAN-C Stations Tan My and Con Son as Coast Guard manned-military units. Coast Guard Southeast Asia section continues to support two civilian-manned LORAN-C stations in Vietnam and three Coast Guard-manned LORAN-C stations in Thailand.

27 January   United States, South Vietnam, and North Vietnam formally agree to a cease-fire in Paris. Coast Guard aids to navigation advisory role to South Vietnam's navigation directorate ends.

30 January   Coast Guard disestablishes Port Security and Waterways Detail.

7 February   Merchant marine detail, Saigon, transfers to Southeast Asia section for administrative control.

11 February   Coast Guard disestablishes Senior Coast Guard Officer Vietnam.

29 March   Last U.S. troops leave Vietnam.

1 April   Last U.S. prisoner of war released.

1 May   Coast Guard disestablishes merchant marine detail, Saigon.

5 May   Last Coast Guardsman leaves Vietnam.

14 July   Last Coast Guard pilots flying rescue missions with Jolly Green Giants in Vietnam depart 40th ARRS, Nakhon Phanom, Thailand.

1975

19 March   North Vietnamese launch major offensive. Tan My LORAN-C Station evacuated.

29 April   Air America helicopter evacuates Con Son LORAN-C Station.

30 April   South Vietnam surrenders.

3 October   Coast Guard disestablishes remaining Southeast Asia LORAN-C stations.

The **Coast Guard**
at **War**

1

Arms from the Sea

Although there have been numerous unconfirmed reports of sea infiltration in the past, none of these have been verified. The event at Vung Ro Bay, however, is considered to be proof positive that sea infiltration is occurring and raises the strong possibility that at least a portion of the unconfirmed reports of the past were, in fact, true. Sea infiltration into RVN [Republic of Vietnam] is now proved.

Vice Adm. Paul P. Blackburn, Jr., USN, Commander, Seventh Fleet
14 March 1965

Vung Ro Bay

On 16 February 1965, 1st Lt. James S. Bowers, U.S. Army, was at the controls of an HU-1B Iroquois medical evacuation helicopter, flying south over Phu Yen province. Bad weather forced the pilot to divert from his inland route and fly along the coast. When he crossed over Vung Ro Bay, 235 miles north of Saigon, he sighted an odd-shaped little island that appeared to be moving. It was 1030 when he circled for a closer look and discovered a 130-foot coastal freighter in a small bay; the ship was camouflaged with trees and bushes. He immediately reported his sighting to the senior U.S. naval advisor, Second Coastal District, at Nha Trang. The information was relayed to Lt. Cdr. Ho Van Ky Thoai, coastal district commander for the Vietnamese Navy (VNN); who confirmed that no friendly vessels were in the area. When a flight of South Vietnamese Air Force A-1 Skyraiders approached the area to investigate, they received machine-gun fire from hills surrounding the bay. The Skyraiders attacked and sank the ship, leaving her just under the surface of the shallow bay.[1]

The next day, a VNN ship arrived at 1430. LSM (landing ship, medium) *Tien Giang* (HQ 405), with a Vietnamese Seal team aboard, attempted to enter the bay to salvage the ship, but was driven back by heavy machine-gun fire from Viet Cong positions ashore. On 18 February 1965, PCE (escort) *Chi Lang II* (HQ 08) joined *Tien Giang*. Together, the ships entered the bay without resistance. After pounding suspected Viet Cong positions with 3-inch and 20mm fire, they withdrew. Later the same day, PC (submarine chaser) *Tuy Dong* (HQ 04) arrived on-scene. That night, *Tien Giang* sailed to Dai Lanh and returned with a company of South Vietnamese special forces. At 0800 the next morning, the three ships attempted to enter the narrow cove, but were forced back by heavy gunfire. After bombarding the beach and surrounding hills, the ships successfully entered the bay on their third attempt and landed troops at 1100. Four hours later, the shore area around the sunken ship was secured.[2]

The reason for the Viet Cong's strong resistance became evident when the troops entered the jungle beyond the beach. In an area the size of three football fields, they found caches containing a hundred tons of weapons, ammunition, and medical supplies. The amount of weapons and ammunition removed by the Viet Cong before South Vietnamese troops finally landed never will be known. Weapons captured included recoilless rifles, dual-purpose machine guns, antitank rockets, heavy mortars, mines, thousands of Russian- and Chinese-made submachine guns and carbines, and more than a million rounds of ammunition.[3]

When U.S. Navy and Vietnamese Seals dove on the ship, they found official North Vietnamese Army and Navy documents aboard, as well as a newspaper from Haiphong, North Vietnam, dated 23 January 1965. The discovery of the ship and the arms caches erased any doubt that North Vietnam was delivering massive amounts of war material to the Viet Cong.[4]

Four years before the discovery at Vung Ro Bay, shipment of war material in support of spreading communist insurgencies in Southeast Asia had become a matter of concern for the United States. Increasingly, overt insurgency activity in South Vietnam caused U.S. military leaders to take a hard look at the situation. A May 1961 interdepartmental task force report recommended that U.S. Navy ships and Vietnamese paramilitary Junk Force vessels begin patrol-

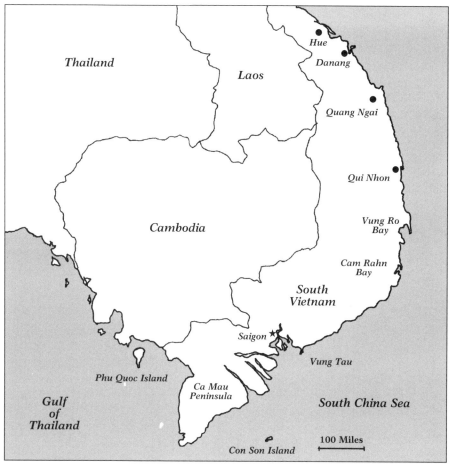

South Vietnam

ing coastal waters to prevent supplies from reaching insurgents. The report recommended that patrols cover South Vietnamese waters in the Gulf of Thailand and the South China Sea, from the Cambodian border to the mouth of the Mekong river.

After evaluating what Navy ships were available for recommended patrols, Adm. Wallace M. Beakley, deputy chief of naval operations for fleet operations and readiness, recommended that 185-foot PCEs and coastal mine sweepers (MSCs) be used. Admiral Beakley recognized that for the mission the ships were "not ideally suited because of speed and draft limitations. But, they are the best available to handle the shallow waters around Vietnam." No immediate action, however, was taken to respond to the task force's recommendation.[5]

Viet Cong military activity continued to escalate during 1961. Fears that insurgents were being supported with arms and ammunition smuggled in by sea increased. To assess the extent of infiltration from the north, the U.S. Navy established a barrier patrol along the 17th parallel separating North and South Vietnam. On completing an exercise in the Gulf of Thailand, five 165-foot ocean minesweepers (MSOs) of Minesweeping Division 73 were deployed for the patrol. On 22 December 1961, a "fixed barrier" was established along a line five miles south of the 17th parallel. The patrol extended from eight to thirty miles offshore. MSOs maintained the barrier with the Vietnamese Navy; two VNN ships and two or three USN ships patrolled continuously. U.S. ships were limited, however, in what they could do. They were not authorized to stop and board suspicious vessels, for example, but had to guide their Vietnamese counterparts to suspects and then stand by while VNN personnel boarded and searched.[6]

On 17 February 1962, the minesweeper division was relieved by five 306-foot ocean escorts (DEs) of Escort Division 72. During their two months of patrolling, Division 73 MSOs did not intercept any ships attempting to infiltrate arms or personnel. But, the MSO Division's summary stated, "to date 52 contacts have turned north upon sighting patrol and have escaped interception." While some senior naval officers questioned the value of continuing the patrol, Secretary of Defense Robert S. McNamara was impressed by the potential deterrent effect of the barrier, and the operation continued.[7]

The recommendation for a patrol in the Gulf of Thailand also was implemented in 1962. On 27 February, escorts USS *Wiseman* (DE 677) and USS *Walton* (DE 361) arrived in the Gulf and began a two-week trial patrol with VNN vessels. Unfortunately, the U.S. ships also were limited in what they could accomplish. South Vietnam and Cambodia both claimed offshore islands along the border, creating a sensitive international situation. At the request of the U.S. State Department, U.S. Navy ships were ordered not to patrol near contested border islands. Shallow coastal waters in the Gulf of Thailand further diminished the effectiveness of patrols; it was impossible for deeper-draft ships to operate close enough to shore to reach coastal traffic. Border and coastal areas—precise locations where coastal infiltration was most likely to occur—were only patrolled sporadically by VNN ships and Junk Force craft. USN ships were relegated to randomly patrolling a north-south line, in open waters 35 miles west of the coast. Their mission was to detect suspicious ships approaching from seaward. When the initial two-week trial period ended, the Gulf patrol was extended at the request of the South Vietnamese.[8]

In the spring of 1962, the Navy evaluated the overall effectiveness of combined USN–VNN patrols. Vice Adm. William A. Schoech, commander Seventh Fleet, concluded, "To date there has been no concrete evidence of massive or even significant infiltration." With no conclusive evidence of infiltration, Adm. John H. Sides, Pacific Fleet commander, recommended that patrols be ended. Adm. Harry D. Felt, commander in chief, Pacific, feared that ending both patrols at the same time would have a negative impact on South Vietnamese morale. He stopped the Gulf of Thailand patrol on 21 May 1962, and continued the 17th parallel patrol until 1 August 1962.[9]

After these patrols ended, no U.S. Navy ships were assigned for anti-infiltration duty. Instead, the United States concentrated on improving VNN capability to meet potential threats. Increased support—in the form of Navy advisors—expanded greatly during 1963. By the end of the year, 742 U.S. Navy personnel were in Vietnam. Navy advisors were assigned to VNN commands, including Sea Force ships, River Force groups, and Coastal Force divisions. Ships received by Sea Force from the U.S. Navy included two LSMs; three landing ships, tank (LSTs); a gasoline barge, self-propelled (YOG); and twelve mine-sweeping launches (MLMs). The first of ten new 100-foot motor gunboats (PGMs) was delivered to the Sea Force in 1963. Coastal Force, or Junk Force as it was commonly called, increased from 80 to 644 junks. The strength of Sea Force and River Force increased to 50 patrol ships and 208 amphibious and riverine vessels. During the period from 1962 to 1964, VNN manpower increased rapidly—Sea Force increased from 3,200 to 6,200 officers and enlisted men; and the Junk Force went from 800 men to a force of 3,900 military and paramilitary personnel.[10]

Despite significant increases in personnel and resources, the ability of South Vietnam's navy to effectively detect and counter infiltration of war material remained questionable; the VNN lacked aggressive leadership. On average, less than half of Sea Force ships and only 40 percent of junks were reported ready for operations—USN advisors believed that even this figure may have been overly optimistic. Despite urgings of U.S. advisors, VNN officers showed little will or ability to conduct sustained patrol operations.

The shocking discovery at Vung Ro Bay in February 1965 had a sobering impact on U.S. military leadership. Vice Adm. Paul P. Blackburn, Jr., commander Seventh Fleet, said Vung Ro Bay was conclusive proof that arms were being smuggled by sea to the Viet Cong. Gen. William C. Westmoreland, commander of the U.S. Military Assistance Command, Vietnam, concurred with Admiral Blackburn's assessment, and called for a conference to plan a combined USN–VNN patrol effort. The conference, which included representatives of commander in chief, Pacific; commander in chief, Pacific Fleet; and the Vietnamese Navy, met on 3 March 1965 to develop concepts for patrol operations. The conference determined that there were two principal infiltration threats: junks moving material along the coast, and trawler-sized vessels bringing large shipments in from sea. Conference representatives decided that the best patrol tactic was for VNN vessels to respond to coastal junk threats, and for the U.S. Navy to defense against trawler threats with ship and aircraft patrols.[11]

The concept for patrol operations was quickly approved by the Joint Chiefs of Staff, and the USN destroyers USS *Higbee* (DD 806) and USS *Black* (DD 666) began patrolling on 11 March 1965. On 15 March, President Lyndon B. Johnson gave formal approval for patrol operations and Vice Admiral Blackburn activated Vietnam Patrol Force, Task Force 71. By the end of the month, a USN force of ten Seventh Fleet ships, four destroyers and six minesweepers, was engaged in patrolling. The surface force was supported with aerial reconnaissance by four Navy SP-2H Neptune aircraft, operating out of Tan Son Nhut airport, and carrier-based A-1H Skyraiders. This small force had the enormous assignment of patrolling not only the 17th parallel but offshore waters along 1,200 miles of coastline. An estimated 35,000 junks and vessels routinely plied coastal waters.[12]

Success of inshore operations was totally dependent on the effectiveness of VNN patrols. USN destroyers and ocean minesweepers, with their deep drafts, could not operate in coastal waters. Continuing South Vietnamese prohibitions against U.S. ships stopping, boarding, and searching vessels further limited the usefulness of destroyers and minesweepers in defending against smuggling by trawler-sized ships. Essentially, U.S. ships and planes were used as radar platforms for detecting suspicious contacts and vectoring (guiding) VNN units, when available, to them.

After Vung Ro Bay, the United States realized that naval participation in inshore operations, beyond advising, was necessary to prevent arms and munitions from reaching the Viet Cong. Adm. Thomas H. Moorer, commander in chief, Pacific Fleet, said, "It is clear that our national policy towards SVN [South Vietnam] is shifting from one in which we attempted to maintain an advisory image in SVN to one of active and overt U.S. participation."[13]

With the anticipation of more direct involvement in coastal surveillance and interdiction, the U.S. Navy began looking for vessels better suited for the mission. In early April 1965, Adm. David L. McDonald, chief of naval operations, met with Adm. Edwin J. Roland, Coast Guard commandant. Admiral McDonald said he was looking for smaller vessels for coastal patrol duties in South Vietnam. He said no such vessels were readily available in the Navy, and it was going to take time to get construction going to build the type of vessel such patrols needed. He asked Admiral Roland if the Coast Guard had any leftover 83-footers from World War II; McDonald remembered 83-foot patrol boats doing rescue work off Normandy during the World War II invasion of Europe. Roland told him the older wooden cutters had all been replaced with modern 95-foot and 82-foot steel-hulled patrol boats. Roland also told him the new cutters were well suited for coastal missions and a number probably could be made available on short notice.[14]

Once a source for coastal patrol vessels was known, events moved rapidly. On 16 April 1965, Paul H. Nitze, secretary of the navy, sent a letter to Henry W. Fowler, secretary of the treasury, formally asking about the availability of Coast Guard cutters for Vietnam. The letter said, in part:

> At the present time, Seventh Fleet units are being employed to prevent sea infiltration into South Vietnam. However, we find such ships suffer major disadvantages in conducting patrols against shallow-draft junks. We are therefore attempting to locate a source of more suitable patrol craft. Such characteristics as high speed, shallow draft, sea-keeping ability, radar and communication equipment are important considerations.

In investigating possible sources of suitable craft it occurred to us the Coast Guard may have some patrol craft available which the Navy Department may be able to use.

I would very much appreciate being informed of such patrol craft as may be suitable and as may be made available to the Department of the Navy to assist in this very important mission.[15]

Fowler replied that the Coast Guard had 82-foot WPBs (patrol boats) and 40-foot UTBs (utility boats) that could be used. On 19 April, arrangements were made for Coast Guard representatives to meet with representatives of the commander in chief, Pacific Fleet, to discuss the use of Coast Guard cutters.

After confirming the number of cutters and crews available for the mission, and discussing additional armament and necessary modifications, a joint Defense Department–Treasury Department "Memorandum For The President" was prepared, proposing that "U.S. Coast Guard operating forces assist U.S. Naval Forces in preventing sea infiltration by the communists into South Vietnam." The memorandum explained:

A conference between representatives of the Treasury/Department of Defense has established that the U.S. Coast Guard has operating forces which are well suited to the mission. . . . They are equipped and trained to prevent sea infiltration. . . . In view of the counter sea infiltration mission assigned the U.S. Navy and the availability of U.S. Coast Guard forces it is requested that you approve the Treasury Department assignment of Coast Guard craft to assist the Department of the Navy. . . .[16]

The memorandum was signed by Treasury Secretary Fowler and Secretary of Defense McNamara. President Johnson approved the proposal, initialing the memorandum on the day it was received at the White House. On 29 April 1965, the president committed the U.S. Coast Guard to service in Vietnam under the operational control of the U.S. Navy.

2

Squadron One Deploys

*The Coast Guard, in response to the request of the Secretary of
the Navy, is providing a squadron of 82' patrol craft for
immediate deployment to Viet Nam. . . . When the assembly of
personnel and equipment enables the designated Squadron
Commander to function as a command, COMWESTAREA
shall establish COGARDRONONE. . . . When appropriate,
direct the commander, Coast Guard Squadron No. One to
CHOP to CINCPACFLT and to carry out such tasks as are
assigned by competent authority.*

Vice Adm. W.D. Shields, USCG, Acting Commandant

"You're Going to Vietnam"

USCGC *Point Banks* (WPB 82327) approached the bulkhead at
Coast Guard Base Woods Hole, Mass. Senior Chief Boatswain's Mate
Bernard C. Webber, at the controls, backed the engines. When the cutter's port bow neared the bulkhead, a seaman jumped ashore with
number one line and dropped the bight over a cleat. The first-class
boatswain's mate payed out ten feet of slack through the chock and
secured the line on the bitts. Webber twisted against number one,
bringing the 82-footer alongside, against the camel. Remaining mooring lines were put ashore. The crew felt a sense of relief as the
engines rumbled to a halt—it had been a long two-week patrol.
Stormy weather did not break until the morning of 29 April 1965, the
last day of patrol. Once mooring lines were doubled up, the crew
turned to, squaring away the cutter for pre-liberty inspection. Webber
intended to grant his seven-man crew maximum liberty; only a security watch would remain aboard.[1]

While the cleanup was in progress, a message arrived from First Coast Guard District headquarters, directing *Point Banks* to "Proceed to Coast Guard Base Boston to receive a new Boston Whaler." Webber shook his head and reached for the phone. He called the duty officer at district headquarters and said, "There's no reason you can't put a boat like that on a truck and send it down to Woods Hole. What's the deal, making me bring a cutter eighty miles to Boston just to pick up a boat? We just got in off patrol. You're messing up my crew's liberty." The duty officer interrupted, "Senior chief, those are your orders. Proceed to Boston, immediately."

Webber canceled liberty, finished taking on fuel and water, and got under way for Boston; by now, the seas were calm. *Point Banks* sailed north through Buzzard's Bay, transitted the Cape Cod Canal, and made her way along the coast to Boston. The base was nearly deserted when *Banks* tied up at 1915. Webber and two of his crew were in the pilot-house getting the mooring message out, stowing charts, and finishing deck log entries, when a Coast Guard lieutenant came down the pier. The officer called to one of the men on deck, asking for Senior Chief Webber.

When Webber stepped out of the pilothouse, the lieutenant looked up and said, "Listen, senior chief, they want you to put on your dress blues and be prepared to meet the press."

"What for, sir?"

"Haven't you heard?"

"Heard what?"

The lieutenant smiled. "Well, you fellows are going to Vietnam."

Webber looked down at him. "You've got to be kidding."

"No. You're going to Vietnam. So get yourself and your crew into dress blues and get ready to meet the press."

Webber immediately went to a telephone on the base and called his wife. "You better sit down," he said. "I was just told we're going to Vietnam. I thought I ought to let you know before somebody else did."

Webber already had orders to retire from the Coast Guard on 1 September 1965. When he found out his cutter and crew were going to Vietnam, he requested that his retirement orders be canceled. At 0800 the next morning, *Point Banks* arrived at Bromfield Shipyard in East Boston for predeployment maintenance and modifications. The cutter was hauled out of the water and worked on for the next ten days. All machinery was checked and outstanding repairs were completed. A unique "piggyback" gun mount, recently designed by the Coast Guard, was installed on the bow. The mount combined a trigger-fired 81mm mortar and a .50-caliber machine gun. Ammunition storage lockers were modified for 81mm rounds and bow lifelines were lowered to provide clearance for the direct-fire mortar. Mounts for four .50-caliber machine guns were installed aft and sound-powered phone circuits were run to all guns. Two extra bunks were installed in the officer in charge's cabin and an extra bunk was put in petty officer berthing. The cutter's 16-foot boat was replaced with a 14-foot Boston Whaler skiff. When Webber was not checking progress of yard work, he finished reports, closed out files, and transferred classified publications. When the shipyard work was finished, *Point Banks* returned to Woods Hole to offload supplies and equipment.

The crew remained in Woods Hole overnight and then sailed for New York in the morning. *Point Banks* entered New York harbor on 18 May and moored at Coast Guard Base St. George, Staten Island. After Webber signed over custody of the vessel at the base, he and his crew took their gear and reported to Third District Coast Guard headquarters in Manhattan, where they were issued travel orders to Coast Guard Base Alameda, Calif. Webber told the personnel officer processing their orders, "We really haven't even had a chance to explain to our families what's going on here." He argued his case and managed to get the crew's group orders amended to allow travel to California by way of Boston. After a brief two-day liberty at home, the crew assembled at Logan Airport in Boston and boarded a plane for California.

Point Banks was loaded aboard the 564-foot United States Lines freighter SS *Pioneer Mist* at Navy Supply Center Bayonne, N.J., on 21 May 1965. She and three WPBs from the New York area were shipped as deck cargo to the Philippines. Two crewmen from each cutter were assigned to travel with the vessels to look after them during sealift.

In 1965, Capt. Elmo R. Zumwalt, Jr., USN, was executive assistant to Secretary of the Navy Nitze. As the Vietnam conflict intensified, Zumwalt participated in a fact-finding trip to South Vietnam to get a firsthand look at the situation. During the trip, the vulnerability of the largely unprotected coast to infiltration of war material to the Viet Cong became obvious. Navy ships patrolling offshore were not able to monitor or control inshore coastal traffic. When Zumwalt returned from the trip, he called his National War College classmate, Coast

Coast Guard cutters Point Orient, Point Lomas, Point Young, and Point Caution are loaded aboard SS Aloha State in New Orleans for shipment to Subic Bay, the Philippines.

Guard Capt. William F. Cass, who at the time was assistant chief of operations for roles and missions at Coast Guard headquarters. Informally, Zumwalt asked him about the availability of Coast Guard patrol boats for use in Vietnam. At about the same time, similar questions were asked by the Navy through the Coast Guard's CNO liaison officer at the Pentagon. Both inquiries were welcomed by the Coast Guard. Cass said, "Admiral Roland [Coast Guard commandant] felt we had capability that should be used. When it first came up, he was about to go to Europe for an IMCO [International Maritime Consultative Organization] conference. He called me in and said, 'I'm very interested in seeing the Coast Guard get involved in supporting the Navy.'" During the Korean war, the Coast Guard had only a minor role. With the Vietnam effort expanding, there were strong feelings in the Coast Guard that its military readiness capability should be used.[2]

In response to queries, the Coast Guard decided that 82-foot Point-class patrol boats (WPBs) would be best suited for the mission. While they were not as fast as the larger 95-foot Cape-class cutters, and, with smaller crews, had less capability, they were considered the best choice, because they were newer, and, with only two main engines, compared with four in the Cape-class cutters, were easier to maintain. Types and manufacture of main propulsion and auxiliary machinery were more consistent throughout the Point class, easing logistic and support requirements. Air conditioning was an important bonus for the 82-footers, considering Southeast Asia's climate and the fact that crews had to live aboard, both on and off patrol. Use of Coast Guard 40-foot utility boats for coastal work was considered, but they were rejected, because they were not designed to operate offshore, had no radar, and lacked messing and berthing facilities.

The Coast Guard next determined which cutters could be deployed. Search-and-rescue coverage requirements in the United States, and alternatives for providing coverage, were determining factors. Seventeen of the Coast Guard's forty 82-foot WPBs and crews were ultimately identified for transfer to the Navy. During initial planning, information about possible deployment was tightly controlled, with a minimum number of people involved.[3]

James A. Reed, assistant secretary of the treasury, and Captain Cass then went to a meeting at the office of the CNO to discuss use of cutters in Vietnam. Cass said, "We got into quite a discussion. There was resentment on the part of some Navy officers. They didn't want the

Coast Guard there [in Vietnam]. One senior admiral said, 'They're just boats. You can only run a boat 10 or 20 percent of the time.' I pointed out that we would run them two-thirds of the time. To the Navy, they were just boats. But, to us they were small ships. They had quarters aboard and were self-sustaining. Then they said, 'It will take forever to get them [cutters and crews] out there.' I said, 'We'll have them ready in thirty days and we'll send the cutters out on ships.' It was quite a discussion." The meeting concluded with the Navy deciding to request the cutters.[4]

Cass and Capt. Cornelius G. Houtsma, chief of the naval engineering division at Coast Guard headquarters, flew out to Hawaii to discuss deployment with the Navy. They took part in a conference at Commander in Chief Pacific Fleet on 23 April 1965. At the meeting were representatives from the CNO; CINCPAC; CINCPAC FLEET, Commander Service Force, Pacific; and Naval Advisory Group, Military Assistance Command, Vietnam. The meeting finalized the type and number of cutters to be provided and developed plans for employment and support.[5]

As a result of the meeting, a joint Coast Guard-Navy agreement was prepared. Cass said, "It was a very simple agreement. It said what the Coast Guard would furnish, what the Navy would furnish, and who would pay for what. Since we were already budgeted for personnel costs, Coast Guard continued to fund that. The Navy said it would pick up the cost of transportation for WPBs and crews. And it would provide the floating base, fuel, ammo, and that kind of support." The Coast Guard provided the squadron staff and prepared cutters and crews for deployment. The agreement was officially signed for the Navy by Victor M. Longstreet, assistant secretary of the navy (financial management), on 2 July 1965, and for the Coast Guard by Rear Adm. P. E. Trimble, chief of staff, on 8 July 1965.[6]

Cdr. James A. Hodgman, the Coast Guard's liaison officer to the CNO in 1965, was involved in discussions about using cutters from the beginning. When the decision was made to deploy patrol boats, Commander Hodgman volunteered to command the squadron. The Coast Guard's office of operations was reluctant to release him from his Pentagon assignment, but his experience as CNO Liaison and familiarity with Navy procedures made him a logical choice for the command. Capt. William B. Ellis, Hodgman's World War II destroyer escort division commander, was deputy chief of the office of personnel at the time, and supported Hodgman's request for the assignment. Lt. Cdr. Richard J. Knapp was named squadron chief staff officer. Hodgman said, "Half an hour after I got selected, Dick Knapp called and said, 'I want to go—in any capacity.'" Lt. Cdr. William E. Lehr, assigned to naval engineering in the Third District, was selected by the office of engineering to be squadron engineer officer.[7]

The crew for a Point-class patrol boat in the United States was eight enlisted men, with a master chief boatswain's mate as officer in charge. For Vietnam, the personnel allowance was changed to include two officers—a lieutenant as commanding officer and a lieutenant (jg) or ensign as executive officer. When asked why the allowance was changed, Cass said, "The feeling was that the presence of an officer was needed for the job of stopping and boarding vessels. We thought there should be a little more seniority." The two seamen in the crew were replaced by petty officers—a second-class gunner's mate to maintain the additional armament and a third-class electronics technician to keep the increased electronic gear operating.

As planning progressed, officers from officer personnel division (PO) in headquarters were called in to meet with Rear Adm. George A. Knudsen, chief, office of personnel. Lt. Stanley J. Walden, assignment officer for deck watch officers through the grade of lieutenant, recalled, "We were told what was going to happen in general. The Navy wanted 82-footers. And they wanted them fast." PO had three weeks to screen and select officers, and issue orders to augment the crews of the patrol boats.[8]

Walden said fitness reports for all officers being considered were reviewed and a minimum score set for selection; any adverse comment in the remarks section was disqualifying. All prospective commanding officers had to have commanded a 95-foot WPB previously. Walden said, "Another criterion was all volunteers. Nobody was to be assigned without volunteering." Since planning for manning the squadron was done in secret—with no opportunity to solicit for volunteers—this criterion meant that not objecting to the orders was the same as volunteering. Walden said, "During the whole experience, I never ever heard one man say, 'I don't want to go.' And, after the word got out, I had people pleading to go."[9]

PO made initial selections, which were reviewed by a senior screening group. Walden said, "They wanted to make sure we sent the very best." After DOD issued its press release on the deployment on Thursday, 29 April 1965, Coast Guard headquarters began issuing orders. Walden said, "There were some very upset commanding officers. We were taking good people away from them." Orders, directing officers to report for duty in California in two to three weeks, arrived at field units without warning.

The 311-foot USCGC *Unimak* (WHEC 379) was such a unit.

"Hereby Detached Immediately"

Unimak took in her mooring lines and got underway from Yorktown, Va., on Friday morning, 30 April 1965. A class of officer candidates from the Coast Guard's Reserve Training Center was aboard for a two-week training cruise. Announcement of Coast Guard 82-foot patrol boats and crews going to Vietnam was a popular topic at the evening meal in the wardroom.

Lt. Alex Larzelere, the cutter's navigator, remained on the bridge to fix the ship's position before going below to eat. Arriving late to the meal, he sat at a side table with the ensigns. When the junior officers asked him if he thought he would get orders to Vietnam, Larzelere said, "No way!" He went on to explain why: "First of all, there are no billets for officers on 82-footers. Second, press releases said crews were specially trained. And finally, I've already got orders. I take command of Group Cape May in three weeks. Do you know how hard it would be to start changing orders now?" Satisfied with the logic of his explanation, the conversation changed to other subjects.

The next morning, Larzelere was standing the four-to-eight watch with his Coast Guard Academy classmate, Lt. Jon C. Uithol, an instructor at the Officer Candidate School. Uithol was training center officer on watch. Just after reveille, the cutter's executive officer, Lt. Cdr. Gilbert P. Sherburne, came onto the bridge and said, "Alex, I'll relieve you of the deck. I want you to go down to radio. There's a message coming in you'll be interested in."

When Larzelere went into radio central, the radioman was at the typewriter, recording a message he was receiving in code through earphones. Larzelere looked over the radioman's shoulder and read, "For LT Alexander R. Larzelere. Hereby detached immediately. Proceed and report CG Base Government Island Alameda for further assignment to Republic of Vietnam. . . ." The radioman continued to clack away at the typewriter, putting down travel order numbers and other administrative details. Larzelere looked back at the message to check the reporting date. "Report no later than 2400, 24 May 1965. . . ." He shook his head and thought, "At sea with less than three weeks to report."

Larzelere returned to the bridge to resume his watch. When he went out on the wing of the bridge, his classmate was scanning the horizon with binoculars. Larzelere leaned against the spray shield and said, "Jon, I just got orders to Vietnam."

Uithol lowered his binoculars. "You're joking?"

"No. I'm serious. I've got to report to Alameda on the twenty-fifth."

The corners of Uithol's mouth curled into a grin. "Don't worry, we'll write. And, we'll send you cookies, too."

Just then, the radioman appeared on the bridge and asked, "Is there a Lieutenant U-I-T-H-O-L here?"

Uithol turned and said, "I'm Lieutenant Uithol."

"Your orders are coming in now, sir," the radioman said.

Larzelere laughed so hard, he almost fell over the side.

Later that morning, in Cape May, N.J., *Unimak*'s home port, Sallie Larzelere got a call from another one of her husband's classmates. He was stationed at the recruit training center and also had received orders to Vietnam.

"Sallie, this is Rex Henderson. I know Al's at sea, so I'll give you a hand if you need help arranging shipment of your household effects."

She said, "Thanks, Rex, but we don't have to move. Alex is going to command the group here."

Henderson paused and then said, "You mean you haven't heard?"

She replied, "Heard what?" and the phone went dead.

Lt. Cdr. Louis H. Mense was chief of enlisted assignments in the enlisted personnel division at headquarters in April 1965. Mense said, "Captain Clark, the Division Chief, was called to a 1630 meeting up in operations. I went with him. At the meeting, we were told we [Coast Guard] were going to send seventeen cutters to Vietnam. They said the deployment was classified and under no circumstances were civilians to participate in the planning." Because the branch kept all enlisted assignment data on a huge status board in the office, military personnel making deployment assignments had to wait until civilian clerical staff went home each day at 1630 before beginning work.

Mense said, "I personally called the various chiefs of personnel divisions in the districts and told them, 'Unless there is a very, very good reason, the crew that is on there [selected WPBs] will go.' Without putting it in writing, I told them, 'If you have a qualified volunteer and want to do a swap, you can.'" He said the objective was to minimize problems for cutters once deployed.[10]

Gunner's mates and electronics technicians were selected by headquarters and did not necessarily come from the same districts as the WPBs to which they were assigned. As far as volunteers, Mense said, "They might not have been volunteers initially, but they certainly weren't unwilling to go. Results in that respect were much better than some anticipated. . . . The Coast Guard has a long tradition of 'You are invited and will attend.'" Same as with officers, once news of deployment was released, enlisted assignment branch was swamped with volunteers. Four spare crews, officers and enlisted, also were selected and prepared for deployment with the squadron.

Officers and men reported to Coast Guard Base Alameda in four groups for processing and training; they began arriving 17 May 1965. Staff and repair force personnel assigned to group four did not receive the training given to WPB crews; they arrived last and, after processing, departed first for the Philippines. The first three groups spent a month on the west coast undergoing training. No effort was made during training to combine officers with specific enlisted crews.[11]

On 27 May 1965, 131 of the squadron's 250 personnel formed up at the waterfront of Base Alameda. The men wore service dress uniforms—officers in khakis and enlisted men in blues. The rest of Squadron One was away at training. From aboard USCGC *Point Comfort*, one of the 82-foot WPBs being deployed to Vietnam, Rear Adm. Christopher C. Knapp, commander western area, ordered Squadron One placed in commission at 1000.[12]

While all three groups did not receive identical training, the programs were basically the same. A week was spent at Navy Amphibious Base Coronado and Marine Corps Camp Pendleton in southern California for briefings and small-arms instruction and training. A second week, by far the most difficult, was devoted to survival and prisoner-of-war training. When crews returned to Base Alameda, they received firefighting and damage-control training at Navy facilities on Treasure Island. The armory at Base Alameda provided weapon training with Thompson submachine guns, .45-caliber pistols, M-1 carbines,

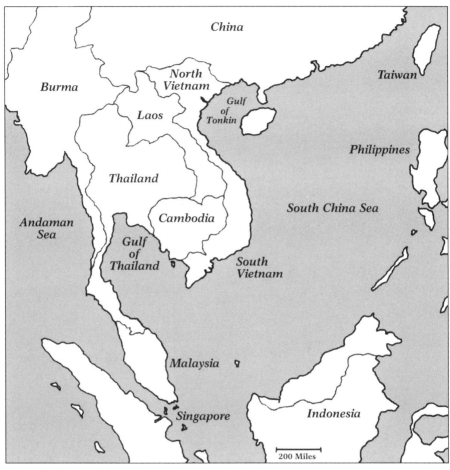

Southeast Asia

AR-15 rifles, and .50-caliber and .30-caliber machine guns; live firing was done at the range at Camp Parks, Calif. Coast Guard ship training detachment 5 was brought in to provide refresher training in radar navigation, maneuvering board (relative motion problems), radio procedures, visual signaling, and gunnery training on the 81mm mortar. Mortar and machine-gun crews received additional training separately at the Camp Pendleton range. C-130 aircraft from Coast Guard Air Station San Francisco transported personnel between training locations.[13]

SERE (survival, evasion, resistance, and escape) training was provided in California's Sierra-Nevada mountains and on Whidbey Island in Washington. Most enlisted personnel, below the rank of chief petty officer, went through SERE training at the Marine Corps Mountain Warfare School, Pickle Meadows, Calif. Officers and chief petty officers were given cold-weather training with the Navy at Whidbey Island Naval Air Station—unusual training for troops heading for Southeast Asia. The deployment took place so rapidly, the squadron had to settle for the best training available, at the time.

During the Navy course, the men learned to make sleeping bags from parachutes and snowshoes from parachute shrouds. During weeklong courses, which involved going for days with only weeds, clams, and an occasional snake to eat, instructors stressed that the primary objective was not teaching specifics of survival, but that "you can survive, regardless of the location." After being sufficiently weakened from lack of food and forced marches, personnel went through all-too-real prisoner-of-war exercises.[14]

Training at Pickle Meadows was received in groups of 25 and began at 0500, with rigorous exercise and then a mile-and-a-half run to the mess hall for chow. For their SERE training with the Marines, the men were dropped off in the mountains for five-day survival treks. They were given a knife, sleeping bag, compass, and map, but no food—they had to survive on what they could find or kill. They were pursued, harassed, and finally captured by the enemy, ending up in a prisoner-of-war compound.

Twelfth Coast Guard District's transient administration unit at Base Alameda was responsible for squadron training and arranged courses and transportation. They made every effort to resolve all medical and dental problems before personnel left the United States. Webber said, "I had four teeth pulled. The dentist told me he didn't have enough time to fix them before we left."[15]

As groups completed training and processing, they were bused to Travis Air Force Base (AFB), Calif., where they joined other servicemen waiting for flights across the Pacific. When it came time to board chartered jets, hospital corpsmen were stationed at the bottoms of the ramps, making final checks of shot records. Personnel found to be deficient were given needed inoculations on the spot, two at a time.

After a brief stop in Hawaii for fuel, the first group of support personnel arrived at Clark AFB in the Philippines on 11 June 1965. The long bus ride over jungle roads from Clark to Subic Bay was their first encounter with the heat and humidity that would become a way of life. A squadron office was quickly established at Subic Bay Naval Base, and at 1 minute past midnight on 12 June, Coast Guard Squadron One "chopped" (changed operational control) to commander in chief, Pacific Fleet, for further chop to commander, Seventh Fleet, and commander Vietnam Patrol Force (CTF 71).[16]

WPB crews and support personnel continued to arrive at Subic Bay throughout June. By 28 June, all commanding officers and executive officers were aboard. The first two patrol boats arrived on 17 June and the last two were off-loaded on 28 June. After arrival, each WPB received a thorough inspection and shakedown. Before being put in the water, bottoms were inspected to check shafts, struts, propellers, zincs, sea chests, and fathometer heads. All transit damage was repaired and bottom paint touched up. Once cutters were in the water, mechanical, ordnance, electrical, and electronic checks were done. Shipyard modifications began as soon as possible. Work included installation of single-sideband, high-frequency transceivers (AN/URC-58); fabrication and installation of gunners' platforms around 81mm mortars; modification of trigger-fired mortars, to allow depression below the horizon for close-range firing; rigging of floodlights for night boarding; installation of small-arms lockers on mess decks; and additional sound-powered phone circuits.[17]

When it became apparent that the squadron would be operating from two widely separated locations in Vietnam, Hodgman recommended that patrol boats be divided into two divisions:

- Hodgman took command of Squadron One and Division 11, which consisted of nine cutters and a Navy support ship, which would be anchored off the island of Phu Quoc in the Gulf of Thailand. WPBs assigned to Division 11 were *Point Banks, Point Clear, Point Comfort, Point Garnet, Point Glover, Point Grey, Point Marone, Point Mast,* and *Point Young.*

- Lieutenant Commander Knapp, originally assigned as Hodgman's chief staff officer, was given command of the eight cutters of Division 12, with its base of operations at the port of Danang in the north. Cutters assigned to Division 12 were *Point Arden, Point Caution, Point Dume, Point Ellis, Point Gammon, Point Lomis, Point Orient,* and *Point Welcome.*[18]

At Subic Bay, crews and support personnel worked seven days a week, well into the night, getting boats ready to sail for Vietnam. Hodgman wrote in the squadron diary on 7 July 1965:

> Continued shipyard repairs and modifications on Div 11 boats only. Div 12 boats commenced underway shakedown; Div 11 boats having limited shakedown pierside. . . . As of today for Div 12 and tomorrow for Div 11, shakedown training has priority on all boats. Yard can work nights and on Saturday and Sunday. I have to deploy.[19]

Beginning the second week of July, emphasis was concentrated on underway drills and training, provisioning, and final preparations for deployment. Division 12 cutters took on their service allowance of ammunition from a barge in the harbor on 6 July; Division 11 loaded the following day. Commissary supplies were loaded on the 8th and by 9 July all cutters had successfully completed full-power trials. Commanding officers continued to receive briefings from Navy personnel returning from patrol duty off Vietnam and all crew members completed a one-day jungle survival course taught by Negrito natives. Boats were under way daily for drills and exercises. All equipment was checked and tested and, as crews became more proficient, nighttime emergency drills and gunnery exercises were conducted.

At 1330 on 16 July 1965, Knapp formally took command of Division 12 in a brief ceremony at the Naval Station. At 1600 that afternoon, cutters of Division 12 got under way. Uithol wrote in his journal, "They lined up in the harbor, eight boats in a line abreast. On the signal 'Corpen Nine,' they all turned and steamed to their fate. As they did, *Point Banks* played 'Cast Your Fate to the Wind' over the radio circuit. It was a sobering affair." The cutters stood out of Subic Bay in column formation. Once clear of the harbor, they rendezvoused with USS *Snohomish County* (LST 1125) for the transit to Danang. The LST was assigned to provide interim support for Division 12 until the arrival of YR-71 (floating workshop, non-self-propelled).[20]

Assistant Treasury Secretary Reed and Coast Guard Commandant Roland visited Subic Bay on 17 July 1965 and inspected Division 11; they went aboard each cutter and talked with crew members. At 0800 on 24 July, cutters of Division 11 unnested and got under way. Before departing the harbor, boats passed in review, rendering honors to Captain Ziegler, USN, commander Task Unit 73.1.2, who was responsible for outfitting and repairs for the squadron at Subic Bay.

The first eight cutters of Squadron One sail from Subic Bay enroute to Danang, South Vietnam, 1965.

Cutters stood out of the harbor into a southwest monsoon. In rough seas, they took station in a circular formation around USS *Floyd County* (LST 762), which would serve as Division 11's interim support ship until the arrival of a landing craft repair ship, USS *Krishna* (ARL 38).

As cutters rose and fell with the swell of the open sea, crew members felt a deep sense of relief; trials and tribulations of shakedown and outfitting were finally behind them. Their minds turned to what lay ahead, beyond the distant horizon. With mixed feelings of excitement and apprehension, they readied themselves to carry out their mission—whatever it might involve.

3

Division 12 on Patrol

I want to make sure that the Coast Guard people in Vietnam know that I am hearing about them often and that I am pleased with what I hear.

Gen. Wallace Greene, Jr., USMC, Commandant
August 1967

Friendly Fire

Point Welcome came about on the morning of 11 August 1966 and headed south, away from the line dividing the waters of North and South Vietnam. The cutter was on the second day of a 3-day patrol in the northernmost coastal area 1A1. She ran without lights, making turns for eight knots. Black seas were calm; a warm breeze blew from the east.[1]

Point Welcome's executive officer, Lt. (jg) Ross Bell, watched the green glow of the coast rotate on the scope of the relative-bearing radar as the cutter turned. He spent most of his time watching the Cua Viet river. Two unlighted contacts loitered just inside the mouth of the river, four-and-a-half miles to the west. Bell waited for the suspicious vessels to clear the river and head south along the coast. At 0300, one of the contacts returned upriver—the other remained at the mouth.

Bell glanced at his watch; it was 0330. He looked forward to being relieved and getting some sleep. Suddenly, two illumination flares popped in the sky off the port beam, 500 yards to seaward. With the United States in control of skies over Vietnam, he knew that the flares, hanging above, were from U.S. or VNAF aircraft. When he heard jet engines approaching, he felt something was wrong. The engines got louder and he hit the general quarters alarm. His hand had just reached the microphone of the radio, when .50-caliber slugs came rip-

24

ping through the aluminum pilothouse. Above the sound of tearing metal, Bell yelled into the microphone, "Article. This is Article India. Am being illuminated and attacked. I believe Vietnamese aircraft. We have received hits." Then, a bullet tore off the front of his left foot and the windshield blew out in front of him. With equipment shattering around him, he heard the Coastal Surveillance Center (CSC) acknowledge his message. The radio went dead.

On the first pass, two cans of gasoline for the cutter's small boat were set ablaze on the stern. Bell said, "I was absolutely amazed at how the crew responded. It was 0330 in the morning and they were up and at their stations in ninety seconds. They had the fire out in less than a minute. It was so fast." Engineman second-class Jerry Phillips, who had been on deck getting some air before going on watch, was hit on the first pass. He died while Seaman O'Connor was trying to stop the blood flowing from a gaping abdominal wound.

The second plane roared in a minute after the first, firing 20mm cannons. Bell said 20mm guns did the most damage. Lt. (jg) David C. Brostrom, the cutter's commanding officer, made it to the bridge. He was reaching for the Aldis lamp to signal the aircraft when he took two 20mm rounds in his midsection; he died instantly. Bell said, "I remember getting hit again. I was picked up, spun around, and then dropped to the deck. I reached up for the chart table. My shoulder went up, but my left hand stayed in my lap. I remember thinking to myself, 'You're really screwed up.' Still, I felt no pain." There was smoke in the pilothouse from detonating 20mm rounds. Bell said, "There was a heavy smell and my ears were ringing, but I don't remember seeing any flashes."

Chief boatswain's mate Pat Patterson, next senior in command after Bell, made it to the bridge and took control of the cutter. Pushing the engine controls forward, he began evasive maneuvers at full speed. He spun the wheel, twisting and turning to avoid the attacking aircraft. Patterson tried to get out from under the illumination, but the forward air controller, call sign "Blind Bat," in an Air Force C-130 Hercules high above, continued to drop flares. A B-57 Canberra and two F-4C Phantom IIs attacked repeatedly, sending bullets and armor-piercing rockets ripping through the cutter.

Bell was lying on the deck in a pool of blood, drifting in and out of consciousness. A large part of his upper left arm was shot away, a round had sliced open his thigh, he had a three-inch gash from shrap-

Interior of USCGC Point Welcome's *bridge after she was mistakenly attacked at night by U.S. Air Force jets, 1966.*

nel in his back over his spine, his head was hit, and part of his left foot was gone. He said, "When I heard the aircraft coming around for another attack, I would bat Patterson on the leg and he would cut the wheel hard. Old Pat really did a number. . . . I remember telling him, 'Take us down to the junk base [South Vietnamese Coastal Group].'"

During the attack, the bridge was wiped out; all three men on watch were hit. All communications, lights, and navigation equipment were destroyed, but steering and engine controls continued to function. The engines never stopped and none of the hits penetrated the hull below the waterline. The ferocious attack by the three aircraft continued unabated. Bell said, "We were under attack for almost 50 minutes. They fired thousands of rocket, 20mm and .50-caliber rounds at us." All during the attack, the U.S. flag continued to fly from the mast of the 82-foot cutter.

At 0415, *Point Welcome* grounded on the sandbar off the junk base and heeled over to one side. Patterson got all the wounded on deck and into life jackets. Every one of the cutter's eleven-man crew, the South Vietnamese Navy liaison officer, and Tim Page, a British journalist, had been hit. Patterson paired up lesser wounded men with more seriously injured and ordered the cutter abandoned. Survivors went over the side in an attempt to swim to the beach. "When we got in the water," Bell said, "They opened up on us from the junk base. Then the VC on the other side of the river began firing at us. We were caught in a cross-fire. Then it all stopped at once. Everything just stopped."

When USCGC *Point Caution* (WPB 82301) heard *Point Welcome*'s brief transmission to the CSC, she left her patrol area and headed north at full speed. Bell said, "I remember trying to swim with my one good arm. Then *Caution*'s boat picked me up. I knew I was messed up, but I didn't know how bad. The last thing I remember was *Caution*'s XO giving me shots of morphine in my thighs." Junks from Coastal Group 11 came out to help pick up survivors and the base fired illumination rounds from mortars to assist in recovering the men in the water. The wounded were taken to the junk base where they were evacuated by helicopter. *Point Welcome* was riddled. She had nine rocket holes in her main deck, five to nine inches in diameter, but her hull was intact and her main engines were still running. At 0630, *Point Welcome* sailed back to Danang under her own power.[2]

Bell woke up in the Marine Corps field hospital at Phu Bai. "I don't know how many days later," he said. "I had over 200 wire sutures holding me together. I looked like a porcupine. I have no idea how many regular stitches I had."

It took three months to repair *Point Welcome*. When the cutter was ready for operations, members of the crew repainted their emblem, "Wile E. Coyote," on the wing of the bridge. Only this time, the coyote had a broken and bandaged tail.

Cutter On-Scene

On 20 July 1965, Coast Guard crews watched distant flashes of artillery fire as they approached the coast of Vietnam. Cutters formed a column astern of USS *Snohomish County* (LST 1126) at 0700 and sailed into Danang harbor; Division 12's WPBs were the first Coast Guard units to reach Vietnam. Lt. Cdr. Richard J. Knapp, Division 12 commander, looked back at the line of patrol boats from the bridge of the LST and thought about his mission and how he would support his cutters. Knapp said, "It was what I didn't know that concerned me. I knew I had eight good boats and crews. But everything else was kind of in flux. Nothing had been set up yet."[3]

The division entered the harbor, turned south, and proceeded to a newly built pier at the VNN base, located on the inside of Tien Sha peninsula below Mon Ky mountain.

Before all the LST's lines were ashore, cutters began nesting along her outboard side. The welcoming party waiting on the pier included Rear Adm. Richard L. Fowler, commander Task Force 71, Vietnam Patrol Force; Rear Adm. Norvell G. Ward, chief naval advisory group, military assistance command; Lt. Cdr. Thong, commander Vietnamese first coastal zone; Lt. Cdr. Chi, commander Vietnamese special forces, Danang; and Lt. Richard Fremont-Smith, USCG liaison officer. The group boarded *Snohomish County* and, after brief introductions, went to the wardroom, where they discussed coastal surveillance in general terms. The admirals then toured the newly arrived cutters and spoke with the crews. When the party left, Knapp was concerned because no operations or intelligence briefings were planned for cutters before departing on patrol the next morning. He wrote in the division diary, "It appears the whole operation, from obtaining VNN liaison officers to actually patrolling, is done on a very casual basis." Knapp realized that naval commanders were coping with a rapidly expanding military

USCGC Point Caution and USCGC Point Gammon moored next to their support ship, USS Snohomish County, after arriving at Danang.

buildup and that Division 12 would have to fend for itself. He contacted the commanding officer of USS *Force* (MSO 445), a surveillance ship in from patrol, and Lt. Cdr. Ackerman from the CSC to arrange briefings for cutter crews that night.[4]

Thong agreed to allow the LST and WPBs to remain moored at the VNN base. Knapp said, "It was a base, but not a support base as we know it. It was comprised of a small building used by U.S. Navy liaison officers as a communications center and one house belonging to the Vietnamese naval commander. That was about it." The base, and a U.S. Navy special operations group across from it, were on a small isthmus, accessed by a causeway. WPB crews berthed and messed aboard their cutters, and division staff members lived aboard the moored LST.

The Han river, running south from the harbor, separated the city of Danang on its west bank from Tien Sha peninsula. Rugged mountains surrounded the large harbor, protecting it from storms. Lt. John M. Cece commanded USCGC *Point Orient* (WPB 82319) with the first deployment. He said, "Danang was an easy harbor to enter and leave. There were no aids to navigation, but the entrance was high on both sides. It was good for radar." When entering at night, lights of large merchant ships riding at anchor in the harbor were hard to distinguish from lights of the city beyond. Cece said, "Sampans were all over the place, crisscrossing the harbor in all directions."[5]

The morning after the division's arrival, five of the eight WPBs prepared to get under way for patrol. Departures were delayed, however, while cutters waited until 1000 for VNN liaison officers to report aboard. USCGC *Point Dume* (WPB 82325) had to wait until 1200, because her liaison officer had to return to Danang to get clothes for the patrol. *Point Orient,* USCGC *Point Lomas* (WPB 82321), and USCGC *Point Gammon* (WPB 82328) sailed north with *Force* to patrol along the 17th parallel. Once clear of the harbor, cutters "chopped" to the commanding officer of the underway destroyer, USS *Savage* (DER 386), who was operational commander for all patrolling vessels in the area. Knapp said, "Surveillance operations were pretty relaxed. The DER stayed offshore and didn't provide a lot of guidance. We kind of set up our own tactics."[6]

On 24 July 1965, *Point Orient* was the first Coast Guard cutter to come under enemy fire. She closed the coast to investigate a junk south of Cua Viet river in moderate seas and hazy visibility. At 0610, tracers streaked toward *Point Orient* from a Viet Cong heavy machine gun, and mortar rounds splashed in the water beyond the cutter. Fire came from hidden positions on shore, 1,200 yards away. *Point Orient* returned fire with .50-caliber machine guns. Cece said, "They were firing from behind a rise back from the beach. We couldn't see the target, but fired at the spot where the tracers were coming from." *Point Orient* took no hits.

After the brief action, the cutter's first-class gunner's mate went to the bridge and handed Cece a .50-caliber shell casing. He said, "This is from the first Coast Guard shot fired in Vietnam." When *Orient* returned to port at the end of her patrol on 24 July 1965, Coast Guard Commandant Adm. Edwin J. Roland was in Danang. *Point Orient's* crew presented Roland with the casing, which later was mounted in plastic and placed in the Coast Guard Academy museum.

When commander Task Force 115 (CTF 115), coastal surveillance force, took over the interdiction mission on 30 July 1965, he designated Division 12 as Danang support group. Cutters on patrol remained under the operational control of the patrolling Navy destroyer. On 8 August, all five cutters on patrol were directed to deploy to seaward along the 17th parallel as radar pickets. This assignment left one WPB near shore to board the large concentration of coastal traffic. Offshore cutters reported no junk traffic in their areas and commanding officers recommended patrolling along the coast. They reasoned that they had a better chance of interdicting and deterring VC shipments by operating where traffic was, rather than offshore where few, if any, vessels were ever seen.

Knapp agreed with his commanding officers, saying, "The deployment doesn't utilize their inshore capability. It places them in a position where their effectiveness is much less than that of two larger units covering the same area." With the approach of northeast monsoon season, all vessel traffic was reduced. Weather on the barrier turned nasty and there was absolutely no traffic offshore. Detection capability for cutters, patrolling as far as 80 miles from the coast, was restricted by heavy seas, low radar antenna heights, and limited height-of-eye. Navigation was a problem.

Cutters managed to stay on station by taking radar ranges and bearings on the WPB patrolling in the next area inshore, using RDF (radio direction finder) bearings, and celestial navigation. Even when the sky was clear enough to see stars, getting sextant angles from the bridge of a WPB tossed in a seaway was no easy feat. Cutters were assigned so far offshore, they came in contact with Navy ships on Yankee Station. When one cutter came alongside a carrier to get supplies, the Navy crew asked if they were the liberty boat to Danang. Open-seas patrols on the 17th parallel took their toll on crews, who went for days without seeing any vessel traffic. Knapp said, "It was not only physical when you had bad weather, but psychological too. It was physical from the beating they took and psychological because they knew they were there for no apparent purpose."[7]

In his first two summary report messages to CTF 115 in Saigon, Knapp worded his recommendations for redeploying cutters along the coast in successively stronger terms. He said, "When I gave the third report to [Lt. Harlan D.] 'Swede' Hanson [Division 12 chief staff officer] to send, he said, 'Are you sure you want to send this?' I said, 'Send it.'" Fifteen minutes after Saigon received the message, CTF 115's chief of staff—a very upset captain—was on the phone to Knapp, asking, "What are you trying to do?" The next day, the commander of Coast Guard Squadron One flew to Danang from An Thoi to counsel Knapp, who said, "I got chewed up one side and down the other. Hodgman told me, 'You can't talk to Navy admirals that way.' . . . But, as a result of that incident, Saigon took another look at the deployment." At 0800 on 24 October 1965, cutters were taken off the line and redeployed along the coast.[8]

Initial crew debriefings indicated that three days on patrol with less than a 24-hour turnaround was about the maximum that personnel could handle. Patrol schedules changed in later years, however, based on weather and the availability of offshore support. In good weather, cutters patrolled for six days before coming in.

In 1965 and 1966, cutters frequently detected small unlighted junks moving south along the surf-line at night. When challenged, the junks would turn through the surf and beach, and their crews would disappear over the sand dunes, dragging materials with them. Frustrated by evasions, cutters became increasingly more daring in attempts to interdict the boats. On 5 February 1966, *Point Ellis* closed to investigate a junk moving along the shore. When the junk, with five men aboard, evaded through the surf and beached, a landing party from *Ellis* went through the surf after them. The party captured one man and confiscated identification papers and belongings of the other four. Some WPBs deployed armed parties in darkened small boats just outside the surf to intercept junks and go through the surf after evaders. In his 14 April 1966 diary, Capt. Robert J. LoForte, commander Coast Guard Squadron One, said, "I had to tighten the reins on Division 12 boats. Skippers were a little too anxious to send landing parties ashore in pursuit of suspect VC fleeing from beached junks." While military supplies were found in some of the deserted craft, most of them were thought to be smugglers transporting illegal contraband. In later years, as fighting in the area intensified, waters along the beaches were declared prohibited zones. Junks detected at night in prohibited zones were taken under fire. Most were quick to return fire, indicating increased VC activity.

When cutters began patrolling, they quickly made contact with coastal groups of the Junk Force. USN advisors assigned to coastal groups were anxious to work with WPBs in their patrol areas. Junks and cutters made joint patrols, combining the junks' ability to work close to shore with the WPBs' radar detection capability and firepower. Junk Force vessels moved along the coast, 100 to 200 yards offshore, while a cutter ran on a parallel course, 1,000 yards offshore. WPBs used their radars to vector junks to darkened targets. While communications during these operations were sometimes difficult, the tactic was effective. Cutter crews maintained good relations with coastal groups throughout their time in Vietnam, conducting joint operations and providing gunfire support when their bases came under attack. Operations with VNN ships of the Sea Force were less frequent, however, and relations were not as cooperative. Sea Force vessels seldom replied to challenges and were difficult to raise on the radio. In a report, Knapp said, "It's a good thing we have their [patrol] schedules or it [identifying them] could be a real problem."9

Operational control of underway Market Time resources in coastal zone I rotated from one deployed destroyer commanding officer to the next. Destroyers, working offshore, had little contact with cutters patrolling along the coast. Control of inshore cutter operations gradually evolved to commander Division 12. While officially designated a support group commander, he had the capability to direct coastal operations and provide continuity. Knapp said, "I was the one who was always there. When DERs rotated in for offshore surveillance, they always checked in with me. We [Division 12] worked [cutter] operations and were doing a lot of active controlling. It never showed up on the organization charts, but the informal organization had us controlling."10

The first six 50-foot Navy PCFs (fast patrol crafts) arrived at Danang on 23 January 1966. The craft, called Swift boats, were assigned to Division 12 for training, orientation, and operational control. Knapp said, "I don't know why I got OpCon of PCFs. They just gave them to me. We took the Swift division in with us. . . . It was a good family." While Division 12 controlled Swift boat operations, it did not officially have control of its own WPBs. In a 10 March 1965 memo to the naval advisory group's operations officer, Capt. John T. Shepherd, Knapp recommended operational control of all Market Time vessels be centralized with a permanent commander ashore.[11]

On 29 April 1966, a new Market Time operation order was published. It followed the centralized organization already in place in the Gulf of Thailand, and put all northern patrol vessels under the operational control of the senior naval advisor, first coastal zone. The operation order assigned Division 12 to—

- Maintain WPBs in high state of readiness
- Provide logistic support to WPBs and associated personnel
- Provide two-thirds of assigned WPBs for inshore patrol operations
- Assist in scheduling
- Train and properly indoctrinate personnel

Division 12 facilities were placed under the operational control of commander naval support activity, Danang. Its operations center was discontinued and returning WPB crews were debriefed by the CSC.[12]

In June 1966, steps were taken at Danang to further cooperation among Market Time elements and develop a better understanding of all aspects of the mission. CSC watch-standers began going on patrol with WPBs and PCFs. Patrol boat crews, in turn, stood watches in the CSC. Persistent communications difficulties caused the CSC watch to be shifted to the former Coast Guard operations center on 15 July 1966. This arrangement lasted until 29 August 1966, when CSC equipment problems were corrected.[13]

Cutters off patrol were frequently used for special operations, such as inserting and recovering marine reconnaissance teams, naval gunfire support, or surveillance missions. On 14 July 1967, *Point Orient* was off patrol, moored alongside YR-71; the crew was painting and doing maintenance. At 1130, her commanding officer, Lt. (jg) Norman T.

Saunders, was told to prepare to get under way for a special operation. The Navy had been shadowing a suspicious trawler for two days; she finally turned west and was headed for the coast. *Point Orient* embarked a Navy psychological warfare team and got under way to intercept the trawler. The team was to talk the trawler into surrendering.

That night, in total darkness, *Point Orient* approached the trawler, *Hon Chon,* as she steamed toward shore. The cutter closed to 120 feet off the trawler; both vessels were running without lights. Saunders said, "Our job was to get really close aboard at darkened ship and play a *Chieu Hoi* [open arms] recording over a sound system we set up. They were supposed to give up. But it didn't make a lick of difference. She just kept steaming." *Point Orient* fired warning shots. The ship refused to stop, and returned fire. The cutter and PCF 79 raked the trawler with machine guns and mortar fire, setting her ablaze. The ship, loaded with arms and ammunition, ran aground and burned. The hull later was towed to Danang.[14]

South Vietnam waters were divided into four coastal zones. Coastal zone I began at the DMZ and stretched 200 miles southeast, and was divided into areas 1 and 2. The first year, Division 12 cutters patrolled to the north in area 1. In 1966, WPB patrols were extended 90 miles further south into area 2. Deployments were then made into areas 3 and 4 in coastal zone II. At least one WPB was always kept on patrol at the 17th parallel, in the area closest to the coast. When intelligence indicated possible infiltration activity, additional cutters patrolled further to sea along the 17th parallel.[15]

With the onset of monsoon weather and heavy seas, WPBs replaced Navy Swift boats on patrol. The PCFs, with lesser sea-keeping capability, were redeployed to more sheltered waters. This change resulted in cutter crews enduring northeast monsoons in the South China Sea until conditions improved, only to be sent to the Gulf of Thailand to face southwest monsoons. Recognizing the hardships that deployments to heavy-weather areas imposed, Rear Adm. Kenneth L. Veth, commander Naval Forces Vietnam, said in a 1967 message to commander Coast Guard Squadron One:

> With the onset of the NE monsoon season, floating units of Coast Guard Squadron One are once again being required to shift operating areas into more turbulent waters to take advantage of the WPBs' superior sea-keeping qualities and the traditionally excellent seamanship of Coast

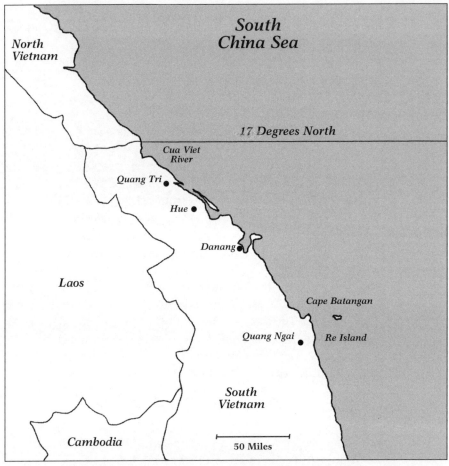

Coast Guard Division 12 operating area

Guard crews. Since their assignment to Market Time in 1965 the WPBs and their crews have borne the brunt of rough-weather assignments, remaining on inshore patrol stations under all conditions of sea and weather.

The Coast Guard contribution to Market Time is recognized and appreciated by Naval Forces Vietnam.

Well done. RADM Veth sends.[16]

The coast in area 1 of coastal zone I, from the DMZ south to Tan My, was edged with sandy beaches and penetrated by two major inlets: Cua Viet river at the DMZ, and Tan My inlet leading to Hue.

South of Hue, the shore gradually became more elevated and rugged. Rocky coastline extended from Danang eighty miles south to Quang Ngai. Sand beaches stretched the last 35 miles to the boundary of coastal zone II.

On patrol, WPBs carried out aggressive boarding programs. Nearly all vessels found in northern areas were fishing junks, working lines and nets close to the coast. The typical junk was wood, about 25-feet long, and powered by a small one-cylinder diesel engine. Boats, open and without cabins, were manned by crews of two or three men, who cooked their food over small charcoal-burning stoves made of clay. Junks were not painted except for "eyes," on the bows and possibly some decorations. Most fishermen used hand lines; a few had monofilament nets. Shark was a common catch.[17]

Cutters usually brought junks alongside for boarding, because they were open and had few places to hide materials. VNN liaison officers and petty officers would check the boat's papers and crew identification cards, occasionally going aboard to check enclosures. Cutters also encountered and boarded cargo junks, carrying rice or other bulk supplies; these were searched by boarding parties. Searchers used .50-caliber cleaning rods to probe through cargoes for weapons or military supplies. When discrepancies were found, vessels or individual crewmen were taken into custody and turned over to coastal groups or taken back to Danang. Cece said, "We didn't have as much [boarding] as down south [Division 11]. We'd go sometimes for days without seeing any boats and then there would be a lot. It wasn't always because of the weather. On some good days we wouldn't see any."[18]

Snohomish County was Division 12's temporary base of operations after arriving in Vietnam. The division established and manned an operations center on the LST. While her facilities were limited, *Snohomish County* provided maintenance for WPBs. USS *Sumner County* (LST 1148) arrived at 0730 on 17 August 1965 to relieve *Snohomish County.* The ships moored together and ammunition, spare parts, and supplies were cross-decked. The new LST had even fewer facilities for maintenance, but cutters continued to operate without serious problems. Lt. Cdr. William E. Lehr, Squadron One's engineer officer, said, "Our guys took care of their own stuff. Even out on patrol, if something broke, they fixed it. As long as they had the equipment and parts, they did the work. They weren't used to having somebody else maintain their gear."[19]

South Vietnamese liaison officer aboard USCGC Point Welcome *checks identification papers of junk's crew.*

After being delayed for several months in Subic Bay during over-haul and outfitting, Division 12's permanent support vessel, YR-71 (floating workshop, non-self-propelled), arrived at Danang on Christmas Day 1965. She had ample workshops for the division's seventeen-man maintenance team, as well as offices and barracks space for division staff. The well-equipped YR gave Division 12 the capability of handling all WPB maintenance, including main engine change-out and overhaul. An operations center with full communications capability was established aboard YR-71 and manned by personnel from spare cutter crews. A large storage barge, YFNB-2, was obtained for cutter spare parts and moored alongside the YR. In the fall of 1967, Division 12 relocated; YR-71 and YFNB-2 moved from the VNN pier to U.S. Navy facilities a mile closer to Danang.

The Coast Guard had the right crews and right vessels for Vietnam. Crews were accustomed to independent operations and knew how to respond to emergencies. *Point Arden's* crew was equal to the challenge they faced on 10 March 1968.

Ammunition Fire

USCGC *Point Arden* (WPB 82309) was in the fifth day of a six-day patrol when she came alongside USS *Patapsco* (AOG 1) to take on fuel. The gasoline tanker was anchored offshore, just south of the mouth of Cua Viet river, pumping gasoline through a pipeline to the naval support activity detachment (NSAD) on the south side of the river. At 0750, *Point Arden's* commanding officer, Lt. (jg) William C. Carr, heard two rounds of mortar fire come from the north side of the river and detonate at the NSAD. Carr said, "At 0805, I began to see fire and hear secondary explosions. I called 'Badminton Three' [3rd Marine Division]. We worked with them quite a bit over the previous months providing naval gunfire support. I asked what was going on and they asked for assistance."[20]

Point Arden secured from fueling, got under way, and set general quarters; the cutter thought the Marines were under attack. The WPB passed over the sandbar at the river mouth and entered the cove to the south, where NSAD was located. As *Arden* approached the landing ship ramp, the crew saw stores burning at the head of the ramp. Cases of C-rations were stacked on top of pallets of 105mm howitzer ammunition. Empty sandbags, small-arms ammunition, and parachute flares were piled on top of the C-rations. Carr said, "The incoming rounds ignited the parachute flares. They were going off, and setting the sandbags and C-rations on fire. Because of the flares, the fire was spreading rapidly. A lot was happening. It was like major fireworks with flares and small-arms ammunition going off."

The Marines asked *Arden* to help fight the fire. A Marine armored personnel carrier (APC) came down to the shore and Carr nosed the cutter's bow up on the beach of the cove. Chief Boatswain's Mate William A. Tugman and his three-man rescue and assistance team scrambled over the bow. They loaded a P-250 pump, hoses, nozzles, fire axes, and two PRC-59 radios aboard the APC. The vehicle went around the east side of the ammunition dump to approach the fire from the south.

Point Arden backed off and came toward the fire from the north. She beached again, next to the LST ramp, and Carr took over as on-scene commander. He had a YTB (large harbor tug), an LCU (utility landing craft), and PCF 81, which he called in off patrol, to fight the fire. He waited until explosions from small-arms ammunition let up before sending parties against the fire. Carr said, "It was 0900 by the time we got three hoses going. The Swift didn't have the equipment, so we used her men on other hoses. We went up the ramp into the dump from the north side." Tugman and his party approached the fire from the south; they were 200 yards from the waterfront. Tugman said a dozen Navy and Marine people were taking shelter from exploding ammunition. "The Navy really couldn't do much about fighting the fire," he said. "They had a semi-fixed system with a bunch of pipes out on the ground and a water tank sitting up in the air. The pumping station for the system was damaged and couldn't be used."[21]

Several wooden shops and sheds were ablaze. Tugman and his men set up the pump, taking water from a pond, and started putting out fires. He said, "They had three big fuel bladders lying on the ground and were worried about them catching fire." Tugman shut off the valves, stopping the flow of fuel to the main ammunition depot, south of the fire, and to the waterfront. Carr said, "He can probably be credited with keeping the whole thing [support activity] from going up." The only communications *Point Arden* had with her fire party on the south side was through a Marine radio operator, who used runners to carry messages to the scene. Carr used a loud-hailer and runners to communicate with fire parties at the ramp.

Carr said, "Pallets loaded with ammunition were stacked in groups about 10-feet square. They covered an area the size of a basketball gymnasium. We had three hoses working at the ramp and were getting the fire under control." Smaller ammunition was continuing to cook off, but Carr considered the risk moderate. Part of *Point Arden*'s crew was ashore manning a hose with an LCU crew. Two more LCUs arrived.

The first large explosion occurred at 1030. The blast blew in all the cutter's bridge windows, sending glass flying. Carr was coming down the ladder from the cutter's pilothouse when it went off; the deckhouse shielded him. He managed to grab the quartermaster, who was thrown across the deck by the blast, and kept him from going over the side. Carr said, "Shrapnel—big stuff—fell for a good 90 seconds so we took cover. . . . People on the bridge were cut by shattered glass, but we were all alive."

Carr and his executive officer, CWO-1 Royce W. Fulcher, went up the ramp to help rescue men wounded by the explosion. Carr said:

I pulled a man from the debris. He had severe wounds in his arms and left leg. He was bleeding from the mouth and in shock. I dragged him back to an LCU. The [LCU's] crew said one of their guys was still up there. I think his name was Golf. I went back up the ramp to look for him by myself. It seemed like an eternity, but I'm sure it was only five or six minutes. I looked all around trying to find a body. But I couldn't find anything. The shell casings were red hot. I could see where the others had already blown. The fire was out of control and I knew it was going to go again. . . . Being up there was, and still is, a vivid memory.

Of the twenty firefighters on the ramp, one was missing and presumed dead, and ten others were wounded—three severely. Wounded were loaded aboard the cutter and other craft, and all vessels backed away from the ramp.

On the other side of the fire, Tugman said, "When the big explosion went, all the stuff on the dock went up. [CS2] Bruce C. Lindberg got cut on the calf and I got hit with shrapnel on the side of the head. I know a lot of Navy guys got hurt." Tugman was taken to the medical tent, where they put a dressing on his head. He said, "They wanted to evacuate me, but I told them I wanted to go back to *Point Arden.*"[22]

The second explosion occurred a half hour after the first. And then a third, right after the second. Tugman said, "After that, there was nothing anyone could do with it. It was gone." Shrapnel falling from the sky caused still more injuries at the waterfront. The second and third blasts did more damage to vessels—exposed in the cove—than the first explosion, when they were behind a rise at the ramp. A Navy doctor arrived aboard an LCU from an offshore LST; he treated severely wounded aboard *Point Arden.* The cutter called for helicopters, and the seriously wounded were hoisted for evacuation offshore to USS *Iwo Jima* (LPH 2).

Point Arden returned to the cove and Carr and one of his crewmen went ashore to look for Chief Tugman and his party; they had not been heard from since the first explosion. When they found them, Tugman was still being treated. Lindberg's wound was more serious; he was evacuated by Marine helo to *Iwo Jima.* Coast Guardsmen returned to their cutter and she backed off to assess her damage. Carr said, "We lost all our firefighting equipment. Four of the crew were wounded and the cutter was banged up. We had shrapnel damage and I didn't know what the concussion did to the hull and superstructure. My PRC-46 [radio] was out so I couldn't talk with other units on-scene. I gave my assessment to the senior Marine officer. I told him that with a third of my crew wounded and no radio to coordinate things, I didn't think there was too much more we could do." At 1300, *Point Arden* departed the Cua Viet river and headed south. Enroute to Danang, GM2 G. T. Landon was evacuated by helicopter to Dong Ha for treatment of a shrapnel wound in his right thigh. Eventually, the fire at NSAD burned itself out. Debris was cleared and the facility was again used as an ammunition dump.

Commander Task Group 115.1's message about the incident said, "The courageous and exemplary performance is without a doubt typical of the type of instant response and action for which the Coast Guard is noted."[23]

Support Operations

Shallow-draft WPBs were well suited for coastal infiltration and exfiltration missions. When the commanding officer of First Force Reconnaissance Company, III Marine Amphibious Force, found out that cutters were operating in the Danang area, he contacted Division 12. The Marines arranged for off-patrol cutters to insert reconnaissance teams into known and suspected VC territory and retrieve them. On the first mission, *Point Arden* dropped three reconnaissance teams off on the northern shore of Danang harbor, just after midnight on 3 October 1965. *Point Orient* picked up the teams after they had scouted the area for three days. From then on, use of WPBs for reconnaissance missions became routine. Cutters also supported Marine amphibious operations by escorting landing craft to shore; acting as blocking forces to prevent VC from escaping over the beach; firing naval gunfire support missions; and providing security patrols to keep local craft from approaching amphibious vessels.

After three years of Market Time operations, no evidence indicated large-scale coastal infiltration of supplies and personnel to the Viet Cong. Boardings of hundreds of thousands of junks yielded insignificant amounts of material and few confirmed Viet Cong or North Vietnamese Army personnel. Most people arrested were draft dodgers avoiding service in the South Vietnamese military or black marketeers. The deterrent effect of massive junk boardings probably will never be known. Infiltration by steel-hulled trawlers was an active, credible threat, but one more effectively countered by different types of solutions. This realization was reflected in a shift in mission emphasis for Market Time patrol boats.

A 10 December 1968 memorandum from the chief of the Military Readiness Division at Coast Guard headquarters said:

> Continued shift in emphasis toward NGFS for inshore and offshore patrol units has again resulted in a significant increase in missions for WPBs. Studies conducted by COMUSMACV early this year indicated that aircraft patrols were the best way to detect infiltration from sea and that both the inshore and offshore patrol units could allocate more time to NGFS without a degradation in effectiveness. Since July of this year, WPBs have conducted an average of 242 NGFS missions per month. The average for all of 1965–67 was only 11 missions per month.[24]

Cutters earned a reputation for their ability to deliver when it came to naval gunfire support. Lt. Cdr. Thomas G. Volkle, Division 12 commander in 1969, received a call from a Marine naval gunfire liaison officer (NGLO), asking him to attend a planning meeting for a Marine operation on Barrier Island. Volkle said,

> When they got to gunfire support, the general asked the NGLO what he wanted for support. He said, "Sir, I want Coast Guard WPBs." When the general asked why, he said, "When I say I got guys in trouble and we need gunfire at this point, I get it. I don't get a lot of questions about whether I have permission from the province chief or how deep the water is or how far can I go in? If I can get other resources fine, but I want WPBs." The general turned to me and asked, "How many can you provide?" I said, "I can give you two, easily." The general asked the NGLO, "Will that be enough?" He replied, "I'd rather have three." I said, "We'll squeeze out another one." When I left the meeting, my chest was sticking out to about here.[25]

4

Market Time in the Gulf of Thailand

They [82-foot WPBs] can operate on patrol 70 percent of the time and can remain on this schedule indefinitely. Even while the cutters undergo their 6,000-hour overhauls and annual dry-dockings . . . the schedule is maintained. To my knowledge, such continued operational utilization off a hostile coast, remote from shore support, halfway around the world from the United States, has not been matched.

Capt. James A. Hodgman, USCG, Commander, Squadron One

Night Action

Point Glover's officer of the deck, Lt. (jg) Joseph Cooley, finished plotting his 0100 fix and clicked off the red light over the chart table. He picked up his coffee mug and turned back to the radar. The 82-foot cutter was on patrol just north of the Balua Islands on Sunday, 19 September 1965. Waters in the Gulf of Thailand were calm under a moonless sky. When the sweep of the radar lit up a small target, Cooley leaned closer. The blip was five miles west of Nui Bai. He adjusted the gain and waited for two more sweeps. Certain that he had a contact, he picked up the sound-powered phone and buzzed the cabin. When Lt. Robert T. Nelson answered, Cooley said, "Captain, I have a small radar contact at 6,000 yards. She's running without lights and heading for the coast." After setting a course to intercept and ordering an increase in speed, Nelson headed for the bridge.[1]

When only 100 yards from the vessel, *Glover* turned on her search-light. Once illuminated, the junk maneuvered erratically in an attempt

44

to evade and the five Viet Cong aboard opened fire. When the guerrillas saw they couldn't escape, they turned to ram the cutter. With the junk heading for a collision with *Point Glover,* the VC jumped overboard into the darkness. Nelson backed hard, successfully avoiding a collision. *Point Glover* pursued the junk and knocked out her engine with .50-caliber machine-gun fire.

Coast Guardsmen boarded the disabled and sinking vessel and made a quick search. No one was aboard. Searchers found a small amount of arms, ammunition, and miscellaneous equipment. They removed the material, took the junk in tow, and headed for Hon Heo, one of the Balua Islands. Unable to control the flooding, they beached the junk in shallow water before she sank. USCGC *Point Garnet* (WPB 82310), on patrol in the adjacent area, heard *Point Glover*'s radio transmissions. She arrived just after the brief action ended and was designated on-scene commander for coordinating a search for the junk's crew. USCGC *Point Clear* (WPB 82315) and USCGC *Point Marone* (WPB 82331) were assigned to assist with the search. When the sun came up, a U.S. Navy patrol aircraft from VP-17 and a VNAF C-47 joined the effort. Cutters used traditional Coast Guard search-and-rescue procedures to conduct a coordinated search. *Garnet* located a Viet Cong survivor and took him prisoner.

A twelve-man landing party from the three cutters went ashore on a small uninhabited island to search for survivors. A search through the heavy growth on the island was negative. *Point Garnet* turned over her prisoner to Vietnamese Junk Force Division 44 at Teksu Island and the cutters returned to their patrol areas.

That night, Division 11's operations center received a terse radio message. At 2330, a voice said, "Barbados. This is Barbados Tango. Taking fire from a junk. We are returning fire. Assistance is enroute. Out." While patrolling south of the Pirate Islands near the Cambodian border, *Point Marone* detected another unlighted vessel on radar. The contact, three-and-a-half miles south of the coastal town of Ha Tien, was heading southeast toward the mainland. *Point Marone* closed the vessel and turned on her searchlight. The cutter's crew saw a 40-foot junk with several men aboard. The junk's cabin and masts were cut off to present a lower profile. Lt. David R. Markey, *Marone*'s skipper, ordered .50-caliber warning shots fired across her bow. The junk attempted to evade while Viet Cong cadre opened fire at close range and hurled handgrenades at the cutter. *Point Glover* heard *Point Marone*'s call and arrived on-scene in time to provide 81mm mortar illumination. Both cutters engaged the junk with .50-caliber machine guns. Heavy fire disabled the vessel and silenced return fire. When the action ended, the junk was disabled and burning. *Glover* came alongside, put out the fire, and took the vessel in tow. Riddled with .50-caliber fire, the boat was taking on too much water to be kept afloat. The cutter's crew attached a marker buoy to the hull before she went down in 15 feet of water.

Eleven Viet Cong were killed in the action. The next day, when the junk was salvaged, papers indicated that twelve men had been aboard. The twelfth VC, though badly wounded, had managed to make it to shore. He was later captured by South Vietnamese regional forces and taken to the U.S. special forces camp at Ha Tien. In addition to rifles, handgrenades, ammunition, and miscellaneous documents, the junk was carrying 10,875 piasters, Vietnamese money. In recording events of the two actions that occurred on 19 September 1965, Cdr. James A. Hodgman, commander Coast Guard Squadron One, wrote in the division diary, "Needless to say, engagements at pointblank range with no warning in the middle of the night are experiences few Coast Guardsmen encounter."[2]

Vietnam

After an 1,100-mile voyage, nine 82-foot cutters of Division 11, in company with USS *Floyd County* (LST 762), arrived in Vietnam on 29 July 1965. For five days, 70-ton patrol boats pounded into 15-foot seas before reaching shelter of Con Son Island, 50 miles from the Vietnamese mainland. Heavy seas and monsoon winds peeled white paint from cutter bows, exposing red lead beneath. The LST, with commander Coast Guard Squadron One aboard, anchored in protected waters; WPBs nested alongside. The division took on fuel, water, and provisions from USS *Currituck* (AV 7), anchored nearby. *Currituck*, a seaplane tender, was at Con Son to provide support for Navy P-5Ms of VP-40. The squadron flew anti-infiltration patrols along the South Vietnamese coast.

To make the transit from the Philippines, cutters refueled from the LST *Floyd County* while under way. With the LST making eight knots through heavy seas, each boat approached from astern, took a 75-foot,

USCGC Point Glover *is towed by USS* Floyd County *while refueling during transit from Philippines to South Vietnam, 1965.*

5-inch nylon towline and then slowed, easing back on the hawser. Cutters made turns for five knots and maintained station astern of the LST. They took a hose from the ship and ran it aft on the starboard side to the fueling connection. Men working on bows of pitching WPBs were frequently airborne. Because of sea conditions, refueling all nine boats took eleven hours.

USCGC *Point Banks* (WPB 82327) was the only cutter to experience engine trouble during the voyage. Fuel oil from loose injector adapters diluted lube oil in one of her main engines; she dropped back with an escort to make repairs. Rough seas and an engine-room temperature of 140° slowed work. Despite conditions, repairs were made without slowing the division. Of the rough transit, Hodgman said, "This was the longest and roughest trip any of the personnel [WPB crews] had taken in this type boat. They obviously took a real beating. But they were proud of it and spirits were high."[3]

Division 11 remained at Con Son overnight to make minor repairs, touch up hull paint, and rest after the arduous trip. The division got underway the next day at 1800. Three Vietnamese Navy liaison officers boarded cutters so patrolling could begin immediately on arrival in the operating area.

On 30 July 1965, while Division 11 was enroute to An Thoi, command responsibility for countering sea infiltration shifted from commander in chief Pacific Fleet to commander U.S. Military Assistance Command, Vietnam. Commander Task Force 115 (CTF 115), Coastal Surveillance Force, relieved commander Vietnam Patrol Force (CTF 71) of operational control of vessels and aircraft engaged in coastal surveillance and interdiction operations. Cdr. Hodgman sent a message placing the squadron under operational control of CTF 115. The message also activated the Gulf of Thailand Support Group (CTG 115.4), with Hodgman as task group commander. The task group consisted of *Floyd County* and WPBs off patrol; it was responsible for maintaining cutters, providing logistic support for operations, and ensuring cutter readiness. On 31 July, when Division 11 rounded Ca Mau peninsula and entered the Gulf of Thailand, three WPBs broke off from the formation and closed the coast to begin patrolling.[4]

Floyd County dropped anchor on the morning of 1 August 1965 in relatively sheltered waters southeast of the village of An Thoi, on the southern tip of Phu Quoc Island. Under a brilliant sun, white cutters—"U.S. COAST GUARD" painted in black on their hulls—nested alongside the LST in clear, blue water. Phu Quoc, roughly shaped like a vertical ice cream cone, was 25 miles long and 13 miles across at the widest point, with a series of small rugged islands trailing off from the southern tip. The four villages on the island were the only territory under control of the government in Saigon: An Thoi, on the southern tip, Duong Dong and Cua Can on the west coast, and Ham Ninh on the east coast. The rest of the sparsely populated island was under Viet Cong control.

The VC, estimated to be 500 strong, had cut roads for overland travel between coastal villages. The only airstrip on the island was at Duong Dong. Troops had to resecure the airfield each time before a plane could land. Construction of a second airstrip was planned for An Thoi. On the Vietnamese mainland to the east of Phu Quoc, only three

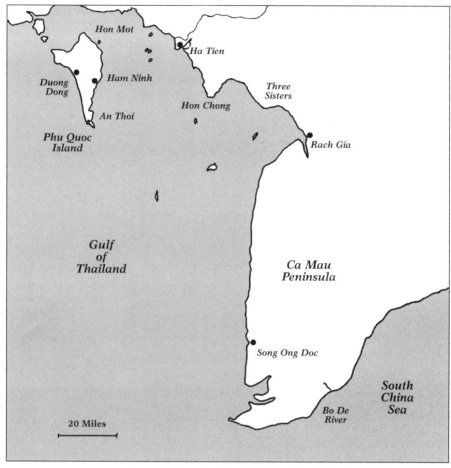

Coast Guard Division 11 operating area

coastal towns were under South Vietnamese control: Ha Tien, 35 miles across the water to the northeast from An Thoi, Rach Gia on the Bay of Rach Gia, 70 miles to the east, and Song Ong Doc on the Ca Mau peninsula, 90 miles to the southeast.

An Thoi, a fishing village of mainly one-room thatch structures, was on the western side of a six-mile sandy cove that gently arched from east to west. Rocky heights on the western end of the cove protected the village from southwest monsoons. A small concrete pier, large enough for junks and small VNN ships, stuck out from the center of the cove. The South Vietnamese naval base, consisting of a few one-story wooden buildings, was east of the village. Modest U.S. Navy facilities—wooden and corrugated-metal structures, and tents—were along the shoreline, west of the base. A coastal surveillance center (CSC), one of five in South Vietnam, was located at An Thoi and jointly operated by VNN and USN personnel. A secure perimeter around An Thoi extended only 1,000 yards inland.

After patrol boats finished nesting next to the LST, Hodgman and cutter commanding officers put on sidearms and went ashore for briefings; wearing .45s when ashore quickly became a way of life. Briefing topics included communications, operating procedures, coordination with South Vietnamese Navy units, recent enemy activity, and navigation hazards in patrol areas. Commander Hodgman, the Coast Guard commander and senior naval officer in areas 8 and 9, exercised operational control over all Market Time units, including the CSC. He spent the entire day in meetings and briefings with personnel from the CSC, commanding officers of U.S. Navy patrol ships, and USN advisors to the VNN Fourth Coastal Zone commander.[5]

To provide a lee suitable for nesting WPBs alongside, *Floyd County* anchored only a half-mile from shore. The anchorage, unfortunately, was in easy mortar range of enemy territory. To reduce the threat, the LST and patrol boats were completely darkened at night. Armed security guards kept watch topside on all vessels and an LCVP (landing craft vehicle and personnel) patrolled around the nest. To control patrol activity, an operations center was established in *Floyd County*'s combat information center. The watch consisted of a Coast Guard officer, two enlisted men from cutter spare crews, and a Navy enlisted man from the LST crew. Because of limited communications capabilities and recurrent electronic problems, the arrangement was only marginally suitable.

On 2 August 1965, Hodgman officially assumed command of Task Unit 115.1.9, with operational control over a Navy ship and six Coast Guard WPBs on patrol in Market Time area 9. The Navy ship, a DER or MSO, was assigned to patrol offshore waters to the south with WPBs working in shallow coastal and island waters to the north.[6]

The assignment of a permanent commander for operations in the Gulf of Thailand was a significant change; previously, the senior officer afloat—commanding officer of a patrolling DER or MSO—had operational control, which shifted to a new ship's CO every two or three weeks. Frequent reliefs made continuity of operations difficult, because commanders did not have time to become familiar with the area or junk traffic patterns and activity.

Area 9 consisted of 150 miles of South Vietnamese coastline on the Gulf of Thailand, from the Cambodian border in the north to the southern tip of the Ca Mau peninsula. Alluvial deposits from the fertile delta shoaled the Bay of Rach Gia and waters adjacent to the peninsula. Shallow muddy waters extended for miles to sea; patrol boats frequently operated with two or three feet of water under the keel and could easily run aground when out of sight of land. Offshore islands scattered throughout the area were mostly inhabited by fishermen and their families. The islands, some with heights of more than 1,000 feet, provided welcome lees for patrol vessels during monsoon season. The only navigational charts available were based on French surveys made in the previous century; fortunately, they proved to be accurate. Uninhabited islets and rocks scattered throughout the northern portion of the area created hazards to navigation, particularly at night and in poor weather.

During the first few weeks after Division 11's arrival, WPB crews explored operating areas and became familiar with junk activities. Some fishing junks were as large as 60 feet with twelve-man crews. Despite initial shortages of VNN liaison officers—the division was down to just one for six boats on patrol by 16 August 1965—cutters carried out vigorous boarding programs. Crews quickly learned enough Vietnamese and sign language to stop, board, and search junks and sampans. Availability of liaison personnel improved when the VNN began assigning petty officers as well as officers to cutters for duty. WPBs had liaison personnel aboard 80 percent of the time. With essentially no visual or electronic navigation aids in the area, cutters relied on their small CR-103 relative-bearing radars for navigation as well as interdiction.

The reality of being in a combat zone was brought home to the division three days after its arrival. The village of Ham Ninh, 10 miles north of An Thoi, was attacked by Viet Cong on 4 August 1965. USCGC *Point Young* (WPB 82303) was called in to evacuate wounded. She returned to An Thoi with twelve South Vietnamese regional force casualties: seven wounded and five dead. When the cutter moored alongside the LST, blanket-covered bodies of dead and wounded were a sobering sight. *Young* also evacuated nineteen dependents, wives and children of casualties. George T. Causey, chief engineman aboard *Point*

Young, said, "We took two of the dead into An Thoi [VNN Base], but nobody wanted them. They looked at them, but no one would take the bodies. We ended up putting them in body bags ourselves and took them out to sea to bury."[7]

Lack of communications between branches of service operating in the area became apparent quickly. On 7 August 1965, USCGC *Point Comfort* (WPB 82317) was boarding sampans off a point north of Rach Gia bay. Boardings took the cutter progressively closer to shore. When one of her crew looked up, he saw a small, single-engine Air Force L-19 spotter plane circling high overhead, dropping various colored flares and smokes. *Comfort's* crew watched the pyrotechnic display for a few minutes and then went back to boarding. With soundings decreasing and the cutter getting uncomfortably close to shore, the commanding officer secured boarding operations. When the cutter turned and headed for open water, a concealed Viet Cong machine-gun crew—patiently waiting ashore—opened up. The cutter quickly moved out of range without damage. *Comfort's* crew did not return fire because sampans were between the cutter and the machine gun. After the incident, the purpose of the plane's pyrotechnics was obvious—as was the need for common frequencies for communications.[8]

USS *Krishna* (ARL 38), relief for *Floyd County,* arrived at An Thoi and anchored on 17 September. The repair ship, specifically outfitted to support WPB operations, was a great improvement over the LST. Facilities aboard the well-equipped ship provided for all levels of cutter maintenance, except drydocking. Lt. Cdr. William E. Lehr, USCG, Squadron One's chief engineer, said, "*Krishna* could pretty well do anything we needed done. They had heavy-lift capability and could overhaul main engines. We had the spare parts and, with our spare boat crews, we had the senior guys who could oversee work. I don't think we had any major problems. The work we did in preparing the boats to go over paid off." In May 1965, while the squadron was forming up, Lehr learned *Krishna* would be assigned to support deployed 82-foot WPBs. He visited the ship in Norfolk where it was being outfitted. He said:

I knew they would have a hard time maintaining 82-footers because Cummins diesel engines had tough fuel systems. Their turbochargers were very tricky to overhaul and care for. They had been a chronic problem. So we literally packed up the entire injector repair shop and turbocharger shop at Staten Island [USCG Base St. George] and shipped

Cutters of Division 11 nested alongside their "mother ship," USS Krishna, *at An Thoi, South Vietnam.*

them down to Norfolk to be installed on *Krishna*. We took the second-class engineman who had been at the shop and sent him to Cummins for a quick six-week course to make him an expert. Then we sent him to *Krishna* as well. He saw that everything was installed and became our turbocharger and injector man.[9]

At the recommendation of *Krishna's* commanding officer, Lt. Cdr Eugene Rueff, USN, the Coast Guard's seventeen-man maintenance detail was transferred to the repair ship and integrated into her crew. *Krishna* then took responsibility for all repairs, modifications, and maintenance beyond the capability of cutter crews. The arrangement worked exceptionally well, with Division 11's chief engineer tasking *Krishna* with maintenance jobs.

To keep WPBs on patrol, hours between main engine overhauls were extended beyond the normal 6,000 running hours. A program of lube oil analysis became an important factor in determining when main engines should be pulled for overhaul. *Krishna* arrived with four spare Cummins engines, which would serve as replacements for engines removed for overhaul. Engine change-outs were accomplished while WPBs were moored alongside. To reduce time required to change engines, cutter crews began disconnecting equipment and removing bolts from main-deck access hatches while returning from patrol. Engine removal began as soon as cutters tied up and was completed in six to ten days. While WPBs were in maintenance status, their patrol duties were absorbed by remaining cutters. The quality of work performed by cutter crews and maintenance details enabled WPBs to sustain high levels of operations in a hostile environment. During the first year, WPBs were in maintenance status less than 6 percent of the time. Adm. John B. Hayes, as a commander, was the second commodore of Division 11. He said, "We were running WPBs at about 80 percent of the time under way. . . . When you think about it, not even the Navy does that with large ships."[10]

An operations center, specifically designed for control of Market Time activities, was constructed aboard *Krishna* while she was enroute to Vietnam. The center, complete with large status boards and surface and air plots, was a major improvement, because it had excellent communications capabilities, including six voice-operator positions.[11]

On 21 September 1965, cutters took on a new look. CTF 115 directed Squadron One to paint over white hulls. The message said, "To increase effectiveness of night patrols paint exterior hull and superstructure of WPB's formula 20 deck gray. Advise originator if aerial identification to be changed. Originator will advise all air activities concerned of foregoing." Deck gray paint was much darker than the haze gray used by USN and VNN vessels; it was better for night operations and gave cutters a distinctive appearance. "COAST GUARD" was repainted on the hulls in a lighter gray.

Raid at Hon Mot

When *Point Marone* moored alongside *Krishna* on 21 September, her commanding officer hurried up the Jacob's ladder; he had intelligence information from the special forces team at Ha Tien. The Viet Cong survivor of the junk engagement two days earlier revealed that his boat came from a VC junk base on the northeast coast of Phu Quoc Island, across from Cambodia. When the special forces detachment at

Duong Dong, on the west side of Phu Quoc, learned of the intelligence, it requested Coast Guard assistance in launching an amphibious raid against the base.

On 26 September 1965, cutters *Point Comfort* and *Point Grey* embarked a raiding party of thirty-six civilian irregular defense group (CIDG) strikers—Chinese mercenaries serving with the Vietnamese Army—their Vietnamese special forces officers, and two U.S. Army special forces advisors. The party, with their two assault rafts, weapons, and ammunition, was divided between the cutters. After a practice landing in daylight on a deserted beach at the south end of Phu Quoc, rafts were hoisted aboard and the cutters headed north. The raiding party, wearing camouflaged uniforms and soft hats, settled down to wait for darkness.[12]

Cutter cooks prepared pots of rice for strikers who stayed on deck; they were uncomfortable below decks. Special forces advisors warned cutter crews not to drink the CIDG's tea—it was laced with a mild narcotic. In calm seas and light winds, the two cutters approached the landing site, a beach west of Hon Mot island. In total darkness, cutters eased in toward shore on 27 September 1965. They stopped when soundings got down to six feet under the keel; the beach was 200 yards away. At 0500, troops climbed down scramble nets into rafts in complete silence, shoved off, and paddled for shore. The cutters slowly backed away, keeping the sound of their stern exhausts to seaward. They stood by 1,000 yards offshore at modified general quarters, ready to provide gunfire support.

The raiding party made periodic reports on its progress with a PRC-25 field radio, tracing each small river it found inland. When the party reached Hon Mot river, it found fresh tracks on the beach. At 1135, the rattle of gunfire shattered the morning calm. The radio speaker blared, "Ambushed. Hit while crossing the river. Heavy firefight. One dead. One seriously wounded." Cutter crews, manning their guns, heard the gunfire and saw muzzle flashes in the jungle. Special forces Sgt. James E. Pruitt, the first man hit, died instantly.

The raiding party was under fire from the other side of the stream and from Hon Mot island; it couldn't move back with the wounded. The remaining special forces advisor requested *Point Comfort* put 81mm mortar fire on Hon Mot. After seven rounds, shooting from the island stopped. No mortar fire was requested on shore, because the raiding party was spread out and the advisor wasn't sure where everyone was. The party put out a colored panel on the beach to mark its location and requested a boat to evacuate the wounded and dead. At 1210, *Point Grey* sent in her small boat. When the Boston Whaler got close to shore, her two-man crew climbed into the water to guide the boat around rocks.

When *Point Comfort* moved close to Hon Mot island to provide covering fire for *Point Grey's* boat, she struck a submerged rock, disabling her port shaft. Once the seriously wounded striker was aboard, *Point Grey* departed for *Krishna* to get him medical attention. *Point Comfort*, operating on one shaft, and *Point Marone*, which had arrived on-scene to assist, provided covering fire while the raiding party withdrew to its rafts. When the party reached the landing site, cutters swept the flanks with .50-caliber fire. *Point Comfort* and *Point Marone* saturated the shore and jungle with mortar fire after the rafts shoved off from the beach, to prevent the VC from moving up automatic weapons.

When the raiding party got back aboard the cutter, it reported the location of the VC junk base. *Point Comfort* and *Point Marone* returned to the vicinity of Han Mot island and blasted the location with mortar fire before departing.

Despite periodic flashes of action, Market Time duty mostly involved long hours of routine boarding. During daylight hours, WPBs spent most of their time near shores, where there were greater concentrations of junks. At night, they conducted radar patrols in their areas to detect moving contacts. Cutters usually made two types of night patrols: along the coastline, about two miles offshore, in the vicinity of prohibited zones; and barrier patrols along area boundaries or between groups of islands and the mainland. WPBs seldom patrolled seaward portions of their areas where there was little traffic or activity; larger ships and air patrols covered those waters.

Cutter commanding officers thought mass boardings, as opposed to selective boardings, were the most effective ways to stop infiltration. Hayes said, "We thought about selective boarding, but we were convinced the best way was to board everything in sight." Priority attention was given to vessels under way and closing the coast. Cutters usually brought junks alongside to board so they could be observed more closely. Junk crews topside, handling lines and fenders, were easier to watch and cover with weapons. Three-hundred-watt floodlights

Author on the bridge of USCGC Point Comfort *during a boarding in the Gulf of Thailand, 1965.*

were installed on the tops of handrail stanchions so junks alongside at night could be illuminated while cutter decks remained darkened. Alongside boardings for larger junks were difficult in rough weather; junk crews had trouble bringing their single-screw vessels alongside stationary cutters. WPB skippers had to be ready to back down hard or move ahead to avoid damage. Cutter small boats also were used for boardings, particularly when checking anchored vessels, but this method was not preferred, because of the vulnerability of boat crews.[13]

Hayes said, "Covering the area [to detect vessels] was an effective operation, but searches were my major reservation." Larger fishing junks put chopped ice on their catches and covered everything with rice hulls for insulation. There was no way to know for certain what was under the fish without removing the catch. Steel probing rods could not penetrate the ice to the bottom. Metal detectors were too sensitive, picking up signals from bolts in the hull and keel. Unloading ice and fish in suspicious circumstances was laborious and time-consuming and caused spoilage. Crews faced similar problems in searching cargo junks loaded with sacks of rice and assorted supplies. Woodcutter vessels also carried logs and charcoal from offshore islands to the mainland.[14]

Active boarding programs, which usually involved all hands, quickly fatigued ten-man cutter crews, who worked twelve- to sixteen-hour days. Crews were divided into three watch sections, with the commanding officer generally not standing watches. When a seaman was added to the complement late in 1965, the cook no longer had to stand watch. Each watch section consisted of an officer or petty officer of the deck, an engineer, and a helmsman. Since 82-footers were designed to run with unmanned engine rooms, all three men stood the watch in the pilothouse. Engineers made half-hourly checks in engineering spaces and monitored gages from the bridge. The helmsman made security checks in non-engineering spaces and above decks. Causey said, "The way we worked it [on *Point Young*], you were on watch for four hours, on standby for four hours, and off for four hours. That made for some pretty long days. Sometimes we'd work for eight hours, be off for four, and then work another eight."[15]

Because crews were small, personnel were cross trained to perform different watch functions, operate communications and electronic gear, fire all weapons, read gages, and handle lines. Depending on the situation, cutters modified their boarding bills to conduct routine nighttime boardings without using oncoming watch sections; COs were up for all boardings. With the heavy emphasis on boarding, crews were constantly reminded to keep up their vigilance and not to let operations become routine. Standing one-in-three watches and conducting nighttime boardings and frequent general quarters left little time for routine maintenance or repair work on patrol. Cutters were relieved on station; transit time after relief decreased the time a WPB had back at the "mother ship" to less than two days. Crews coming off patrol were debriefed, performed maintenance, took on fuel and supplies, and completed paperwork—while resting up for the next patrol.[16]

While high humidity was a problem for all electronic gear, the CR-103 radar proved to be effective and reliable. Newer SPS-53 radars were installed in the spring of 1967. Radar ranges were limited by low antenna height and types of targets; ranges for wooden junks were only three miles for boats under thirty feet and four-and-a-half miles for junks larger than that. Radars detected steel-hulled ships of one hundred feet at ten miles. Visual detection ranges during daylight were only slightly better than radar. Small junks could be seen at three-and-a-half miles and larger vessels at five-and-a-half miles. Small 100-foot steel hulls could be seen at nine miles. Against coastal backgrounds, however, visual detection ranges for all kinds of craft were much less.[17]

In addition to boarding, cutters provided naval gunfire support for shore units. *Point Clear* was called on for naval gunfire support on 20 October 1965, when a South Vietnamese popular force outpost south of Ha Tien came under heavy attack. The platoon manning the outpost was running out of ammunition and was about to be overrun. They made a desperate plea for help to the special forces at Ha Tien. The special forces detachment asked *Point Clear,* patrolling offshore, if she could help. By the time the cutter moved into firing position, Viet Cong had reached the final defenses; government troops had retreated into their command bunker. Defenders used the last of their tracer ammunition to fire into the advancing VC to spot for *Point Clear.* The cutter's crew poured .50-caliber fire into the oncoming guerrillas, but it failed to stop them. Lt. Jon C. Uithol, *Clear's* commanding officer, said, "We fired our port guns until they were red and then used the starboard [guns]." Finally, in desperation, the platoon called for high-explosive mortar rounds to be fired on the compound. Using flashes from hand-grenades as points of aim, *Clear* pumped out 81mm rounds, which broke the Viet Cong attack, and they retreated. A visit to the outpost the next morning by Capt. William E. Angel, USA, in command of Special Forces Detachment A-421, confirmed that Coast Guard fire was the prime factor in turning back the VC attack. He said:

> The 81mm HE [high explosive] and illuminating fire in addition to .50-caliber [machine-gun] MG fire was in my opinion the turning point of the VC attack. At the time the Coast Guard started firing, the VC were on their final assault to the perimeter of the PF [popular forces] defenses. The Coast Guard placed effective fire into the VC while illu-

Cutters engage in first combat action in Gulf of Thailand on 25 August 1965. USCGC Point Comfort's *gun crew fires 81mm mortar at Viet Cong staging area north of An Thoi on Phu Quoc Island.*

minating the area, enabling the defenders to fire their small arms at targets.[18]

Requests for naval gunfire support missions in the gulf continued to increase as action ashore intensified. Commander Naval Forces Vietnam proposed assigning a DER to area 9 for NGFS, but shallow coastal waters in the northern part of the area put most targets out of range for 3-inch guns. WPBs responded to requests for support with their 81mm mortars. Rear Adm. Norman C. Venzke, who took command of Division 11 in 1967, said of the increasing naval gunfire support missions, "It got to a point where we were having an [81mm] ammunition supply problem at An Thoi. We were running dry. They had to fly it in."[19]

When 50-foot Navy fast patrol craft arrived at An Thoi, they were used for closer patrols. Cutters began operating at greater distances from the support ship. CTF 115 was anxious to get more patrol presence on both the east and west sides of the southern Ca Mau peninsula. In January 1966, cutters began continuous patrolling in southernmost portions of areas 8 and 9—120 to 210 miles from An Thoi—which were wide open with little protection during heavy weather. Venzke said, "Basically, if you needed long legs or the weather was heavy, you had to use a WPB. . . . During monsoon season, crews took a hell of a beating, particularly in the open waters during southwest monsoons." While on extended operations, WPBs came under operational control of the destroyer patrolling in the area, receiving fuel, water, and provisions from her. Eighty-two-footers, with six-and-a-half-foot drafts, were the first U.S. vessels capable of probing unsurveyed water along the southern coast. They explored river mouths and charted soundings for future operations.

Market Time's First Trawler

Point Grey was in her last day of a long-range patrol in area 8 on 9 May 1966. The patrol was extended from four to six days when *Grey's* replacement developed mechanical problems. High winds and heavy seas battered the cutter for most of the patrol; cooking hot meals was impossible and sleep was difficult, at best. On the last night of the patrol, winds died down and seas finally let up, but were still running at eight feet. Heavy rain, which had been falling from a moonless sky, also was slackening. At 2200, the watch in the pilothouse spotted what appeared to be two fires on shore just north of the Bo De river. *Point Grey's* commanding officer, Lt. (jg) Charles B. Mosher, said, "We saw the fires and were suspicious. Why would fires be burning in the rain? It wasn't cold."

Mosher decided to stay in the area to see if there was any activity. *Point Grey* closed to three miles offshore and waited; she had 10 feet of water under her keel. Mosher said, "Besides being suspicious, it gave us a reason to heave to so we could ride better." *Point Grey* waited for three hours. When the fires died out and nothing had happened, the cutter got under way after midnight and headed south for the patrol area boundary to meet her relief. *Point Grey's* XO, Lt. (jg) Roger R. Rosnoski, had the deck.[20]

At 0050, the watch picked up a radar contact closing on the port bow; the vessel, at a range of nine miles, was heading northwest on a converging course. Mosher said, "We picked her up so far out, she had to be steel. We knew it wasn't [USS] *Brister* [the DER in the area], so it could only be one of two things: A South Vietnamese patrol boat—they never talked to us—or somebody interesting." *Point Grey* only had to alter course slightly to intercept the contact. At 0120, with the crew at general quarters, the cutter closed on the ship, which was running without lights. When the contact did not respond to flashing-light challenges, *Point Grey* turned on her searchlight. The vessel was a small coastal freighter, about 120-feet long, riding low in the water, with no markings on her blue-gray hull or white superstructure and no flag flying. A boxy cabin and short stack were aft and what appeared to be fishing nets were in her well deck. Mosher said, "We made a tentative ID that she was Chinese Nationalist. We called in a standard sighting report. They [operations center] sent back a contact designation of 10-E1."

Mosher decided it was too rough to board, particularly at night with rain obscuring visibility. He said, "She slowed and started to maneuver on different courses. We thought she was lost. We took up a position inshore of her and just sat there. We waited for what seemed an eternity. We weren't sure what we had."

Point Grey was facing a new situation: this was the first suspicious trawler interdicted by a Market Time unit. There was no intelligence about infiltration trawler activity near Ca Mau. The last trawler action had been at Vung Ro Bay in February 1965. When the ship picked up speed and headed for shore, *Point Grey* fired 81mm illumination rounds and followed. Mosher said, "I didn't want to open fire on her. We still thought she was Chinese Nationalist." The ship ran aground two miles from the coast at 0500. *Point Grey* closed to 100 feet and put a light on her. Mosher said, "We could see people aboard. One guy was in the waist and a couple of people were walking around on the stern." *Point Grey's* VNN liaison petty officer tried to communicate with the people, but they did not reply. Mosher stuck with his decision to wait for daylight to board. Seas were becoming more calm all the time. He said, "Even though I didn't have any indication they were bad guys, I didn't like the tactical situation." Mosher told the operations center that the ship was aground and they would board at 0700.

When the sun came up, it was a clear day; seas had calmed and there was hardly any wind. The ship, pushed toward shore by a rising tide, was 1,000 yards from the coast. The shoreline was swampy and covered with growth except for a small sandy spit. When the cutter approached the ship to board, the crew saw lines over the side. While they were investigating the situation, the cutter came under fire from ashore. Mosher said, "Firing was coming from three locations, automatic and rifle fire. We could see ricochets in the water. I don't think we took any hits. Most of the splashes were short of us." *Point Grey* backed off and reported what had happened.

While waiting for USS *Brister* (DER 327) to arrive, *Grey* made firing passes on the shoreline to prevent Viet Cong from reaching the ship. The cutter made three runs, firing her 81mm mortar and .50-caliber machine guns. When return fire came from the spit, *Point Grey* replied with 81mm high explosives rounds, fused for airburst. The firing stopped. *Brister* arrived at 1145 and a coastal minesweeper, USS *Vireo* (MSC 205), came on-scene in early afternoon. At 1325, three USAF F-100 Super Sabers made air strikes on the shoreline, dropping napalm and firing 20mm cannons. When Mosher went aboard *Brister,* he said "I got together with the CO and Ops officer. We developed a plan of action. There wasn't much *Brister* could do. She was at maximum gun range. The plan was for us to go in, cover ourselves as best we could, and get aboard. If it was too shallow for us to reach the ship, *Brister's* small boat would try and we would cover them."

Point Grey headed for the ship with *Brister's* motor whaleboat following at a good distance. The tide had now pushed the trawler to 100 yards from land; she was perpendicular to shore, bow in. The cutter was pushing mud with her bow when she got close to the trawler. A four-man boarding party, with the XO in charge, waited aft of the pilothouse. Two members of the boarding party were from the forward gun crew; they were replaced on the mount by Major Gillespie, U.S. Army—he was aboard for transportation to An Thoi—and the VNN liaison petty officer. Mosher said, "They let us get awfully close [to the beach]. Then they hit us with everything, including heavy machine guns. Rounds went right through our steel hull. We tried to come in so the trawler was protecting us [between the cutter and the beach], but they were firing from a wide-ranging front." The three men manning the forward gun all went down in a matter of seconds. Petty officer Kepler, the cook, was hit first; he took a .30-caliber round through his thigh. The Army major also got a clean hit through the thigh. The VNN petty officer was the worst casualty: He had been bending over, opening a box of ammo, when he was hit; the round caught him in the back of the left shoulder, at the opening to his flak jacket, and went under his collarbone, up his neck, and out his cheek.

The boarding party ran forward, cleared the gun, got it firing again, and dragged the wounded to safety. Mosher backed hard and the screws dug into the mud. The tachometers were up, but the cutter was hardly moving. The crew could feel the cutter shudder as she fought her way through the mud. Black smoke poured from the stern exhausts. Mosher said, "When I got her back to where she was floating, I twisted around to get the port guns firing. I still hadn't given up [on boarding] yet. That's when the radar quit. I was looking at the scope, checking the range to the beach. A slug came through the front of the pilothouse, hit the console, and went through the outer case, tumbling. It shattered on the end of the sweep motor, right in front of me. An inch lower and it would have gotten me between my belt and my crotch."

The Army major, with his trouser leg cut off and a tourniquet around his thigh, took over the starboard quarter .50-caliber mount. With three .50s firing, Mosher's ears were ringing; the smell of gun smoke was heavy in the air. He said, "The major was angry. He put six or seven belts of ammo through, just taking his thumb off the trigger long enough to reload. He would walk it [gunfire] up to the tree line. When he got on target, he kept it there." When Mosher looked around for the motor whaleboat, she was headed back toward *Brister*. He decided to pull back too.

Mosher said, "There wasn't any confusion during the action, because everybody knew their job. We had been under fire before and that probably helped." *Point Grey* cleared the area and went alongside the coastal minesweeper to pick up a corpsman to treat the wounded. Mosher said, "When we came alongside, the Navy was a little awed because we had quite a few bullet holes."

When *Point Grey*'s crew did a damage assessment, they found the cutter had been hit more than thirty times. Mosher said, "Our bridge was pretty well shot up. We had hits in the superstructure and a few through the hull—one right at the waterline. The forward ammo lockers took hits, but nothing detonated. We had to get rid of some 81mm rounds. Bullets went through the canisters. We lowered them into the water and let them go. When we went to put our boat over the side, we found the motor had been hit."

After *Point Grey* pulled back, three VNAF A-1 Skyraiders came in and struck the beach with high explosives and napalm. Late in the afternoon on 10 May 1966, CTF 115 ordered the trawler destroyed. The Viet Cong's aggressive defense of the ship indicated the value of her cargo. CTF 115 knew the trawler, probably loaded with arms and ammunition, could not be left that close to shore overnight. *Brister,* with her 14-foot draft, could not get close enough to reach the trawler with her two single-mount, 3-inch-50 guns. *Point Grey* and USCGC *Point Cypress* (WPB 82326)—which arrived on-scene from Division 13— were given the job of destroying the trawler.

Mosher said, "Her *[Brister]* shots fell short. So *Grey* and *Cypress* went in. Since my radar wasn't working, *Cypress* gave me ranges to the target. We went after her [trawler] with 81mm HE. We fired about twenty rounds apiece. We scored hits and set her afire. But there were no secondary explosions. When we pulled back, she was burning." The cutters were alongside the destroyer escort when, at 2030, a violent explosion ripped the trawler apart. Mosher said, "It was almost dark when the ship blew. We were out at *Brister* and it shook us. You could see there wasn't very much of her left."

Throughout the night of 10 May and the morning of 11 May 1966, *Point Grey* and *Point Cypress* fired illumination over the remains of the trawler to prevent any VC from reaching her. Junks from Coastal Group 41 arrived at 2300 and swept the beach with harassing fire. In the morning, South Vietnamese troops established a beachhead. Unable to repair her radar, *Point Grey* transferred her remaining ammunition to *Point Cypress* and headed back to An Thoi.

An accurate assessment of the effectiveness of Market Time patrols in stopping infiltration of arms and supplies to the Viet Cong was very difficult. The number of actual contraband seizures was relatively small and there was no way of knowing the preventive impact of vigorous interdiction and search programs. During the first ten months after the arrival of Squadron One, approximately 80,000 junks were detected— visually or on radar—by U.S. forces. Of these junks, more than

40,000 were either boarded or inspected. As a result, only 30 suspicious junks and 140 suspects were turned over to South Vietnamese authorities because of discrepancies in identification papers.[21]

Hayes said, "To the extent that we had no intelligence information to the contrary, I would have to conclude we were fairly successful. I say that because I think the people we were supporting ashore, our Army and Navy advisors, sooner or later would have gotten word of something. It would have filtered back through the Vietnamese, particularly if it [infiltration of arms] was happening regularly. . . . We had both Vietnamese intelligence and Navy intelligence people. They certainly had their networks and something would have come back through them. My conclusion is that it was pretty darn tight."[22]

Venzke said, "I theorize that it would be stupid for a trawler to bring a load down [from North Vietnam or China] and then try to come through the 4th coastal zone when they could go north to Kep or Sihanoukville [across the border in Cambodia], unload there, and bring the material south across the border. In fact, material was intercepted coming from Cambodia into the 4th coastal zone by truck. I think our aggressive patrolling made them use alternate routes."[23]

Extensive river and canal systems, running through rural regions of the country, were a safer means for transporting troops and supplies than attempting to move them through heavily patrolled coastal waters. As the war continued, the threat of arms and war materials being infiltrated from sea was reevaluated. On 30 September 1968, Vice Adm. Elmo R. Zumwalt, Jr., relieved Rear Adm. Kenneth L. Veth as commander Naval Forces Vietnam. He redirected the focus of interdiction operations to controlling the infiltration threat on internal waters. He used his three task forces, with in-country resources, to respond to the threat: TF 115, Market Time, with 26 WPBs and 81 PCFs; TF 116, Game Warden, with 197 PBRs (river patrol craft); and TF 117, Riverine Assault Force, with 161 armored river craft. The program he initiated was called SEA LORDS (Southeast Asia Lake, Ocean, River, and Delta Strategy).[24]

PCFs, because of their shallower draft and limited capability for working offshore, were increasingly used for incursions up rivers and canals on SEA LORDS operations. Cutters in the gulf, restricted from working inland because of their size and draft, covered coastal areas previously patrolled by Swifts. CTF 115 shifted WPBs from Division 11 to Division 12 at Danang and to Division 13 at Cat Lo, where the threat of infiltration from offshore was considered greater. By 1968, Division 11 was reduced to four WPBs and one 105-foot Royal Thai Navy patrol boat. The division continued to patrol the Cambodian border and the northern portion of area 9 with its limited resources.

Each division of Squadron One operated under unique conditions. Cutters in the Gulf of Thailand worked in muddy shallow coastal waters, patrolling offshore island groups and carrying out operations with the Army's special forces. Division 11 cutters and crews, at the end of a long supply line with few facilities or amenities, boarded thousands of craft of all description and engaged in all types of operations.

5

Patrolling the Delta

From Vietnam, we learned that we [the Coast Guard] should be very aware of our military mission and that we bring to bear something that this country needs. The Coast Guard is a very capable war-making service in a specialty area—it has the expertise and experience to run patrol boats. Anytime there is a war that needs patrol boats, the Coast Guard ought to be there as the source of boats, experience and people.

Adm. Paul A. Yost, USCG, CTG 115.3, CTG 115.4, and 4th coast zone advisor

Co Chien

Point League's **petty officer of the deck** called Lt. (jg) Stephen T. Ulmer to the bridge just before midnight on 20 June 1966; the 82-foot cutter was in shoal waters at the mouth of the Co Chien river. Ulmer, on his first patrol in command of the WPB, went up the ladder to the pilothouse. Scheduled for rotation back to the United States after a year in Vietnam with Division 12, Ulmer volunteered to extend for the opportunity to command a cutter.[1]

The night was hot and the air still; seas were calm. There was no moon. After clearing the shoals, Ulmer returned to the cabin, only to be called two hours later. This time, the bridge reported a large radar contact—inbound. The vessel, believed to be a steel-hull, ran without lights. Ulmer put on khaki shorts, slipped on some moccasins, and went up the ladder to the bridge. In the darkened pilothouse, he watched the radar contact get stronger as the range decreased. He picked up the microphone to the high-frequency radio and said, "Grainy Lamp, this is Sepia Mike. I have a contact inbound for Co Chien river. She's eight miles offshore and running without lights. I'm going to challenge. Will keep you informed." The Coastal Surveillance Center (CSC) at Vung Tau rogered for the report.

The ship, closing the coast on a westerly course, was making six knots. *Point League* was between the vessel and shore, just to the north of her track. The cutter's crew went to general quarters and Ulmer set a course to intercept. When *Point League* was broad on the ship's starboard bow, at a range of two miles, Ulmer began signaling with a hand-held Aldis lamp. He challenged the ship with flashing light four times without response. *Point League* then closed to 600 yards off the ship's starboard beam and turned on her searchlight. Ulmer said, "She was a coastal cargo vessel, about 100 feet long with a dark-green hull. Her pilothouse was aft and she had two cargo hatches forward. She was towing a 20-foot wooden junk on her starboard side." When the light hit the trawler, she stopped. Then she got under way and headed for the river, leaving the junk behind. The trawler quickly increased speed to 12 knots.

Point League put two bursts of .50-caliber machine-gun fire across the ship's bow. The trawler responded immediately with intense heavy machine-gun fire and continued toward the river. The cutter doused her searchlight, passed under the ship's stern and came up on her port side. When broad on the trawler's port quarter, *Point League* turned on her searchlight and opened fire with three .50-caliber machine guns. North Vietnamese gunners, manning Chinese communist .51-caliber heavy machine guns, were waiting.

Ulmer said, "All she could see of us was our searchlight on top of the pilothouse. I was right below it, controlling the light from inside. Bullets came right through the pilothouse. They were firing incendiary rounds. They lit up when they hit, but didn't start any fires." Lieutenant junior grade Markle, the cutter's executive officer, went down with a head wound. Ulmer and BM1 Clyde K. Wooddell, on the helm, were momentarily blinded by flashes of detonating rounds.

After *Point League*'s initial report of action, the CSC was on the radio demanding more information. The cutter was too busy engaging the trawler to respond. Ulmer said, "I handed the mike to our [VNN] liaison officer. He didn't have a GQ billet. I told him, 'Here, you answer them. Tell them we're in the middle of a fight. We'll give them information later.'" Ensign Tung took the mike, and in careful English, said, "Sorry, we are very busy. Call back later." Then, when the ensign could not find the bracket to hang up the mike, he stuck it in an empty coffee mug in a cup holder. When he pushed the mike into the cup, the transmit button depressed. The open mike jammed the circuit; other units could hear bits and pieces of the action, but no one could transmit. The situation lasted until *Point Slocum,* coming from the adjacent area to assist, got close enough to raise *Point League* on FM radio and tell her she had an open mike.

The trawler steamed toward shore while exchanging fire with the cutter. Ulmer saw the shoreline on radar and knew the ship was heading for shoal water; he turned off the searchlight and let her run aground. *Point League* backed off to 1,000 yards and used her 81mm mortar to illuminate the vessel, which grounded 75 yards from shore. The cutter continued to pour .50-caliber fire into the ship; return fire stopped. Ulmer said, "By now, we were getting all kinds of communications. We were told the Air Force was getting ready to do their thing." During the action, only two of *Point League*'s crew were wounded—the bow gunner's leg was grazed by a bullet and the XO suffered a scalp wound from a sliver of shrapnel. Ulmer said, "We were very fortunate. God was with us."

One of the Air Force's C-47 gunships, known as "Puff the Magic Dragon," arrived on-scene. The plane, a military version of the DC-3, was armed with three 7.62mm miniguns. She made a pass, dropping flares and then raining fire down on the ship. At 6,000 rounds a minute, tracers came down from the sky like a shaft of light. Ulmer said, "It looked like a downpour in the water around the ship." Helo gunships arrived next and blasted the ship with rockets. When dawn came, *Point League* took fire from shore. Ulmer said, "They were firing from behind a sand dune, just back from the beach. We could see muzzle flashes and splashes in the water. I told our gunners to suppress the fire. They did a great job. I was amazed at their accuracy from 1,000 yards."

Just after dawn, crews of *Point League* and *Point Slocum* saw the trawler erupt in a ball of flame. The explosion, probably a scuttling charge, left the ship on fire. The two 82-footers attempted to approach the burning trawler, but took heavy fire from the beach. Ulmer said, "We returned fire as best we could and called for air support." Jets came in and dropped antipersonnel munitions behind the sand dunes; the firing slowed but didn't stop. When two coastal group command junks arrived, *Point League, Point Slocum,* and *Point Hudson*—a third cutter that arrived on-scene—used the junks to trans-

Crewmen from USCGC Point League *and USCGC* Point Slocum *fight fire aboard North Vietnamese ammunition trawler. Ship was forced aground by USCGC* Point League *during engagement off entrance to Co Chien river.*

port firefighting parties to the trawler. WPBs moved in and laid down covering fire, while the junks approached the ship, one on each side. The burning ship, loaded with an estimated 100 tons of ammunition and 1,200 weapons, was grounded perpendicular to the shore—bow in. Ulmer said, "There was a lot of smoke. She was burning pretty good. We were worried about exploding ammo." When USS *Tortuga* (LSD 26) arrived offshore, she sent in a landing craft with another firefighting party. By 1100 the fire on the ship was under control. *Point League* and *Point Slocum* made up alongside the smoldering ship, one on either side. With the cutters heading to seaward and the trawler pointing toward shore, they attempted to refloat the hulk.

As word of the trawler action spread, Ulmer said, "All kinds of people came, including South Vietnamese Navy ships." At 1335, the VNN ship *No Than* (HQ-225) ignored warnings to keep clear while the cutters tried to refloat the trawler and came alongside. In his report Ulmer said, "Her seamen poured across our decks, grabbing souvenirs from the vessel like it was a bargain sale." When *No Than* finally moved off to let the cutters continue, she left several of her crew behind. With *Point League* on one side and *Point Slocum* on the other, the cutters tried to break the ship free; an ebbing tide made it impossible. As more ships and personnel arrived to look at the trawler, the two 82-foot cutters gathered up their gear, recalled their crews, and departed.[2]

On 5 August 1965, COMUSMACV requested more vessels to patrol the Vietnamese coast. The request resulted in a study of the overall infiltration threat. After meeting from 2 September 1965 to 18 September 1965, representatives from CINCPAC, COMUSMACV, CINCPACFLT, OPNAV, and CHNAVADVGRP recommended more ships for offshore patrolling, a doubling of aircraft effort, and an increase in the number of patrol vessels for inshore coverage. The study called for 50 percent increase in the number of Coast Guard WPBs.[3]

On 22 October 1965, in anticipation of a request for more patrol boats, Coast Guard Commandant Adm. Edwin J. Roland ordered preliminary preparations for deploying another division of WPBs. His message called for the reassignment of smaller cutters, 44-foot motor lifeboats and 40-foot utility boats, to fill gaps in search-and-rescue coverage created by deploying 82-footers. Coast Guard headquarters, on 29 October 1965, directed its districts to implement the planned deployment of nine more cutters to Squadron One.

Barham F. Thomson was a lieutenant junior grade, serving as executive officer aboard the 125-foot cutter USCGC *Cahoone* (WMEC 131) when his orders arrived. The cutter was in a shipyard at New Orleans. He said, "My CO was on leave somewhere in upstate New York, hunting. His wife had to get hold of him to get him back to the ship. I was literally gone in three days."[4]

Enlisted crews for the new division stayed with their cutters, just as was done with Divisions 11 and 12. Gunner's mates and electronics technicians again were added to complements. Lieutenants junior grade selected to command cutters were volunteers. In contrast to the first two divisions, in which all COs had previously commanded WPBs, only three of the eleven new commanding officers had WPB command experience. Remaining COs came from assignments as executive officers aboard 125-foot medium endurance cutters or coastal buoy tenders. COs were five years junior to lieutenants assigned to command boats with Divisions 11 and 12.

Officers assigned to command cutters with the first deployment were experienced lieutenants; many had two previous commands—a WPB and a LORAN station. They developed initial tactics and procedures for operations in hostile coastal waters. Added maturity was beneficial in establishing relationships with other services and the Vietnamese. Rear Adm. Marshall E. Gilbert was a lieutenant when he deployed with the first cutters to Vietnam. He said, "They wanted to make sure we [the Coast Guard] went over there and performed. That was the right decision. There was a lot of pressure that we perform successfully. It was appropriate to back off and use less senior COs after the initial experience."[5]

Cdr. James A. Hodgman, commander Squadron One, assigned Lt. Cdr. William E. Lehr, Squadron One's engineer, to command newly formed Division 13 during outfitting. Lehr said, "They were the shortest set of orders I ever got. They said, 'Go to Subic Bay. Assemble boats and crews. Outfit Division 13. When ready, sail to Cat Lo, Vietnam.'" Lehr asked Hodgman to assign Lt. Eugene J. Hickey from Division 12 and Lt. Gilbert from Division 11 to go with him to Subic Bay; he wanted some Vietnam experience in the division. Lehr said, "They had both been on the line and knew what the heck was going

Division 13's USCGC Point Cypress *being loaded aboard SS* Pioneer Myth *for shipment to the Philippines*

on. They could explain the operation probably better than I could." Lehr arrived at Subic Bay Naval Station on 10 December 1965 and established Division 13 two days later. The division, with nine patrol boats, had a complement of 161 personnel—26 officers, 24 chief petty officers, and 111 petty officers and nonrated personnel.[6]

After processing and training in California, Division 13 staff and repair personnel began arriving at Subic Bay on 14 December 1965. Boat crews, who received additional weapon and survival training, started arriving three days after Christmas. Twenty-one of Division 13's personnel were sent on to Divisions 11 and 12 in-country in exchange for crewmen with Vietnam experience.

While waiting for their cutters at Subic Bay, crews received jungle survival and evasion training, and weapon practice. Cutters arrived as deck cargo aboard ships: four on board SS *Pioneer Myth* on 24 January, one on SS *Transcaribbean* on 27 January, and the final four aboard SS *Ocean Cloud* on 2 February. Crews spent six weeks at Subic Bay training, outfitting their cutters, and conducting underway exercises and gunnery practice. They painted their WPBs dark gray before departing Subic Bay. Lehr said, "It was basically the same routine as before, with crews arriving by plane and boats coming on ships. But this time, the boats were better fitted out back in the states."[7]

Two last minute casualties threatened to delay Division 13's departure. A galley reefer on one boat broke down right before deployment. When a replacement could not be found in the Navy supply system at Subic Bay, Lehr said, "We went to the Navy Exchange and bought a commercial refrigerator. We cut a hole in the cutter's deck, lowered the reefer into the galley, and the boat went to Vietnam with a Fridgidaire. I forget how we paid for it."[8]

The other problem was more serious. On 13 February 1966, *Point League* was under way finishing training exercises. Suddenly, her main engine alarm sounded on the bridge; it was Sunday afternoon—five days before deployment. Main engine lube oil samples revealed water dilution. Cutter engineers began tearing the plant down to determine the extent of damage. Working into the night, they discovered three scored pistons and scored cylinder liners. They found more damage early Monday morning. By Monday afternoon, with the engine jacked up and the crankshaft exposed, it was apparent that a complete overhaul was required.

An urgent request went out to Squadron One for parts to be shipped to Subic Bay. Division 12, with the best parts inventory, responded to the request. At Danang, parts and tools were assembled into complete "ready for installation" kits to speed up repair work. Division 12's repair force delivered crated equipment to the airport at Danang for shipment to Cubi Point Naval Air Station at Subic Bay. Division 12 engineers slept on the crates at the runway to make sure they got out on the first available flight. A truck from Division 13 was waiting at Cubi Point when the Marine C-130 with the parts aboard landed.

The damaged engine was stripped down, literally to the foundation. Enginemen from all cutters worked in three shifts, each under the supervision of a chief petty officer; CWO-1 George W. Fenlin was in overall charge of the repair. Crews worked around-the-clock and rebuilt the engine in 72 hours. Partial load run-in was made on Friday morning, 18 February 1966. The division, including *Point League,* rendezvoused as scheduled with USS *Forster* (DER 334) at 1600 that day near the entrance to Subic Bay to begin the transit. *Point League's* engine run-in was completed during the voyage.

In preparing for deployment, Lehr made an advance visit to the South Vietnamese naval facility where cutters would be based. It was at Cat Lo, a village on the main highway, 35 miles southeast of Saigon on the eastern edge of a large delta swamp. After visiting the base, Lehr said it was:

> Six kilometers north of Vung Tau on Highway 15 on a narrow strip of land between the highway and the river. The base is 75 yards wide by 300 yards long. There are a number of buildings on the site occupied by the South Vietnamese Navy. Unlike Danang, there will be no clear boundary between Vietnamese and U.S. living and working areas. Lieutenant Commander Son is base commanding officer and commander of the 3rd coastal zone. He is cooperative and easy to work with. I am impressed with the cleanliness of base. It is the best South Vietnamese facility I have seen.
>
> H-shaped Quonset huts are under construction. Five will be built for barracks. A fuel facility is also under construction. Construction of storage and shop buildings has been held up.
>
> There is a 125-foot concrete dock at one end of the base. It is only available to the U.S. Navy on a part-time basis. It is owned by the South Vietnamese Navy and used as a commercial pier. The tidal range is twelve to fourteen feet with a current of four knots. There are several curves in the six-mile channel to the base.
>
> Security is integrated, VN–U.S. U.S. mans some defense positions and stands some security watches. An unsecure mangrove-covered island is directly opposite the base.[9]

On 10 February 1966, Division 13 sent three men with aids-to-navigation experience to Cat Lo to evaluate and mark the channel. Using begged-and-borrowed equipment and supplies, they sounded the channel in the Song Dinh river and set markers. The division's outfit and a 26-man advance party arrived aboard the light cargo ship USS *Mark* (AKL 12) a week later and made preparations for the division's arrival.

Division 13 cutters enjoyed good weather during an uneventful transit to Vietnam; they refueled once from their escort. When the formation arrived off Vung Tau on the morning of 22 February 1966, *Forster* anchored and cutters nested alongside. Late that afternoon, cutters—spaced 1,000 yards apart—went up the river on a strong flood tide to the South Vietnamese Naval Base. WPBs nested three deep at the fuel pier, paralleling the stream. Capt. Robert J. LoForte, the new Coast Guard commander of Squadron One, and Lt. Cdr. Axel J. Hagstrom, who would take command of the division, were waiting on the pier when the cutters arrived. The division was greeted by the mayor of Vung Tau (an ARVN lieutenant colonel), the 3rd coastal zone commander (a VNN commander), an honor guard, a police band, and a group of school girls. The teenaged girls, wearing white traditional *ao-dai* dresses, carried small U.S. flags and presented each cutter's commanding officer with a flower lei. After welcoming speeches and a brief reception, six WPBs returned down river to the anchorage at Vung Tau, lessening the attractiveness of a target for a VC attack. Six cutters departed on patrol at 0800 the next morning. They patrolled coastal areas extending from 60 miles north of Vung Tau to 120 miles south.[10]

Cutters tied up end-to-end along a 300-foot wooden bulkhead, paralleling the river. When additional cutters were in port, they nested outboard. Surging muddy waters of the Song Dinh river, driven by unusually high tides, made mooring difficult. Thomson said, "The tide was tremendous. At times, I could literally climb onto the bridge [of the cutter] from the pier and at other times I had to go up a gangway to get on the main deck." When Navy Swift boats began arriving at Cat Lo, they moored at a floating pier made of small barges. Very little junk traffic passed between the base and a mangrove island 200 yards away. VNN ships also moored at Cat Lo, but Division 13 had little contact with them.

Division 13's headquarters was in a cinder block building, and maintenance shops and warehouse spaces were in another. Division staff and maintenance personnel were billeted in long Quonset huts that ran perpendicular to the highway, ending just inside the perimeter of the base, which was congested with little open space. It had paved roads, but no sidewalks; paths were worn through the weeds between buildings. Trees grew inside the compound at the Vietnamese end, but not at the U.S. end. Initially, South Vietnamese were responsible for base security and assigned all personnel to stations for defense of the base. Gilbert said, "My GQ station was in a watchtower.

Sandbagged guard tower near cutter and Swift moorings at Cat Lo, 1966.

I put together a kit for GQ with extra clips, flashlight, water, and food. If we got hit, I wanted to be ready." Security later was taken over by the U.S. Navy. BMCM William J. Miller was a BM1 when he was stationed aboard *Point Slocum* in Division 13 in 1968. He said, "We all felt the base was secure, until we got hit during the 1968 Tet offensive."[11]

Topography varied greatly in Division 13's patrol areas. Littoral regions from Vung Tau south to the tip of the Ca Mau peninsula were dominated by major river systems. Delta land was low and offshore waters shallow. Mud stained the South China Sea for miles to seaward until the stains ended abruptly, giving way to clear blue water; a distinct line marked the division. North of Vung Tau, the land was rugged; mountains ran down to the sea. Waters were deep up to the surf-lined shores. Thomson said, "You could go right up to the shore. You could almost put your bow on the sandy beach. It was like California." In some places, cliffs with caves lined the shore. While the north portion of the area was scenic, patrols there were usually bor-

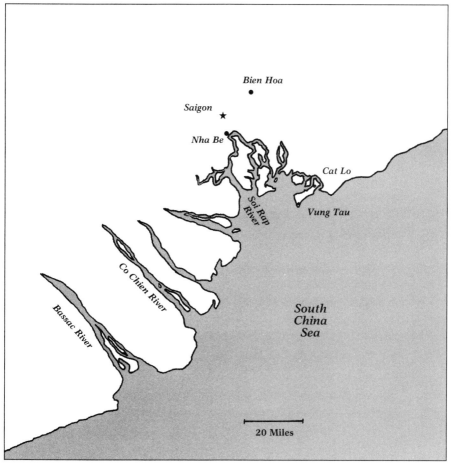

Coast Guard Division 13 operating area

ing; time passed slowly because there was little or no traffic to board.[12]

When cutters got under way for patrol, they chopped to the Navy CSC at Vung Tau, where patrol areas were assigned. As with Divisions 11 and 12, the initial emphasis was on boarding. Thomson said, "Everything we saw we boarded. Sail, motor, fishing, cargo, whatever. That was the name of the game. We were big into numbers." Most vessels were small fishing boats, 20 to 25 feet long with three-or-four-man crews. They were boarded alongside. Same as in the other divisions, large cargo junks were searched by boarding parties while cutters stood off. Probe-type metal detectors were worked down into bulk cargoes to check for weapons or ammunition. Miller said, "We never found any, but we did find small amounts of medical supplies."[13]

The number of cutters assigned to Division 13 varied between nine and twelve, depending on areas to be patrolled, mission emphasis, weather, and maintenance requirements. WPBs patrolled from four to six days with a two-day in-port break. Underway times were often extended, however, when relief vessels were used for other missions or had maintenance problems. When patrols were extended north to Cam Rahn Bay, cutters made double patrols. Miller said, "We would patrol north for four or five days and then pull into Cam Rahn Bay. We'd spend a day or two there and then work our way south for another four or five days. We did that because the enroute time to get on-station was so great." Crews liked to pull into Cam Rahn Bay, which had a large facility with ample supplies and one of the best exchanges in Vietnam.[14]

Division 13's well-armed, shallow-draft, 82-foot WPBs had excellent potential for use in rivers of the delta. The vast 400-square-mile swamp extended from south of Saigon to the coast and was known as the "forest of assassins." Designated the Rung Sat Special Zone (RSSZ), the swamp, covered with mangrove and nipa palm, was infested with Viet Cong. It contained VC ammunition factories, training camps, rest areas, and medical facilities, all in continuous operation. The region was particularly important because supply ships had to pass through it to reach Saigon. Ships using the two main rivers to reach the city—the Long Tau and the broader but shallower Soi Rap—were vulnerable to attack. South Vietnamese Army troops were not able to dislodge the VC from the difficult terrain, which was crisscrossed with thousands of interconnecting rivers and streams. Stepped-up attacks on merchant shipping in January 1966 coincided with the rapid increase in the amount of military material being shipped to Saigon. Vulnerability of the waterways became an important consideration in the buildup. Planning for a Marine amphibious operation in the RSSZ, beginning in January 1966, was accelerated after the freighter, SS *Lorinda,* was ambushed in February 1966.[15]

The Viet Cong's major vulnerability in the RSSZ was the lack of food and water; supplies had to be brought in by junk. Provisions were received from VC-controlled territory on the other side of the Soi Rap river. In advance of Operation Jackstay, a Marine operation to "Sweep the Rung Sat and remove hostile forces adjacent to the channels," Division 13 cutters were ordered to patrol the lower reaches of the Soi Rap river. After two days of daylight patrols, WPBs began patrolling around-the-clock on 10 March 1966, making the first continuous U.S. river patrols in Vietnam. LoForte said in the squadron diary, "I plan to be aboard the first 24-hour patrol in the innermost area because I sense some concern on the part of crew members for the danger involved. Both banks of the Soi Rap are hostile. The entire area is a VC stronghold."[16]

LoForte flew to Cat Lo to discuss the operation with the division commander, his staff, and patrol boat commanding officers. Hickey, in command of *Point White,* said, "Being the senior underway guy in the division, I figured it was my privilege, honor, or whatever to be the first up there. I didn't think we would be very successful on the rivers. The enemy could attack from cover on either bank. The French tried and weren't successful. I didn't think it would take the VC very long to figure out WPBs had aluminum superstructures and thin steel hulls."[17]

Cutter patrols on the Soi Rap stopped large-scale movement of VC troops and supplies in or out of the zone and were used to gauge the strength of resistance that could be expected during Operation Jackstay. Beginning with the first 24-hour patrol, cutters intercepted VC junks crossing the river and engaged in actions almost nightly. Fire, routinely taken from ashore, included mortars and recoilless rifles. Actions on the Soi Rap river caused March 1966 to be the heaviest combat month since Squadron One arrived in Vietnam.

During one action, a Viet Cong senior official being protected by an armed escort was blown overboard by an explosion aboard his junk. The crew of *Point White* saved the badly burned man from drowning and treated his wounds. Hickey said, "He told us, 'Up until now, I considered Americans to be my enemies. They saved me. If I live, they will be my friends.'" He lived and, in advance of the operation, provided valuable intelligence about the location of VC activities throughout the RSSZ.[18]

When Jackstay began, WPBs were pulled in from coastal Market Time areas to patrol rivers in support of the operation. Capt. John T. Shepherd, operations officer for the naval advisory group in Saigon, directed river patrol activities of six WPBs and four PCFs from aboard the flagship. On the morning of 26 March 1966, ships of the amphibious ready group moved into the muddy waters off Long

USCGC Point Hudson *patrols the Soi Rap river in the Viet Cong–infested* Rung Sat *special zone, 1966.*

Thanh peninsula and put the Marine special landing force ashore. In describing patrol-boat support, Lt. Cdr. Robert E. Mumford, Jr., USN, on the staff of Commander Amphibious Squadron One, said:

> Patrols were conducted by day and by night. Some boats patrolled a single point, and others patrolled a stretch of river. Their mission was to stop enemy movement. The continuous boat patrols also prevented the enemy from planting as many mines as he might have, particularly since the only ones he had were of the command-detonated variety, which take a long time to emplace and require a continual watch if they are to destroy a victim.[19]

When the operation ended on 6 April 1966, most WPBs returned to coastal patrol duties, but some still patrolled the rivers. *Point Partridge* was patrolling the Soi Rap on 19 April 1966, when she picked up an unlighted target at 1940. She increased speed to intercept the junk crossing the river. When the cutter turned on her searchlight, two men in a 16-foot sampan opened fire. *Point Partridge* returned fire with .50-caliber machine guns. Both Viet Cong were knocked overboard. When *Point Partridge* closed on the boat, her crew saw one of the VC struggling and threw him a lifering. The man in the water tried to grab the ring, but couldn't—his right hand was severed at the wrist and his left arm was severed below the shoulder. BM1 Edward P. Owens immediately jumped into the water, pulled the VC to the ladder at the cutter's side, and passed him up to others on deck. The cutter's crew stopped the bleeding, treated the prisoner's wounds, and gave him morphine. He was turned over to the South Vietnamese Navy. While patrolling the Soi Rap river from 1 May 1966 to 6 May 1966, *Point Partridge* shot it out with enemy junks or took fire from river banks every night.[20]

Cutters also took fire from ashore while patrolling rivers to the south. In December 1966, *Point Grace* went up the Bo De river alone. When she turned and headed back, the VC launched a coordinated attack, firing recoilless rifles from both sides of the river. The cutter was 200 yards from the south bank when she was hit by three of several 57mm recoilless rifle rounds fired. One struck her starboard bow at frame seven, three-and-a-half feet above the waterline; it detonated in the crew's head. A second round hit in the same area, just above the waterline; it ripped an 8-inch hole in the hull, but did not explode. The third penetrated the cutter's hull amidships on the starboard side, one foot below the main deck; it went into the engine room, passed through a lube oil storage tank, ripped out some wiring, rattled around inside a vent duct, and finally dropped out into a trash can— it never detonated. LoForte wrote in the squadron diary, "We were lucky—very lucky!! If the rounds hadn't been duds or fallen short, we would have had our first Coast Guard prisoners of war and been down to 25 boats." The explosive-ordinance-disposal trained commanding officer of the SEAL team at Cat Lo told Division 13's commander that it was extremely rare for a 57mm round to fail to explode. He said a dud had not been seen in months.[21]

Point Grace was lucky again on the afternoon of 17 September 1967 while patrolling off Long Toan secret zone, an area of heavy VC activity. She was 1,000 yards from shore when she came under heavy fire from automatic weapons and recoilless rifles from bunkers on the beach; *Point Grace* returned fire and opened to seaward. The cutter was hit by two of the more than 25 rounds of 57mm recoilless rifles fired at her. One round blasted an 8-inch hole in the steel deck at the base of the mast and sent shrapnel ripping through the aluminum deckhouse. Another round hit the starboard side at frame 13, just above the waterline; it detonated in the crews' quarters, only six feet from where an earlier round hit. The action brought the total to six recoilless rifle hits suffered by *Point Grace* in nine months—without any personnel casualties.[22]

Desperate Straits

Point Banks was on patrol in area 5C south of Cam Rahn Bay on 21 January 1969. Just before midnight, the bridge watch intercepted radio traffic from ashore; South Vietnamese Army (ARVN) soldiers were surrounded by VC and desperately calling for help. Lt. (jg) Gerald L. Underwood, in command of the cutter, was asleep in the cabin when the watch reported the action ashore. He went to the bridge and listened while the soldiers described how they were cut off by two platoons of VC. They were surrounded on three sides, backed up to the beach, and were pleading for someone to come to their rescue.[23]

Underwood made direct contact with the ARVN soldiers, who in rapid broken English described their condition and where they were. Underwood called CSC at Vung Tau, reported the situation, and requested permission to attempt to rescue the nine troopers. A Navy Swift, patrolling in the area, heard the cutter's transmission and also volunteered to attempt the rescue. CSC came back and directed *Banks* to take action. Underwood said, "When we first intercepted the traffic, we were about ten miles away. By the time we got the go-ahead, we were not more than a mile offshore, perpendicular from where we thought they were."

By the time Underwood came down from the bridge, Gunner's Mate second class Willis J. Goff and Engineman second class Larry D. Villarreal had the small boat ready to go. Underwood said, "Goff and Villarreal were two of my best men. They were aggressive and liked doing stuff like that. When I asked for volunteers, I pretty much expected they would be the ones to go."

Just under a mile from shore, *Banks* put her 14-foot Boston Whaler into the water. Goff was in the bow with an M-60 machine gun on a mount he designed; Villarreal was at the controls of the boat—both men wore flak jackets and helmets. The boat pulled away from the cutter, increased speed, and headed for shore. The night was warm with light winds; seas were unusually calm for area 5. Before disappearing into the darkness, the bridge made a radio check with the boat's PRC-59 portable FM transceiver—it was the last radio communication they had. Just after the boat left the cutter, the radio went dead. Unable to talk to the boat, Underwood got under way to be as near to shore as possible. He said, "We started closing the shore while watching the fathometer. We got to within a half-mile and stopped." Underwood feared in the back of his mind that he might have been baited into a trap. Unable to communicate with the boat, his concerns were heightened. Underwood said, "Sometimes down in the southern areas we got radio calls that we could tell were not legitimate."

The ARVN troops said they would show a light to mark their location, but when Goff and Villarreal approached shore, there was not one but three lights in separate locations. They picked the middle one and headed in. With waves breaking over the gunwales, the boat fought her way through heavy surf to the sandy shore. When the bow grounded on the steeply sloped beach, nine South Vietnamese soldiers came running out of the jungle. Just then, the Viet Cong opened fire on the boat with automatic weapons. Goff replied with rapid bursts from the M-60 machine gun, suppressing enemy fire.

In the darkness, the soldiers climbed aboard with their gear; Goff continued firing into the jungle. After four men got in the boat, Villarreal had to forcibly stop the others from crowding aboard—he promised to return. The five ran back to the jungle and provided covering fire while the boat fought her way back through the surf.

Underwood said, "It was one of the darkest nights I can remember. There was no moon. We never saw anything ashore. We couldn't see the surf. I think it was just pure luck when we went in and almost hit the exact spot where these guys were. If they had been 100 yards either way we never would have found them."

Point Banks used her 81mm mortar to lob rounds into the jungle, behind the beach. She swept the night air above the jungle with .50-caliber machine-gun fire, keeping her fire high to avoid hitting her own men. Two Navy Swifts were offshore and an Air Force C-47 gunship was in the air for support. Underwood said, "I had never seen so much tracer firing in all my life. There was shooting from the shore, to the shore, back and forth and all around. . . . Every few minutes, I had my crew stop firing. We would sit and listen. We were at darkened ship and had no comms [communications] with the boat. I was trying to hear if they needed us to come in. I thought we might be able to hear them holler."

The boat made it back to *Point Banks* by steering for the flashes from the cutter's guns. When they came alongside, the ARVN troops climbed aboard the cutter and collapsed on deck. Underwood said, "When I looked down at the boat, I didn't want them to go back in. The Whaler was swamped up to the gunwales. The only thing keeping her up was the flotation in the hull. But they told me they promised the other five they would be back for them. They felt they had to go back in."

On the second run, the boat nearly capsized several times. When the motor stopped while going through the surf, Villarreal calmly restarted it and continued to the beach. When the boat approached, the VC were waiting; automatic weapon fire was even more intense than before. Goff laid down a steady stream of M-60 fire as the five men ran through the surf and dove into the boat. Villarreal maneuvered the heavily ladened boat safely back through the surf and out to the waiting cutter. With everyone aboard, *Banks* headed for sea. Underwood said, "To sum things up, the nine guys we brought aboard were probably the nine happiest people I've ever seen in my life. They were exhausted, but smiling. They just collapsed on the fantail as we headed for Cat Lo."

Citations for Silver Star medals awarded by the Navy to Goff and Villarreal said, "The nine men would have met almost certain death or capture without the assistance of the two Coast Guardsmen."

Working along the coast and in the rivers brought cutter crews in contact with U.S. advisors at South Vietnamese bases and outposts. The WPB's ability to provide accurate and substantial gunfire support was appreciated; many requests were received for fire-support missions. WPBs also frequently provided illumination for outposts. Miller said, "We would call them and say we were in the area and would be dropping some rounds of illumination for them. Then we'd pop off a few rounds to keep the VC off balance. When they confirmed they had people [VC] in the wire, we'd drop in HE for them. U.S. advisors with the ARVN appreciated it."

In 1968, the focus of operations for Division 13 shifted from coastal interdiction to more aggressive inshore activity. Capt. John G. Busavage, who was a lieutenant junior grade when he commanded *Point Comfort* in 1968, said, "From the time I got there in August 1968, our patrol areas were actually up the rivers and canals. We were only supposed to go offshore to rendezvous for supplies or if there was an indication something was going on. This was even before SEA LORDS [Southeast Asia Lake, Ocean, River, and Delta Strategy] came in."[24]

On the afternoon of 26 October 1968, Lt. Cdr. Joseph F. Smith, in command of Coast Guard Division 13, volunteered to lead a raid on a Viet Cong staging area. He was officer in tactical command for a raiding party of two WPBs, two PCFs, and two Seawolf helicopters. The small force went up the My Thanh river in area 7D, at the southwestern entrance to the Bassac river. Before reaching their objective—a Viet Cong village—Smith embarked in a 17-foot Boston Whaler and led the boats up the river. They took the village and the surrounding area under fire. Smith said, "I was skimming around, running the show from the Boston Whaler. We went in and destroyed their boats. We dropped grenades in the sampans." The raiders destroyed three bunkers and damaged three others. Fifteen boats were destroyed or damaged including eleven motorized sampans. Fifteen huts and 150 gallons of fuel oil were burned. Smith said, "We didn't get any resistance until we were withdrawing. We took some fire when we were leaving." Smith was not too impressed with the tactic; he was concerned about the vulnerability of the crews. He said, "During the debrief, I told them, 'You couldn't see anybody in the foliage. In those narrow canals, if I had an M-16, I could've knocked down everybody on the bridge before they knew what hit them.'" Commander Coast Guard Activities Vietnam described the My Thanh raid as SEA LORDS Mission No. 1.[25]

After October 1968, WPBs engaged in more joint operations with Swift boats, going up rivers and canals. Underwood said, "We went up some rivers like the Bassac that were a mile wide. But we also went up canals so narrow you had to back in, because you couldn't turn around to get out if you were ambushed. We had to watch the tide to make sure we could get back over the bar." The purpose of river and canal incursions was to return fire and inflict casualties. Cutters took hits and suffered damage, but fortunately none were disabled in waterways and casualties were surprisingly light. Underwood said, "I saw an intelligence report that was based on VC prisoner interrogations. It said the VC were very suspicious of the 82-footers because anything that went that slow was sure to have some special armament, weapons, or troops aboard. They understood the Swift that came, did its shooting, and left. But the plodding 82-footer baffled them. They were suspicious." Actually, the cutters did have formidable firepower and could fire from both sides at the same time. Of the river and canal incursions, Underwood said, "I'm not sure we felt it was an effective tactic, but we thought we were doing our duty and operations relieved the boredom. It was better than boarding junks all day. As CO, I felt if we planned one operation a day, it would give the crew something to focus on and prepare for."[26]

Busavage went to a patrol boat commanding officer conference at CTF 115's headquarters in Cam Rahn Bay. At the conference, Coast Guard WPB and Navy PCF skippers questioned the value of going up canals. When one young lieutenant (jg) raised the question with the commodore, Busavage said, "I still remember the captain looking down the table with his cigar and saying, 'Son, this is the only war the Navy's got and we've got to make the most of it.'"[27]

There was no doubt that 82-foot cutters were the right resources for the coastal interdiction mission. But the mission changed and Division 13 WPBs were increasingly used for raids in rivers and canals—a role they were neither designed nor suited for. Cutters were too big, too slow, and drew too much water, and did not have armor to compensate for their lack of speed. Smith said, "Why we never got hurt more in those canals, I'll never know."[28]

As the conflict dragged on and opposition to the war mounted in the United States, increased Vietnamese participation in operations was considered. Smith, who was uncertain about the appropriateness of the incursion mission for WPBs, sent a rapid draft letter to Capt. John M. Austin, commander Coast Guard Squadron One in Saigon, asking Austin if anything was being done to turn cutters over to the Vietnamese. "I volunteered our division to provide operations, engineering, and supply training to the South Vietnamese Navy so they could take over the cutters," he said. The turnover program began at Division 13 in December 1968.[29]

6

Command in the Gulf

I thought the combination of Coast Guard and Navy people worked very well. It was a very interesting situation. It demonstrated that you can have Navy officers commanding Coast Guard people and the reverse just as in World War II. There were negligible differences. Leadership is leadership no matter where you are.

Adm. John B. Hayes, USCG, CTG 115.4 and COMCOGARDIV 11

Ambush at Rach Goc

Despite high winds, weather was warm when six U.S. Navy Swift boats (PCFs) cast off from the floating SEA LORDS base before dawn. The 50-foot boats formed a column and headed for Duong Keo river in the morning darkness of 5 May 1969. Coast Guard Lt. Cdr. John C. Spence was in command of the small force of PCFs, MSF (mobile strike force) troops, UDT (underwater demolition team) personnel, and Seawolf helicopters. At 0640, boats were four miles from the eastern tip of Ca Mau peninsula. Spence said, "As we approached the river mouth, we saw a white flare. The Viet Cong knew we were coming. Everyone in the boats saw it. Word spread among the troops, 'They know we're coming, let's turn back.' But I told them we couldn't. When the mercenaries [MSF] saw we were going ahead with the mission, I began to smell incense burning."[1]

Spence, commander of Coast Guard Division 11, was temporarily assigned as officer in tactical command (OTC) of SEA LORDS' assets in the southern Gulf of Thailand. He and U.S. Navy Lt. Cdr. George Elliot, in command of the Swift boat division at An Thoi, rotated as OTC. The SEA LORDS base consisted of an LST, two Seawolf helicopters, ninety Chinese mercenary troops and their Green Beret advisors, and a SEAL team. Spence said, "Who ever was down there commanded everything. We would go down, stay a week or two, and then be relieved by the other. It became a permanent operation." Floating resources for SEA LORDS operations were drawn from the WPB and PCF divisions in the Gulf. Staff support for the base was provided by Gulf of Thailand Surveillance Group (CTG 115.4).

As part of Operation Silver Mace II, an assault landing force went up Duong Keo river in the late afternoon of 12 April 1969. The force, made up of eight Swifts, Seawolf helicopters, SEAL and explosive ordnance disposal teams, and troops from the Vietnamese marines' 6th Battalion, was commanded by Cdr. Paul A. Yost, USCG, who commanded the surveillance group and was senior naval officer in the Gulf of Thailand. Four miles upriver, boats were ambushed while approaching the village of Rach Goc. Action began when two claymore mines detonated from the northwest bank, spraying lead Swifts with shrapnel and signaling ambushers to open fire. The enemy, estimated to be two companies strong, fired B-40 rockets, recoilless rifles, machine guns, and small arms. PCF 43, the last boat in the column, was hit with recoilless rifle fire and B-40 rockets; she went out of control and grounded at full speed on the river bank in the middle of the ambush. Yost took two Swifts and returned to the beached vessel.[2]

Under fire, the boats moved in and picked up PCF 43's crew. The Swift was left in flames and later blew up. When the battle ended, three U.S. Navy men were dead and thirty-three wounded; two Vietnamese marines were killed and thirteen wounded.[3]

Spence said, "It was my turn as OTC and Captain Hoffman [Roy F. Hoffman, commander Task Force 115] said he wanted to get even [for the 12 April 1969 ambush]. He wanted the VC village attacked." For the operation, Spence used six Swifts—he kept one in reserve at the LST—one WPB, two Seawolf helicopters, and ninety troops. The raid was scheduled for dawn. He said, "We had aerial photos showing bunkers along the river. My plan was to draw out the enemy. The name of the game was to get them to expose themselves and then use the Seawolfs."

The South Vietnamese Army district chief at An Thoi had told Spence about VC river ambushes. He said ambush kill zones were usually no more than fifty yards wide. Spence divided his PCFs into two groups of three boats each; he spaced the groups 500 yards apart. "I knew we would get hit," Spence said. "My plan was for the first three boats to fight their way through the ambush. The second three would stop before reaching the kill zone and put their troops ashore to flank the ambushers. Surviving lead boats would land and flank from the other side." Spence was in PCF 23, the second boat of the first group.

When Swifts reached the river mouth, Seawolf helicopters were still not airborne; a combination of the LST twisting in the current and high winds prevented them from taking off. With the deeper-draft WPB standing by offshore, the raiding party made its way up the river. The waterway narrowed to only 100 feet wide as the PCFs neared Rach Goc. Just as the lead boats—PCFs 22, 23, and 45—rounded a curve in the river, they were hit. Spence said, "All of a sudden the sky lit up. Rockets hit the first boat. Then they opened up on us with everything." The lead boat, PCF 22, took three B-40 rocket hits—one in the main cabin, one in the engine room below the waterline, and another in the hull just forward of the pilothouse—knocking out the boat's steering and setting her on fire. Somehow, PCF 22 managed to make it through the ambush before veering out of control and beaching on the south bank. Spence said, "They were heaving grenades at us from tall grass along the river. They would run at us, throw grenades, and then flop into the grass." The next two boats fought their way through the ambush and pulled into the bank, one on either side of the crippled Swift; they were spaced about 10 yards apart. Spence said, "As soon as we beached, we were mortared. I saw poles with ribbons tied to them along the bank and realized they were range markers. I ordered strikers ashore. They knocked down the markers as they set up a perimeter around the boats. There were bunkers on our side of the river, but they were empty. Thank God!" Heavy fire continued from the other side of the river. During breaks in fighting, men on the Swifts could hear the enemy moving toward them through the tall reeds across the river. Beaching on the opposite bank put the PCFs in good defensive positions with stern-mounted 81mm mortars and .50-caliber machine guns in firing positions. They fired their .50s low into the grass and heard cries from enemy casualties.

The second three Swifts—PCF 71, 9, and 5—landed on the north side of the river before reaching the ambush; their troops closed on the left flank of the ambushers. Spence said, "It was a good ambush. I don't know what their total force was, but it was relentless. Air support was the only thing that broke it. Seawolfs came in and put down some effective fire. Then we were able to get a jet. It was one of the first times. An Air Force F-4 Phantom made two napalm runs and a couple of strafing runs. They really did a nice job, right on target." Air strikes were only 25 yards from the boats.

After the air strikes, enemy fire let up and Swift boat crews were able to take care of their wounded and work on PCF 22. Spence said, "We were there for about an hour before the firing let up enough that we could call in Seawolfs to 'dust off' our wounded." When the remaining enemy withdrew, UDT personnel blew up interconnecting concrete-and-stone fortified bunkers. Temporary repairs to PCF 22 were completed at 1700. She was taken in tow and the raiders returned to the LST.

Swifts Deploy

On 31 October 1965, two of the Navy's new class of 50-foot PCF (patrol craft, fast) arrived at An Thoi. The boats, called Swifts, were part of Boat Division 101. PCF 3 and PCF 4, the first of 17 Swift boats planned for the Gulf, reported to CTU 115.1.9 for Market Time operations with the WPB division. Aluminum-hulled PCFs were a military version of crew boats used for offshore oil rigs in the Gulf of Mexico. Swifts, which drew three-and-a-half-feet of water and displaced nineteen tons, were powered by twin diesel engines; they were capable of twenty-five knots in calm waters. Boats were manned by crews of six: a lieutenant junior grade as officer in charge and five enlisted men. They were well armed, mounting a piggyback 81mm mortar and .50-caliber machine gun aft, and twin .50-caliber machine guns in a tub on top of the pilothouse. The next six Swifts arrived in the Gulf on 24 December 1965.

To moor new patrol boats, a pontoon causeway was anchored perpendicular to the beach at the Navy base at An Thoi. Navy crews, who did not live aboard their boats as Coast Guard crews did, berthed and messed in tents ashore at the advisory compound; the support ship *Krishna* did not have enough space to accommodate additional personnel. Living in tents was difficult for crews in hot, humid weather. Conditions improved on 8 June 1966 when APL 55 (barracks craft, non-self-propelled) arrived at An Thoi. The APL was anchored with a four-point moor in the lee of Hon Roi island, just south of An Thoi; *Krishna* moored alongside. The barracks craft and support ship shifted

Coast Guard cutters, Navy Swifts, and Thai Navy motor gunboat moored at barracks barge anchored south of An Thoi in the Gulf of Thailand.

anchorage closer to An Thoi when weather permitted. PCF crews moved aboard the air-conditioned APL (called "apple") and opened their own mess; Swifts moored alongside. Maintenance teams on the two vessels overhauled patrol boat main engines; WPB engine work was done on *Krishna* and PCF engines were overhauled on the "apple."

At 0800 on 12 May 1966, CTF 115 Operations Order (OPORDER) 201 went into effect, designating Commander Task Group 115.4 as the operational commander in the Gulf of Thailand and changed the task group name from support group to surveillance group. The OPORDER separated the support ship *Krishna* from the task group and placed her under control of Naval Support Activity, Saigon.

Manning U.S. Navy Swifts was more complicated than single-crewed Coast Guard WPBs, because three Navy crews were assigned for every two Swift boats. Adm. John B. Hayes, a commander when he was in command in the Gulf of Thailand from 1966 to 1967, said, "One of the problems with Swifts was that a permanent crew was not assigned to a particular boat. I had a lot of problems as did their division commander. He had a heck of a time with his crews. It was hard to develop much esprit de corps when crews didn't own their own territory."[4]

PCF hull design—light-weight and shallow-draft with a short bow—made open-sea interdiction operations difficult; boats were severely limited in seaways of six feet and above. In all but calm waters, aluminum hulls did not provide stable platforms for boarding. With small crews of only six men, endurance was also a problem for Swifts. To get maximum patrol time out of PCFs, and not expend their endurance on transiting, they were assigned 24-hour patrols in areas close to An Thoi. Later, they deployed to the southern end of the area with a destroyer as mother ship. While limited in open-sea operations, Swifts proved to be very effective on inland waterways. They were used extensively for incursion operations up rivers and canals in later phases of the Vietnam war. Adm. Paul A. Yost, who commanded Task Group 115.4 in 1969, said, "PCFs never were any good for offshore work. They constantly got driven to shelter. . . . It was a good thing we found another mission and pulled them off [interdiction patrols]."[5]

PCF 4 Mined

A coastal group Kien Giang–type junk was on patrol on the afternoon of 14 February 1966 when, just after 1600, her crew heard an explosion. When they turned, they saw a smudge of black smoke rising from the water offshore from Three Sisters. The area, dominated by three prominent hills—Nui Hon Dat, Nui Hon Me, and Nui Hon Soc—was a known VC stronghold. The junk came about and headed for the smoke to investigate. When she got closer, her crew saw PCF 4's guntub and the top of her cabin sticking out of the muddy water; the sea was strewn with bits of debris. The junk's crew pulled the Swift's officer in charge and two crewmen from the water—one of the enlisted men was dead. The other three crewmen were missing. On shore, 250 yards to the northeast, Viet Cong prepared to come out to the wreckage of the Swift. Junkmen quickly reported their situation and, using their .30-caliber machine gun, bravely made several firing runs to force the VC back.[6]

The blast had occurred as the Swift's crew was cutting a Viet Cong flag from a bamboo pole stuck in the mud. When the command-detonated mine exploded under the bow, the explosion lifted the boat and tore a 10-foot hole in her hull. In seconds, she was sitting on the muddy bottom in ten feet of water.

USCGC *Point Clear* (WPB 82315) was on patrol 25 miles west of Three Sisters when she received a FLASH message, directing her to proceed at maximum speed to the site of the sinking. Her commanding officer, Lt. Jon C. Uithol, was on the bridge when the message arrived. He set a course and ordered full speed. *Point Clear* arrived just after sunset and Uithol was designated OTC; five Swift boats—PCFs 3, 5, 10, 11, and 12—also converged on the scene.

Point Clear anchored 500 yards off the coast. On shore, dense jungle began just beyond the rocky coastline, sloping up a small rise. Tall palms towered over the lush vegetation. Uithol said, "We formed a half-moon around the wreckage. We could direct fire from different angles." When coastal group junks arrived, he put them into the line. Uithol requested air support and when gunships arrived on-scene, he gave them targets. He said, "'Puff the Magic Dragon' gunships hosed the area down all night. When they fired, there was a loud humming-buzzing noise. Tracers were so many and so close together, it was like a pink light coming down from the plane to the ground. It was continuous, almost like a laser beam. When one plane got low on ammunition, it left and another arrived." Uithol stayed up all night, working with the aircraft. When it started to get light, the planes left; they were too vulnerable to ground fire during daylight.

The sun came up hot and bright under a clear sky; muddy waters were calm. In the morning light, Uithol saw the damage that the gunships had done. He said, "They made tossed salad out of the whole area. They just pulverized everything." Boats on the line provided cover while divers from *Krishna* worked from a rubber raft within rifle-range of the shore. They removed the mortar and machine guns and some of the ammunition from the wreckage of PCF 4, and recovered the bodies of two more crewmen. Fire from ashore intensified when an LCM-8 (landing craft, mechanized) with a crane aboard came out from Rach Gia to attempt to raise the hulk. The equipment was borrowed from RMK (Raymond, Morrison-Knudsen) Construction Co., which was working in Rach Gia. At 1400, two WPBs, four PCFs, and eight junks closed to 400 yards from the beach and opened fire while the LCM moved in with the crane. Uithol said, "There was a lot of shooting. Lots of noise and smoke. We were beam to, firing mortar and machine guns." Two armed helicopters attacked with machine guns and rockets. Uithol retained command of patrol units even after more senior officers arrived on-scene. He said, "My recollection is that I kept it [OTC] the whole time. They told me, 'You've handled it this far, go ahead and keep it. We're busy getting the boat [PCF 4] out.'"

While the VC were pinned down, the 74-foot LCM hooked onto the Swift with its crane. Uithol said, "They tried to lift the wreck, but couldn't. But they did manage to break it loose from the muddy bottom. The other 82-footer [Point Mast] went over and put a towline on the LCM-8. While the crane kept the wreck partially off the bottom, she [Mast] towed the 'mike boat' [LCM-8] out 2,000 yards."

An old stone structure used by the VC for firing on salvage efforts was destroyed; it turned out to be a Buddhist monastery. Hodgman said, "We had no time to be particular. That's where the firing was coming from." Later, USCGC Point Mast (WPB 82316) towed the submerged wreckage another eight miles offshore into twenty-four feet of water where Krishna could get to it. When Krishna raised the Swift, she was a total loss.

Four days after PCF 4 sank, crews from three inport WPBs came ashore in an LCM to the advisory compound on 18 February 1966. They joined Swift boat crews at a memorial service for their compatriots killed in the blast. Men stood under a searing morning sun, waiting to take their seats on folding metal chairs, arranged in ragged rows in the sand. The air was still and hot, and the temperature was in the nineties by the time the memorial service began for the four Navy crewmen—BM2 Tommy E. Hill, GMG2 Dayton L. Rudisill, EN2 Jack C. Rodriguez, and SN David J. Boyle. The chaplain opened with, "The Lord is my shepherd; I shall not want." Crews lowered their eyes to avoid the glare of the sun; the camp mascot dogs wandered aimlessly among the rows of chairs. Crews sang "Onward Christian Soldiers," squinting at the words on the backs of mimeographed programs; their hesitant musical strains, faint in the open air, drifted over the water. Men shifted their weight on chairs that tilted in the soft sand; their shirts were wet with perspiration. When the service ended, they got up and moved back toward the water, talking in lowered voices and lighting cigarettes. They thought about their shipmates and the words in the program, "May we who live, live in such a way that we may die in honor before God and man."[7]

After the incident, there were several reports of VC flags sighted on poles in the water along the coast. Small brightly painted sampans, flying VC flags, were also spotted anchored near shore. Warnings about probable booby traps were widely circulated among patrol forces.[8]

Advisory Role

In October 1965, Rear Adm. Norvell G. Ward, USN, commander Task Force 115 and chief of the naval advisory group in Saigon, explored the possibility of consolidating operations and advisory efforts in the Gulf of Thailand. On 15 November 1965, he put his plan into action by assigning Cdr. James A Hodgman, Coast Guard Squadron One's commander, to his staff with the additional duty of senior naval advisor to the Vietnamese commander of the fourth coastal zone. Hodgman said the consolidation was intended to "strengthen coordination between naval forces by making the U.S. and Vietnamese naval commanders true counterparts." The assignment gave commander Squadron One several new responsibilities.

In addition to Market Time operations in the Gulf of Thailand and maintenance and administrative support for Division 11 at An Thoi and Division 12 at Danang, Hodgman took charge of the U.S. Navy's advisory program in the fourth coastal zone. This command involved working closely with the South Vietnamese Navy commander and included responsibility for operational readiness of Vietnamese units, supply support for U.S. advisors and Vietnamese forces, operation of the Coastal Surveillance Center (CSC), coordination of the military assistance program (MAP), support for the USN section of the VNN base at An Thoi, liaison with Vietnamese public officials, and oversight of the extensive military construction program. Construction projects included building a 4,000-foot airstrip, and rebuilding the compound at An Thoi and a Coastal Force repair base near Rach Gia.[9]

While the scope of the task group commander's duties varied over time, the advisor role was always the most unique experience. When Hodgman took on the assignment, he had forty U.S. Navy officers and enlisted men in the program. His two deputies were Navy lieutenant commanders, one assigned as assistant fourth coastal zone advisor at An Thoi and the other as assistant fourth coastal zone advisor at Rach

Gia. Remaining advisory personnel were assigned with VNN units, primarily coastal groups (Junk Force), operating throughout the Gulf of Thailand. Hodgman personally advised the Vietnamese Navy officer in command of the fourth coastal zone. Coastal zone forces included three patrol ships—a rotating mix of PGMs, PCEs, LSILs, LSSLs, or MSCs—deployed from Saigon, seven coastal groups (Junk Force), two bases, a command center, and a junk repair facility. Bases were located at An Thoi and Rach Gia. The repair facility was located at Rach Soi, south of Rach Gia.

USN and VNN personnel jointly operated the CSC at An Thoi. Three coastal groups were based at An Thoi, three at Kien An—up the river from Rach Gia—and one at Poulo Obi, a group of small mountainous islands near the tip of Ca Mau peninsula. Each coastal group was authorized two USN officers and two enlisted men as advisors. A group usually consisted of three motorized command junks (Yabuta class) and seventeen smaller motorized junks (Kien Giang type). Junks ran from thirty-seven to fifty-four feet in length, made between five and eight knots, and carried machine guns (one .30-caliber on Kien Giangs and .30- and .50-caliber on Yabutas), and small arms. Kien Giangs were phased out as more Yabutas were built and assigned to coastal groups.[10]

Personnel turnover and shortages were a continuing problem for both the USN and VNN. The Vietnamese did not have enough officers to man their coastal groups and bases and still provide liaison officers for U.S. units. Rapid turnover of coastal group officers and low levels of enlisted training made continuity of operations difficult. Of the U.S. advisors, Hodgman said:

> One-year tours and the shunting of talent to fill new needs in an expanding operation made it difficult for the United States to keep its 40 officer and enlisted advisory billets filled and stabilized—to say nothing of the problem of keeping people assigned to advisory tasks working on them, rather than on the myriad details connected with operating the crowded advisory compound ashore.[11]

Navy intelligence liaison officers (NILOs) also were assigned to the senior advisor. An intelligence specialist with the rank of lieutenant commander was on the staff at An Thoi and NILOs were assigned at Ha Tien and Ca Mau. A manned radar site was constructed on Poulo

Motorized coastal group junk alongside an 82-foot cutter.

Obi to support surveillance operations. While it was difficult for senior advisors to break away from the press of daily operations, they recognized the importance of getting out into the field to visit their advisors. Hayes said, "I tried to visit the outlying sites about once a month. . . . Of all of our people, they [advisors] were most exposed to danger." They also were on their own, immersed in a foreign culture.[12]

The objective of the naval advisory program in the gulf was to work itself out of a job and turn surveillance operations over to the VNN. Differences in culture and motivation had a direct impact on the success of the effort. Americans, with one-year tours of duty in Vietnam, were anxious to get the job done and in a hurry to see results. The Vietnamese, for whom the war had gone on for years and was likely to continue well into the future, had a different outlook. They adjusted to functioning within the limits of existing situations and were not overly motivated to seek change, especially when the impact of change was uncertain.

The VNN fourth coastal zone commander and his officers were very conscious of their status; they resisted pressures for action from their result-oriented American advisors. They particularly avoided situations that might appear as though they were taking orders from advisors. Yost said, "There was no doubt that they [the South Vietnamese] did not think we Americans understood the war. And when we pressed to do things, like give up siestas and get things moving to fight the war, they would say, 'You don't understand our problems. You don't understand our ways. We don't do things that way. You can't get that kind of thing done.'" Ceremonies and preparations for visits by dignitaries were more important than running operations. Improving poor housing at junk bases and raising chickens and livestock took precedence over patrolling. Yost said, "Fighting the war was not their major concern. Even after we turned PCFs over to them, they never considered them as fighting resources, tools to wage war. Their attitude was that this is a wonderful gift we got from the Americans and we have to be sure we don't damage it or endanger it. Because, if we do, Navy headquarters will be very mad at us."[13]

To get Vietnamese to run operations, U.S. personnel learned they had to indirectly and discretely suggest the idea. It was important for initiatives to come from the Vietnamese commander. Rear Adm. Norman C. Venzke, a commander when he had command in the gulf in 1967-68, said, "The advisory business was like pushing a wet noodle. I had absolutely no hammer." Hodgman reported in a November 1965 squadron diary, "The South Vietnamese Navy presented a proposal for an 'Operation Roundup' to be held later in the week. This is a coupe. Lt. Cdr. Hagstrom [from Division 11] made up the OPORDER two weeks earlier and implanted the idea with the South Vietnamese who are now proposing it."

Operation Roundup

Coast Guard Division 11's operations officer, Lt. Alex R. Larzelere, climbed aboard the VNN coastal minesweeper (MSC) *Ham Tu II* (HQ 114) at 2115, on 6 April 1966. He was OTC for U.S. forces during an operation roundup scheduled to begin at 0600 the next day. Larzelere wore a .45-caliber automatic and carried a PRC-59 portable VHF FM radio to communicate with WPBs and PCFs. The operations order, a razor, and a toothbrush were stuck in the radio carrying case. The MSC's officer of the deck, a young VNN ensign, appeared on deck and saluted smartly. When Larzelere followed the ensign below, he noticed the ship was freshly painted and appeared well maintained.[14]

While having tea with the ensign, Larzelere counted nine large rats roaming the small wardroom, brazenly walking across the deck and sitting on overhead pipes, their long tails dangling down. The ensign appeared not to notice their presence. After tea, Larzelere was shown to the stateroom where he would sleep. He was told, "*Dai uy* [lieutenant], the room is empty. The officer who lives here has gone to Saigon. He is at hospital with tuberculosis."

Larzelere twisted vent controls in an effort to get air into the stifling compartment, without success. He stripped to his underwear and climbed onto the upper bunk. In the darkness, he felt the flat ventilation duct that ran just above his face. He dismissed thoughts of rats using the duct as a runway and went to sleep. He awoke a few hours later when he felt bugs crawling over him. The insects weren't biting so, in the dark, he assumed they were roaches; he brushed them away and went back to sleep. When he awoke in the morning, the ship was under way heading for an anchorage in the Balua Islands. He discovered that the bugs that shared his bunk during the night were Asian termites aboard the wooden-hulled minesweeper. In the officers' head, Larzelere had to dip water from a big pot into a sink to shave, because the minesweeper had no running water.

After a breakfast of dried fish and beer, he went to the bridge and met the ship's commanding officer, Lt. Thong. The two lieutenants discussed the upcoming operation on the bridge wing and then their conversation shifted to foreign affairs. Thong talked about the implications of the recent tricontinental communist conference in Havana. The South Vietnamese lieutenant, speaking fluent English, discussed an article he read in a French magazine. Larzelere was impressed with Thong's intellect and linguistic ability, but surprised to see that the ship's captain wore no shoes or socks with his uniform—apparently his usual attire. The operation, conducted in island waters and Cay Duong bay, involved a VNN MSC and PGM, two USCG WPBs, two USN PCFs, and coastal groups 44 and 45. Vessels converged on the area at daylight, systematically corralling and boarding all junks in the area. The operation was successful in terms of coordination and logistics, but yielded little more than minor discrepancies in identification papers and a few draft dodgers.

Hodgman reported an example of the sensitivities he faced in dealing with the VNN commander in the squadron diary. On 15 December 1965, he said one of his advisors knocked loudly on the door of the fourth coastal zone commander during his siesta, startling him. The VNN commander complained to Hodgman and, after the incident, decided his English was no longer good enough for him to receive his briefings in English; they would have to be translated into Vietnamese. Hodgman said in his report, "I have handled the incident without an international flap."[15]

While juxtaposition of eastern and western cultures was difficult and often frustrating, personnel serving in the advisory program found it to be rewarding. Venzke said, "It was the best tour of my whole career. It was a balancing act. Lots of operations. The advisory business. It was so diverse. It was an exciting challenge." Social amenities were also a challenge. After a dinner with his counterpart, Hodgman reported, "I have gone through fried pigs' intestines, goat testicles, ginseng wine, dog and calf skin—all for the cause of better international understanding—and I have enjoyed it. But my stomach rebelled tonight at a mixture of cold duck's blood, red peppers, and duck giblets." Hayes said, "Closely associating with a culture different than your own can be quite a shock. But that was the most interesting part of being senior advisor, without question."[16]

On 2 October 1966, the fourth coastal zone advisor moved ashore from the support ship anchored offshore to the advisory compound at An Thoi. The Market Time operations center moved ashore at the same time and was combined with the CSC. Hayes said, "I felt I would be more effective with my counterpart. My rationale was to get closer to him and his people and bolster the advisory part of our effort." U.S. operations center and headquarters were in a one-story, white wooden building, connected to VNN headquarters by a briefing room, which was used by both Americans and Vietnamese. The U.S. operations center had full communications capability.[17]

The objective of the advisory program was to bring Vietnamese up to a level of effectiveness where they could take over surveillance operations. Hayes said, "As a commander, this was my greatest concern. It was certainly the most difficult aspect of the job. Trying to develop, with such a different culture, people who didn't think the same way we did with respect to operations and maintenance. Their motivation was quite different." By the time Hayes left Vietnam, he and his staff felt they had been successful, but only partially. He said, "We felt we were never going to see the Vietnamese doing it the way we would. It was not that they were not receptive, they just had different motivations and objectives than we did." Of the reluctant receptiveness of his counterpart, Venzke said, "I could appreciate his feelings. I used to think to myself, 'How would I like someone always looking over my shoulder?'"[18]

When Cdr. Adrian L. Lonsdale took over as senior naval advisor, he found himself in an unusual situation; Cdr. Dang Cao Thang, the VNN officer he was to advise, had been the vice chief of naval operations for the South Vietnamese Navy. Because Thang took part in a failed coupe attempt, he had been assigned out of the country as naval attache in Korea. When Thang, who graduated from the Vietnamese Naval Academy in Hanoi and the Naval War College in the United States, returned to Vietnam, he was assigned to Phu Quoc—a location sufficiently remote from the seat of power in Saigon.

Lonsdale said, "I was more of a coordinator than an advisor. I still had the power, but he'd been fighting the war for twenty-two years and didn't need a lot of advising." All planning and coordination for operations had to be handled through U.S. systems. South Vietnamese Navy communications were so badly compromised, they could not be used for operations. South Vietnamese nationals with access to communications systems passed information to the Viet Cong, in hopes of improving their position should the communists win the war. South Vietnamese units participating in missions received their orders through U.S. Navy advisors, just hours before operations began.[19]

Lonsdale, who made several trips with Thang to visit local Vietnamese Navy units, said, "He could go to a unit and look at the people's shoes and tell if there was graft and corruption there. If the men were wearing good shoes, he knew money the commander was getting was going to the troops. If they were all wearing sandals, it meant the commander was diverting the funds, probably to his own pocket, and there would be hell to pay."[20]

Surveillance Task Group

The Coast Guard commander in the Gulf of Thailand wore three hats: he commanded the Gulf of Thailand surveillance group and Coast Guard Division 11, in addition to serving as senior naval advisor to the Vietnamese fourth coastal zone commander. He was responsible to three separate bosses—captains who had differing opinions about mission priorities. He reported to CTF 115, commander Coast Guard Squadron One, and the senior naval advisor. Venzke said, "It was an impossible situation. I had to satisfy three four-stripers. I handled the jobs in the following priority: the operations job as task group commander came first. The advisory job was second. And I essentially turned over [Coast Guard] Division 11 to my chief staff officer. I couldn't do all three." When Venzke was scheduled to leave Vietnam in April 1968, he recommended command of Division 11 be separated from the other two jobs. In ceremonies on 4 April 1968, Lonsdale relieved Venzke as CTG 115.4 and senior advisor; Lt. Cdr. Alan C. Peck, who had been Venzke's chief staff officer, took command of Division 11.[21]

By 1968, no evidence indicated that significant amounts of arms and supplies were being smuggled to the VC through gulf waters; the infiltration threat had not materialized. Toward the end of 1968, focus of operations shifted from defensive patrolling to offensive actions. Lonsdale said:

> Incursions from sea just sort of came about. . . . We had a lot of Navy lieutenants who, on dares, started running up the rivers and seeing if they could get from one place to another. It was contrary to doctrine, but they did it. They went through and found out it wasn't so bad. When our task force commander found out what we were doing, he said, 'Let's start doing more of that. Let's start taking the territory back.' So we did. We wrested control of the canals and most of the inland waters, at least along the coast, back from the communists. We were running freely wherever we wanted to. Probably the last [communist] stronghold was the tip of Ca Mau peninsula.[22]

With the approval of the task force commander, Lonsdale began planning and executing coastal operations. Initially, only U.S. forces were authorized to take part in the actions. Later, CTF 115 approved the use of South Vietnamese Navy vessels and troops. Operations, conducted almost daily, were usually amphibious raids on VC villages and staging areas along the coast of the mainland. Some raids, using canal and river systems, penetrated well inland. Lonsdale did not need prior clearance for missions, as long as they took place in "free fire zones." He said, "I just planned them and did them. . . . We pretty much ran our own show. We made reports afterward. . . . Captain Hoffman was CTF 115. He let us go ahead and do what we thought we could do." Task group forces also made landings on the northern coast of Phu Quoc Island. But when little VC activity was found, they were discontinued. Operations usually began with naval gunfire from Market Time ships softening up the objective. Next, WPBs and Swifts moved in and provided covering fire while coastal group junks or VNN landing craft put troops ashore. When available, helicopter gunships were used to support landings.[23]

Lonsdale said, "Occasionally, I'd go on operations. But I couldn't go on all of them; I was too busy planning the next one. Around 1100, I would start on the next day's operation. In the afternoon, I would get reports on the one we did that morning. I made my reports to Saigon and did press releases. Through the night, probably to midnight, I worked on the next day's operation." In preparing for missions, CTG 115.4 requested intelligence information about prospective landing sites from Saigon. "After we sent a request," Lonsdale said, "It wouldn't be long before we got a query through intelligence channels asking what we knew about activity in that particular area so they could respond."[24]

Cdr. Paul A. Yost relieved Lonsdale as U.S. commander in the gulf in 1969. He commanded the task group for three months before turning it over to the South Vietnamese, as part of the Vietnamization program. During Yost's time in command, offensive operations pressed further into the river systems of the mainland. Yost said, "I tried to plan five operations a week. Five a week stretched our capacity for logistics, maintenance, and repair. We never did more than five and some weeks, I'm sure, we did less. Our missions depended on the availability of ground forces, which were usually [Vietnamese] regional and popular forces." Swift boats were the primary resources for inland operations; WPBs drew too much water to get into many of the river systems and were too big to maneuver in narrow waterways. Yost said cutter crews were eager to get involved in inland actions, "But they weren't suitable for that mission. They weren't handy [in the water-

Coast Guard crew prepares to board junk near shore in Viet Cong–controlled territory.

ways] and you put them at a risk beyond what made sense for that costly a weapon system."[25]

Yost made a point of going out on operations. He said, "Early on I decided if you led missions you planned them well. People who didn't lead missions could get into a habit of sloppy planning and taking more risks than they should. To keep myself involved and keep the risk factor very well known to me, I tried to lead between a third and a half [of the operations]." When patrol boat activity shifted from defensive patrolling to offensive operations in 1968, commanders began devoting more time to planning and executing missions and less time to advisory functions. Lonsdale spent twice as much time on task group operations as he did advising the coastal zone commander. Three-fourths of Yost's time went into task group work.[26]

In a major effort to Vietnamize the war, South Vietnamese Navy fleet command units assumed sole responsibility for surveillance operations in areas 8 and 9 on 1 June 1969. The Vietnamese commander of the fourth coastal zone took command of the Gulf of Thailand surveillance group (TG 115.4). After his relief as CTG 115.4, Yost was reassigned to command a newly created floating base on the Cua Lon river in Ca Mau peninsula. On 5 July 1969, Yost relieved Cdr. Charles M. Plumly, USN, as commanding officer of "Sea Float" and commander Task Group 115.7. Sea Float—called *Tran Hung Dao III* by the Vietnamese—was a combined U.S. Navy and South Vietnamese Navy operation; a U.S. officer was in command with a South Vietnamese Navy officer second in command. The fortified base—complete with patrol-boat moorings, helicopter pads, maintenance shops, and berthing and messing—was built on nine "ammi" pontoon barges and anchored in the middle of the river; operations from Sea Float began on 27 June 1969. Sea Float supported operations on local river systems. Yost was next assigned to Vung Tau, where he commanded Market Time operations in the third coastal zone as CTG 115.3 for his last six months in Vietnam.[27]

Coast Guard Division 11 was disestablished after four years of operations in the Gulf of Thailand. The division's remaining four WPBs and a Thai PGM were reassigned to Division 13 at Cat Lo. The feared sea infiltration of arms and supplies to the Viet Cong through the Gulf of Thailand never materialized. Aggressive coastal patrolling denied the enemy the use of gulf waters as a supply route.

7

The Coast Guard
Role Expands

This will be my last [Squadron One] diary entry. Real mixed emotions. . . . sure hate to relinquish the reins on what has been the finest assignment of my career. To those who read this diary, let me say that the Coast Guard's ability to deploy large numbers of top-drawer officers and men to a combat zone has been proven in Vietnam. My job has been easy because I have had a magnificent breed working for me.

Capt. Robert J. LoForte, USCG, COMCOGARDRON ONE

Rung Sat Special Zone

With the sun setting on 9 March 1966, *Point White* turned south in the Soi Rap river and headed for open water. Lt. Eugene J. Hickey, Jr., the cutter's commanding officer, increased speed. Her wake fanning out across the muddy water, the WPB made an obvious show of leaving the river for the night.

Two WPBs began patrolling the Soi Rap on 7 March 1966. Coastal Group 33 assigned two junks to work with each cutter. The river marked the western boundary of the Rung Sat Special Zone (RSSZ), a mangrove-covered swamp, known to be infested with Viet Cong, who had ammunition factories, extensive training camps, and medical facilities in continuous operation in the area. The South Vietnamese Army (ARVN) had not been able to dislodge the VC from the difficult terrain. Lack of fresh water and supplies were the guerrillas' major vulnerabilities; all their provisions had to come into the zone by junk from VC-controlled territory on the west side of the river.

After two days of daylight patrols, cutters commenced 24-hour operations. Hickey waited until dark and then slowly cruised back upriver. Capt. Robert J. LoForte was aboard the WPB. He recently had taken command of Coast Guard Squadron One and was the senior Coast Guard officer in Vietnam. "Because it was a new and more restricted area of operations," LoForte said. "I went along on *Point White* when she patrolled the upper part of the area, north of Ly Nhon peninsula."[1]

At 2215, *Point White* was 17 miles south of Saigon, approaching the entrance to Vam Sat canal; the night was dark and moonless. Vam Sat twisted its way into the RSSZ; it was known to be a departure point for VC junks and sampans crossing the river. Engineman first class Joseph E. Moody manned the forward .50-caliber machine gun. He said, "We were definitely expecting trouble. We knew we had VC on both sides of the river. All day long we saw lots of activity. . . . We could hear mortars going off."

When Hickey detected a westbound radar contact leaving Vam Sat, he set general quarters and increased speed. The crew felt the cutter surge through the muddy water toward the darkened junk two miles away. Hickey said, "I timed my approach to intercept her in the middle of the river. I didn't want her to turn around and get back to the canal."

The siren wailed and the Vietnamese liaison officer ordered the junk to stop with a loud-hailer. When she ignored the orders, Hickey called the target's bearing down to Moody on the mount. Moody said, "I could see something dark in the water. The very second I trained on it, they opened fire. I could see muzzle flashes and returned fire with the .50-caliber." At 150 yards from the junk, Hickey turned on the searchlight. The VC aboard the vessel responded with intense fire from automatic weapons and rifles. *Point White*'s crew returned fire with .50-caliber machine guns and M-16s.

Seaman Buzzele was asleep in the crews' quarters when the general alarm sounded. He said, "We all headed up the ladder. This was my first time in combat and I was a little shaky. I went up on the bow to my GQ station." As Buzzele was taking the cover off a box of .50-caliber ammunition, enemy rounds slammed into the mortar ready box, four feet behind him. Buzzele said, "There was smoke and sparks in the ready box. If it had gone up, there wouldn't have been anybody left because the box was full of ammo. We couldn't get rid of it right away because we had to keep fighting the VC."

As the cutter closed in, sixteen men on the junk kept up a steady stream of fire. ET2 Gerald M. Sampont said, "I emptied the rest of my [.50-caliber] ammo into her side. Every one of them [bullets] from those three .50s were hitting the junk. I could see splinters flying and tracers going right into her side."

When the firing started, Hickey took the wheel. He turned the cutter to bring the after guns to bear, and stopped. He said, "The fire was very heavy. . . . I don't know how they did it. We had three .50s working them over plus a couple rifles. They kept taking the .50-caliber fire directly into the junk and it didn't even slow their rate of fire." Hickey knew if he continued to shoot it out with the junk, some of his crew would get hit. He said, "I decided to run over him. I had to stop them from shooting."

When the searchlight went out, Hickey said, "LoForte grabbed the M-16 on the bridge. It was loaded with tracer rounds. He could see where the junk was and used tracers as spotting rounds for the machine guns. It was very effective." When the chief boatswain's mate who had taken over the bow .50 reached down to get another box of ammunition, a bullet from the junk knocked the wood off the handle of the machine gun. The chief was not hurt.

Hickey headed the cutter toward the junk, steering directly into her fire, and increased to full speed. At the last second, he put on hard left rudder. The cutter struck the junk a glancing blow with her starboard bow and sent a six-foot bow wake sweeping over the junk's deck, knocking some of the VC overboard. As *Point White* passed the junk, fire from GM2 L. K. Gates's machine gun set off an explosion. Moody said, "There was a big flash and I saw a body go up in the air and into the water. The firefight stopped and we picked up survivors." Hickey went over the side and helped recover one VC who was badly burned and about to go under. The man turned out to be a key VC leader in the RSSZ; he was traveling with an armed escort.

Point White pulled alongside the swamped and sinking junk; her crew took two prisoners from the vessel's stern sheets. When a Coast Guardsman attempted to help a wounded VC lying on deck, the man suddenly turned and fired; a crewman on the cutter shot and killed him. The WPB's crew tried to recover intelligence material before the junk went down, but a VC, holed up in the forward cockpit, continued to fire sporadically through a narrow opening. Finally, one of the

USCGC Point White*'s commanding officer, Lt. Eugene J. Hickey,
examines an 81mm mortar round casing struck by Viet Cong gunfire during night action on the Soi Rap river.*

cutter's crew got into a position where he could get a clear shot into
the cockpit; he fired a burst from an M-16 and the shooting stopped.
The cutter picked up a fourth prisoner from the water. When the fighting was over, Hickey checked the mortar ready box, which had been
hit. He said:

> At least three white phosphorous rounds and an illumination round had
> quite a bit of damage to their cases. I moved everybody back from the
> area. Not that it would have done any good, because if the box went up
> it would have blown the whole boat up. They weren't smoking any
> more, but they were hot. I tried to get the rounds out without jarring
> them. Every time one would bump, my heart would stop. . . . I left them
> in the cases and threw them over the side. A 7.62mm slug fired from the
> junk fell out of one of the white phosphorous projectile cases.

After the action, Hickey said, "LoForte was cool under fire. He went right for that M-16 and got into it. I'll give him credit; he never told me what to do. He never gave any orders. He said, 'I'm here. Let me know if you need any help.' He acted like one of the guys."

When rumors of more Coast Guard forces deploying to Vietnam began circulating at the end of August 1965, Cdr. James A. Hodgman, in command of Squadron One, wrote to Coast Guard headquarters. In his 9 September 1965 letter, he said, "If there is any increase in Coast Guard forces assigned to Vietnam, I believe a centralization of control in Saigon is essential." In the letter, he quoted from his 28 August 1965 squadron diary, which said:

> I am aware of the possibility of additional Coast Guard port security forces and ships being sent to Vietnam. The squadron concept is stretched to its limit now due to the location of squadron headquarters, the large separation of divisions, and centralization of naval operational command in Saigon. If additional forces are sent to Vietnam, I recommend that a commander, Coast Guard Forces Vietnam (or similar title) be established to provide administrative supervision of all Coast Guard forces and serve as the Coast Guard advisor to chief, naval advisory group, MACV. The billet should be a captain and he should have a suitable staff.[2]

Once the decision was made to deploy a third division of 82-foot WPBs to Vietnam, the chief of the naval advisory group in Saigon made a formal request for assignment of a senior officer to his staff to coordinate Coast Guard activities. He wanted the officer to handle requests for Coast Guard assistance with other mission areas in addition to coastal surveillance. On 15 December 1965, the Joint Chiefs of Staff (JCS) notified Commander in Chief Pacific (CINCPAC) by message that Coast Guard Capt. Robert J. LoForte was being assigned to Saigon as commander Coast Guard Squadron One with additional duty as senior advisor to the chief naval advisory group for Coast Guard–related matters.[3]

LoForte arrived in Hawaii on 4 January 1966 and remained in Honolulu for six days. In preparation for his assignment, he attended meetings and briefings at CINCPACFLT and 14th Coast Guard District headquarters. After landing at Clark AFB in the Philippines, LoForte traveled to Subic Bay to meet with U.S. Navy commanders providing support for Squadron One and checked on Division 13's preparations for deployment. On 15 January 1966, LoForte landed at Tan Son Nhut airport on the outskirts of Saigon and went directly to the naval advisory group and coastal surveillance force headquarters on Phan-Dinh-Phung Street. He called on Rear Adm. Norvell G. Ward and met with senior staff members and the Coast Guard liaison officer. LoForte moved into two small offices set aside for Squadron One on the second floor, down the corridor from the admiral's suite of offices. Lt. Harlan D. Hanson, Squadron One's liaison officer with the naval advisory group, briefed LoForte on his duties and efforts to resolve supply and logistic problems.[4]

Nine days after his arrival, LoForte flew north to Danang to review operations and support requirements for Division 12. At the same time, he sent Lt. Richard J. Clements from his staff to An Thoi to work on shifting administration of the squadron to Saigon. During his visit with Division 12, LoForte inspected cutters and facilities, met with Navy officials and was briefed on division operations by Lt. Cdr. Richard J. Knapp. On 29 January 1966, LoForte landed in a Navy UF-1G Albatross in calm water off An Thoi. He boarded USS *Krishna* (ARL 38) and for the next two days received briefings, reviewed squadron files, met with cutter crews, inspected vessels, and discussed squadron business with Hodgman.

At 1600 on 31 January 1966, with all hands mustered aboard *Krishna,* LoForte relieved Hodgman of command of Squadron One. Hodgman then relieved Lt. Cdr. Axel J. Hagstrom as commander of Division 11. As one of his first official acts, the new squadron commander reassigned Hagstrom to command Division 13 when it arrived in Vietnam. Hodgman recommended Hagstrom for the assignment; his time in command of Division 11 and as chief staff officer gave him invaluable experience for initiating operations at the new division. Lt. Cdr. William E. Lehr, who commanded Division 13 during organizing and outfitting, became LoForte's chief staff officer in Saigon. Because of his naval engineering experience and background, Lehr also was designated squadron repair and logistic officer. Throughout Squadron One's service in Vietnam, it was common practice for officers assigned to command a division to spend some time gaining in-country experience in a chief-staff-officer billet before taking command.

Cdr. Risto A. Matilla had arrived at Saigon in September 1965 in response to COMUSMACV's request for "services of a Coast Guard officer experienced in port security work" to advise the Vietnamese. After LoForte arrived, Matilla was assigned to Squadron One while doing his survey. The request for the security survey was initiated by commander, naval advisory group after he observed the lack of security at the port of Saigon. Ward was alarmed by the vulnerability of waterfront facilities critical to resupplying the war effort. A Vietnamese Navy officer, designated commander of the Capital Military District, was charged with "proper security of the river, along the waterfront, and in the port." Unfortunately, several different Vietnamese government agencies not under his authority also were involved. Saigon police, harbor police, Vietnamese customs, and ARVN all participated in enforcement and patrol activities. The sprawling, congested port area, with uncontrolled access, was a disaster waiting to happen.[5]

While conducting his port security survey, Matilla became aware of a potentially disastrous situation at Nha Be, the munitions arrival port south of Saigon. Vietnamese stevedores unloading explosives had little or no training in safe handling of dangerous cargo. The busy ammunition anchorage was next to South Vietnam's largest fuel farm complex; an accident at one could destroy the other. At Matilla's recommendation, the chief of the naval advisory group proposed to MACV, "that a channel for ocean-going ships be laid out from Nha Be to Cat Lai . . . eliminating the grave threat to the fuel farm."[6]

On one inspection trip, Matilla observed a Vietnamese truck carrying a load of high-explosive projectiles. When the vehicle reached its unloading area, he watched the driver get out, lower the tailgate, and get back in the cab; the truck then quickly backed toward the delivery point and the driver slammed on his brakes. The truck stopped with a jolt, causing projectiles to tumble to the ground in a pile. While the shells were unfused, they still contained high explosives and could initiate an explosion that would have destroyed the entire facility. When asked about this bizarre procedure, the driver shrugged his shoulders and said, "It would be easier with a dump truck."[7]

With the advice of COMCOGARDRON ONE, COMUSMACV sent a message on 17 February 1966 to CINCPAC stating, "US Coast Guard has capability of providing explosive handling supervisory teams. Commanding general USARV [U.S. Army, Vietnam] has an urgent need for two teams." In response to the request, which was forwarded to the Coast Guard commandant through the JCS, the Coast Guard made preparations to deploy two explosive loading detachments. Each detach-

Saigon's congested waterfront is vital for resupplying the war effort.

ment consisted of an officer and seven enlisted men, specially trained in explosive handing.

Once a Coast Guard captain was attached to the naval advisory group, he was assigned to handle matters involving Coast Guard missions and expertise. In April 1966, LoForte met with the director of the Vietnamese navigation directorate to encourage improvements in aids to navigation; improvements were needed to support increased shipping activity. LoForte expended considerable effort in attempting to get the Vietnamese to address the problem. Unfortunately, they were not able or not willing to get required work done in a reasonable time. On 19 December 1966, a three-man Coast Guard aids to navigation team was assigned to Squadron One to assess in-country requirements.[8]

Expanding Navy roles and responsibilities in Vietnam resulted in creation of a new command. On 1 April 1966, Ward took command of Naval Forces Vietnam (NAVFORV) in Saigon; LoForte continued to serve as his Coast Guard advisor. When NAVFORV was established, Market Time operations became a separate command. On 19 April 1966, Capt. Clifford L. Stewart, USN, took command of Market Time as CTF 115. Ward honored the Coast Guard by holding the task force relief ceremony aboard the 82-foot USCGC *Point Grace* (WPB 82323) moored at Cat Lo. LoForte noted in the diary, "The squadron was proud to have one of its vessels selected for the change of command." After creation of NAVFORV, LoForte became more involved in the Coast Guard's expanding role in Vietnam.[9]

On 8 February 1966, LoForte met with Captain Jacques, USN, chief of the Military Sea Transportation Service (MSTS) office in Vietnam, who was plagued with problems caused by merchant-ship crews during long layovers in Vietnam. He told LoForte a Coast Guard merchant marine detachment (MMD), with authority and experience to deal with merchant mariners, was needed. The State Department officer in charge of the consular section at the U.S. Embassy, Robert Lewis, was adamant, however, that he did not need or want Coast Guard assistance. Lewis apparently had a bad experience with a Coast Guard MMD while serving in Greece in the 1950s.[10]

LoForte got an opportunity to address the need for an MMD in Vietnam while at Tan Son Nhut airport on 25 April 1966. Frank H. James, a representative of Lykes Lines—a large shipper transporting supplies to Vietnam—was passing through the airport and recognized LoForte's Coast Guard cap device; he came over and talked to him. During their conversation, need for an MMD was brought up. LoForte told James of the reluctance at the U.S. Embassy to ask for assistance and suggested that a request might be initiated though the State Department in the United States.[11]

The Navy attempted to get MACV to address the need for a Coast Guard MMD. On 31 August 1966, commander MSTS Far East, a Navy rear admiral headquartered at Yokohama, Japan, wrote to COMUSMACV requesting assignment of an MMD. The letter said:

> During the course of the Vietnam operations, and particularly since the big buildup commenced early this year, MSTS has been confronted with an increasing number of problems involving merchant ships and crews. Under peacetime division of authority and responsibility most of the problems arising do not fall under MSTS cognizance though they seriously affect our capability to perform our assigned mission. . . . The problems of the discipline of merchant seamen, repatriating seamen who have deserted ships in Vietnam ports, hearing complaints, and conducting judicial hearings are unresolved. . . . Since the latter problems are properly a matter for U.S. Coast Guard jurisdiction, it is strongly recommended, and requested, that a Coast Guard Merchant Marine Detail with one or two officers be established in Saigon.[12]

On 6 October 1966, Gen. William C. Westmoreland replied to MSTSFE. He denied the request, saying it was an Embassy function. But he did say the problem would be monitored.

With the build up of U.S. forces in Vietnam, the demand for shipment of ammunition supplies increased steadily, and unresolved problems with merchant seamen manning the ships also increased, creating a pressing need for the services of an MMD. To circumvent objections of the U.S. consul, the Coast Guard established a new entity: Coast Guard Shipping Advisory Unit, Vietnam. The one-man unit was attached to commander MSTS Far East Area and assigned to Saigon. Cdr. Edward F. Oliver, a marine investigation specialist, arrived on 3 December 1966, and took on the daunting task of looking into incidents aboard all U.S. merchant ships transporting supplies to Vietnamese ports. He handled matters of ship safety, seaworthiness, and inspections, crew qualifications, and enforcement of discipline. With more than 300 U.S. flag ships engaged in a continuous Vietnam sealift, it was an extremely busy undertaking for one individual.[13]

As an advisor to NAVFORV, COMRONONE participated in the search for a follow-on to the Navy Swift boat. COMNAVFORV was concerned about the Swift's limited capability. In a letter to the Chief of Naval Operations (CNO), he said:

> The PCF has definite limitations in terms of range, endurance, and sea-keeping capabilities. A patrol of greater than 24 hours results in excessive crew fatigue and decreased effectiveness of patrol units. . . . The PCF is ineffective in seas greater than five feet, resulting in a further degradation of patrol capability in the area where such seas are common.[14]

On 25 July 1966, LoForte met with Captain Stewart, Market Time's task force commander, and Capt. John T. Shepherd, NAVFORV's operations officer, to review a proposed design for a 65-foot second-generation Swift boat. LoForte said, "It was decided it [the proposed design] would not be enough of an improvement over the 50-foot Swift. It was shot down because they needed a vessel for sustained operations of a minimum of four days, can handle 8- to 10-foot seas, and has a top speed of eighteen to twenty knots. Crew must number at least eleven, preferably twelve. Requirements indicate a vessel of a minimum of eighty to eighty-five feet and a 6-foot draft." LoForte observed in the squadron diary, "In other words, just about what the WPB is."[15]

In recognition of its performance, Coast Guard Squadron One received the Navy Unit Commendation in November 1966. LoForte traveled to An Thoi to accept the award on behalf of the squadron. On 2 November 1966, Adm. David L. McDonald, the CNO, presented the award to LoForte at the VNN base at An Thoi. He made the presentation at a ceremony at the end of the tee pier, with *Point Banks* and *Point Glover* as a backdrop. After the festivities, Admiral McDonald and Rear Admiral Ward visited *Krishna,* anchored offshore. While the admirals were returning to An Thoi aboard a Swift boat, two WPBs steamed by in column formation. With crews manning their rails, the cutters rendered passing honors to Admiral McDonald. LoForte said, "They looked very sharp, especially since both boats were sporting their newly authorized commendation ribbon on their bridge wings. Fast work!"[16]

That evening, back in Saigon, NAVFORV's staff held a briefing for the CNO and his party. LoForte wrote, "Throughout the Market Time part of the briefing, the excellent role of the WPB was continually apparent. They said, 'We never have to pull them off station because of weather. They have the lowest CASREP [equipment casualty report] rate in the entire Market Time–Game Warden fleet and the highest operationally ready ratio, best communications capability, greatest firepower, and maximum number of successes.' It was sweet music!"[17]

Throughout 1966, the Coast Guard's role in Vietnam continued to expand with the addition of another patrol boat division; a port security and waterways detail; explosive loading detachments; a shipping advisor; an aids to navigation team; LORAN-C stations; and deployed 14th District buoy tenders. On 11 January 1967, to more accurately describe its expanded role, Coast Guard organization in Saigon was designated Coast Guard Activities Vietnam (CGACTV).[18]

While other Coast Guard roles increased, support of Squadron One remained the major mission for CGACTV; the captain retained the title of commander Squadron One. Administrative and logistic support for the three divisions of patrol boats continued to require the majority of the staff's attention. Lt. Cdr. Richard A. Bauman, who served as CGACTV chief staff officer in 1967 before taking command of Division 12, said, "About 75 percent of our job was to get people in and to the [WPB] divisions. We would pick them up at Tan Son Nhut [airport] and bring them in overnight. Then we would get them out on a Market Time flight the next day. Squadron One also handled arrange-

ments for shipyard availabilities for WPBs and assisted with administrative and logistic support as well as public affairs."[19]

During the years the Coast Guard was in Vietnam, CGACTV functioned with a minimum of staff personnel. With only slight variations
over the years, the complement consisted of a captain (0-6) as commander; a commander (0-5) as chief staff officer—the billet was upgraded
from lieutenant commander in 1967; a lieutenant (0-3)—alternately
titled administration officer, operations officer, or readiness officer;
two warrant officers—a chief machinist as engineer and supply officer
and a chief ship's clerk as personnel officer; a chief or first-class yeoman who ran the office; and a chief or first-class journalist, who handled public affairs. An aids to navigation (ATON) team, consisting of
a lieutenant commander and two or three enlisted personnel, also
was assigned. While the ATON team was attached to the U.S. Agency
for International Development (USAID), it usually worked out of
CGACTV's office when not in the field.[20]

Capt. Charles B. Hathaway, a commander when he reported as
chief staff officer in November 1967, said of CGACTV's organization,
"Everybody did everything because there was always somebody out
on the road. There weren't that many of us." With regard to CGACTV's
relationship with the Navy, Hathaway said:

> The squadron commander was expected to attend the admiral's staff
> conferences, but we really weren't under them in any way. . . . We just
> kind of fit in and did our thing. We were independent of them as much
> as the Coast Guard is independent of the Navy at all. . . . We took care
> of our own people. That's why we were there, so the Navy didn't have
> to worry about taking care of the Coast Guard people. . . . If they could
> give us any help, they did. They helped us a lot with public affairs. We
> only had one journalist and they had a whole organization. . . . We
> helped them and they helped us.[21]

Hathaway said CGACTV served as an administrative base for Coast
Guard personnel assigned to other armed forces and agencies. They
checked on the well-being of the people and helped them with matters
peculiar to the Coast Guard. Hathaway said, "We were their home
base, a place they could come and talk to other Coast Guard people."[22]

On 15 May 1967, Coast Guard Squadron Three's high-endurance
cutters arrived in Vietnam waters and joined Operation Market Time.
The squadron's five deployed cutters operated out of Subic Bay in the

Philippines, where commander Squadron Three had his headquarters. CGACTV served as an in-country coordination point for cutter support. By 1968, CGACTV was providing support for Coast Guard personnel serving with the Navy in Squadron One; the Army in the port security and waterways detail and explosive loading detachments; the Air Force in the 37th and 39th Aero Rescue and Recovery Squadrons; the U.S. Embassy in the MMD; and USAID in the ATON detail. While not under CGACTV's administrative control, support was provided for personnel at Tight Reign LORAN-C stations at Tan My and Con Son Island. CGACTV also supported and exercised operational control over buoy tenders deploying to Vietnam. Administrative control of buoy tenders remained with the Fourteenth Coast Guard District, but they received support from CGACTV when in-country.

8

Squadron Three

It is requested that the Treasury Department assist the Department of the Navy by assigning five high-endurance cutters to augment Market Time forces.

Paul H. Nitze, *Secretary of the Navy*
10 March 1967

Trawler SL-3-70

By the time the small boat from USCGC *Rush* (WHEC 723) came under the falls and hooked on, the 378-foot high-endurance cutter's main diesel engines had rumbled to life, the special sea detail was set, and the anchor was at short stay. The boat was hoisted and her gunwale brought against the ship's hull; the cutter's captain, Capt. Robert W. Durfey, stepped aboard. He returned his executive officer's salute and headed for the bridge. *Rush* was anchored off the southern tip of Phuc Quoc Island in the Gulf of Thailand while Durfey and ship's officers attended Operation Market Time briefings at the CSC at An Thoi. While briefings were in progress, the center received a message that a Navy P-3 Orion patrol aircraft had sighted a suspicious steel-hulled trawler 50 miles east-northeast of Con Son Island in *Rush*'s patrol area.[1]

The cutter weighed anchor at 1330 on 17 November 1970 and headed south to round Ca Mau peninsula before heading northeast. Gas turbines were put on the line and Durfey ordered a speed of 25 knots. Word of the trawler's sighting quickly circulated through the ship. Excitement mounted as the crew heard the high-pitched whine of 16,000-HP turbines and felt the ship surge forward.

Patrol aircraft from Task Group 72.3 kept the suspicious vessel, identified as a possible SL-3 infiltration trawler, under observation while *Rush* was enroute to conduct covert surveillance. At the same time,

USS *Tacoma* (PG 92), one of the Navy's new 165-foot patrol gunboats, closed the target from the east. Communications between surveillance ships and aircraft were good during the day, but deteriorated rapidly at night. *Tacoma* arrived on-scene first and took station seven miles astern of the trawler. *Rush* rendezvoused with *Tacoma* on the morning of 18 November 1970 and took over surveillance at 0800. She remained out of sight at a range of twelve miles. *Tacoma* was released to return to her patrol area.

For the next three-and-a-half days, *Rush* shadowed the suspected infiltrator. The cutter maintained radar surveillance from a range of between 10 miles, just out of sight, and 14 miles, the limit of firm radar contact. The cutter's officers of the deck (OOD) and combat information center (CIC) teams got plenty of practice in station keeping, as Durfey continually varied the cutter's relative position from the suspect; if the trawler had radar, he did not want it to appear she was being followed. At night the cutter ran darkened ship. In CIC, radarmen were assigned during each watch to maintain a continuous dead reckoning tracer plot on the trawler—they had no other duties. They ensured that the cutter did not get close enough to be seen, and prevented the trawler from becoming confused with other ships on radar.

The trawler first headed east-northeast away from Vietnam, passing through vessel traffic in trade routes between Hong Kong and Singapore on the afternoon of 18 November 1970. That night, while the midwatch was in the process of relieving, an urgent call came over the 21 MC from CIC, "Bridge. Combat. Trawler closing rapidly." The suspect had suddenly reversed course and, with a relative speed of 20 knots, was closing at a rate of one mile every three minutes. The trawler got to within five miles of the darkened cutter before *Rush* could open range. The near miss prompted the captain to stagger reliefs of bridge and CIC watch sections.

On 19 and 20 November 1970, the trawler ran a racetrack pattern on the eastern edge of the shipping lane, mingling with traffic. Making turns for between eight and ten knots, she gradually worked her way to the southwest by running longer southwest than northeast legs. On the evening of 20 November 1970, the trawler, now designated SL-3-70, broke from her pattern and headed northwest toward Vietnam. With brief exceptions, she maintained a steady course and speed.

When it was apparent that the trawler was going to attempt to infiltrate on the evening of 21 November 1970, commander Task Force

115 assigned additional forces to assist *Rush;* Durfey was designated officer in tactical command (OTC) for the intercept operation. *Rush* remained darkened as she followed the trawler toward the entrance to the Co Chien river, 70 miles south of Saigon. USCGC *Sherman* (WHEC 720), sister ship of *Rush,* was enroute from the northeast. Under a moonless sky, the 172-foot ocean minesweeper USS *Endurance* (MSO 435) waited between the coast and trawler to make the initial challenge. *Tacoma,* approaching from astern of *Rush,* was ordered to proceed and assist *Endurance.* With the suspect nine miles from shore—well within South Vietnam's 12-mile limit—Durfey directed *Endurance* to "close and challenge the trawler." At 2235, *Rush* commenced illuminating the area with 5-inch star shells and all units were ordered to turn on navigation lights.

When the trawler failed to answer *Endurance's* challenge, the MSO fired two rounds from her 40mm deck gun across the ship's bow. The trawler then turned seaward and took evasive action. *Endurance* signaled, "Trawler not stopping. Request permission to open fire." *Rush* replied, ordering *Endurance* to take the trawler under direct fire. The trawler immediately returned *Endurance's* fire with automatic weapons and 75mm recoilless rifles, and then turned and attempted to ram the MSO. At 2325, *Rush* ordered *Endurance* to break off her attack and told *Tacoma* to close at maximum speed and take the trawler under fire with her 3-inch gun. *Rush* continued to illuminate the trawler with star shells. At 2329, *Tacoma* reported a gas turbine flameout and mechanical failure with her 3-inch, .50-caliber deck gun. When Navy OV-10 Black Pony aircraft arrived on-scene to provide illumination, *Rush* went into action. Over the sound-powered phone, the command was given, "Surface action port. Trawler bearing 335. Range six thousand, five hundred yards. Commence tracking." When the reply came back, "On target," the command was given to load. The bridge talker looked at the OOD and repeated, "Bridge. Fire Control. Mount 51 loaded. Request permission to commence firing." *Rush* adjusted her shots until the trawler was bracketed and then fired for effect. The cutter expended 25 rounds of 5-inch ammunition, scoring two probable and two possible hits before ceasing fire. *Sherman,* which had closed from the north, next opened fire. She landed three hits before the trawler went dead in the water. At 0017, infiltration trawler SL-3-70 disappeared from radar.

Endurance searched the area where the trawler was last seen, but found no survivors. During the brief engagement, *Endurance* was the only U.S. ship hit, sustaining topside damage from the trawler's 75mm recoilless rifles and small arms; she suffered no personnel casualties. *Rush* and *Endurance* remained in the area overnight while other ships were released to return to their patrol areas.

High-Endurance Cutters

In the beginning of 1967, U.S. troop strength in Vietnam had reached almost 400,000. President Lyndon B. Johnson continued to pursue a policy of applying increased military pressure in an attempt to force North Vietnam's leaders to the negotiating table. On 25 February 1967, CINCPAC forwarded a request to the JCS for seven additional U.S. Navy destroyers. Their 5-inch guns were needed to conduct naval gunfire support missions for ground forces in South Vietnam and naval gunfire against North Vietnam. In the request, CINCPAC indicated that CINCPACFLT had seven radar picket escorts (DERs) that could be reassigned from Market Time operations to the fleet, but they would require suitable replacements. Two new 165-foot *Asheville*-class patrol gunboats were available as Market Time reliefs, but the rest of the ships in the class were still under construction, and would not be available for another year.[2]

In a 10 March 1967 memorandum to the Treasury secretary, Navy Secretary Paul H. Nitze requested assistance of additional Coast Guard forces for Vietnam. He said:

> The U.S. Navy forces in Vietnam have an urgent requirement for additional naval gunfire support. To provide such support it will be necessary to release U.S. Navy destroyers from other fleet missions. In order that the overall defense posture of the United States is not degraded, it is planned to assign destroyer escorts now on Market Time operations to replace these destroyers. Liaison between representatives of the U.S. Navy and U.S. Coast Guard has established that five high-endurance cutters can be made available to relieve the DERs.[3]

Assistant Treasury Secretary Joseph V. Barn replied on 14 March 1967 that the Coast Guard was preparing to assign five ships, and that details were being worked out between the Coast Guard and the Navy. In a message sent to area and district commanders, Coast Guard Commandant Adm. Willard J. Smith designated five 311-foot *Casco-*

class high-endurance cutters for deployment to South Vietnam with Market Time. The message directed five cutters—*Half Moon* (WHEC 378), *Yakutat* (WHEC 380), *Barataria* (WHEC 381), *Bering Strait* (WHEC 382), and *Gresham* (WHEC 387)—to sail in time to arrive at Pearl Harbor, Hawaii, by 23 April 1967 and Vietnam by 10 May 1967. The message indicated that the cutters would be gone from home ports for ten months. Navy support for deployed ships was arranged by amending the Department of the Navy–Coast Guard support agreement for 82-foot patrol boats (WPBs) already deployed for Market Time.[4]

Squadron Three Deploys

Gresham had just returned from Pacific ocean station patrol and was moored at Coast Guard Base Alameda, Calif. On 6 March 1967, her commanding officer, Cdr. Norman L. Scherer, was called to Twelfth Coast Guard District headquarters in San Francisco. In a brief conference, he was told to prepare his ship for deployment to Vietnam. *Gresham* immediately went into a shipyard for a short maintenance availability; additional communications equipment and .50-caliber machine-gun mounts were installed. Scherer said, "They froze our crew and we were allowed to pick to fill vacancies. We took experienced people who had just gotten transferred from the ship." The crew was augmented with additional communications personnel and CIC watchstanders.[5]

The five cutters proceeded independently to Hawaii and moored at Pearl Harbor Naval Station. On 24 April 1967, cutter crews formed up under a glaring Hawaiian sun, wearing dress-white uniforms. In a brief ceremony, commander Fourteenth Coast Guard District officially established Squadron Three. Capt. John E. Day took command of the squadron, designated Task Unit 70.8.6. Two days later, the cutters departed Pearl Harbor enroute to the Philippines. Day and his staff were embarked aboard *Gresham;* Scherer was senior cutter commanding officer.

Enroute to Subic Bay, cutters conducted general quarters drills, station keeping, and, above all else, underway replenishment exercises. Cdr. Richard M. Morse, commanding officer of *Barataria,* said, "Squadron Three held a dozen [replenishment] exercises as we steamed

The first five high-endurance cutters of Squadron Three nest next to USS Jason *after arriving at Subic Bay, the Philippines, on 10 May 1967.*

westward: conning officer approach practice, rig practice, bolo [weighted line] and shotline practice, night-lighting checks, night approaches, and finally, night rigging." When not conducting GQ drills, station keeping or replenishment exercises, the ships sailed in column formation. Enroute, the squadron reported to commander Seventh Fleet for Market Time duty on 4 May 1967. Cutters joined nine Navy DERs of Escort Squadrons 5 and 7, maintaining the outer barrier patrol. On 10 May 1967, cutters completed their transit and entered Subic Bay. Day established Squadron Three's office at the naval station and wrote the commandant, via commander Western Area, that, "All cutter operations are on schedule and no major difficulties have been encountered. . . . Liaison has been established with all local commands." Cutters of Squadron Three wasted no time in commencing operations; three were on patrol in Vietnam on 15 May 1967.[6]

The organization changed on 1 October 1967: Squadron Three and the deployed Navy escort squadron were combined to form a single task unit, with Day designated task unit commander. With a staff of four Coast Guard officers, four Navy officers, and three Coast Guard and ten Navy enlisted personnel, the task unit was responsible for scheduling Market Time patrols, training and readiness of task unit ships, coordination of logistic and personnel support requirements, port visits, and upkeep periods. It also was responsible for control, maintenance, and transfer of twenty-five different types of portable equipment used by Market Time ships on patrol. Equipment included such items as body armor, portable electronic equipment, and training devices.[7]

In addition to task unit commander, Day was designated commander Cruiser-Destroyer Group Seventh Fleet representative, Subic Bay (COMCRUDESREP). As such, he represented an average of sixty-five cruiser-destroyer–type ships assigned to commander Cruiser-Destroyer Group Seventh Fleet for matters concerning personnel, material, repairs, and readiness. He expedited location and delivery of vital parts and supplies needed by ships.[8]

On Patrol

Scherer said Squadron Three's primary mission was "interdicting supplies being infiltrated to Viet Cong irregulars and naval gunfire support." With Subic Bay as home port during deployment, cutters made three-week patrols off the coast of South Vietnam. WHECs and DERs rotated in the different coastal patrol areas. One WHEC was always kept in the Gulf of Thailand where she could provide naval gunfire support for forces ashore with her longer-range 5-inch gun. Scherer said, "We patrolled randomly, fifteen to twenty miles offshore." Outer barrier ships (Coast Guard HECs and Navy DERs, PGs, and MSOs) were under operational control of commander Coastal Surveillance Force CTF 115 while on patrol. The barrier was supported by long-range Navy P-2 Neptune and P-3 Orion patrol aircraft, searching further offshore for suspicious vessels approaching the coast. Cutters conducted boarding programs while on patrol. Scherer said, "We boarded twelve to fifteen junks a day. Just in the event we could run onto some contraband. . . . Sometimes with Vietnamese liaison officers. Sometimes without." Five cutters and five escort ships continuously manned four Market Time stations off Vietnam and two Taiwan patrol stations (Navy-manned), and served as Hong Kong station ship. The two escort squadrons rotated on six-month deployments to Subic Bay from their home port in Hawaii.[9]

The second deployment of WHECs consisted of two 327-foot *Bibb*-class and three 255-foot *Owasco*-class cutters. These cutters had more time to prepare and underwent predeployment shipyard availabilities and refresher training. East coast cutters completed three weeks of training with Fleet Training Group Guantanamo Bay, Cuba, enroute to the Pacific. Cutter replacements were staggered over a two-month period—December 1967 through January 1968—to provide continuity for squadron operations.[10]

The second deployment was in place and on patrol when North Vietnam launched its Tet offensive on 31 January 1968; North Vietnamese and Viet Cong troops attacked cities and villages throughout South Vietnam. To provide supplies to continue the offensive, North Vietnam sent trawlers to infiltrate arms and ammunition to their forces ashore in South Vietnam.

Tet Trawlers

A P-2 Neptune aircraft detected the first trawler 150 miles south of the demilitarized zone. When it became probable on the afternoon of 29 February 1968 that the ship would attempt to infiltrate, the 255-foot USCGC *Androscoggin* (WHEC 68) was directed to take the vessel under surveillance. Cdr. William H. Stewart, in command of *Androscoggin*, kept out of sight while he followed the trawler toward the coast. The ship was headed for the vicinity of Cu Lao Re island, 70 miles southeast of Danang.[11]

Closer to shore, Coast Guard 82-footers *Point Welcome* and *Point Grey* and two Navy Swifts, PCF-18 and PCF-20, waited. Lt. Cdr. Richard A. Bauman, COMCOGARDIV 12, aboard *Point Welcome*, was the inshore barrier OTC. Bauman, call sign *"Permeate,"* spaced his units two miles apart in a line four miles offshore. They waited in the darkness in the path of the trawler. Seas were calm with a gentle breeze blowing from seaward. Commander, Northern Surveillance Group ordered *Androscoggin* and patrol boats "to block the trawler infiltration attempt with capture of the vessel highly desirable, but with stopping the infiltration attempt the primary mission."[12]

Androscoggin waited until the trawler, running without lights, closed to six-and-a-half miles from the coast before intercepting. The cutter challenged the ship with flashing light at 0112 on 1 March 1968. When there was no response, *Androscoggin* illuminated the trawler with three 5-inch star shells. The vessel, positively identified as an SL-class North Vietnamese trawler, began firing recoilless rifles and machine guns at *Androscoggin* and then turned toward the cutter. *Androscoggin* opened fire with her 5-inch gun. Stewart said, "Our main battery scored a direct hit on the after starboard side of the vessel and she turned again and headed for the beach."[13]

Bauman, who was waiting with patrol boats, said, "She [the trawler] laid down a stream of heavy black smoke from her stern and disappeared behind it as she angled in toward the beach. . . . *Androscoggin* continued in with the trawler and told the inner barrier to clear. . . . I called *Androscoggin* and said we were ready to engage."[14]

When *Androscoggin's* line of fire became fouled by a southbound cargo junk, caught in the middle of the action, Stewart ordered helicopter gunships to attack. At 0129, two gunships—"Shark 6" and "Shark 9"—made firing runs with 2.75-inch rockets and 7.62mm miniguns. They were met with intense fire from the trawler's guns. At 0140, with the trawler rapidly closing the coast, Stewart ordered her taken under fire by the 82-footers and Swifts.[15]

Bauman said, "As she [the trawler] came in, there was a lot of [machine-gun] fire coming from her, particularly at the aircraft. They did a lot of firing at everybody. . . . *Point Welcome* pursued from directly astern [of the trawler], firing illumination rounds from her 81mm mortar while *Point Grey* and two PCFs poured in extremely accurate .50-caliber machine-gun fire." Under fire, the trawler headed into the surfline and grounded on the sloping sandy shore at 0210. She was 50 yards from the beach near the mouth of the Song Tha Cau river.[16]

Patrol boats closed to 500 yards off the beached trawler. *Point Welcome* opened fire with her 81mm mortar, scoring two direct hits with her first four high-explosive rounds. The other boats laced the ship with .50-caliber machine-gun fire. Accurate shooting silenced the trawler's guns. A small explosion occurred in the bow of the trawler at 0229; but it did not seriously damage the vessel. While the patrol boats maneuvered to maintain positions in a northerly setting current, a horrendous explosion ripped through the night. In his after-action report, Bauman said, "WPBs and PCFs were showered with shrapnel. Large pieces flew overhead to land well to seaward. Despite large amounts of missiles flying about there were no personnel casualties." *Point Welcome* had the forward pilothouse windows completely shattered by the blast. The portside window was smashed from the inside by a piece of shrapnel. A rifle bayonet, bent into a perfect "S"-shape, landed between the 14-foot Boston Whaler and the stern. Four crewmen dove under the boat for protection from the rain of metal. When smoke from the explosion drifted away, no trace of the trawler could be seen.[17]

The second trawler was sighted by patrol aircraft off the southern tip of South Vietnam and covert surveillance of the vessel was handed off to USCGC *Winona* (WHEC 65) at 1400 on 29 February 1968. Cdr. Herbert J. Lynch, in command of the 255-foot cutter, said, "We followed her all day. Just after midnight, she turned and made for the coast. We were in continuous communications with the surveillance center. As we approached Ca Mau peninsula, we started to run out of water. I told the Center, 'I can only stay with her for another 20 minutes.' That's when they told me to halt and board her." At 0200, *Winona* closed to 500 yards, lit up the trawler with her 24-inch searchlight, and ordered the ship to stop. Lynch said, "She kept going so we put a 5-inch round across her bow. She answered with machine-gun fire." When the cutter's searchlight went out, Lynch said, "We fired at the flashes from her machine guns." After twelve rounds, the trawler exploded. The cutter was so close that debris from the ship, including fragments of bone and flesh, fell on the decks. While the trawler had been closing the coast, two Coast Guard 82-foot WPBs waited just offshore and two Navy PCFs were at the mouth of the Bo De river, believed to be the trawler destination. Lynch said, "The patrol boats had radar, so they knew where we were. I told them, 'Just don't get down my line of fire.' We weren't going to worry about them. They had to worry about themselves."[18]

The third trawler was found in a cove 10 miles north of Nha Trang and was attacked by Navy Swifts, a VNN 100-foot motor gunboat, and Junk Force units. When hit by the fifth mortar round, the trawler exploded. A fourth trawler, under surveillance by USCGC *Minnetonka* (WHEC 67), turned back to sea before entering South Vietnamese waters. Trawlers were known to be rigged with self-destruction charges, but it was difficult to tell if explosions were self-detonated or the results of explosive cargo being hit by gunfire. While *Androscoggin* and *Winona* took several hits from trawler guns during actions—bullet holes ran across *Androscoggin*'s port bow, spray shield, and bridge area—neither vessel suffered personnel casualties.[19]

◆   ◆   ◆

A boarding party from USCGC Yakutat *prepares to board and inspect a motorized fishing junk.*

In addition to interdicting steel-hulled ammunition trawlers, cutters boarded coastal junk traffic. A 1969 publication, *Lessons Learned by Squadron Three Cutters,* cautioned crews to "Stay loose because the unexpected is routine. Do not hesitate to close and board any Vietnamese vessel you see. Even the slightest thing out of order could signal an infiltrator. Lack of [North Vietnamese] success with the so-called 'classical' trawler-type infiltrator has quite probably led to much more devious disguises." WHECs used small boats to put boarding parties on vessels, or took junks alongside. In discussing boardings, *Lessons Learned* said, "When boarding fishing junks, don't let the smell of rotten fish keep you from checking thoroughly. After a few minutes, you won't smell a thing."[20]

Initially, heavy emphasis was placed on WHECs patrolling the outer barrier and boarding. But as combat actions in coastal areas intensified and the capability of a cutter's 5-inch gun was realized, requests for naval gunfire support increased. Ships on later deployments spent more of their patrol time providing gunfire support. Cutters were called on to destroy enemy encampments and caches of war materials and to support engaged forces ashore. Lynch said, "It was nothing to fire 50 rounds of shoreside support. We did so much shooting, we had to rebarrel the gun. We wore out the grooves on it." During four-and-a-

High-endurance cutters of Squadron Three fired more than 77,000 5-inch projectiles during naval gunfire support missions in Vietnam.

half years of squadron operations, cutters fired an average of 41 naval gunfire missions each, expending a total of 77,036 rounds of 5-inch, .38-caliber ammunition. USCGC *Dallas* (WHEC 716), in Vietnam with the fifth deployment, did the most shooting: she fired 6,640 rounds during 163 separate gunfire missions during her deployment. Replacing worn gun barrels became common for cutters. Sometimes cutters, particularly in the Gulf of Thailand, had to go into dangerously shallow waters to reach their assigned targets. Durfey, who was with the seventh deployment, said, "We had difficulty getting within range because of our 22-foot draft. Sometimes we would have to go into areas with only one or two feet of clearance. Fortunately, the bottom was mostly mud." At first, almost all gunfire support was fired during daylight. Later, as Viet Cong became more aggressive and night attacks increased, gunfire support was called for at all hours. "We provided most of our gunfire support at night," Durfey said. "Perhaps 60 percent was after dark."

Cutters were called on for naval gunfire support in close proximity to friendly forces. During the period from April to December 1970, a Squadron Three high-endurance cutter was continuously assigned as Song Ong Doc Naval Gunfire Support unit. The cutter provided on-call protection for the U.S. Advanced Tactical Support Base at the mouth of the Song Ong Doc river in the Gulf of Thailand. On 18 May 1970, USCGC *Sherman* (WHEC 720) was on station off the base when at 0345, the base picked up activity on a "duffel bag" (detection device) and requested fifteen rounds of fire (five airburst and ten surface-detonating) on a target just north of the river. Tragedy struck when *Sherman* fired the mission. After ten rounds, the cutter received an urgent cease-fire—gunfire had fallen among U.S. forces. Misdirected gunfire killed a Navy petty officer and wounded nine others—three seriously. Wounded were evacuated by helicopter to *Sherman* for treatment by the cutter's doctor.[21]

While on patrol, WHECs provided logistic support for Coast Guard WPBs and Navy PCFs. Cutters provided fuel, water, medical support, and commissary supplies to patrol boats. Engineers and technicians also helped with mechanical and electronic repairs. When weather in the Gulf of Thailand was good and seas were calm, Navy PCFs could operate further from their base at An Thoi. WHECs provided berths for two spare PCF crews. When patrol boats came along side each day to refuel and reprovision, crews would change. Coast Guard WPBs required fuel and water when their patrols were longer than five days.

When operations permitted, Squadron Three cutter crews supported local Vietnamese villages in their operating areas; ships sent medical and civic action program (MEDCAP) teams ashore. Lt. Cdr. Richard H. Beiter, executive officer of USCGC *Owasco* (WHEC 39), said, "I got ashore for . . . a MEDCAP trip with our doctor to a village about eighty miles south of Danang. . . . We reached the beach by a series of transfers from *Owasco* to a Swift boat to a motorized junk. . . . We did have one bit of action on our arrival. Apparently 'Nguyen Charlie' sent his welcoming party to greet us. A few enemy mortar rounds came whistling into the . . . encampment as we arrived." Cutter doctors provided medical treatment while the rest of the team helped villagers with mechanical or structural repair projects.[22]

USCGC Mendota *takes on fuel and supplies while under way on Market Time station off the coast of South Vietnam.*

Underway replenishment (UNREP) was a way of life for Squadron Three cutters on patrol. Eighty percent of their logistic support—from ammunition and fuel oil to ice cream and mail—was provided while under way. During early deployments, cutters replenished two or three times a week. During *Barataria's* first sixty patrol days, for example, she had thirty-two UNREPs: seven times from oilers (AO), six day and one night; three times from ammunition ships (AE), two day and one night; four times from stores ships (AF), one day and three night; two daytime vertical replenishments from combat stores ships; and sixteen other freight and passenger transfers. Cargo came aboard so fast that cutters had to use hydraulic pallet trucks to clear receiving stations. Five-inch projectiles came in racks of a dozen, weighing more than 600 pounds. UNREPs were done at twelve knots and course changes were frequently made while receiving supplies.[23]

Operation Market Time began phasing down in the spring of 1969. Navy personnel from the deployed escort squadron were detached from the task unit staff on 16 May 1969, reducing the staff to five Coast Guard officers, four Coast Guard enlisted, and five Navy enlisted personnel. After the reduction, the task unit continued to support cutters and destroyers on Market Time operations and still functioned as cruiser-destroyer group representative in Subic Bay. A month-and-a-half later, Navy destroyer escorts were withdrawn from Market Time, leaving five WHECs as the only large ships maintaining the outer barrier.[24]

The first of the new and more capable *Hamilton*-class cutters arrived for deployment in Vietnam in November 1969. These 378-foot ships were equipped with helicopter flight decks and had top speeds of 29 knots; increased capability partially made up for the loss of Navy DERs. Durfey said, "In the later phase of Operation Market Time, we inspected a lot of vessels, but didn't board much." Because *Hamilton*-class cutters had helicopter flight decks, they were frequently called on to assist with medical evacuations. Durfey said, "We would take injured people aboard from other vessels and provide a platform for MEDEVAC helos. Back then, there weren't many patrol ships with flight-deck capability." He said *Rush* worked medical evacuations at least once a month and provided other types of medical assistance even more frequently.[25]

Final Trawler Action

Just after midnight on Easter Sunday morning, 11 April 1971, patrol forces closed in on another suspicious trawler off Ca Mau peninsula, 175 miles southwest of Saigon. Three Market Time ships, the cutters *Rush* and *Morgenthau* and USS *Antelope* (PG 86), waited until the 150-foot trawler entered South Vietnamese waters before intercepting. *Rush* ordered *Antelope* to close and challenge the vessel. When she got no reply, *Antelope* fired warning shots across the ship's bow. *Rush* then fired illumination rounds and ordered *Antelope* to take the trawler under fire.[26]

When the ship returned fire and headed for the open sea, *Rush* engaged the trawler with her 5-inch gun. The trawler took several hits and turned again, heading for the coast. *Morgenthau* was waiting and opened fire with her main battery. Under fire from three Market Time ships, the trawler suddenly stopped two miles from shore; heavy black smoke billowed from her deck. *Rush* gave "cease-fire" and ordered

Antelope to approach and investigate. *Rush's* press release said, "As *Antelope* closed the trawler, a devastating explosion was observed after which the trawler disappeared from all radar scopes. No survivors nor debris were observed in the area following the sinking."[27]

As the phase down of Market Time operations continued, USCGC *Mellon* (WHEC 717) outchopped without relief on 2 July 1970, bringing Squadron Three down to four WHECs. In the spring of 1971, remaining Navy billets were transferred from task unit staff; COMCOGARDRON THREE could no longer carry out duties as COMCRUDESREP Subic. The function was reassigned to the commanding officer of the deployed destroyer tender, USS *Dixie* (AD 14), on 1 May 1971. The eighth and final Squadron Three deployment arrived at Subic Bay in July 1971.

During Squadron Three deployments, high-endurance cutters spent 75 percent of their time under way, 20 percent in upkeep—a 10- to 14-day upkeep period each quarter—and 5 percent on port visits. Patrols were scheduled for 21 days, but actually averaged 33 days, and some patrols ran as long as 49 days. From April 1967 to January 1972, 4,500 officers and men participated in 32 deployments with Squadron Three. Cutters, which remained painted white during deployments, steamed 1.3 million miles.[28]

Durfey, reflecting on his tour in Vietnam as commanding officer of *Rush,* said, "I don't think the Coast Guard motto, *Semper Paratus* [Always Ready], ever had a more significant meaning than it did over there. Every few days it was something completely new, completely different, and in a different world. We got called on to do all manner of things. And we were never unable to respond to a request or order for a mission. That's what sticks with me."[29]

9

With the Jolly Green Giants

I am personally aware of the distinguished record achieved by the [Coast Guard] pilots flying in combat with our "Jolly Greens." They have flown many difficult and challenging missions and have consistently demonstrated their unreserved adherence to both our mottos, "Always Ready" and "That Others May Live." . . . They are indelibly inscribed in the permanent records of the stirring and moving drama of combat air crew recovery in Southeast Asia.

Gen. Howell M. Estes, Jr., USAF, Commander, Military Airlift Command
24 February 1969

Combat Rescue

Smoke streamed from the Air Force F-105 Thunderchief as it flew south toward the demilitarized zone separating North and South Vietnam. It was 1535 on 1 July 1968 when Lt. Col. Jack Modica made his decision to eject. His aircraft was losing altitude rapidly, and he knew he would never make it across the line. After calling in his position, he punched out seventeen miles northwest of Dong Ha. The low-altitude ejection left him unconscious on the floor of dense jungle. When he came to, he could not move—the ejection, hard landing, or both—had injured his back. He made sure his emergency-locater beacon was on. Looking up at the thick jungle canopy, he waited.

Two 37th ARRS HH-3E helicopters lifted off the pad at Danang Airbase and headed north. When the Jolly Green Giant helicopters arrived on-scene, they were driven off by heavy ground fire. With darkness rapidly approaching, another rescue attempt was made an hour later. Lt. Cdr. Lonnie L. Mixon, a Coast Guard exchange pilot fly-

137

ing with the ARRS, was at the controls of "low bird," the primary recovery helicopter. When he made his approach on the downed pilot's location, he took several hits and had to pull out. He evaluated his damage and went in for a second try; he was met with even more intense fire. The helicopter's electrical system was knocked out, a hydraulic line was ruptured, and the fuel tanks were hit. Faced with leaving Modica in the jungle overnight, Mixon decided to take the damaged helo in for one more rescue attempt. With darkness settling over the jungle, he brought the helicopter around and headed in. Enemy tracers, streaking through the night, found their target and the helo was hit again. Mixon broke off and headed his crippled "Jolly" for home. Rescue operations were suspended for the night.[1]

At daybreak, two Jolly Greens were launched. When they reached Modica's position, the enemy was waiting; North Vietnamese Army (NVA) gunners had moved into the area in force. Ground fire, much heavier than the day before, greeted the helicopters. An A-1E Skyraider flying cover for the mission was hit and went down, killing the pilot. Helicopters—one with an unexploded B-40 rocket lodged in a belly fuel tank—were pulled out of the area while fighter-bombers came in to pound enemy positions.

A debrief of flight crews involved in rescue attempts indicated that Modica was on the floor of a small valley under a thick jungle canopy. Crewmembers said that NVA gunners were positioned close to the pilot's location. Fire had come from all around and directly below their helicopters. The North Vietnamese apparently were using the injured pilot as bait; as long as he was alive and free, they knew that Americans would keep coming for him. Flight crews agreed it would be foolhardy to put a pararescueman on the ground to help Modica—the rescue helicopter pilot would have to do the job. He would have to lower the jungle penetrator, a 26-pound bullet-shaped device with three narrow folding paddle seats, close enough for Modica to reach and pull himself aboard.

Three hours after the first rescue attempt on 2 July 1968, two Jollys took off from a forward strip just below the DMZ. Lt. Lance A. Eagan, USCG, was flying "low bird." "High bird" would be his backup. "As soon as I entered the area," Eagan said, "I came under very heavy antiaircraft fire from 37mm guns." The aircraft was shaken by airbursts while dumping fuel to lighten the load. When Eagan got over the downed pilot's location, he said, "It was impossible to see him because of the dense jungle. But we could see smoke he was sending up." Unfortunately, the smoke was scattered as it filtered up through the jungle, making it impossible to pinpoint the pilot's location. When low bird got closer, Eagan made radio contact with "Scotch Three," Modica's call sign. The downed pilot told him, "I've got a broken back. I can't move."

Enemy gunners held their fire while Eagan closed in on Modica's position and went into a low hover. He used his helicopter's rotor blades to clip off the soft tops of the jungle trees in an attempt to see through the canopy and spot the pilot. When the crew still could not locate Modica, Airman First Class Joel Talley, the mission's pararescueman, volunteered to go down and look for him. The twenty-year-old Talley, on his first mission, said he would find the pilot and get him to a place from where he could be lifted. Despite Eagan's reluctance to put Talley on the ground, he realized it was the only way to get the injured man out. Eagan also knew that as long as his helicopter was flying, he could not leave without his crewman.

Talley was lowered into a small clearing near where smoke was sighted; he disappeared into the jungle. The pararescueman spotted Modica when the pilot fired a pen gun flare. Talley reached the man, who was becoming delirious, and treated him for shock, while Eagan repositioned the helo for the hoist. The penetrator was lowered again and Talley carried the pilot to it. He quickly strapped Modica and himself onto the paddles and signaled for pickup. With the hoist cable down, Eagan's Jolly Green was committed to a stationary hover just over the tree tops.

The first bullet smashed through the center windshield, passing between Eagan and his copilot; it came from a North Vietnamese sniper in a tree directly ahead of the helo. Eagan said, "When the bullet hit, I could see shattered Plexiglas coming toward me in slow-motion. It was a stop-motion sensation, then everything went back to normal. I'll never forget that part of it. Then," he said, "the whole world erupted. They opened up with everything. They were shooting at us from every angle." He could hear the hits. He said, "They sounded like very dull thuds." With the helicopter rocked by gunfire, Eagan waited until the penetrator cleared the jungle. "Once they were above the tree line," he said, "I took off with the two of them swinging fifty feet below the aircraft."

The helicopter landed at Dong Ha, where the rescued pilot was taken to the hospital for observation. Eagan said, "When I got on the ground, I counted forty hits in the aircraft. I guess they were intent on stopping us. I had several hits in my rotor blades. A few more inches

Lt. Lance A. Eagan, a Coast Guard exchange pilot flying with the Air Force's 37th aero rescue and recovery squadron, checks his HH-3E helicopter after returning from a mission.

either way and my Jolly would have gone down." There were nine hits in the helicopter's fuel tanks and four of the five rotor blades were hit. The helicopter had to be airlifted back to Danang. For their conspicuous gallantry during the mission, Talley received the Air Force Cross and Eagan the Silver Star Medal.[2]

Exchange Program

As the war in Vietnam escalated after 1965, the United States placed more emphasis on aerial bombardment. Rescue support for increased air strikes put a heavy strain on the relatively small Air Force combat rescue community; helicopter pilots were being rotated back to Vietnam for second and third tours. While demand for rescue pilots to

support missions increased, the number of aviators available for assignment got smaller. Experienced pilots were opting to get out of the service rather than continue to serve repeat tours in Vietnam. To meet
demands, the Air Force stepped up its training for replacement pilots.

In 1967, the Coast Guard needed to train instructor pilots in preparation for receiving a new class of helicopters. Construction of Sikorsky
HH-3F medium-range recovery helicopters for the Coast Guard began
in 1967, with the first aircraft to be delivered in 1969. Quotas for H-3
training at Air Force schools were impossible to obtain because of
demands for pilots for Vietnam.[3]

In March of 1967, the Air Force and Coast Guard reached an agreement that addressed the needs of both services. While not specifically
stated in the "Memorandum of Agreement Concerning an Exchange of
Rescue and Recovery Officers," the intent was clear. The Air Force
would train a number of Coast Guard officers to the instructor level
in H-3 helicopters and, in exchange, the Coast Guard would then make
the newly trained, rescue-experienced aviators available to the Air
Force for duty. Coast Guard pilots were to receive a year of training
and then serve one-year tours of duty with the ARRS in Vietnam. They
would use the combination of their training and actual rescue experience to accomplish the rescue squadron's primary mission—behind-
the-lines jungle recovery of strike pilots.

Officially, the objectives of the agreement—which included exchange
of fixed-wing as well as helicopter pilots—were:

- Acquaint each service with the tactics, techniques, operating
  and maintenance procedures, and development activities of the
  other service insofar as they relate to joint rescue forces.

- To provide each service with experience in using the special-
  ized search, rescue, and recovery equipment employed by the
  other service.

- To develop a potential in exchange officers to assume higher
  command and staff positions.[4]

The agreement, which called for "a one-for-one exchange of not
more than five officers in the grade of 0-3 [captain/lieutenant] or 0-4
[major/lieutenant commander]," specified that exchange officers would
be attached to overseas locations of the U.S. Air Force Aerospace Rescue and Recovery Service, and continental United States units of the

U.S. Coast Guard. The agreement was signed by the Coast Guard commandant, Adm. Willard J. Smith, on 14 March 1967 and by the Air Force chief of staff, Gen. John P. McConnell, on 31 March.

In a 15 May 1967 message, the Navy also requested Coast Guard helicopter pilots for duty in Vietnam. The message said, "Coast Guard participation in the armed helo game warden mission would be most helpful as it is in Market Time. Such participation would be a significant contribution to the river patrol effort." The commandant replied in a 16 June 1967 message, "After extensive study and examination current operations, regret Coast Guard unable participate in armed helo Game Warden mission due requirements maintain SAR [Search and Rescue] and other expanding commitments."[5]

Prerequisites for Coast Guard volunteers for the Air Force rescue pilot program included qualification as an aircraft commander, current assignment as a rescue helicopter pilot, and at least one prior tour as a rescue pilot. The ARRS training cycle began at Sheppard AFB in Texas, where Coast Guard and Air Force officers received transition training in H-3 helicopters. The first groups of Coast Guard officers went through training with classes of twenty pilots. Later, when rescue pilots were being trained for assignment to the 37th ARRS in Vietnam and the 40th ARRS in Thailand, class sizes doubled to forty. After Sheppard, training continued at Eglin AFB in Florida, where aviators attended combat crew training school. Lt. Cdr. James M. Loomis, a member of the second group of Coast Guard exchange pilots, said, "That's where they basically told us, 'Forget everything they taught you at Sheppard. Now, we're really going to teach you how to fly this thing.' And they did. It was probably the best military school I ever went to." In 1971, the 37th ARRS began flying larger Super Jolly Green Giant HH-53C helicopters. Additional training in these aircraft was received at Eglin. Coast Guard fixed-wing exchange aviators received six weeks of C-130E basic training at Sewart AFB in Tennessee before going to rescue crew commander school at Eglin for C-130H (Surface-to-Air Recovery System) and C-130P (Air-to-Air Refueling) training.[6]

Two survival schools completed ARRS training for helicopter pilots. The first was a rigorous month-long course at Fairchild AFB in Washington, where aviators underwent SERE training, which included survival, prisoner-of-war compound, and escape and evasion. The second was a week-long jungle survival course at Clark AFB in the Philippines just before going to Vietnam. After training, helicopter pilots reported

*Jolly Green Giant HH-3E, flown by Coast Guard Lt. James M.
Loomis and Lt. Robert T. Ritchie, refuels over Vietnam from an
Air Force HC-130P, piloted by Coast Guard Lt. James C. Quinn.*

to Vietnam. Fixed-wing aviators went to the 31st ARRS in the Philippines to fly C-130Hs out of Clark AFB and to the 39th ARRS at Tuy Hoa, Vietnam, to fly C-130P tankers. Aviators in Vietnam were assigned to the Air Force for operations and to commander Coast Guard Activities Vietnam for administration.

Danang

Eagan, Mixon, and Lt. Jack C. Rittichier reported to the 37th ARRS for duty at Danang Airbase on 3 April 1968. Once "in-country," things moved rapidly for helicopter pilots. During their first week, "newbies," as they were called, went out on each of the different kinds of missions they would be expected to fly. They received additional hoist training and geographical familiarization, and learned safe areas where they could put down in emergencies. They also had the opportunity to get down on the deck—25 to 50 feet off the ground—and sharpen their low-flying skills, something they could never do in the United States because of FAA flight rules. During their second week, they phased into the alert sequence as extra pilots and went onto regular duty rotation the third week.[7]

Two months after their arrival, on 9 June 1968, Rittichier was killed while attempting to rescue a pilot downed behind enemy lines, 27 miles southeast of Khe San in Quang Tri province. The pilot of an A-1E Skyraider, flying cover for Rittichier, saw his helo hit by ground fire and go down. When it hit the ground, the helicopter burst into a ball of flame; it was reduced to ashes in 30 seconds and there were no survivors. At the time of his death, Rittichier was already recommended for six awards for combat rescues—an Air Force Cross, three Distinguished Flying Crosses, and two Air Medals.[8]

ARRS facilities at Danang Airbase were located on the Vietnamese side of the runways. The squadron occupied former French Air Force buildings; they were old but better than the pilots expected. Their hangar, located just north of the control tower, was a weather-worn structure made of cinder block with a sheet-metal roof; it was open on both ends. Like all other buildings, it was protected with sandbags. Rocket attacks on the base were frequent, particularly during later phases of the war. Two covered and sandbagged revetments were used by squadron mechanics while they performed maintenance on helicopters. When not on alert, squadron aircraft were dispersed in pairs in sandbag-protected revetments. Personnel were billeted in former French bachelor officer's quarters. The white cinder block building was constructed in the shape of an "H." Two three-story berthing wings were connected with a crossbar that contained heads and showers. Officers ate at the Danang officers open mess, affectionately known as the "DOOM" club. Initially, squadron offices were located on the upper level of the hangar, but later were collocated with a South Vietnamese Air Force wing in a separate building. In 1971, when the United States was drawing down its forces, Air Force activities were consolidated and the 37th ARRS moved to the U.S. side of the base, where facilities were newer and better.[9]

The organization of a rescue squadron was unique in the Air Force, which traditionally is organized into wings, with separate flying and maintenance commands. These functions in an ARRS were under a single commanding officer. The combined flying and maintenance organizations, commanded by a lieutenant colonel, was similar to Coast Guard air station organization. The operations officer, a major, was second in command. Squadron administrative duties were handled by an executive officer, a non-flying billet, with a staff of enlisted specialists.[10]

Personnel complement of the squadron varied over the years, but generally remained at approximately one hundred personnel—seventy flying and thirty maintenance. Their goal was to keep nine full crews, with approximately twenty pilots, ready to fly. Within the squadron, Coast Guard officers were often junior in rank, but senior in terms of aviator qualifications. They usually were designated as instructor pilots and flight examiners, based on their experience, flight checks, and examinations. The Air Force qualification system was different from the Coast Guard's; each qualification, such as instructor pilot or flight examiner, had to be earned separately. In the Coast Guard, these qualifications were incorporated in the overall qualification as aircraft commander. Collateral duties were also different—in the Air Force all of an aviator's duties were directly related to the flying mission. Collateral duties for exchange officers usually included working in standardization, intelligence, operations, or safety.[11]

The 37th ARRS operated twelve helicopters. Initially, the squadron flew Sikorsky HH-3Es. Powered by twin General Electric turbines delivering 3,000 shaft horsepower, the H-3 had a maximum speed of 145 knots and an unrefueled range of 425 nautical miles. Helicopters were manned by crews of four (pilot, copilot, flight engineer, and pararescueman) and armed with two 7.62mm M-60 machine guns—one mounted on either side. In 1971, the squadron began flying larger Sikorsky HH-53C helicopters. The new Super Jolly weighed a third more than the older aircraft, but it had better than twice the horsepower (6,870 SHP), giving it a maximum speed of 170 knots. The unrefueled range was extended to 550 nautical miles. An additional pararescueman was added to the crew of the more heavily armed Super Jolly. New helicopters mounted three 6-barreled Gatling guns. The 7.62mm miniguns had a rate of fire of 2,000 rounds per minute, with each helicopter carrying 12,000 rounds. H-53s also had M-60 machine guns and carried an assortment of shotguns, rifles, and pistols for protection in case they were forced down behind enemy lines.[12]

Coast Guard exchange pilots in Vietnam began flying larger HH-53C Super Jolly Green Giant rescue helicopters in 1971.

In November 1968, bombing in North Vietnam was halted while negotiations to end the war were in progress. Eagan and Mixon were transferred from Danang to Nakhon Phanom, Thailand, where they were assigned to Detachment 1 of the 40th ARRS at the Royal Thailand AFB. The detachment's nine Jolly Greens supported clandestine bombing strikes against the Ho Chi Minh trail, passing through Laos. Jollys stood "strip alert" at the airbase or were deployed into Laos to Air America strips, known as "lima sites." Eagan said, "When we went into Laos, we had to cover the 'stars and bars' on the helo and remove all insignia from our uniforms." While in Laos, Eagan made the ARRS's 1,500th combat save. Reports of the mission to the media made no mention of location. When he received a Distinguished Flying Cross for another mission in Laos, the Air Force sanitized the citation to remove any specifics of the rescue. The award simply stated that he was "audacious and tenacious in the face of opposing hostile fire."[13]

As the war continued, Air Force pilots from the Strategic Air Command and Military Airlift Command were given helicopter transition training and were sent to rescue-and-recovery squadrons. After a nine-month helicopter program, they reported to Vietnam. Capt. Joseph L. Crowe, a Coast Guard exchange officer in 1971–72, said, "Transition pilots were trained to work with one set of tactics. And they became very proficient in handling that situation. But they lacked the experience needed to handle unusual situations." If a mission were different, such as mountain flying, a more experienced crew would be assigned out of rotation. Coast Guard aviators handled missions at sea; Air Force pilots were not trained in overwater navigation and were not familiar with the intricacies of hoisting from a rolling ship.[14]

Throughout the war, the 37th ARRS's primary mission was the rescue of strike pilots. How that was accomplished changed over time. In 1969, strike objectives were so varied, with targets in Laos, North Vietnam, and South Vietnam, that Jollys were held on strip alert waiting for missions. Two helicopters were kept on primary alert and two on secondary alert at Danang. Two more H-3s were assigned to the Quang Tri alert, standing by at the Marine base near the DMZ from sunrise to sunset. A seventh helo orbited over the southern Tonkin Gulf during peak periods. Loomis said, "We didn't have a duty rotation. There weren't enough crews to even stand port and starboard duty. We basically flew six days a week." The routine called for alert crews to get intelligence briefings in the morning and then the Quang Tri alert and Tonkin Gulf orbit helos took off. Primary alert helicopters at Danang were preflighted and then "cocked." When cocked, the helos were ready to take off with the push of a button; no one was allowed near them. Crews stood down from alert after dark.[15]

In 1971, strike missions were more focused. The squadron kept two helicopters on alert, with two alert crews and one standby crew ready at all times. Flight crews stood 48-hour duties, on a one-in-three rotation. During the first 24 hours, an alert crew was "high bird" with backup responsibility for spontaneous rescue. For the second 24 hours, the crew was "low bird" with primary rescue responsibility. The crew was off duty for two days and then on standby for the next two days. Scheduled bombing strikes were supported with an airborne rescue package. A typical mission in support of a strike involved crews getting up between 0430 and 0530 and going into strike operations with the fighter-bomber wing for briefings on the air tasking fragmentary order, called the "Frag." ARRS intelligence and operations personnel looked at strikes planned for F-4 Phantoms and F-105 Thunderchiefs and decided how to position the "rescue package," which usually included: King, airborne mission coordinator, in a C-130P Hercules tanker; Jollys holding airborne; Sandys, A-1E Skyraiders, flying cover; and Covey, a forward air controller in a light single-engine 0-1 Bird Dog spotter aircraft or the larger twin-engine Bronco OV-10. The "package" was airborne during fighter-bomber ingress to the target and then repositioned for egress. Locations for holding were selected on the basis of terrain and enemy threat. If a strike pilot went down and was not recovered the same day, a recovery mission was planned overnight; follow-on rescue missions were over and above requirements to stand alert for the next day's strikes.[16]

The tempo of operations for Coast Guard pilots flying Jolly Green Giants varied. Initial groups had continuous high-tempo work loads, accumulating 450 to 550 flight hours in a one-year tour. Later, as efforts were made to end the war, the tempo varied from periods of no activity during bombing halts to frantic activity in response to enemy offensives. Pilots in later groups logged from 300 to 350 flight hours.

Near the end of the war, as the United States was withdrawing its troops, ARRS missions changed. On 30 March 1972, the communists mounted a major military offensive. In a three-pronged attack, 15,000 troops, supported by Soviet artillery, rockets, and tanks, converged on the northern province capitol of Quang Tri. As the city's defenses crumbled, eighty American advisors and several South Vietnamese Army troops retreated to the Citadel, a walled military compound in the middle of the city. Surrounded by an overwhelming enemy force, there was only one way out for the advisors—helicopter airlift.

Crowe, who was promoted to lieutenant commander during his tour, was assigned operations planning for the 37th ARRS. With the situation in Quang Tri becoming desperate, he was tasked with planning a mission to rescue Americans trapped in the Citadel. He said, "When I first tried to plan the mission, I felt it would be impossible to complete. But we were ordered to try."

Quang Tri Rescue

On 1 May 1972, Crowe briefed six Jolly and ten Sandy crews. He knew 25 percent losses were expected and the mission would be considered a success if no more than 50 percent were lost. Crowe said, "Sending those guys out on the Quang Tri mission was the most difficult thing I had to do in Vietnam. We thought they were going to be wiped out." Crowe was not permitted to fly the mission because of his familiarity with classified plans and the risk of capture.[17]

Jolly Greens orbited over the coastline for an hour while A-1E Sandys strafed and bombed enemy positions to clear a path for them. Maj. Jackson R. Scott, pilot of the lead helicopter, asked the forward air controller where they could expect ground fire. He was told, "After you're over the city, it will come from all over." There was only one landing zone at the Citadel and it was only big enough for one helicopter at a time; enemy gunners already had it zeroed in. The plan called for three rescue helos and two airborne backups. Sandy Seven, the A-1E leader, said, "I'm going to put a smoke rocket on the beach where I want you to enter." The lead Jolly came in low at 170 knots. An Army helicopter pilot, who had landed HU-1E helicopters at the Citadel several times, was aboard to guide the aircraft in. As they approached, heavy yellow smoke was rising from the Citadel; waiting U.S. advisors blanketed three sides of the landing zone with a smoke-screen. The helicopter touched down and troops rushed up the back ramp. With thirty-seven aboard, the after helicopter crewman said, "Take her up!" In the process of stopping more troops from climbing aboard, the crewman fell off the ramp and was left behind. As the first Jolly Green lifted off the next was on its way in; they were spaced four minutes apart. The second helicopter picked up forty-five people, including the missing crewman. The third helicopter loaded fifty people aboard and barely made it over the wall. Enemy troops were making their way into the Citadel as the last helo left. When the mission was over, Jollys had rescued 132 people—the largest aerial evacuation of the Vietnam War. In what became known as the "miracle mission," not a single person was injured, none of the helicopters took a single hit, and only two fixed-wing aircraft were shot down, a forward air controller and a Sandy. Both fixed-wing pilots bailed out safely and were rescued, one by friendly ground forces; the other was picked out of the sea by an Army helo.[18]

The Vietnam era was a difficult time for the United States; it was a time of conflicting emotions and internal turmoil. Perhaps these were the reasons the Coast Guard did not take full advantage of experiences gained by its aviators who flew with the Aerospace Rescue and Recovery Squadron. Exchange pilots said when they returned from their tours, not only did the Coast Guard fail to recognize what they had done in Vietnam, it failed to learn from their experiences. There were no debriefings or special efforts to find out if Air Force rescue equipment or procedures had application for the Coast Guard. They were never asked about their familiarity with Doppler navigation, air refueling, surface-to-air refueling from ships, low-light-level TV, infrared side-looking optics, special sensors, or the value of pararescuemen in aiding survivors. Unfortunately, the objectives of the memorandum of agreement between the Air Force and the Coast Guard were not accomplished—exchange officers simply rotated to their next duty stations as if their previous tours had been routine assignments.

While exploits of these rescue pilots may have gone unheralded, they wrote an important chapter in Coast Guard search-and-rescue history. And they experienced the indescribable sense of satisfaction that comes from knowing that people lived because of what they did. After one particularly harrowing rescue of a downed pilot who faced certain capture or death, a Coast Guard aviator flying with the 37th ARRS said, "I cannot describe the sensation of victory I had as we rode wing on King [airborne mission coordinator] taking fuel with fighters making aileron roll passes and loops around us. The sky was never quite so blue or the clouds so puffy and white."

10

Explosive Loading Detachments

These [Explosive Loading] Detachments have provided invaluable support and advice to elements of the 1st Logistical Command in the matter of explosive safety. . . . Attesting to the success of their tireless efforts is the fact that despite many adverse conditions, explosive safety and port security at our ports has been maintained at a remarkably high level, and no serious incidents have occurred. . . . Their accomplishments here in the Republic of Vietnam merit the highest praise and add luster to the reputation of the United States Coast Guard.

Maj. Gen. C. W. Eifler, USA, 1st Logistical Command
13 June 1967

Cat Lai

The ammunition ship SS *U.S. Tourist* was the only vessel in the anchorage at Cat Lai in the early morning hours of 14 February 1968. Moored fore-and-aft to buoys, she was headed downstream in the Nai river, with dark muddy water flowing past her weathered hull. Vietnamese stevedores worked in shifts, unloading ammunition from the holds of the ship. Cargo lights hid stars dotting the clear night above.[1]

BM1 David Shields, a member of Coast Guard explosive loading detachment no. 1 (ELD 1), went into the deckhouse to wake his partner, BM1 J. William Berry. The two men were assigned to the ammunition ship until her cargo was discharged. They stood port-and-starboard watches as safety supervisors, relieving each other. Berry slept in a bunk in a spare stateroom on the port side of the 0-1 level.

151

It was just after midnight when Shields stuck his head in the stateroom, woke Berry, and left.

Berry sat up on the side of the bunk and put on his boots. Just as he went through the door, Viet Cong recoilless rifles opened fire from the darkness on the other side of the river. Berry said, "The first round came in at deck level. It went through the bulkhead under the bunk just as I stepped into the passageway. It blew the bunk into a million pieces. The blast blew paint off the bulkhead. I had paint chips stuck to my back from where my hat was right down to my boots." A second 75mm recoilless rifle round hit a foot above the porthole, but failed to detonate; it bounced off the steel bulkhead and rolled over the side.

Shields ran back down the passageway to check on his partner. He found Berry stunned and deafened by the blast, but not hurt. Berry said, "Rounds were still landing. There was a lot of smoke and it was noisy as the devil." When shells slammed into the hull and superstructure, Vietnamese stevedores panicked and fled. They left cargo hatches open and pallets of 105mm howitzer ammunition exposed. Berry said, "We went out on deck and secured the ammunition they left. We darkened ship in case something else happened."

When the attack started, Lt. James P. Ruff, Jr., ELD 1's officer in charge, asked for a volunteer to go out to the ship. He and EN1 Richard J. Yered left the Army compound on the riverbank in a Boston Whaler while rounds were still landing; he wanted to prepare the ammunition ship to get under way. The barrage lasted for twenty minutes. Together with Berry, Shields, and an Army sergeant, Ruff and Yered manned winches, restowed ammunition, and closed hatches. Then they checked the ship's crew and stevedores for casualties and inspected the vessel for damage. Nine rounds had hit the ship, but none had ignited any of the ammunition aboard. The action caused minor personnel injuries and damage.

Berry said, "All the fire came from the village straight across [the river] from us. They brought in helicopter gunships and they did a lot of firing around the village. But they didn't fire on the village. That's where the rounds came from." Off-loading operations resumed at daylight.

Four nights later, on 18 February 1968, Vietnamese stevedores were still nervous about the shelling. When they stopped loading operations at midnight to eat, they looked cautiously toward the village a half-mile away. They couldn't see beyond the glow of cargo lights, but they knew it was there; memories of the earlier attack were fresh in their minds.

Yered said, "I was in my cabin cleaning up when explosions erupted all around the ship. I rushed out on deck with my helmet and flack jacket." Guerrillas were firing 75mm recoilless rifles from across the river. The barrage came out of the darkness from the same place as the earlier attack. Projectiles hit both SS *U.S. Explorer* and SS *Neva West* moored in the anchorage. Nineteen rounds struck the Army compound at Cat Lai on the northwest bank of the river.

An Army barge alongside SS *Neva West* was three quarters filled with 150 tons of high explosives—pallets of 81mm mortar ammunition; two rounds hit the barge. Yered checked for casualties and then ran to the barge. He said, "The after end of the barge was billowing smoke and flames and there were secondary explosions. I assumed they were mortar shells going off. I ran to hatch three and charged a firehose." He hosed down the fire for fifteen minutes but could not put it out.

Sgt. Douglas Box, in charge of the Army detail aboard the ship, was on the radio in the wheelhouse. Yered said, "I called up to Box and told him I had to go on the barge to put the fire out. There were still sporadic explosions going off all the time. I went over the side and climbed down the Jacob's ladder with a firehose." When Yered found the hose would not reach the fire, he started throwing buckets of water on the flames. Box, using a firehose from the main deck, kept flames away from Yered, who pushed burning ammunition over the side and doused the fire with buckets of water. Mortar shells were ruptured and red hot. Yered said, "I used water coming out of the main engine overboard discharge. I don't know how many buckets it took. I know it was a lot. We finally got the fire out." By the time the fire was extinguished, six pallets of ammunition were burned through on one side. While Yered fought the fire, guerrillas fired at him with small arms from the other side of the river.

After his burns were treated, Yered went back on the fantail of the ship. "It was then," he said, "that I started to think how close it was. My wife and kids were uppermost in my mind. I started thinking of them." Yered was awarded the Silver Star Medal for his gallantry and the Purple Heart for injuries.

Port Security

When Coast Guard Commandant Adm. Edwin J. Roland stopped in Saigon on 23 July 1965, during a trip to visit cutters of Squadron One, he met with Rear Adm. Norvell G. Ward, chief of the naval advisory group (NAVADGRU). Ward asked Roland if it would be possible to get an experienced port security officer assigned to NAVADGRU for temporary duty. Roland assured him that the Coast Guard would "do all it could to help as long as a need exists."[2]

After Roland's visit, the commander of the military assistance command (MACV) formally requested port security assistance on 4 August 1965. The message to CINCPAC said:

> It is understood here that the U.S. Coast Guard is responsible for port security in the United States. . . . It is considered that the Coast Guard could lend valuable assistance in improving security in the Port of Saigon. It is requested, therefore, that the commander United States Coast Guard be requested to make available to the chief of the naval advisory group, MACV, for temporary assignment of about three months, an officer experienced in port security work.[3]

When the request reached Coast Guard headquarters, Rear Adm. William W. Childress, chief of the office of operations, called Cdr. Risto A. Matilla into his office; Matilla was chief of the ports and waterways division. Childress told Matilla that the Defense Department needed a Coast Guard port security expert in Vietnam as soon as possible. Matilla received orders and departed for Saigon in a matter of days; there was no time for special training enroute.[4]

When Matilla arrived in Saigon, he reported to MACV, from where he was sent to the NAVADGRU to work for Admiral Ward. His assignment, broadly stated, was to look into all aspects of port security. Previously, port security was left to the South Vietnamese.

Matilla immediately began surveying waterfront facilities in and around Saigon. He was shocked by what he found. "There was no real security program except at the ammo dumps," he said. "They [the Vietnamese] had no concept of [port] security. They didn't grasp the importance of it and didn't pay much attention to it." About 10,000 people entered and left the Port of Saigon each day; a third of them had no legitimate business there. The custom house was located in the middle of the port area. To gain access, people only had to say they were going there to pay taxes or take care of other customs business. No identification was required.[5]

Pilferage at the port was estimated to be 5 to 10 percent of military cargo and up to 50 percent of USAID and commodity import program cargoes. Matilla said, "Pilferage was rampant. They lost a whole shipload of cement while I was there. It just disappeared. The ship arrived and was supposed to be loaded with cement, but they couldn't find the cement." He said Vietnamese stevedores claimed they couldn't use cargo-unloading equipment and insisted on hand-carrying cargo. "When they carried sacks of rice on their shoulders," Matilla said, "one stevedore would position himself over a hole in the deck of the pier and another would make a hole in the sack with a knife. The rice would pour down through the hole into a sampan waiting under the pier."[6]

Waterfront facilities, which extended along the west bank of the Saigon river, were old and inefficient. Small entrances and narrow roadways, built by the French in the previous century, limited access to wharves that had limited space for staging cargo. Facilities, barely adequate for handling routine flows of cargo, were quickly over-whelmed by the military buildup. The sprawling port, with little or no control over access, was extremely vulnerable to sabotage or attack. Matilla said, "You really didn't know who was working for you and who was [Viet Cong] working against you. They had no identification system."

When Matilla completed his survey of the Port of Saigon and out-lying ports, he identified problems and recommended corrective action. The potential for a disastrous ammunition explosion was the most seri-ous problem he observed. Hundreds of tons of ammunition, arriving daily, were off-loaded by inexperienced Vietnamese stevedores using inadequate equipment. Matilla recommended that Coast Guard explo-sive handling experts be assigned to Vietnam to supervise ammunition loading.

The need for explosive loading detachments was supported by an entry in NAVADGRU's "Historical Review" for November 1965, which said:

Merchant Marine officers have reported that ammunition unloading procedures at Nha Be are not carefully or safely performed. The Vietnamese stevedores are totally inexperienced. They either lack the proper tools or use improper equipment to handle various classes of ammunition. Lack of supervisory personnel is most glaring.

NAVADGRU's "Historical Review" went on to say:

To combat this situation CHNAVADGRP proposed to COMUSMACV that requests be made for two Coast Guard port safety units. These teams consist of eight men (an officer and seven enlisted) who have special training and practical experience in handling ammunition. They would train the local stevedores in proper handling procedure and observation of safety regulations.[7]

In a 20 February 1966 message to CINCPAC, MACV reported that the Army in Vietnam urgently needed two Coast Guard "explosive handling supervisory teams." CINCPAC forwarded the request to the Joint Chiefs of Staff, requesting that action be initiated to get teams deployed. The Coast Guard responded to the request, assigning two ELDs to Vietnam. Detachment members were given two weeks to relocate their families before reporting to Coast Guard Base Alameda, Calif., for training and processing. ELDs departed for Vietnam together aboard a chartered Continental Airline flight. After brief stops in Hawaii and the Philippines for fuel, the plane landed at Tan Son Nhut airport at 1700 on 3 June 1966. Men emerged from the air-conditioned plane into Vietnam's heat and humidity.[8]

Lt. (jg) Edward G. O'Keefe, the most senior of the group, was officer in charge of ELD 1. He was older, with fifteen years of prior enlisted service as a gunner's mate, and was well-experienced in explosive loading and port security. Lt. (jg) Gerald T. Willis, commander of ELD 2, had gone to the Army's hazardous cargo and stevedoring schools at Fort Eustis in Virginia after commissioning. Willis gained his practical experience while assigned to Captain of the Port, Jacksonville, Fla. For three years, he had supervised explosive loading at King's Bay depot in Georgia, where ammunition ships loaded-out for Vietnam. Each team had seven enlisted men, ranging from chief petty officer to seaman. Petty officers were boatswain's mates, gunner's mates, enginemen, and damage controlmen with dangerous cargomen (DG) designators. In addition to explosive loading training, all petty officers had practical experience, working at ammunition loading facilities such as Port Chicago in California.[9]

Detachments gathered their gear and climbed aboard an Army bus. At Kopler transit compound in Saigon, men were assigned three to a room. They spent the next two days going through Vietnam orientation programs. O'Keefe and Willis met with COMCOGARDRON ONE on 6 June 1966. Next, they went to Army's 1st Logistical Command, headquartered near Tan Son Nhut airport. O'Keefe said, "The Army wasn't ready for us. We had to make our own contacts. We had to find out just what the heck they wanted us to do and where they wanted us to do it." Willis said COGARDRON ONE "gave us orders saying, 'You are hereby detached from the U.S. Coast Guard and attached to the U.S. Army.'"[10]

At 1st Log, they met with officers of the 11th Transportation Battalion, which was responsible for moving ammunition in Vietnam. After familiarization visits to different loading sites, the decision was made to assign ELDs to the director of transportation for duty at two major ammunition ports—Nha Be and Cam Rahn Bay. "It took three weeks to establish ourselves," O'Keefe said. "We were totally new and the Army wasn't receptive to us being there. They looked at us like a bunch of regulatory people who were going to tell them what to do." On 11 June 1966, Willis flew up to Cam Rahn Bay to meet the Army colonel for whom he would be working. He met him at a hail-and-farewell party at the officer's club. Willis said, "He told me, 'I don't need any wet-behind-the-ears lieutenant telling me how to handle ammunition. I've been doing it all my life.' It was an embarrassing scene."[11]

ELD 1 was assigned responsibility for operations at Nha Be. The port, little more than a civilian junk landing south of Saigon, was at the junction of Long Tau and Soi Rap rivers. A road ran 11 miles from Saigon to the landing and stopped. O'Keefe said, "There were no docks at all. We built ourselves a facility out of dunnage next to the road to work out of." Across the road to the south was the Vietnamese Navy base. U.S. Navy river patrol craft (PBRs) operated out of the base as a tenant command. Vietnam's largest commercial fuel-oil farm was on the north side of the road, next to the river.[12]

Ships anchored three at a time in the river while ammunition was off-loaded into barges for distribution. Vessels kept their steam up, ready to get under way in case of attack or emergency. The combination of river flow and tides caused currents at the anchorage to reach six knots. When ELD 1 first arrived, ships anchored randomly on the north side of the channel. When the tide turned, vessels swung at anchor and rode down on each other. O'Keefe worked with the pilot's association at Nha Be to establish specific anchorages to permit better security and eliminate collisions.[13]

Personnel from the Army's 124th Terminal Service Company handled ammunition distribution from the anchorage. They lived in a compound next to the river with a second lieutenant in charge. O'Keefe said, "When I saw the way those troops were living, there was no way I was going to have our people in there. We kept our Navy billets in Saigon and commuted the whole time I was there. We got away with a little bit more because we were the first detail. Nobody really knew what we were doing."[14]

While ammunition was being off-loaded—which was most of the time—everyone in the detachment worked every day; one man remained on each ship overnight. The rest of the ELD drove back to Saigon before the road closed at dark. O'Keefe said, "At night, we couldn't move barges around, so we loaded ammo as late as we could into the evening. When we ran out of barges, we stopped. . . . The men could work a 24-hour shift and still get some sleep." ELD members drove from Saigon in the morning and boarded ships with the new shift of Vietnamese stevedores. O'Keefe said, "Approximately ninety stevedores were needed for three ships. Enough for six on each of a ship's five hatches, though not all hatches were worked at the same time."[15]

When ELD 1 personnel began work at Nha Be, they quickly learned that Vietnamese stevedores had little or no appreciation for safety and lacked basic knowledge and experience in modern cargo-handling techniques. O'Keefe said, "They [the stevedores] were like a pack of rats. After they pulled ammunition out of accessible places, they got the rest out any way they could. They'd wrap a line around a four-high stack of pallets and pull on it. The ammunition would fall on the metal deck. Boxes would break open and stuff would go flying. You'd get a knot in your stomach that wouldn't go away." The job of Army personnel was the distribution of ammunition; they did not get involved in cargo-handling or safety. Specialists 4/C and privates tallied ammunition as it was unloaded into barges. A sergeant or sergeant first class was in charge of checking the manifested cargo coming from each ship.

In addition to being extremely hazardous, Vietnamese stevedoring operations were inefficient. It took as long as a month to unload a single ship. ELD personnel realized the Vietnamese would have to learn basic cargo-handling techniques before the Coast Guard could even think about enforcing explosive-loading regulations. When they showed stevedores better and safer procedures, ships were unloaded faster. O'Keefe said, "Vietnamese [stevedores] didn't resist changes. They would do whatever we wanted them to. The Vietnamese straw bosses would pretty much do what we told them or asked them to do."[16]

ELDs also improved operations by upgrading equipment. They replaced manila slings with wire slings and rope cargo nets with stronger nylon nets. Hand-forged cargo hooks, which were cracked and bent, were replaced with drop-forged safety hooks. With little or no oversight, the detachments used their initiative to obtain equipment needed to get the job done faster and safer. Most of the gear came from the ammunition ships themselves; masters were only too happy to give the ELDs equipment to make operations safer.

O'Keefe said, "One of the things that gave us some advantage as the first team was that they [the Army] . . . figured we were just going to be sheriffs and cops and get in the way of their operations. When we started showing them you can rig your gear differently, you can get the cargo out without breaking it up, and move it out faster, then we started being the golden boys. They just let us run the place." Capt. Robert J. LoForte, commander Coast Guard Squadron One, said, "They [the U.S. Army] did not want the Coast Guard butting into their stevedore operations. But such fears were allayed and our Army compatriots are glad to have our assistance."[17]

O'Keefe recommended using electric forklifts below decks to speed up unloading and get ships out faster. He went to the Port of Saigon to look for equipment. Among stored cargo at the port, he discovered forty-four electric forklifts still in their crates, complete with batteries. LoForte said, "No one knew they were there. Or, at the least, they didn't know what to do with them." In praising the work of ELDs, LoForte said, "Activities are so new here in-country and support conditions so austere that the imagination and conscientiousness of our individual Coast Guardsmen are the keys to our successful accomplishments."

When O'Keefe tried to get a 100-ton barge from the Port of Saigon as a facility for supporting forklifts, he said, "The colonel in charge of the port said I would get it [the barge] over his dead body." O'Keefe went to 1st Log's special project officer responsible for moving ammunition and told him he needed forklifts; O'Keefe said, "If we keep doing things the way we are, this thing is going to blow up. We'll be picking up pieces of ships a mile away." The issue went to the general and ELD 1 got its barge. They set up a shop on the barge and rigged a generator for recharging batteries. The barge was kept alongside one of the ships or moored in the anchorage. Once they started using forklifts, the stevedores began unloading so much ammunition that barge ports were overwhelmed by the outflow. In the first six months in Vietnam, the tonnage of ammunition handled increased by 66 percent. The 1st Logistical Command implemented O'Keefe's recommendations for inventorying, distributing, maintaining, and replacing mechanical ammunition handling equipment at all ports.[18]

The second detachment, ELD 2, deployed to Cam Rahn Bay on 15 June 1966. The crew was assigned to live in tents with the 606th Transportation Company. Enlisted men were split up and billeted by rank. Willis said, "We did that for two nights and then I said, 'The hell with this, I'm getting my people together.' We got a tent and set it up and then started scrounging around for materials to build a hooch. Eventually, the men ended up with one of the nicest places in Dodge City." The quarters they built had a plywood floor, plywood and screen sides, and a tent top. Ammunition ships they worked on gave them mattresses and bedsprings from unused passenger staterooms. They even got the first wringer washing machine at Cam Rahn Bay; it was donated by one of the ships. After a visit to Cam Rahn Bay, the commander of Squadron One said, "They constructed an outdoor shower with a 55-gallon drum and they're working on getting a refrigerator, electric grill, coffee maker, and tape recorder."[19]

The Army facility at Cam Rahn Bay was located on the west side of a point of land north of the entrance to the bay. The area was relatively secure, protected by South Korea's White Horse Division, which was deployed around it. Except for a few old French buildings, Cam Rahn was a tent city. Willis said, "There was a lot of sand and scrub bushes. It was like being in the desert of the Southwest [United States]. . . . The sand was fine and it was windy. It blew around and got into everything."[20]

When ELD 2 arrived, there were no piers for off-loading; ammunition ships were unloaded while anchored in the bay. The detachment began work on their first ship, SS *American Packer,* on 22 June 1966. Ammunition was off-loaded from the ships into Army LARCs (lighter, amphibious, resupply cargo) and transported ashore for shipment to various ammunition depots. ELD personnel traveled back and

Coast Guardsman from explosive loading detachment 2 observes
artillery projectiles being offloaded at Cam Rahn Bay.

forth to ships aboard LARCs until they got a spare 14-foot Boston
Whaler from Coast Guard Division 13. Ships anchored at Cam Rahn
Bay were used as floating warehouses; ammunition was off-loaded as
needed. Willis said, "When the Air Force and Army needed ammo,
napalm, shells, or whatever, they would say, 'Okay, we're going to
open up these ships.' Then we would load out of one, two, or three
ships. The off-load went to several ammo dumps." Detachment members stayed aboard ships, working 12-hour shifts. They didn't mind the
duty because they ate and lived better on the ships than most troops
ashore. Uniforms for the detachment consisted of lightweight, olive-
drab, jungle fatigues and white safety hardhats. Before long, Army personnel working on ships began wearing hardhats, as well. Men carried
small arms only when they left Cam Rahn Bay. Willis said, "I felt safer
at Cam Rahn than I did in Saigon."[21]

Army stevedores who unloaded ammunition at Cam Rahn Bay were
better trained and more disciplined than Vietnamese stevedores at
Nha Be. Sergeants supervised cargo handling and Coast Guard per-

sonnel served as safety supervisors, making sure explosives were handled in accordance with safety provisions of the Code of Federal Regulations. Problems were relatively minor. Willis said, "Officers on the merchant ships loved us. They had heard all kinds of horror stories about how ammunition was handled before we got there. . . . After a while, when they [the Army] found out we weren't there to make trouble and we knew what we were doing, we got along fine." Armed military police (MPs) were aboard each ship to provide security; LARCs and LCMs with MPs aboard provided waterside security.

At Cam Rahn Bay, Willis worked with the Army during the installation of prefabricated De Long piers. The piers, made up of 300-foot sections, 90 feet wide, were towed to Vietnam from the United States. They accommodated four ammunition ships at once, off-loading directly to shore. Willis provided input on pier operation and safety precautions. COMCOGARDRON ONE said the Army was enthusiastic about Willis's input and agreed to operate piers under Coast Guard safety standards established for explosive loading operations in the United States. They specifically agreed on installation of fire pumps, hydrants, first aid stations, and more sophisticated firefighting equipment. Willis was asked to draft recommendations for controlling traffic, load limits, and smoking areas.[22]

When piers were first finished, masters refused to take ammunition ships up the bay without pilots. They were concerned because there were no recent charts nor buoys, and ships were loaded with explosives. The Army asked Willis to pilot the first ship, SS *Mormack Dove,* to the pier. Willis said when he went aboard, the master told him, "Come on son, you stay on the bridge with me and I'll take her on up. If there's a screwup, I want someone who can support my side of the story." When the ship moored—after an uneventful transit—an Army general was waiting for them with a band on the pier. After the general congratulated the master for being the first ship to arrive at the new port facility, the old skipper put his arm around Willis's shoulder and said, "I never could have done it without Lieutenant Willis, here." Then he poked Willis in the ribs with his elbow. Willis said, "The next thing I know, I'm the pilot for the next five ships to arrive."[23]

Initially, the eight men of ELD 2 were enough to handle the work load. But as the tempo of operations increased and the value of ELDs was recognized, their services were requested at more sites. They were asked to check explosive-loading operations at Qui Nhon, Nha Trang, and Danang. Willis or another member of ELD 2 went to other sites about once a month to check on operations and provide advice. At times, the ELD did not have enough men to cover all ships off-loading. While the work load at Cam Rahn Bay was hectic, Willis said, "We pretty much had it made. We were by ourselves. The Coast Guard wasn't bugging us and the Army wasn't bugging us. We had a job to do and we did it."[24]

Ammunition anchorage at Nha Be, south of Saigon, was finally relocated seven miles up the Nai river at Cat Lai in 1967. The Coast Guard had been recommending the move away from the fuel farm since 1965. The Navy's military sea transportation service (MSTS) held up the move because Cat Lai was not considered secure enough. When Viet Cong guerrillas kidnapped the mayor of Nha Be from his residence, MSTS reconsidered the relative safety of the two locations. ELD 1 moved to Cat Lai on 1 May 1967. The wisdom of the move was confirmed four months later when the Viet Cong launched a major attack against Nha Be on 2 and 4 August 1967. Facilities were heavily damaged by 75mm recoilless rifle and 81mm mortar fire.[25]

At Cat Lai, detachment personnel ate and slept at the Army compound. Berry said, "It was a pretty large facility with a sandbag and barbed-wire perimeter, patrolled by [U.S.] Army MPs and some Vietnamese. There were a dozen or more tents and a couple old French stucco buildings. There were Vietnamese inside the compound. A lot of civilian labor." Enlisted members of the detachment slept on cots in a single wooden-floored tent. The officer in charge bunked in the bachelor officers quarters (BOQ) in one of the French buildings.[26]

Men worked in two-man teams. Berry said, "When we went to work on a ship, we stayed with it until it was completely off-loaded. Sometimes we would go directly to a second ship and maybe a third and a fourth. We lived aboard, slept aboard, and ate aboard [the ships]. The two men on the team worked out the rotation, however they wanted." When an ammunition ship arrived, a team went right aboard, sometimes with the officer in charge or chief petty officer. They met with the captain and his mates and gave them information about mooring, preparations for getting under way, off-loading routines, and potential threats. As soon as meetings were over, ammunition off-load began. Ships moored parallel to the stream heading downriver.[27]

The Army had enlisted "checkers" at each open hatch, checking off inventory as it was unloaded. A more senior noncommissioner officer, called "super cargo," was in charge of checkers on each ship. The company that was contracted to provide local stevedores used Koreans as foremen. Berry said, "Koreans were straw bosses for the Vietnamese. . . . I enjoyed working with them. They were sharp. We mostly worked with them because they could speak English and Vietnamese." Stevedores worked around-the-clock in two crews; half worked while the other half slept. They operated winches and did everything with regard to cargo handling. Berry said, "I don't think they [the Vietnamese] ever worried about safety. They were constantly trying to take shortcuts. They had a number of accidents." Navy PBRs and South Vietnamese river assault group (RAG) boats made random patrols though the anchorages for security. Concussion grenades were periodically dropped over the side, next to the ships, to discourage underwater attacks by sappers. Berry said, "When I was on watch, I was constantly on deck. I made rounds of the ship every thirty minutes—if I wasn't down in one of the holds."[28]

BMC Ronald W. Kinkade, a Coast Guard reserve port security specialist, worked on the Seattle police force. He came on active duty as a first class petty officer in 1968 and volunteered for Vietnam. When he arrived in-country, he was assigned to ELD 1. Kinkade said, "Vietnamese stevedores were easy to work with. But sometimes they'd horse around with each other like a bunch of kids. We had to watch that." In addition to ensuring that safe procedures were followed, ELD personnel continually checked the condition of equipment and rigging. Kinkade said, "The ships were old. Most had been laid up since World War II, but the equipment didn't break down as much as we thought it would."[29]

The volume of explosives unloaded under supervision of ELDs continued to increase. In their first six months of operations, the two ELDs supervised the off-loading and back-loading of 235,420 tons of explosives from 176 vessels. In 1967, the numbers increased to 906,327 tons from 499 ships.[30]

The commanding general of the 1st Logistical Command was enthusiastic about using Coast Guard explosive loading detachments. His confidence in the detachments was reflected in the disposition report (DR) he sent to all his commands, which said:

At the request of this headquarters, U.S. Coast Guard Squadron One has made available to this command a Port Security and Waterways Detail.

Subordinate to this unit are two U.S. Coast Guard Explosive Loading Detachments. One is presently stationed at Nha Be and one at Cam Rahn Bay.

The primary mission of the Port Security Detail is to provide advice and assistance in Port Security matters including the handling of explosives.

The personnel of this unit have had a wealth of experience and are experts in their field. Commanders are encouraged to seek their advice and assistance and to give careful consideration to their recommendations. Explosive Loading Detachment personnel are authorized to make on-the-spot corrections of unsafe conditions and their recommendations will be adhered to by all concerned.[31]

Subsequent commanding generals issued similar letters. Lt. Cdr. Emanuel Schneider, officer in charge of the Coast Guard Port Security and Waterways Detail (PS&WD) in 1968, said, "General [Joseph M.] Heiser issued a letter to all his commanders, telling them that the Coast Guard [Explosive Loading] Detachment assigned to them spoke for him and anything they directed in the terms of physical security was to be carried out. That's a damned handy letter to have. Fortunately, we never had to use it, but they [Army] all knew it was there. It was a tremendous compliment [to the Coast Guard]."[32]

Because of the independent nature of duty and the high level of responsibility and authority given EDLs, the original detachments were replaced with more senior officers and enlisted men. Detachment officers in charge were full lieutenants; enlisted members were a master chief petty officer (E-9) and six petty officers, primarily first class (E-6). Schneider said, "The smartest thing the Coast Guard did was assigning senior petty officers to ELDs. The year I was there, we had only one disciplinary procedure among the fifty or sixty men assigned. Senior petty officers were rock-solid and very dependable." Replacement ELD personnel were trained at Army and Navy ammunition-handling schools and in port security at the Coast Guard Training Center at Yorktown, Va. They had been assigned to dangerous cargo and port security units in the United States before going to Vietnam. Enlisted men had DG designators.[33]

In 1967, the explosive loading mission expanded. When the ammunition ship SS *Gamon* arrived at Nha Be after being partially off-loaded at Qui Nhon, ammunition was loose and scattered about the hold because of poor shoring. The officer in charge of the PS&WD said in the unit diary, "This substantiates my recommendation to 1st Log for an ELD Qui Nhon." In June 1967, anticipating a JCS request, Coast Guard made preliminary plans to deploy a third ELD to Vietnam for assignment to Qui Nhon. The new detachment received training with replacement personnel ordered to ELDs 1 and 2. Training consisted of three weeks of explosive loading school at Coast Guard Port Security Station Concord and a week at the Navy cargo handling school at the Naval Supply Center Oakland.[34]

Near Disaster

On 24 October 1967, ammunition was being off-loaded from SS *Berea Victory* anchored in Qui Nhon harbor. As a pallet of 750-pound bombs was swung over the side, it slipped out of the single-wire, double-choke sling. The bombs crashed to the deck of the LCM taking on ammunition alongside. Two bombs broke open, causing a low-order explosion aboard the boat. Two stevedores were blown overboard by the explosion and two managed to make it up the ship's ladder; a fifth man, the boat's coxswain, was killed by the explosion. The dead man was thrown against the engine controls, causing the boat to get under way. The LCM, which was not secured with lines, moved away from the port side of the ship with her rudder hard right. She made a wide turn, crossing the ship's bow from port to starboard.[35]

On fire and trailing smoke, the boat headed into open water, midway between *Berea Victory* and the ship in the adjacent anchorage, 600 yards away. A second small explosion detonated, followed immediately by a devastating blast that blew the LCM to pieces. Miraculously, the boat moved clear of ammunition ships before exploding, averting a major disaster. An Army transportation command board of inquiry determined that the accident was caused by a lack of knowledge and faulty off-loading procedures.[36]

ELD 3 arrived in Vietnam for assignment to Qui Nhon at the end of March 1968. Some of its members were temporarily assigned to Cat Lai for brief in-country indoctrination with ELD 1. At Qui Nhon, ELD 3 personnel moved in with the 394th Transportation Command and built themselves quarters. They began supervising off-load operations on 1 April 1968. Ammunition was off-loaded at two ship anchorages in an open roadstead, an LST landing beach, and a dock in the village of Qui Nhon.[37]

Complaints about ammunition handling operations at Danang prompted the Navy to take action there. The master of SS *Longview Victory* complained about unsafe ammunition handling procedures at the port and recommended action to "station U.S. Coast Guard here and make stevedores go by safety rules." The master of SS *North Platte Victory* said in his 21 May 1967 report:

> In Danang every known rule of safety was violated in the discharge of ammo. . . . Danang is the only U.S. Navy operated port in Viet Nam and the only port in Viet Nam that does not have a USCG Inspection detail. Recommend that a USCG Inspection group be established in that port before a major accident or catastrophe occurs.[38]

At the request of commander Naval Support Activity (NAVSUPP-ACT) Danang, Coast Guard Division 12 formed a dangerous cargo advisory team to assist the Navy with recommendations concerning ammunition-handling operations. In April 1967, as a result of Coast Guard recommendations, NAVSUPPACT separated the explosive-loading anchorage from POL (petroleum-oil-lubricants) moorings in the harbor. On 31 August 1967, COMNAVSUPPACT sent the following message to COMNAVFORV concerning Coast Guard assistance with explosive loading inspections:

> With increasing volume [of] explosive cargo being handled [at] Danang, and continuing concern for safety in handling explosives, very desirable to have Coast Guard assistance assigned in form of inspection and advisory team.
>
> COMDIV ONE TWO now provides inspection and advisory service on not-to-interfere basis with primary mission. Service is periodic inspection aboard working ammunition ships and ramps. Although limited, service very professional and of immeasurable value.
>
> It is requested that action be taken to formalize Coast Guard inspection and advisory assistance with commensurate staffing to provide 24-hour coverage for three ammunition ships working at anchorages and two ramp off-load/back-load sites. Inspectors would not be tasked with line responsibility but would be empowered to stop operations considered to be unsafe.[39]

ELD 4 was established at Danang on 9 July and limited operations began on 17 July 1968. The detachment was fully operational on 22 July 1968. ELD 4 had the capability for continuous twenty-four-hour supervision of loading operations on two deep-draft vessels and supervisory personnel on a twelve-hour basis at various LST ramp sites.[40]

A fifth explosive-loading operation was conducted at Vung Tau. While never officially established, ELD 5 was made up of personnel temporarily assigned from the other four detachments. In 1968, ELDs supervised off-loading and back-loading of 1,456,278 tons of ammunition from 454 vessels.

11

Shipping and Port Security

Disabling of a Panamanian freighter by a mine while the ship was moored at Nha Be, plus the discovery of additional mines affixed to anchor chains of other vessels, forced a reappraisal of GVN-US port security. CGUSARV [commanding general U.S. Army, Vietnam] has been assigned responsibility for all matters pertaining to port security. . . . In order to assist and advise CG [commanding general] 1st Log Command in this most complex task, an urgent requirement exists for COGARD personnel trained in port security. These personnel will be utilized in determining port security requirements, coordinating input of personnel and equipment of participating commands, and monitoring readiness posture of port security units.

Commander, U.S. Military Assistance Command, Vietnam
20 July 1966

SS *Enid Victory*

Coast Guard Commander Frank Oliver climbed down from the Marine C-130 Hercules at Cubi Point Naval Air Station in the Philippines on 20 December 1966. Puddles from a late morning shower still stained the runway. He got into a waiting car and headed for Subic Bay Naval Station. (Oliver had reported as shipping advisor to the Military Sea Transportation Service [MSTS] command in Saigon three weeks earlier.) The driver brought the car to a halt at the gangway of an aging, rust-streaked Victory ship, SS *Enid Victory*.[1]

The 439-foot ammunition ship was enroute to Vietnam when an explosion tore through her engine room, disabling the ship and killing the second assistant engineer. Navy tugs brought the vessel to the U.S.

169

shipyard at Subic Bay. Repairs were almost complete, but the ship did not have enough crew to get under way. One watch engineer was dead and another had deserted to Manila. Only the chief engineer, who was making his first voyage on his license—and, according to him, his last—and an elderly third assistant engineer were available to run the plant.

When MSTS in Saigon told Oliver that the ship's cargo of bombs was urgently needed to support Operation Oregon under way in central Vietnam, he caught a flight to the Philippines. When he boarded the freighter, he found that the master and first assistant engineer had gone to Manila, five hours away, to track down the ship's missing engineer and persuade him to return. If that failed, they intended to recruit new engineering talent. Oliver was aboard *Enid Victory* when the shipyard foreman reported repairs were completed; the ship had to get under way for sea trials. With the master gone, Oliver said, "In view of extenuating circumstances, it seemed appropriate for me to take the ship to sea and conduct sea trials without delay."

At first, *Enid Victory*'s crew was reluctant to put to sea with the Coast Guard commander. But when they learned that he held a merchant marine master's license, they cooperated; crewmembers wanted to complete their voyage and return home. Oliver had graduated from the California Maritime Academy and had sailed in merchant ships, including Victories, before coming in the Coast Guard; he kept his master's license current. To get additional engineers for sea trials, Oliver contacted other Victory ships lying at anchor in the Bay by radiotelephone. "It was a situation calling for moral suasion," he said. In a matter of minutes, four experienced engineers volunteered their services.

When Navy port control told Oliver that no pilots were available to take the ship out of the harbor, he said, "I asked the Navy if there was any objection to me acting as pilot. There was none." A Navy tug moved the 7,600-ton ship away from the pier. With her single screw churning the green water of the bay, *Enid Victory* headed for the South China Sea. The one-day voyage was uneventful, but Oliver said, "Tons of ammunition in the hold seemed to have a visceral effect on all hands. I experienced an uncontrollable urge to give all traffic a wide berth regardless of privileged-vessel concept."

Trials were successful and Oliver anchored the ship in the ammunition anchorage at the entrance to the bay. Next he went to Manila and found the master. "Red Mahun [the master] wanted to send a message to MSTS saying he couldn't sail because the chief engineer was incompetent," Oliver said. "I think the death of the second assistant [engineer] bothered him [the master] more than he realized. But I convinced him that the chief engineer was competent. I got the agent's doctor to prescribe tranquilizers for Mahun and got him headed back to Subic." Four days later, bombs were being off-loaded from *Enid Victory* at Nha Be.

Shipping Advisor

In November 1966, Cdr. Edward F. Oliver was assistant chief of public affairs at Coast Guard headquarters in Washington, D.C., serving in a rotational tour out of his specialty as a merchant marine inspector. When he heard reports from his marine inspection colleagues that the Coast Guard was considering assigning an officer to Vietnam to resolve merchant vessel delays, he volunteered for the job.[2]

The billet was created and Oliver was selected for the assignment. His experience in a similar position as merchant marine detail officer in Naples, Italy, made him particularly well suited for the job. Because the U.S. consul in Saigon continued to resist assignment of a Coast Guard merchant marine detail (MMD) to the Embassy, the billet was officially described as a technical advisor to the Navy's MSTS. Regardless of title, Oliver knew he was being sent to Saigon to carry out the functions of a one-man MMD.[3]

Need for the services of such a detail increased with the escalation of U.S. efforts in Vietnam; more and more vessels loaded with ammunition, weapons, and supplies arrived daily. An estimated 97.5 percent of all materials delivered to Vietnam came aboard ship—surface costs were only a tenth of air transportation. By 1966, sealift had increased to 300 freighters and tankers in a supply line that stretched halfway round the world. An average of 75 ships, with more than 3,000 merchant seamen, were moored or anchored in Vietnamese ports every day. Many ships, particularly those activated from the national defense reserve fleet, were old and in poor condition. Southeast Asia's hot humid weather made ships uncomfortable without air-conditioning. Liberty and recreation facilities for crews were poor if they existed at all. Long layovers resulted in boredom and crew problems.[4]

After being briefed about the job by MSTS and the Coast Guard, Oliver said:

Information about the new billet only raised more unanswered questions: the job had no name, mission guidelines were nonexistent, reporting date was indefinite, commanding officer was unknown, base of operations was not known, and area of operations was not known. . . . I realized I was about to acquire the ideal job, one where you are expected to call the shots and write the rule book. It was all mine for better or worse.[5]

Oliver assumed the title of shipping advisor. At the suggestion of a friend at MSTS, he arranged to be attached to commander MSTS, Far East (COMSTSFE), a Navy rear admiral, rather than commander MSTSO Vietnam, a captain. The backing of an admiral was important in dealings with senior officers of other services in Vietnam. Two weeks after he was told he had the job, Oliver was on a plane heading for Japan. He met with his new boss, Rear Adm. Lucien B. McDonald, COMSTSFE, at his headquarters in Yokohama on 2 December 1966. At the brief meeting, McDonald gave Oliver a broad mandate to keep ships moving and blanket travel orders for all Southeast Asia.[6]

The Air France 727 carrying Oliver arrived at Tan Son Nhut airport at 1800 on 3 December 1966. He was assigned to a BOQ in Cholon on the outskirts of Saigon. His first night in Vietnam included standing the midwatch with an M-16 rifle on guard post and the spectacle of a 120mm mortar attack on the airport. The next morning, Oliver reported to MSTS Vietnam's offices located in an old French building by the river. The commanding officer, Capt. Carl Pfeiffer, USN, welcomed Oliver with open arms; he had been anxiously awaiting Coast Guard assistance to handle merchant marine problems. Pfeiffer arranged for Oliver to move out of the BOQ and into a downtown apartment with two maritime administration officials on Tu Do Street. Oliver said, "He also handed me the keys to what was to be my most important possession and badge of office, a 1943 model Jeep. I called it the 'Sopwith Camel.'"[7]

On 5 December 1966, Oliver made a courtesy call at the consular section of the U.S. Embassy; and had a cordial though reserved meeting with Mr. Robert Lewis—the official who strenuously resisted assignment of an MMD—and Mr. Ralph H. Cadeaux. Oliver said, "Mr. Lewis asked me to work closely with Mr. Cadeaux. . . . The interview went well and he [Lewis] warmed up by the time I departed." Oliver called on COMNAVFORV, the provost marshal of the 716th MP unit, and the provost marshal of the port police before returning to the MSTS offices. When he got back, Pfeiffer had files of casualty reports— collisions and strandings—waiting for him to review. When he went to his office, Oliver found a stack of more than 100 reports of seaman misconduct on his desk. When he sat down to begin work, he was struck by the magnitude of the job he faced: He had the overwhelming task of personally looking into incidents aboard all U.S. merchant ships transporting supplies to Vietnam, as well as other Southeast Asian ports.[8]

He was wading into the stack of misconducts when two MPs brought in a merchant seaman who had wrecked a bar and stolen a girl's purse. Oliver asked the MPs to confine the seaman until he could arrange to get him out of the country. When he looked into the case, he found that the man, whose ship had sailed from Danang without him, had been arrested seven times in the past three weeks. The Embassy had taken no action to repatriate him. Oliver persuaded the master of a ship leaving the next morning to sign the seaman on. In his unit diary, Oliver noted, "One less problem in Saigon." Masters were not particularly happy with this method of getting troublesome seamen out of the country, but they cooperated. On ships with full complements, seamen were signed on as minimal salary "workaways" for the purpose of repatriation.[9]

On 23 December 1966, Oliver arranged a luncheon for Cadeaux aboard SS *President Taylor*. During the meal, he suggested to Cadeaux that the U.S. consul might want to bring to the attention of Saigon police officials that police in Japan and the Philippines charge troublemaking seamen who do not sail with their ships for expenses. Merchant mariners who fail to join (FTJ) ships when they sail are charged for room and board, escorts to airplanes, arrest warrants, and other expenses. Oliver pointed out that amounts could be substantial and made an errant seaman's stay in the country much less enjoyable. He said in the shipping advisor diary, "Cadeaux thought it was a great idea and will act on it. If Saigon police go for it, it will have a sobering effect on FTJs. As it is now, Saigon is a paradise compared to Manila or Yokohama." When Cadeaux asked Oliver to move his shipping advisor operation into the new Embassy when it opened, Oliver said, "If you're serious, put the request into writing."[10]

On 5 December 1966, the military was granted authority to take disciplinary action against merchant mariners. U.S. seamen became subject to the Uniform Code of Military Justice (UCMJ) in accordance

*Commander Oliver, shipping advisor to the U.S. Navy's Military
Sea Transportation Service command in Saigon, boards a merchant
ship to conduct an investigation, 1967.*

with Article 2, which stated, "In time of war, all persons serving with
or accompanying the armed forces in the field . . . are subject to the
UCMJ." Seamen were considered to be accompanying the armed
forces. Application of the code and actions taken to remove the attractiveness of Saigon as a port for seamen who jump ship were effective—
FTJ cases dropped from a peak of twenty a week to five a month.[11]

Oliver's area of responsibility included the deep-water ports of
Vietnam—Saigon, Vung Tau, Nha Trang, Qui Nhon, Vung Ro, Cam Rahn
Bay, and Danang, and the seaports of Singapore, Bangkok, Hong Kong,
Manila, and Keelung, Taiwan. Lane C. Kendall, commercial shipping
advisor to commander MSTS said of the Coast Guard shipping advisor:

His authority extended to all Vietnamese ports and was intended to
assure that, at all times, American ships and seamen met minimum stan-

dards of the Coast Guard. From the day he took over, there was the closest coordination between the Coast Guard, MSTS, and Mar Ad-V [Mar-
itime Administration–Vietnam], and the active and aggressive exercise
of Coast Guard supervision in Vietnamese waters aided materially in
improving operations.[12]

A magazine article described the shipping advisor's one-million-
square-mile operating area as the largest maritime police beat in the
world. During his first months in Vietnam, Oliver traveled almost continuously. When not traveling, he was handling cases by radio or telephone. He said, "At times it seemed to be one continuing series of
assaults with a deadly weapon—straight razor, stevedore hook, meat-
hook, roast knife, serving fork, and knives of every description including switch, sheath, pocket, butcher, paring, French, and butter." He
traveled to ports all over the country to remove assailants, because
masters feared further violence from them or from friends of victims.
Oliver escorted recalcitrant seamen back to Saigon for repatriation to
the United States. He said, "Fortunately, the Air Force was cooperative
and passenger terminal sergeants were understanding. When I
appeared with a disgruntled prisoner in tow, they always found two
seats on the first aircraft heading south."[13]

Responsibility for U.S. merchant seamen in foreign countries rests
with the State Department, so a Coast Guard merchant marine detail
assigned to an embassy derives its authority to act from the State
Department. Oliver, in his capacity as MSTS shipping advisor, did not
have embassy affiliation; he continually pushed the limits of his legal
authority in efforts to resolve problems. He knew that supply ships
had to keep moving, so he did what had to be done to get them in and
out of port. Three months after his arrival in Vietnam, Oliver moved
into an office at the U.S. Embassy, but retained the title of shipping
advisor, and also kept his office at MSTS. The Embassy forwarded a
formal request to the State Department in Washington, asking that a
Coast Guard MMD be officially assigned.[14]

SS *Loma Victory*

SS *Loma Victory* was moored at a De Long pier in Cam Rahn Bay
with 5,000 tons of retrograde ammunition in her hold for return to the

United States. The master, after not being seen for a number of days, emerged from his cabin the night of 23 March 1966; he was intoxicated with barbiturates and alcohol. He staggered around on deck armed with a .38-caliber pistol; he was looking for his first mate so he could shoot him. Army MPs halted ammunition handling operations and withdrew all military personnel from the ship. The provost marshal did not permit MPs to become involved in problems aboard merchant ships.

When Lt. (jg) Gerald T. Willis, officer in charge of ELD 2 at Cam Rahn Bay, heard of the situation, he contacted Oliver in Saigon by radio just after midnight. Oliver quickly dressed, grabbed the travel bag he kept packed, headed for the airport, and caught a jet heading north. Willis was waiting at the airstrip when he landed; it was still dark. When they got to the pier, they heard loud music coming from *Loma Victory.* MPs at the head of the pier kept people from approaching the ammunition-laden vessel. Oliver and Willis chambered rounds in their weapons, walked down the pier to the ship, and climbed the gangway. They found the master in his cabin, calmly sitting with his pistol next to him. He wore sunglasses and had a large drink in his hand; an Akai tape deck blasted at full volume from the corner. Oliver said, "After I turned the volume down, I informed him he was no longer master and his chief officer had been appointed acting master." Oliver ordered him to surrender his .38, which he did, reluctantly. Oliver escorted the man to Saigon where he arranged for his repatriation. His master's license was subsequently suspended in the United States by a hearing examiner.[15]

When word that a Coast Guard officer was in Saigon to handle merchant vessel problems spread through ports of southeast Asia, radio messages started coming in around-the-clock. The work load increased steadily as Oliver went from one ship to the next. He quickly realized that even working seven days a week the job was too much for him to handle alone, and he requested help. On 19 June 1967, Lt. Cdr. Joseph L. Hamilton, a marine inspector, and YNC Robert Clark, a court recorder, were sent from COMSTSFE in Yokohama to assist Oliver. He said, "When I got the other two people, it was a different story. It was the difference between night and day."[16]

In its first year, the three-man shipping advisory unit traveled the length of South Vietnam's coast from the DMZ to the Cambodian border. Using every means of transportation from jet to sampan, they boarded more than 500 ships and investigated 263 serious cases, including mutiny, deaths and accidents, narcotics, groundings, assaults, and desertions. On twenty occasions, sailors were removed from ships and taken to Saigon for repatriation—not all peaceably. Sixteen merchant mariners voluntarily surrendered their licenses in lieu of having hearings, and seventeen seamen's documents were deposited with the Embassy pending hearings. In reflecting on his Vietnam duty, Oliver said, "I'm grateful for a once-in-a-lifetime assignment. It will always be satisfying to remember that after the Coast Guard unit was established a ship was never delayed because of an unresolved crew problem."[17]

The U.S. State Department approved creation of an MMD at the Embassy while Cdr. William T. Sode was serving as shipping advisor. Merchant Marine Detail Saigon was established on 1 July 1968, and in that year, the detail investigated 164 casualty cases—collisions, groundings, death and injury, and equipment and hull failures affecting seaworthiness. The number dropped in 1969 to 100 cases. Improvement was credited to better aids to navigation and increased emphasis on shipboard safety by the Coast Guard and shipping companies. Demands for investigation of personnel cases—such as assault and battery, attempted murder, mental and physical incompetence, flagrant disobedience of orders, and so forth—fluctuated but always remained high. There were 336 cases investigated in 1969 and 428 in 1970.[18]

As U.S. involvement in Vietnam drew down, it became more difficult for investigating officers to arrange transportation to ports. They had to rely on Coast Guard personnel at ELDs in port areas to assist them with investigations, relying heavily on telephone and radio communications to conduct investigations and resolve problems.

The Coast Guard's unique capability in merchant marine investigations contributed significantly to sustained resupply of military operations in Vietnam. Shipping advisors and, later, merchant marine details exercised initiative and judgment in removing personnel and resolving problems to keep ships moving. They had experience and authority to function as an effective liaison for the Embassy and military commands with merchant ships and crews in-country. In addition to enforcing discipline, MMDs also protected individual rights of merchant mariners.

Port Security

A floodtide of war materials to support the buildup of U.S. forces began arriving in Vietnam in the summer of 1966; port facilities, strained to their limits, were increasingly vulnerable to Viet Cong sabotage and attack. In a 20 July 1966 message, Gen. William C. Westmoreland, COMMACV, announced his decision to make the Army responsible for all matters pertaining to port security; the message eliminated any doubt about which service—Army or Navy—had the mission. Westmoreland assigned USARV primary responsibility for physical security at ports throughout Vietnam, with the exception of Danang—a port primarily supporting Navy and Marine operations in I Corps. While the Army had the mission, it had few personnel trained or experienced in port security to carry it out; Westmoreland requested Coast Guard port security assistance.[19]

Cdr. Raymond C. Hertica was executive officer at the Coast Guard's busy Los Angeles/Long Beach captain of the port office in California. On the evening of 15 September 1966, he was called to the office from his home to see a classified message. When Hertica arrived, the officer of the day handed him the dispatch ordering to him to Vietnam as officer in charge of the Port Security and Waterways Detail (PS&WD). He was detached on 26 September 1966 and given nine days leave to settle his family before reporting to Coast Guard Base Alameda for processing. Other members of the PS&WD—Lt. Cdr. Donald G. Kneip, BMC (DG) Charles D. Wise, and YN2 Harris—received orders to report to Alameda on equally short notice. Need for the detail was considered so urgent that the men did not receive the usual pre-Vietnam training before departing.[20]

PS&WD personnel traveling in work uniforms arrived at Tan Son Nhut airport on 15 October 1966 and were met by a driver from Squadron One and taken into Saigon. Hertica said, "It was a hot humid afternoon and there were a million Vietnamese around. My first thought was, 'What have I gotten into?'" The detail stopped briefly at COGARDRON ONE's office and then went for indoctrination and processing with the Army.

The Army, increasingly aware of vulnerability of port facilities, feared disruption of vital resupply efforts. Port and waterway security became a high-priority issue. Hertica said:

Facilities and ships at the Port of Saigon, thirty-five miles from the sea, are vulnerable to sabotage and attack.

First they took us over to meet General Westmoreland, MACV. He briefed us about the problems they were having. He talked to us a little bit about our backgrounds and training and said we were going to be attached to the 1st Logistical Command for operational control. We were surprised when we met with Westmoreland. We really didn't know what was going on until we got in-country and found out about Captain [Risto A.] Matilla's recommendation that Coast Guard port security advisors come over. Apparently the Army, very uncharacteristically, zoomed us up [to the general]. It was quite a rush.[21]

The detail then met with Maj. Gen. Charles W. Eifler, commanding general of 1st Logistical Command, at his headquarters in Saigon on 17 October 1966. 1st Log was responsible for port and waterway security in II, III, and IV Corps. Hertica said, "When we talked to Eifler, he knew there were problems. But he was so far up the chain of command, he wasn't sure what they were. There had been a lot of incidents with things being blown up by sappers. It was getting to the point where it was very serious as far as he was concerned. His people couldn't seem to get a handle on it. The general wanted us to go out and look at every port and barge terminal. He wanted us to make a survey, brief the local commander on what we found and our recommendations, and then come back and brief him." The detail was then given a brief tour of the Port of Saigon. Their initial impression was that port security, by stateside standards, was very poor.[22]

Officially, 1st Log defined the detail's mission as the following:

- Advise 1st Log command staff and subordinate commanders, through the provost marshal, on matters pertaining to the safe handling of explosives and port and waterway security.
- Coordinate with U.S. Coast Guard, commander naval forces, 18th MP brigade, and other agencies as appropriate on port and waterway security.
- Advise and assist subordinate commanders and the 18th MP brigade on the technical operation and employment of river patrol boats and other small craft employed in port and waterway security.[23]

PS&WD was assigned to the Army for operational control and COGARDRON ONE for administrative control. The two Coast Guard ELDs were put under command of officer in charge, PS&WD. While the detail was assigned to the 1st Log provost marshal, Hertica was told to report directly to General Eifler.[24]

The next day, Hertica and his team received briefings about Army port security efforts. Hertica said, "They [1st Log] were given responsibility for port security in June 1966; however, they had never done this type of operation before. . . . We discovered they didn't know beans about it. There was a lot of enemy activity in port areas and nobody really knew what they were doing." The detail spent the rest of the day going over 1st Log files and directives.[25]

On 19 October 1966, PS&WD toured port facilities at Saigon, Newport, Cat Lai, Nha Be, and connecting waterways by boat. Newport was a deep-water port facility being built upriver from Saigon to handle diverted military cargo. It had berths for four ships, mooring buoys for three more, and landing facilities for LSTs and LCMs. During the tour, particularly at Saigon, the detail observed a mass of confusion, with ships and barges moored at every possible place. Hundreds of uncontrolled junks and sampans plied the waters.[26]

The detail was given an office in 1st Log's 4th Transportation Command headquarters and was issued a jeep; members began making detailed surveys of Saigon port and Newport by road and on foot. While they were impressed with the volume of cargo moved under very difficult circumstances, they were discouraged by operations they saw: facilities were poor, wharves were run down, and almost all cargo was hand-carried. The detail then went by helicopter to ammunition barge unloading sites in the greater Saigon area. "Conditions are primitive in all cases," Hertica said in the shipping advisor diary. "It's a miracle there hasn't been an explosion either through accident or otherwise. . . . Port security is practically nonexistent."[27]

After his visit to Newport, Hertica made several recommendations for improving physical security. He said the facility needed more lighting, more and higher metal perimeter fencing, and log booms on the river, north and south of the facility. When he saw tree branches and other debris floating past and under newly constructed piers, he told the Army commander that sappers could use the debris to float downriver with explosives and get under the piers. Hertica recommended putting heavy metal mesh down into the water around piers and installing lights under them. He said, "The local commander didn't do anything about it. Then the VC came in and blew up one of his piers. That kind of got his attention."[28]

Harris, PS&WD's yeoman, was not trained in port security and did not go into the field. He stayed in Saigon and prepared reports on the results of surveys. While the detail had an office at 1st Log, Harris usually worked at COGARDRON ONE's offices where he helped out with Coast Guard duties when not doing PS&WD work. Hertica, with the assistance of Kneip and Wise, embarked on a vigorous inspection program at port facilities on rivers near Saigon. Inspections included barge sites at Cogido—ammunition and supplies for the airbase at Bien Hoa; Long Binh—a potential ammunition handling point; Thu Duc—dry cargo for Saigon; Buu Long—ammunition resupply; Binh Trieu—ammunition resupply; Cau Binh Loi—JP-5 fuel for Tan Son Nhut; and Cat Lai—recommended as an alternate explosive loading port for Nha Be. Recommendations for improving security at ports and barge sites included—

- Greater control over access for stevedores and other personnel
- Higher chain-link fences
- More barbed wire
- Improved lighting
- Relocation of generators away from perimeters
- Defoliation around perimeter fencing
- More fire protection with trailer-mounted pumps
- More bunkers for personnel protection
- Guard towers
- Restricting unauthorized vessels to at least fifty feet away from all mooring buoys, barges, and piers
- Buoys to moor empty barges
- Roving waterfront patrols
- Boat patrols
- Log booms upriver and downriver from facilities to limit access and divert floating mines
- Minesweeping
- Twenty-four-hour guard watches

Eifler was pleased with the detail's work and ordered all recommendations implemented. When Hertica raised the continuing issue of dangers of having explosive-loading operations next to the fuel farm at Nha Be, the general said he would personally recommend moving explosive loading to Cat Lai with USARV and MACV.[29]

While Eifler was enthusiastic about PS&WD's surveys, local commanders were not; they resented Coast Guardsmen inspecting their facilities and making recommendations about their security. "I didn't tell Eifler about it [the resentment]," Hertica said, "because I didn't want to get them in trouble. I could understand how they felt. . . . They were all good people. Specialists in their fields. But they weren't very security conscious."

At Qui Nhon, an anchored tanker was pumping fuel ashore when an explosion erupted amidships, and the ship sank in shallow water. The local Army command investigated the incident and reported that the ship had been sunk by an engine-room explosion and that the Viet Cong had nothing to do with it. Eifler sent PS&WD to Qui Nhon to take a look at the ship. Kneip, who was a qualified diver, borrowed equipment from a Navy underwater demolition team stationed nearby and got the team's help in diving on the wreck. He made pictures of the hole in the hull, showing that the blast came from an external explosive charge. After the incidents at Newport and Qui Nhon, Hertica said, "Eifler put out the word to all local commanders that they were to do anything we recommended unless he specifically told them not to."[30]

The detail spent a lot of time, particularly in the first months, gaining the confidence of Army field personnel with whom they worked. Hertica said, "We had to convince them we weren't sneaking around behind their backs trying to get them in trouble. We didn't have any ax to grind and nothing to gain. We had to be very diplomatic and not get people all upset. Later, it got better because they found out we knew what we were doing."[31]

When word got around that security surveys could help commanders protect their units and operations, PS&WD visits were welcomed. Hertica said, "In most cases, they looked forward to us coming. They wanted to find out what their problems were before they got up the chain of command. Security got a whole lot better." The detail set its own schedule and was independent in making inspection trips. Members traveled throughout Vietnam and were on the road 70 percent of the time; when they went to a unit, they paid their respects to the commander and then looked around. After they finished, they met with the commander, told him what they found, and gave him their recommendations. On returning to Saigon, the detail made a personal report to the general if it found anything significant; otherwise, it submitted a report to him through the provost marshal.[32]

PS&WD saw a glaring security deficiency when it first began making surveys: facilities lacked adequate waterside patrols. While the Army patrolled on shore, surveillance also was needed on the water—

particularly at night. Hertica advised Eifler that 31-foot PBRs (river patrol craft) like those used by the Navy would be ideal boats for security patrols. He calculated that thirty-nine boats would be required for waterside security throughout Vietnam. Until PBRs could be obtained, Hertica recommended using Boston Whalers; Eifler approved the recommendations and sent an urgent request for boats.[33]

The Army obtained and armed 17-foot Boston Whalers for use as port security boats until PBRs could be deployed. 1st Log tasked PS&WD with training Army MPs as coxswains. Hertica said in the unit diary, "In addition to our regular duties, the Port Security and Waterways Detail is fast becoming the Army's small-boat experts." On 20 February 1967, the Army sent Hertica back to the United States for two weeks to participate in a patrol boat conference and evaluations of a boat for riverine operations. Coxswain training first began in May 1967. When the first twenty Boston Whalers arrived on 10 July 1967, PS&WD set up a training school for coxswains; waterside security patrols began three weeks later.[34]

Once the detail finished its initial port inspection program, it began making follow-up surveys. Hertica said, "When we reinspected Port of Saigon's waterfront facilities, we found many deficiencies corrected. We were surprised at the amount of progress they made in a 3-month period." In addition to improved security at Saigon, authorities also implemented recommendations for weekly warehouse and storage-area inspections. Workers separated dangerous cargo by types, reducing the risk of fire. New firefighting systems were installed and old systems updated. Hertica said in the PS&WD diary, "The fire department at Newport got a new 1,000-gallon pumper truck. Five months ago Newport didn't even have one fire extinguisher. Now they have a fire department." In looking back at how PS&WD made improvements in security, Hertica said, "Frankly, we did a lot of things by assuming authority and telling people what to do. It was the only way to get the job done."[35]

Sabotage by infiltrating Viet Cong was a constant and major threat to port installations. The problem was complicated by the lack of an effective identification system. Hertica said, "We couldn't tell the good guys from the bad guys. Dock workers, stevedores, and even people in security could all be Viet Cong in disguise. It was a very difficult proposition. They could move around in some areas without fear of detection. They didn't have an identification system from what I could determine." While personnel security was a constant concern for PS&WD, it was primarily the responsibility of MP brigades. The detail had little direct contact with South Vietnamese military and civilian agencies dealing with access and personnel security.[36]

Lt. Cdr. Emanuel Schneider went to Vietnam in 1968 with orders to be assistant officer in charge of the PS&WD. When he arrived in-country in June, he was told the Army had downgraded the officer in charge billet to lieutenant commander and he was in command. After checking in with NAVFORV and COGARDACTV, Schneider went by Jeep to 1st Log's new headquarters at the huge Army complex at Long Bien, ten miles northeast of Saigon. The headquarters was located in a two-story building on one side of "headquarters hill"; USARV headquarters was on the other side.

In addition to the usual training for Vietnam, Schneider attended Vietnamese language school and a refresher course at the Coast Guard's explosive loading school, Port Chicago. The detail's personnel complement also was changed to upgrade the chief petty officer billet to a master chief petty officer. BMCM (DG) Ralph H. Carr was Schneider's senior enlisted man. The yeoman's billet was changed to a quartermaster because of the amount of chart work required of the detail.[37]

On headquarters hill, PS&WD was located with 1st Log's provost marshal. Schneider said, "That's who I reported to on a daily basis. But, in point of fact, I was really given free rein." The three-man detail had one long office on the second deck. PS&WD met incoming personnel for ELDs at Tan Son Nhut and brought them to Long Bien before assigning them to detachments. The number of people working at the office varied, depending on vacancies to be filled at ELDs.

The extensive Army complex at Long Bien, covering several square miles, was not totally secure. Schneider said, "We were directly penetrated and attacked several times. And we weren't immune from rocket attacks either. We had attacks almost nightly. One or two rockets or a barrage." The road to Saigon went "red" at 1500 every day and stayed closed until 0900 the next morning. The area the road passed through was a free-fire zone at night.[38]

The PS&WD was given responsibility for preparing merchant vessel dispersal plans for all 1st Log ports. If a port came under attack, and the attack lasted longer than a set time, ships were to disperse on their own in accordance with these plans, which specified where ships would go and where they would rendezvous. In carrying out its duties, detail personnel continued to travel extensively, making security inspections. Because of the work load, inspections usually were made by a single person rather than a team. Schneider said, "When we showed up [at a facility] there was never a problem. The Army was always very willing and interested in hearing our viewpoints. There were times, as I think back, that I was embarrassed by how much they thought we knew and how much we were playing off-the-cuff." The Army was good about providing air transportation. When PS&WD had to get somewhere, the transportation office at Long Binh set up a flight, either fixed-wing or helo. Occasionally, members of the detail found themselves in strange surroundings. Once they were sent into the mountains with indigenous Montagnard troops to survey ammunition supply points (ASP) and make recommendations about security.[39]

Schneider said, "We used to joke that the Army wanted us to handle anything wet. They wanted us to inspect patrol boats and train crews, and make patrols with them." In December 1968, 1st Log's commanding general had the PS&WD inspect the 159th Transportation Battalion's 5th Heavy Boat Company and the 231st Medium Boat Company. He wanted to make sure the battalion's 118-foot LCUs and 56-foot LSMs were ready to support Operation "Speedy Express," planned for the Mekong delta. In preparation for providing logistics for the operation, the detail was tasked with surveying waterways in the delta to determine navigable routes, test communications, and plot landmarks that could be used as navigation aids. In conducting surveys the detail traveled the entire lengths of the Mekong and Bassac rivers from the South China Sea to the Cambodian border; its recommendations were incorporated into 1st Log's operations orders.[40]

When LCU 1088, an Army resupply vessel on a mission up the Bassac river, accidentally crossed into Cambodia, she and her crew were captured by Cambodians. After the incident, 1st Log sent Schneider up the Bassac in another LCU to follow the route taken by 1088 and find out how she could have gotten into Cambodia. He was to make recommendations for marking the area so it could not happen again. Schneider said, "I used the same chart as 1088, an old French Michelin rubber plantation chart. It wasn't very accurate. I retraced her route and went clear up into Cambodia. Then I submitted my recommendations."

What Schneider did not know was that the U.S. Navy was responsible for patrolling the river and preventing boats from crossing the border. When his report went up the chain of command, it caused a row among Navy and Army commanders. When Vice Adm. Elmo R. Zumwalt, Jr., COMNAVFORV, found out that a Coast Guard officer had piloted the Army vessel that penetrated Navy security, Schneider was summoned to Saigon to explain his actions. He said, "[Captain John M.] Austin [COGARDACTV] told me, 'Put on some steel pants. You're going to see Zumwalt and he's really upset.'" At the meeting, Schneider said, "The admiral said to me, 'I want to know whose side are you on? Are you on the Navy's side or are you on the Army's side?'" At that point, Austin stepped in and explained to the admiral that Schneider was under Army control, carrying out Army orders. Austin said Schneider was doing what his operational commander told him to do. "And that was the end of it. I didn't even speak," Schneider said.[41]

The first ten PBRs arrived in Vietnam in April 1969. Schneider said, "As fast as PBRs came in-country, my master chief and I were going out training their crews. I transferred a chief engineman from one of the ELDs to what I called the headquarters unit to help get PBRs ready." Crews were trained and boats were fitted out and tested as quickly as possible. A boat company assigned to the 18th MP Brigade operated the PBRs. The radar-equipped boats, capable of 25 knots, were powered by water jets for operating in shallow water. They mounted twin and single .50-caliber machine guns and a grenade launcher. Mission commanders and machine gunners for each boat were military police; craft operators were from the transportation command.[42]

When PBRs came on-line, Boston Whalers were shifted to patrol smaller outports. Whalers began patrolling a port near Danang just in time to stop a Viet Cong sapper attack. Schneider said, "I think the sappers were shocked to find armed Boston Whalers where there hadn't been any when they did their recon a couple of days earlier. Sappers were all captured in the water."[43]

Toward the end of his tour, Schneider began working with the South Vietnamese. He said, "They [the South Vietnamese] realized the importance of port security, but they had higher-priority agendas." When USAID sent over thirty 30-foot patrol boats for Vietnamese customs patrols, they were never used. Schneider said, "The boats came off the ship and stayed tied up to the pier where they were unloaded the whole time I was there. . . . There were too many times where equipment was turned over, but never got into play." Schneider was scheduled to participate as an advisor on a night ambush mission with two

Vietnamese marine police PBRs. On the night of the operation, he said, "As we were leaving the dock, a Vietnamese accidentally fired off a .50-caliber machine gun and shot up the boat ahead of us. That ended the operation for that night. I was glad to be rid of that particular part of the job."[44]

Thinking back about his year in Vietnam, Schneider remembered the daily sight of thin columns of black smoke climbing into the blue sky from all over the area. Every morning, cutoff 55-gallon drums used as latrines were hauled outside, doused with diesel fuel, and set on fire. "I'll never forget the sight and smell of burning 'grunt pots,'" he said. "Or the constant sound of the thump, thump, thump of outgoing artillery and mortar fire."[45]

12

Operation Tight Reign

We [U.S. aircraft] were able to operate in adverse weather because of LORAN. . . . When LORAN was introduced . . . , it became feasible to strike into most areas of North Vietnam regardless of weather. . . . During the 1968–72 [air] campaign, . . . LORAN became the preferred technique for all-weather bombing in RP1 [Route Package One—DMZ to above 18th Parallel]. . . . LORAN techniques offered two advantages: the accuracy was better and a formation could bomb at the same time as the lead aircraft.

Gen. William W. Momyer, USAF, Commander, 7th Air Force

Bangkok

Pan American flight number 1 lowered its wheels and touched down at Bangkok's Don Muong international airport at 0200 on 15 January 1966. Six officers from the Coast Guard's Operation Tight Reign came down the ramp and walked to the terminal. Dress khaki uniforms felt warm in the humid night air. After collecting their gear, they climbed into taxis and headed into the city. The group, led by Capt. Thomas R. Sargent, III, was embarked on a secret Defense Department mission to build an electronic navigation system in Southeast Asia. The system, when completed, would provide all-weather aircraft positioning data—accurate to within yards—covering North and South Vietnam.

Sargent and CWO3 Baker Herbert, the project's contracting officer, first went to the U.S. military assistance command, Thailand (MAC-THAI). Sargent told them, "I'm here to get land and I need an office." An Army colonel told him there was no room at MACTHAI and, with the buildup in Southeast Asia, office space anywhere in Bangkok was impossible to obtain. Sargent said, "Look, I need an office and a telephone." When the colonel told him he would probably have to wait six months for an office, Sargent turned to Herbert and said, "Mr. Herbert, I want you to get us an office. We need two desks, three chairs, and a telephone." Herbert said, "Yes, captain," and left. Sargent stayed at MACTHAI to brief senior staff about the project. When he told them he was going to buy land, clear sites, construct four stations in Thailand and Vietnam, and have the system up and running in eight months, they told him, "You Coast Guard guys are nuts."[1]

After checking at MACTHAI for possible leads on office space, Herbert went to the U.S. Navy's officer in charge of construction for Southeast Asia (OICC SEA) in Bangkok, where Navy personnel confirmed the critical shortage of office space. Herbert finally talked to a Thai civilian working for the Navy; the man told him about a new building that might have offices available.

The taxi pulled to the curb in heavy traffic; Herbert got out in front of the Bangkok Bank building at 300 Silom Road. The four-story building, with a light blue finish and modern facade, reminded Herbert of a movie theater. Inside, he met Mr. Kathchit, an assistant manager who had been educated in the United States and spoke perfect English. He told Herbert there were still two vacant offices, but Thai owners of the building did not want to rent to the U.S. Government. He said it took too long to get paid by the Embassy.

Herbert said, "Mr. Kathchit, I have $25,000 in my briefcase. It's in a cashier's check. If you can cash it, I can pay you for office space this minute." Kathchit looked at the check. He smiled and said, "Yes. I can cash this. Let me take you to the manager." Herbert met the manager and then looked at adjoining offices on the third floor. After negotiating a price, Herbert told Kathchit, "I'll take the two offices for a year and I'll pay you in advance." A contract was signed, a phone installed, and furniture ordered.

Sargent was still at MACTHAI when Herbert called. Sargent got on the line and Herbert said, "Captain, we have two offices at the Bangkok Bank building. The telephone's installed and furniture arrives today. I'm sorry, but I can't get typewriters until tomorrow." Sargent took out a pen, wrote down the address and phone number, and said, "Thank you, Mr. Herbert. Carry on." Sargent handed the paper to the Army colonel and said, "Here is our address and the phone number where you can reach me." Sargent said, "From that day forth, MACTHAI never questioned us. At all. Never."

LORAN

In the spring of 1965, U.S. bombing in North and South Vietnam intensified. Monsoon weather and inaccurate geographical charts limited effectiveness of air strikes. The Air Force needed a navigation system that would permit reconnaissance planes to locate and mark enemy targets so bombers could return and strike them at night and in any kind of weather. The returnability problem was discussed at a meeting of electronics specialists at the Pentagon in March 1965. A Coast Guard electronics engineer at the meeting told the group that LORAN-C, an accurate, large-area marine navigation system operated by the Coast Guard, could provide the required capability.

LORAN-C was an enhanced version of the hyperbolic radio navigation system first used in World War II. LORAN, an acronym for long range aid to navigation, used the time difference between receipt of synchronized electronic pulses transmitted from paired stations—master and slave. Time differences, measured in millionths of a second, provided lines of position; crossing lines from two sets of stations fixed the position of an aircraft or ship. The new system, LORAN-C, used lower frequencies (90 to 110 kilohertz) and provided longer-range coverage, reliable over water out to 1,200 nautical miles. It also was considerably more accurate than earlier versions; in best-coverage areas, positions were accurate to plus or minus ten yards. Bombers equipped with LORAN-C could continuously track their positions enroute to objectives and, if necessary, accurately drop their ordnance without ever seeing the target.

Recognizing potential applications for such a system, the Air Force asked the Coast Guard if it would be possible to construct a LORAN-C chain covering Vietnam. The Coast Guard studied the problem and, in June 1965, told the Air Force that a system to meet their requirements was feasible and could be on the air in August 1966. Operation Tight Reign was launched.

Captain Sargent was chief of the Coast Guard's civil engineering division at headquarters in 1965. He also was the civil engineering LORAN program coordinator. He said, "The Air Force had to go to the

Department of Defense to get funds to build stations. We needed three stations and a monitor. As usual, funds were at a premium." Once the decision was made to build the chain, the Coast Guard was anxious to get started; they made a commitment to have the system on-air by August 1966—the clock was running. Sargent told the Air Force that Defense Department funds were available from a canceled Navy LORAN project. The Navy no longer needed the LORAN chain, which had been planned for the entrance to the Straits of Gibraltar. Even after funds were identified, however, getting the Pentagon to transfer them to the new project was time-consuming.[2]

Aware of the Defense Department's strong interest in the project, Coast Guard Cdr. Harold R. Brock, a civil engineer, and Lt. Cdr. Maynard J. Fontaine, an electronics engineer, began working on plans for a Southeast Asia LORAN-C chain. Brock said, "Without authority, we started doing clandestine work on the system. Ned Fontaine and I put it all together. We worked on our own time at night, just trying to get things going. The time frame was so compressed, if we hadn't, it never would have happened." In the fall, they began more detailed planning and the initial contract work.[3]

In October 1965, Sargent went to the Pentagon in an attempt to get the project moving. He said, "The on-air date was specified. It was imperative that we start as soon as possible. But they said they couldn't get $14.5 million transferred from the Gibraltar chain right away. It was more than a transfer from one location to another. It was different services, as well." When Sargent told DOD he had administrative funds left over from other LORAN projects that he could use to investigate possible station sites in Southeast Asia, the Pentagon quickly approved a survey trip.[4]

Coast Guard electronics and civil engineers reviewed Air Force requirements, and determined geographical areas where stations would provide needed coverage and still be accessible for construction and support. Locations were selected for two transmitting stations in Thailand and one in Vietnam. Danang was initially selected for the monitor station.

Sargent said, "In November 1965, I departed with Cdr. Carl S. Mathews, Cdr. William R. Fearn, and an Air Force lieutenant colonel named Harper. We went to Bangkok because it was easier to fly into. I left Mathews and Fearn in Thailand to look for two station sites and I took Colonel Harper with me to Saigon." The group traveled on priority orders with special passports. The project was so sensitive, Sargent could not tell his wife where he was going, so he told her he was going to Japan. Mathews and Fearn picked Sattahip and Chiengmai for sites in Thailand and Sargent and Harper decided on Con Son Island and Danang in Vietnam. Once general site areas were selected, the team returned to the United States, arriving just before Thanksgiving.[5]

On 13 December 1965, Secretary of Defense Robert S. McNamara sent a letter to Treasury Secretary Henry W. Fowler, requesting that the Coast Guard build the LORAN-C chain. Despite the delay in approval, the on-air date remained August 1966. Brock said, "Once we got official word from DOD, we pulled out all stops." Coast Guard Commandant Adm. Edwin J. Roland personally gave the order to "get it on the air." Sargent said, "I don't recall what the [project] priority was, but I had a red flag that said I could do anything I wanted to get it done. I had to get it done."[6]

The Project Begins

The Coast Guard initially estimated that construction of the LORAN-C chain would take fourteen months. The six-month delay in authorization, however, reduced the time available to complete the project by more than 40 percent. Some preliminary design and logistic work had begun, but no commitments could be made to suppliers and contractors until funds were authorized. The compressed time frame, station locations—in remote areas halfway around the world—and a logistic system stressed by the Vietnam buildup complicated an already difficult situation. Site selection and preparation, equipment contracting, material staging and shipping, in-country transportation planning, and training for station crews all had to be done concurrently. It was imperative that each element of the work be accomplished as programmed for the overall project to succeed; all four stations were vital and had to be in operation for the system to be of value. If any station was not on-air with the others, the chain would be broken.[7]

CWO3 Baker Herbert, a finance and supply specialist, was at his mother-in-law's house with his family when he received a phone call from Coast Guard headquarters on 29 December 1965. The personnel assignment officer said, "How would you like to go to Southeast Asia?

I can't tell you what the mission is, but are you interested? You did volunteer for Vietnam." Herbert said yes and was told to be in Washington, D.C., on 3 January 1966, ready to go overseas. Herbert said, "I went back to Michigan, put my gear in storage, moved my family, and flew to Washington. I met Captain Sargent as soon as I got to headquarters. He greeted me and asked if I was sure I wanted to go to Southeast Asia. He said, 'There's shooting over there and a possibility you could get hurt.'"

Sargent returned to Bangkok on 15 January 1966 with four civil engineers—Lt. Cdr. Arthur E. Gerken, Lt. Cdr. Daniel C. Olson, Lt. Cdr. Raymond E. Womack, and Lt. Everett L. Crowell—and the contracting officer, CWO3 Herbert. Brock and Fontaine arrived in Bangkok six days later; Brock was commander, Tight Reign construction detachment, and Fontaine was his executive officer and electronics officer. Lt. Cdr. Everett G. Walters, Ens. J. C. Erikson, and six seamen arrived with Brock and Fontaine. Walters, a representative of the Coast Guard office of operations, was there to look into support requirements for Tight Reign; Erikson, a former enlisted electronics technician, scanned frequencies at sites for potential interference. Seamen were surveyor's assistants, serving as rodmen, chainmen, notetakers, and, in some cases, surveyors.[8]

Once an office was established in Bangkok, the detachment began final site selection and land procurement. MACTHAI and MACV provided support for the project. Herbert said:

> The higher-level people at MACTHAI were difficult to deal with. If you wanted something, you had to talk to the noncommissioned officers in charge. I told them we needed help. I said, 'There's something I can do for you. This is a high-priority project and I can get you a letter of commendation from the commandant of the Coast Guard. That's not something every sergeant will have in his file when it comes time for promotion.' I told them I'd write them a letter and sign it 'by direction.' Before I left Washington, I took a whole stack of commandant's stationery. It worked every time. We got aircraft, trucks, whatever we needed.[9]

The team selected specific station locations in Thailand. They selected Sattahip, 80 miles south-southeast of Bangkok on the Gulf of Thailand, for the LORAN chain's master station. The land, on a slight

Tight Reign LORAN-C stations

grade sloping toward the water, had been used for growing tapioca and was near, but not on, the shore. Sargent said, "It was somebody's farm. We paid $40,000 for it. I don't know where the money went, but we paid it. And nobody bothered us." Slave I was located in north-central Thailand. The site was shifted from Chiengmai 45 miles southeast to the vicinity of Lampang, a city of 30,000 people; the site location was 300 miles north of Bangkok, between Lampang and the village of Hang Chat. The land was on a plain, covered with dense growth. Crowell said, "Trees were a hardwood called Peng, a wood similar to teak. They were small, less than ten feet tall. And there was a lot of brush. It was very tropical." The team selected the Royal Thai AFB at Udorn for the monitor station; it was a more secure location than sites available at Danang.[10]

After selecting sites in Thailand, Sargent flew with Brock and Fontaine to Saigon to confirm the site for slave II. Con Son, a 5-mile long island 45 miles southeast of the delta, was the largest of a group of fourteen islands belonging to South Vietnam. The site for the station was a level area of mixed sand and dense jungle on the northwest side of the island. A prison, first established as a penal colony by France in 1862, continued in operation a mile-and-a-half south of the site on the other side of a mountainous ridge; it held 4,000 inmates. Sargent said, "After we landed on Con Son, I went down to the prison and met with the Vietnamese commanding officer. . . . I signed a contract for using the land. There were graves there and I signed an agreement saying we would rebury any remains we had to disturb." Arrangements also were made to hire prisoners to clear the site.[11]

After staying overnight in Saigon, Sargent attempted to get a car to take them to the airport for the flight back to Bangkok. When he finally reached the Army motor pool, a Vietnamese woman told him captains did not rate transportation and hung up. He called back and asked to speak to the woman's supervisor, an Army sergeant. When the man came on the line, Sargent explained, "I'm Captain Sargent, U.S. Coast Guard, and I need a car to take me to the airport." The man said, "Look, I'm a sergeant, too. I don't rate transportation and neither do you," and hung up. In frustration, Sargent called back and told the woman he was Col. T. R. Savage, U.S. Coast Guard. A car was promptly sent to pick him up. He said, "From then on, whenever I had to telephone a motor pool or dispatcher, or make a first-time contact with military offices, I used the 'Colonel Savage' identity."[12]

Once land was arranged, the construction detachment went to individual sites to make detailed surveys and prepare topographical maps; each survey took five days. They did not survey the monitor station site, however, because it did not require a transmitter tower or ground system. Monitor station components were self-contained in air-transportable vans. Commander Fourteenth Coast Guard District deployed a C-123 Provider aircraft from Air Station Guam to Don Muong airport for use by the detachment during construction. Lt. Cdr. Ronald D. Stenzel, aircraft commander, and his crew shuttled people and material to sites. All locations had airstrips capable of landing cargo aircraft. The survey phase of the project lasted from 25 January 1966 to 5 March 1966.[13]

While Brock handled civil engineering aspects of the project and Fontaine the electronics, Sargent provided the horsepower to keep things moving. When the Air Force failed to provide a plane as agreed, holding up departure of the survey team for Con Son, Sargent sent a message to Washington saying that Tight Reign was delayed due to non-cooperation of Air Force. The chief of staff of the Air Force replied with an "Immediate" precedence message directing Air Force commands to provide all available support for the project. Brock said Sargent played an important role in representing Tight Reign at higher levels.[14]

When surveys were completed, a civil engineer was sent to each site to begin clearing operations; Gerken went to Sattahip, Womack to Con Son, and Crowell to Lampang. Brock and Fontaine coordinated construction operations, working out of the Bangkok office; Herbert handled contracting and YN1 Donald L. Fallis and SK2 Edward A. Daniels provided administrative support. Once sites were determined and surveys were under way, Sargent returned to the United States in early March 1966. Back at headquarters, he coordinated staging of materials and preparations for shipping.

Lampang

Lt. Larry Crowell stood with his two suitcases and watched the gray-and-white Thai Airways DC-3 taxi down the short runway, dust swirling behind it. He was the only one who got off the plane at Lampang on 29 March 1966; other passengers—all Thais—continued on to Chiengmai. A driver from the hotel was waiting when Crowell entered the small but modern terminal building.[15]

It was 1030 when the Jeep started down the gravel road toward town. Thick jungle lining the road occasionally gave way to rice paddies and water buffalo wallows. The Jeep passed ox- and horse-drawn carts, bicycles, and a few trucks on the level road. Most people wore loose-fitting black clothes. By the time the Jeep reached the outskirts of Lampang, Crowell's wash-khaki uniform was stained with perspiration; the temperature was 94 degrees. "I was looking forward to making contacts and getting on with the work," he said. "I was excited by the challenge."

Crowell had a broad mandate: As resident engineer for Tight Reign I, he had to carve a clearing out of the jungle, supervise the laying of foundations, build roads, get building materials from the railhead to the site, construct three large buildings, and erect a 625-foot tower. And he had to do it all in four months.

His two-page order concluded: "It is practically impossible to stipulate all the requirements of the resident engineer. It is therefore incumbent upon you to judiciously perform your duties to the best of your abilities insuring all the while that the interests of the government are fully protected."[16]

The Jeep pulled off the road through a gate into a small parking area in front of a three-story pastel-blue-and-pink stucco building. Crowell walked through a small garden into the lobby of the only hotel in Lampang, where he had stayed during the site survey. He spoke to the clerk, using the small amount of Thai he had learned during his two months in-country. After registering, he carried his bags to a second-floor room, at the rear of the building. "It was stark," he said. "A bed, some wicker furniture, and a washstand. There was a small bathroom with a Thai-type toilet in the floor. A shower nozzle came out of the wall; there was no enclosure. Windows had no casings. They were square holes in the stucco wall with shutters that closed over the outside."

Crowell picked up the Land Rover the survey team had left at the Thai Army compound and drove to the site. When he got there, he said, "The only thing done was survey lines. We had hired some natives to clear the lines. They hacked down trees and bushes along boundary lines and along a radial or two for the tower location. The site was still covered with trees and bushes. I was the only one there." Crowell's first job was to get soil core samples to Bangkok for analysis and conduct soil-compression tests. But he could not begin until the borings team subcontracted by Citra, Thailand Co., Ltd. in Bangkok arrived.

After walking the site, he drove to Hang Chat to see Dr. Niyom Srihanok, a respected member of the community. Half German and half Thai, he spoke English. He lived in a large two-story house and had several people working for him. While not actually a medical doctor, he treated the local population. Crowell said, "We got reacquainted and I met his family. We went to a little dining room off the main part of his house and had tea. I told him what I was there to do and he said he would help. He saw an opportunity and was interested in contracting some of the construction work."

Crowell drove back to Lampang. After a meal of water buffalo steak and fried rice at an open-air restaurant, he drove to the hotel. Back in his room, he was struck by how alone he was: no communication with Bangkok was available after 1430. The Lampang communications building only made radio contact with Bangkok four times a day, at 0830, 1030, 1300, and 1430. Crowell said, "There I was, by myself. Alone in a place I'd never heard of four months ago. It was a very lonesome feeling. Nobody to talk to. I was isolated. I began to have second thoughts about what I was doing. I thought, 'I can just disappear and no one will ever know.'" Then he reflected on the enormity of his responsibility and the challenge he faced.

He turned out the light at 2200 and went to sleep.

Supplies

While sites were cleared in Thailand and Vietnam, construction materials, equipment, and supplies were assembled in the United States. The Coast Guard Supply Center Brooklyn was the primary staging point for Tight Reign. The volume of material arriving for the project quickly overwhelmed the supply center, which had neither space nor people to handle the influx. The Coast Guard ordered additional personnel to the supply center and took over a large area of the marine operating terminal in Brooklyn.[17]

H. H. Robertson Inc. delivered fabricated materials for construction of pre-engineered buildings. Trylon Inc. provided three 625-foot transmitting towers, broken down into sections. Engines, generators, and spare parts for power plants came from Caterpillar. LORAN transmitters, timers, and associated electronic components were prepared for shipment, along with vehicles, galley equipment, furnishings, and everything needed to allow stations to operate independently. Brock said, "We outfitted the stations with equipment, spare parts, and consumables for a full year, right down to the toilet paper. They had enough fuel capacity for two years of operation." Chicago Bridge and Iron Company Inc. shipped twelve 63,000-gallon fuel tanks, four for each station, and six 25,000-gallon water tanks to San Francisco for delivery to sites.[18]

The office of the Navy officer in charge of construction (OICC), Thailand, completed design and layout work for the project in February 1966. The three transmitting stations had the same basic layout, consisting of three one-story buildings: a barracks, built on-site; and two pre-engineered buildings—a combination signal-power building and a galley-mess building. Brock said, "We did grading and topographical work so they [the stations] were a standard layout." The large 200-foot-by-40-foot signal-power building was closest to the tower. Construction crews erected a galley-mess building and a barracks side by side, 100 yards from the signal-power building. The 100-foot-by-30-foot buildings were 30 feet apart and connected by a covered walkway. Fuel tanks were located between the signal-power building and the other buildings. At Lampang, the signal-power building was built closer to the tower, inside the ground system. The monitor station at Udorn was a smaller operation, consisting of three small prefabricated buildings.[19]

OICC also prepared plans and specifications for a barracks building suitable for construction at all three transmitting sites. A combination electronics workshop and warehouse also was designed for the master station at Sattahip; it served as a storage facility for common materials for all stations. A spare tower also was stored at Sattahip. On 24 March 1966, a contract was given to Citra for site preparation and construction of barracks at the two Thailand locations. Construction on Con Son began in April 1966 with work being done by the joint venture, RMK-BRJ Corps., contractors handling construction for the military in Vietnam.[20]

At Thai stations, local laborers cleared the land for construction; their wage was 90 cents a day. Prisoners clearing land at the Con Son site received $1.25 a day. Herbert traveled to sites in Thailand and paid laborers in cash. After a Thai worker was murdered at Lampang, Herbert became concerned about carrying large sums of money into the field. He opened an account with the Bangkok Bank and transferred funds to branches at Lampang and Sattahip to pay workers. Sargent was not aware that putting U.S. funds in a foreign bank account was illegal unless approved by the U.S. government. He said, "When I came back [to the United States] the second time, the [Coast Guard] comptroller wrote me a very nasty memo saying what I was doing was completely illegal and I should stop it immediately. I wrote back and said, 'I won't stop it. I don't want my agent-cashier killed. Get me the authority for the account.' And he did."[21]

Construction

The phased construction project called for preliminary work to be completed before buildings, towers, and electronic equipment arrived. Brock said, "The site work was done so that when the material came in, footings, foundations, floor slabs, and everything underground would be in place. All we had to do was erect buildings and install equipment."[22]

Equipment and construction materials were delivered in three shipments. Communications equipment, hardware and piping to be installed under concrete slabs, and tower anchors arrived by air in late March 1966. Over 100,000 pounds of material arrived on Air Force C-141 Starlifter aircraft. Water and fuel tanks, copper ground wire, and the balance of the underground equipment arrived at Bangkok aboard the first ship, SS *Andrew Jackson,* on 17 May 1966; heavy construction equipment and a contingent of contractor personnel also arrived aboard the ship. Tankage and materials were transported north to Lampang by train. *Andrew Jackson* off-loaded equipment and supplies for Con Son at Bangkok; USCGC *Nettle* (WAK 169), a Coast Guard cargo ship deployed from Sangley Point, the Philippines, delivered materials to the island, landing supplies over the beach. From Bangkok, *Andrew Jackson* went to Sattahip and off-loaded the shipment for the master station.

The main delivery of Tight Reign materials arrived in Thailand on 14 June 1966 aboard SS *Mayo Lykes,* a C-3 freighter. The entire ship was contracted by Coast Guard and loaded with cargo for the LORAN chain. "Getting [construction] materials to the sites was the most difficult part," Sargent said. "It took a great deal of coordination." The entire rail line from Bangkok to Lampang had to be leased. Everything on the single-track rail line had to stop while construction materials were shipped north. To know the exact time the shipment would arrive, the detachment tracked the vessel's progress using the Automated Merchant Vessel Reporting System (AMVER). Ninety-four railroad cars were needed to deliver material to Lampang. A road had to be built to get heavy equipment from the rail siding at Hang Chat to the site.[23]

Mayo Lykes was off-loaded and under way from Bangkok in thirty-six hours. Her next stop was Sattahip, where she moored at a De Long pier while cargo for the master station was off-loaded and trucked to the site. The ship then sailed to Vietnam, where she anchored off Con Son Island. Construction equipment, materials, and supplies were transferred to two LSTs, which landed them over the beach. Sargent said, "I had trouble getting LSTs from the Navy. Without them, I was afraid I would get two stations and a monitor on air, but no third station. We pulled some strings and got LSTs."[24]

Additional Coast Guard engineers arrived with the main shipment; they had worked in the United States expediting contracts and assembling materials for the project. Lt. Cdr. William F. Roland, an electronics engineer, coordinated the shipment and installation of electronic equipment; Lt. Cdr. John R. Ehrmann, a civil engineer, was responsible for erection of towers at all sites. An additional civil engineer also was assigned to each station to assist the resident inspector: Lt. Cdr. Gilbert L. Aumon went to Con Son and Lt. William M. Devereaux was assigned to Lampang; Lieutenant Commander Gerken and Lt. (jg) Alger M. Pully worked at Sattahip.[25]

The first LORAN-C station crew members reported aboard in July 1966. Brock said, "Crews arrived in stages. We brought in engineers and electronics technicians first. We didn't want the commanding officers right away. I didn't want any unnecessary people out there. Conditions were difficult. They were living in tents." Chief radio electricians, assigned as station executive officers, directed the installation and testing of electronic and power-plant equipment. When two crewmen at Con Son contracted falciparum malaria, personnel were moved out of tents and into the galley-mess building. The recreation room became a dormitory.[26]

Theft was a problem at Thai stations, where tons of material were stockpiled during construction. At Lampang, Crowell said, "We had to get all that material there without having something stolen. That's where the doctor [Niyom] helped. He gave us a hand with security." When a generator was stolen, Crowell went to Niyom. He said, "I complained to him that he was supposed to be providing security for us." Two days later, the generator reappeared at the station. When Crowell asked Niyom what happened to the men who stole it, he was told, "It is better that you don't ask." After stations were completed, facilities were added for detachments of Royal Thai infantry to provide security. LORAN-C stations were technically Royal Thai military installations.[27]

One night at Lampang, thieves stole the antenna ground system by cutting heavy copper-wire radials, buried just below the surface at the base of the tower. Then the thieves pulled the 600-foot wires out of the ground. A few nights later, a Thai guard shot and killed a thief. The shooting and a new security fence brought the problem under control. Security at Con Son was not a problem—until there was a prison break. Three companies of South Vietnamese regional forces, 450 men, were stationed on the island to provide security at the prison.[28]

By the end of July 1966, stations were fully manned. Crews completed installations, tuned equipment, and inventoried and stowed spare parts. Lt. Albert E. Kaufmann, Jr., commanded the master station at Sattahip, which was manned by two officers and twenty-six enlisted men. Slave stations had complements of two officers and twenty-three enlisted men. Slave I at Lampang was commanded by Lt. Angus McKinnon and slave II, on Con Son Island, by Lt. Cdr. Ralph W. Judd. Lt. James L. Mueller commanded the monitor station at Udorn with a crew of two officers and fourteen enlisted men.[29]

Lampang was the first station to begin transmitting. It went on air on 8 August 1966, less than eight months from the time Operation Tight Reign was authorized. Sattahip was up and running a week later. On 2 September 1966, United States and South Vietnamese flags were hoisted at Con Son and that station was commissioned. After testing and calibration, the chain was declared fully operational on 28 October 1966. To support LORAN-C stations, the Coast Guard established a Southeast Asia section (SEASEC) in Bangkok with a captain in command. Unlike other Coast Guard units in Southeast Asia, SEASEC and LORAN-C stations were under operational control of commander Fourteenth Coast Guard District, headquartered in Hawaii. MACV and MACTHAI provided logistic support for the stations.[30]

The Coast Guard completed the Tight Reign LORAN-C chain, from start to on-air, in eight months. Planning and management were critical to success of the project. The project staff was intentionally kept to a minimum and authority, as well as responsibility, was delegated down to working levels. Brock said, "Officially we worked for headquarters, but actually we were completely autonomous. That's what made the program such a success. Nothing was done by committee and headquarters didn't interfere. Tom Sargent played an important role. He got us complete support and total autonomy. We couldn't have done it any other way." Sargent had the complete support of Coast Guard headquarters and, with his four stripes, the rank to get the project going; he knew how to overcome obstacles. Looking back at Tight

Coast Guard LORAN-C station on Con Son Island, paired with other stations in Vietnam and Thailand, provides accurate long-range electronic navigation for U.S. forces.

Reign, he said, "Everything worked out very well, but it wasn't because of me. It was Harold Brock and Ned Fontaine and all the rest of the people who did the work."[31]

When the chain went into operation, CINCPAC Adm. U. S. G. Sharp sent a message to the Coast Guard commandant:

> Announcement of operational status of the Southeast Asia LORAN-C chain is noted with admiration. Real estate acquisition and equipment procurement goals were met in record time. Please pass my personal congratulations to the officers and men of the U.S. Coast Guard who contributed to this outstanding accomplishment.[32]

Tan My LORAN Station

In 1968, the United States increased its efforts to disrupt the flow of troops and material coming south from North Vietnam. Defense Communications Planning Group worked on a secret project to establish an electronic detection system to monitor southward movements. Seismic, magnetic, and acoustic sensors were placed in bomb-shaped devices equipped with small radio transmitters. LORAN-C receivers, incorporated in devices, provided accurate locations of sensor units. Air Force aircraft dropped sensors along infiltration routes to detect enemy troop and supply movements.

Plans for the system were initially limited by lack of LORAN-C coverage along northern portions of the Ho Chi Minh trail. The Defense Department requested that the Coast Guard extend LORAN-C coverage and increase accuracy with the addition of a transmitting station north of Danang. Capt. William F. Roland was a lieutenant commander when he served as SEASEC executive officer. He said, "When I got back to Washington, one of the first things I did was start the ATLS [Air Transportable LORAN System] program. The program consisted of [ETC] Larry Sartin and me. We worked on putting transmitters in packages that could be delivered by air." Components for a LORAN-C station were installed in 8-foot-by-8-foot-by-24-foot trailers mounted on skids. Units were sized for delivery aboard cargo aircraft.[33]

In November 1968, a survey team selected a site six miles east-northeast of the old imperial capital of Hue, forty-two miles south of the DMZ. The location was a point of land on the south side of the mouth of the Perfume river. The site was a level area, only three feet above high water, built up from spoil material dredged from the river. It was surrounded on three sides by water or rice paddies. The little village of Tan My was two miles west of the site. A few small pines were the only trees in the area. The land was marshy and had to be built up with fill dirt. The location had the advantage of being close to a landing that could handle LSTs and was only 15 miles from Phu Bai airbase.

In late December 1968, the Defense Department officially requested that the Coast Guard establish a LORAN-C station at Tan My. The classified project, code named "Combat Aid," was to be completed as soon as possible. Coast Guard engineers developed a critical path method (CPM) network with a start date of 31 December 1968 and a completion date of 23 August 1969. The project consisted of three major systems: LORAN-C transmitting system, operations system, and personnel support system. A standard 625-foot antenna-tower was used. The operations system, prefabricated by Litton Communications Inc., was contained in eighteen ATLS units. Porta-Kamp Manufacturing Company Inc. provided thirty prefabricated shelters for personnel support. The cost of the project was $5.2 million.[34]

RMK–BRJ began site preparation and antenna foundation work on 12 March 1969. The site was built up with 100,000 cubic yards of fill, much of it required for the raised-perimeter road. Roland said, "To install the 625-foot antenna, they had to drive a number of steel pilings as far as 185 feet into the spoil." Trylon Inc. erected the tower in twelve days, "topping off" on 21 June 1969. Air Force C-141 Starlifters flew components for the station from McGuire AFB in New Jersey to Danang Airbase in June 1969. Barges transported components and tower sections to the site at Tan My. After the ground system was put in, the station's crew installed fiberglass-over-wood ATLS units under the direction of civil and electronics engineers. Four 250-kilowatt engine-generator sets, mounted on covered concrete slabs, provided power for the station. On-air testing began on 13 July 1969, and the station commenced full operation on 15 August 1969.[35]

Steel frame, aluminum-covered Porta-Kamp trailers provided berthing, galley, mess, recreation, and office spaces. Rear Adm. Ernest R. Riutta, USCG, was a lieutenant when he commanded Tan My LORAN-C station in 1971. He said, "With the Porta-Kamps, we were able to put them together side by side and knock out walls. We put four or five together and made a big galley. They were basically pre-fab buildings like you see on industrial sites." ATLS units usually were connected end to end. Porta-Kamps were white and ATLS units were beige; tops of all buildings were painted aluminum to reflect heat. Buildings with heavier equipment were mounted on cement slabs.[36]

A 10-foot-high berm, just outside of the 600-foot-radius ground system, encircled the entire complex. A perimeter road ran along the top of the wide berm. Inside, buildings were protected by five-foot-high concrete revetments. Sandbagged shelters also were available for personnel. Riutta said, "We kept trucks, everything, inside the berm. It was all on the ground system. Nothing was outside the berm." Beyond the berm and fighting bunkers, the station was protected by a 12-foot-high chain-link fence surrounded by rolls of concertina razor wire. Electronic sensors, motion detectors, trip flares, and claymore mines were implanted around the perimeter. Three manned-guard towers were equipped with .50-caliber machine guns and night scopes. A battery of four 81mm mortars inside the compound provided heavier firepower.[37]

The normal complement of the station was 73 men: 35 Coast Guardsmen; a 35-man Air Force air police security unit from the 366th Weapons System Security Detachment, Danang; and a 3-man Marine naval gunfire support liaison detachment. When threat to the station increased, Army platoons were brought in to provide additional protection. With reinforcements, the number of people living at the compound reached 160. The 101st Airborne Division was based at Camp Eagle, five miles from the station. Riutta said, "When the 101st stood down four months into my tour, we became the northernmost U.S.-manned installation in Vietnam. We kind of hung out there like a little thumb. We had to count on the Vietnamese to protect us. It wasn't a very comforting thought."[38]

In the spring of 1972, North Vietnam launched a coordinated attack on Quang Tri, thirty-two miles north of Tan My; 15,000 NVA troops, supported by tanks and artillery, converged on the city from three directions. The 4th ARVN Division, which stood between the North Vietnamese and the LORAN-C station, broke and fled. Quang Tri fell to the North Vietnamese on 1 May 1972. Riutta said, "I was worried about the vulnerability of the station. When Quang Tri fell, battles were so close we could see them from the station. We knew how intense the fighting was, because helicopters brought wounded into our pad. Our first-class corpsman was doing triage for U.S. casualties before sending them to Danang." The North Vietnamese swept south, cutting the station off from Danang. Riutta said, "We were literally in a pocket. The only way in and out was by air." Quang Tri was retaken by the South Vietnamese in September 1972.[39]

Air Force B-52 Strato Fortress bombers from Sattahip, Thailand, pounded the Ashau valley and the area around Hue and Quang Tri. They came in over the coast at Tan My, turned at the tower, and followed a LORAN-C line out over the valley on Arc Light strikes. When station personnel saw bombers coming, they manned the LORAN-C timers. Ground shock from nearby bombing caused timers to trip off the line. They had to be reset within a matter of seconds or aircraft would lose "lock" on the signal and have to abort missions. Riutta said, "You'd always know when an [F-4] Phantom raid was coming. The [Air Force] LORAN bird out of Nakhon Phanom or Udorn would come right over the tower at low altitude and head to sea. He'd pick up a stick of Phantoms and they'd come screaming in, right over the tower, and head for the Ashau to drop their bombs."[40]

Because of helicopter traffic in the vicinity of Hue, the 625-foot LORAN-C tower was marked with flashing red lights. It was the only thing lighted in the area and could be seen for miles. While the station and tower provided vital electronic navigation guidance for U.S. bombers and sensor location data, North Vietnamese or Viet Cong never attacked it. Roland said, "I think the NVA and VC didn't take out the tower because they used it. Nobody gave them credit for using the LORAN-C system, but I think they used the tower and lights for visual navigation in the hills behind Hue." Riutta said, "Our cover story was that we were Voice of America, which had several large towers not more than a mile away from us. Everywhere we went, we told anybody who would listen to us that we were transmitting the Voice of America. It was the best cover we could think of."[41]

13

Aids to Navigation

A large number of aids to navigation buoys are being installed throughout RVN [Republic of Vietnam] in connection with channel dredging and port improvement projects. Maintenance and servicing requirements for these aids to navigation are beyond the capability of RVN Directorate of Navigation. The U.S. Coast Guard has performed these functions on a temporary basis since December 1966. Recommend the U.S. Coast Guard be tasked with the interim responsibility for installation, maintenance, and servicing of U.S.-sponsored aids to navigation in RVN until the RVN Directorate of Navigation, with USAID [U.S. Agency for International Development] assistance, can assume the responsibility.

Commander in Chief, Pacific
27 August 1967

Tanker Moorings

On the morning of 28 March 1966, the 180-foot Coast Guard buoy tender USCGC *Planetree* (WLB 307) sprung out on her number-two line and backed away from her mooring under a blue sky. She turned and headed for the Pearl Harbor ship channel and the open sea beyond. The crew, in work uniforms, stood down from mooring stations and waved a final farewell to families on the pier at Coast Guard Base Sand Island. They were not told their ultimate destination, but from the urgency of their mission and the classification of message traffic, they assumed it was Vietnam. Morale was high.[1]

The 1,025-ton cutter had been loading for an aids-to-navigation trip to Samoa when her commanding officer, Lt. Cdr. Glenn F. Young, was

Crew on USCGC Planetree's *buoy deck prepare tanker mooring for setting off the coast of South Vietnam.*

unexpectedly called to Fourteenth Coast Guard District headquarters. He was told the Samoan trip was canceled and his ship had a new mission. He was to prepare for a three-month deployment to an undisclosed location and be ready to set tanker mooring assemblies.

Mooring assemblies consisted of three anchors, a sinker, and a mooring buoy, deployed in a crow's-foot array; *Planetree* had never set such an assembly. Young said, "The Coast Guard wasn't sure a [180-foot class] tender could do the job. We were approaching our [weight] limits." After the tender's buoy deck was strengthened and stoppers enlarged to accept larger chain made from 2-inch-diameter steel stock, a practice mooring was attempted in Pearl Harbor's West Loch. "It was an absolute disaster," Young said. "It just didn't work. That night, we went back and figured out a better way to do it."

The next day, on 26 March 1966, *Planetree* cleared the Pearl Harbor channel entrance and turned west. Beyond the reef, where water turned a deep blue, the ship lowered her small boat. While the boat put out marker buoys for anchor locations, the ship's deck force made final preparation for the second practice mooring. A 15,000-pound stockless anchor hung over the port side from bitts, just forward of the deckhouse. An 8,200-pound concrete sinker hung from a chain stopper forward on the buoy deck. Two 750-pound anchors hung off bitts on the fo'c'sle deck and a 9 1/2-foot-diameter mooring buoy rested on wooden chocks near the buoy port. The weight of the rig caused the ship to heel 30 degrees to port. Hundreds of feet of chain were faked down across the buoy deck and stopped-off.

Planetree slowed as she approached the first marker. The chief boatswain's mate in charge of the buoy deck signaled and a seaman swung a sledge hammer, tripping a chain stopper. The huge stockless anchor plunged into the water; chain rattled with a roar as it snaked over the gunwale. The single-screw ship crabbed toward the second marker, streaming chain behind her. When the 400 feet of chain fetched up, she stretched it taut and let go the block of concrete at the center of the array. Turning to port, *Planetree* paid out 400 feet of lighter 1 1/2-inch chain on a 45-degree angle and let go the first 750-pound anchor. Getting a 90-degree spread with the second 750-pound anchor was the most difficult part of the procedure. Chain hung up on coral heads and rocks when it was dragged across the bottom. After the second mooring, Young said, "It almost worked. It was close enough. I thought we could do it. We actually sailed without knowing whether we could really set a mooring or not."

Coast Guard Assistance

To support U.S. involvement in Southeast Asia, an increasing number of ships—military and merchant marine—sailed into Vietnamese waters and called at Vietnamese ports. When vessels began going into unmarked and poorly charted harbors and rivers throughout the country, the immediate need for aids to navigation (ATON) became obvious. Since the Coast Guard was responsible for ATON in the United States, the commander of the naval advisory group in Saigon looked to Squadron One for assistance in establishing new aids and resolving problems of missing, off-station, or extinguished Vietnamese aids. Capt. Robert J. LoForte, commander Coast Guard Squadron One (COMCOGARDRON ONE), met with Nguyen Van Dat, South Vietnam's director of navigation, on 26 April 1966 to discuss more aids to support U.S. operations; an estimated forty additional buoys and fixed aids were required. While the directorate only maintained thirty buoys—most without lights—and ten lighthouses, Director Dat said it would be impossible for his buoy tender to take on any additional work. Vietnam's aids-to-navigation organization, unlike the Coast Guard, was not a military service. It had a low priority for supplies and trained personnel were difficult to retain; employees were subject to the draft and their pay was meager—only a fourth of what U.S. contractors paid. The Vietnamese also had a different appreciation for the importance of accurate and reliable aids. It was not unusual for a Vietnamese aid, even a manned lighthouse, to be extinguished for weeks or even months at a time.[2]

The Vietnamese Navigation Directorate had only one buoy tender and one buoy depot. The directorate's 170-foot tender, *Cuu Long,* homeported in Saigon, was built in 1943. She had been a U.S. Army cargo vessel and had only minor structural and tackle modifications for working buoys. A large cargo hatch remained in the middle of her buoy deck; only five feet of space on either side of the raised coaming was available for working buoys. The configuration was inefficient at best and deadly dangerous at worst. Crew shortages frequently rendered the vessel incapable of getting under way. The small buoy depot at Phu An on the Saigon river maintained and repaired aids. The depot had equipment capable of fabricating nun and can buoys—if manpower and steel were available.

LoForte worked with USAID officials advising the directorate of navigation and got Dat to agree to provide limited cooperation in meeting U.S. needs for more aids. LoForte wrote in the squadron diary, "But everything we do will have to be cleared by Mr. Dat, a 'can't do' kind of guy." COGARDRON ONE's administration officer, Lt. Richard J. Clements, who was assigned to pull the ATON effort together, inventoried supplies and materials at Phu An depot and found buoys, chain, ballast balls, and swivels at a U.S. contractor's staging area. By 1 July 1966, twenty-three buoys—ten lighted, six nuns, and seven cans—had been located. LoForte said in the diary that the buoys "should be enough to handle [marking] Cat Lai, Chu Lai, and about two other ports. The problem now is to get the Vietnamese to prepare the buoys and set them. . . . We have to nursemaid them all the way. For the past week, Lieutenant Clements has done nothing but ATON. We can't spare this much effort."[3]

First Tender Deploys

The Coast Guard's first employment of a buoy tender in Vietnam occurred in April 1966 when *Planetree* deployed out of Honolulu to establish fuel mooring assemblies for tankers along the Vietnamese coast. Neither the Navy nor U.S. contractors had the capability to handle the size buoys, anchors, and sinkers involved. The tender sailed for the Philippines with orders to be ready to set twenty-five moorings. Mooring assemblies were shipped separately. *Planetree* departed Subic Bay naval station on 22 April 1966 and headed west. "It was one of those things," Young said, "where I couldn't open my orders until I was actually under way and enroute. When I opened the orders, they referred to plans I didn't hold, talked about frequencies I didn't have, and told me to go to Cat Lo, a port I couldn't find. We looked on the charts and Cat Lo wasn't there. We checked the Sailing Directions and there was no such place. We were under radio silence, so I turned around and went back to Subic. I pulled alongside a Navy destroyer and they gave us a chart with Cat Lo on it. Then we sailed for Vietnam."[4]

Planetree arrived off Vung Tau at first light on 26 April 1966. She signaled the old French tower at Cape Saint Jacques, but got no answer. The chart showed only eight feet of water in the channel to Cat Lo, not deep enough for the tender's 13-foot draft. Young approached the merchant ship anchorage off the cape and saw a Coast Guard 82-footer alongside a freighter. *Planetree* came abeam of the cutter and hailed her. Young said, "A man came out of the pilothouse, looked up, and said, 'What the hell are you doing out here?' I told him, 'I'm lost.' Which I was." The cutter gave *Planetree* a corrected chart showing a deeper channel and led her to the base at Cat Lo. The next day the tender sailed for Phan Rang to begin setting mooring buoys.[5]

When *Planetree* arrived offshore at Phan Rang, she was still unable to contact anyone ashore by radio. She obtained PRC-25 VHF-FM field radios at Cat Lo, but did not know the frequencies used at Phan Rang; Young sent a boat into the beach to make contact. When the boat could not get through the surf, the boat officer stripped to his shorts, dove over the side, and swam through the breakers to the beach. As

Young watched through binoculars, five armed men rushed out of the trees and dragged the officer into the woods. Fortunately, he quickly reappeared with the U.S. troopers who captured him and contact was made.

Planetree set twenty-one buoys for tanker moorings at Phan Rang, Nha Trang, Qui Nhon, Chu Lai, and Danang. An additional mooring buoy was set off the LST ramp at Chu Lai. The work load and need to stand additional watches in the combat zone quickly fatigued the cutter's small crew. At night, *Planetree* ran at darkened ship. When the crew could not find "Dog Zebra" covers for portholes, they simply painted the glass black. *Planetree* set her final mooring buoys at Danang on 8 June 1966 and departed, having demonstrated the Coast Guard's capability to deploy a large buoy tender for operations in Vietnam.[6]

Advisors

Discussions with USAID officials in November 1966 resulted in agreement that a three-man Coast Guard ATON detail—one officer and two enlisted men—was needed to assist and advise the Vietnamese in establishing new aids at Chu Lai, Qui Nhon, Danang, and Cam Rahn Bay. COMCOGARDRON ONE requested that ATON personnel be assigned temporarily to Vietnam for three months, beginning in mid-December 1966. Lt. Cdr. Everett G. Walters and two enlisted ATON specialists arrived on 18 December 1966 to work with USAID. LoForte described Walters' mission in the diary as, "He will act as an advisor, cajoler to GVN [Government of Vietnam] ATON people in an effort to get them to be responsive to U.S. Forces aids to navigation requirements. He is not going to push anyone around. He is going to be the most subtle and diplomatic pressurer the Coast Guard has ever put on the job. Although we must see the work gets done, we must develop the capability, enthusiasm, and interest of the GVN people for doing for themselves. This is the essence of U.S. involvement in RVN."[7]

Walters and his two first-class petty officers—a boatswain's mate and an electrician's mate—met with USAID advisors to the directorate of navigation. After discussing the situation with USAID's ports and waterways director, a civil engineer from Indiana, Walters said, "He is interested, but has no knowledge of aids to navigation. As a matter of fact, I am coming to the conclusion that no one in Vietnam other than the Coast Guard knows anything about ATON." When Walters

South Vietnamese buoy tender, Cuu Long, *with buoy on deck.*

inspected *Cuu Long,* he said, "I have never seen a more dangerous buoy-working area. If she *[Cuu Long]* is to work buoys extensively, the hatch coaming will have to go and a flush hatch cover installed." Walters made arrangements with the Navy at Saigon shipyard to repair the ship's radar, fathometer, and gyro compass.[8]

A week after its arrival, the detail flew to Danang and Chu Lai to discuss aids to navigation needs with local commanders. When word that Coast Guard advisors were working with the Vietnamese Navigation Directorate spread, U.S. commanders felt they had a responsive point of contact for ATON problems; requests for more and better aids came pouring in. The Coast Guard detail was caught between commanders who had legitimate needs and a Vietnamese directorate that was unwilling or unable to provide services. When *Cuu Long* sailed to mark the Bassac (Hau Giang) river south of Saigon, she took forty-two days to set eight buoys.[9]

Walters' first challenge was to get *Cuu Long* to mark the channel into Chu Lai for the Navy. The ATON detail located required buoys and hardware at Phu An depot, got them repaired and painted by

Coast Guard aids to navigation detail uses Navy LCM-8 to set buoy to mark channel at Chu Lai, 1966.

depot workers, and prepared plans for marking the channel. The avail-ability of *Cuu Long* remained questionable. With Tet holidays approach-ing, it was uncertain whether the ship's crew would leave their home port. Buoys eventually were shipped to Chu Lai on a cargo vessel and set, as well as possible, using a jury-rigged Navy LCM. *Planetree* returned to Vietnam on 11 March 1967 to provide needed services for expanding port operations. She installed channel buoys at Danang and corrected the position of buoys at Chu Lai.[10]

Direct Involvement

On 6 March 1967, COMNAVFORV designated Capt. William N. Banks, COMCOGARDACTV, as his aids to navigation advisor, and tasked Banks with coordinating ATON efforts among all agencies. Banks headed a working group that completed an aids to navigation study on 31 March 1967. It determined that Vietnamese capability, even with USAID input, was inadequate to meet navigation needs. It concluded that direct U.S. aids to navigation assistance was required to support military operations and recommended full-time use of a Coast Guard 180-foot WLB (buoy tender, seagoing) for Vietnam. USAID was to continue working to upgrade navigation directorate capabilities with an objective of having South Vietnam take over the mission by January 1969.[11]

Commander Fourteenth Coast Guard District in Hawaii began assigning tenders to 30-day Vietnam deployments in July 1967. *Ironwood* (WLB 297) was the first buoy tender to deploy under the program. She sailed from her home port of Agana, Guam, arriving in Vietnamese waters on 5 July 1967; her deck was loaded with buoys for additional channel projects. *Ironwood* first sailed to the Bassac river to service Vietnamese buoys. She replaced unlit larger buoys with cans and nuns, and repositioned buoys at the mouth of the Bassac, an important navigable waterway into the interior, leading to the cities of Can Tho and Long Xuyen. It also was in hostile territory; *Ironwood's* crew manned machine guns and wore flak jackets while working topside. The Bassac river project, including running time, took *Ironwood* four days, compared to *Cuu Long's* forty-two days. Relieved buoys from Bassac river were repaired, fitted with lanterns and batteries, charged, and used to mark a channel to the De Long pier at Vung Tau.[12]

After *Ironwood* serviced aids at Danang, she went north to the Cua Viet river, five miles below the DMZ to mark a newly dredged channel. The Army Corps of Engineers' dredge working on the project had come under enemy fire on 9 May 1967. Hit twice, the dredge managed to beach herself. COGARDACTV reported on *Ironwood's* work in the river, saying:

> Cua Viet was her final project. She constructed a shore light on a wrecked and beached tug which the VC used as a forward observation post during mortar attacks on the Marines. The new shore light makes everybody happy. The Navy will use it as a navigational aid, the Marines will use it as a reference point for their harassing fire, and the VC will probably use it as an OP in the belief the Marines won't blow it up.[13]

ATON Coordinator

The Joint Chiefs of Staff authorized an increase in COGARDACTV staff for ATON, adding an officer and three enlisted men. Lt. Cdr.

David H. Freeborn reported as aids to navigation coordinator on 28 September 1967. His mission was "advising COMNAVFORV with regard to ATON matters which are of concern to the Navy in RVN and with obtaining coordination in the field with other commands and agencies." While efforts to prepare the Vietnamese to participate more fully in setting and maintaining aids continued, U.S. ATON focus shifted from advising to implementing.[14]

Freeborn said, "By the time I got there, it was very clear that it [ATON] was going to be done by ourselves." He had one man assigned to him, a first-class electrician's mate named Candido Rosado. Freeborn said, "Rosado was the perfect man for the job. We only had a 12-volt system, so we didn't really require an EM1. But Rosado was the kind of petty officer who could, and was willing to, do everything. He fixed vehicles, did carpentry, whatever." The detail worked independently and had a broad mandate to improve aids to navigation in Vietnam in support of U.S. operations.

Freeborn's first task was to find out where and what kinds of ATON systems were required. "To do this," he said, "I'd find out where a harbor project was under way and who was in charge. We'd get on a plane and fly there. I'd say, 'I understand you're building a harbor. What are you doing about aids to navigation?' After meeting with contractors and a couple of days of dialogue, we'd pretty well understand the project and would come up with a plan for aids." The detail also responded to requests from Army and Navy field commanders who called, asking for help.[15]

The detail started from scratch, establishing initial aids in many areas. They filled urgent needs first, setting up markers in harbors. Most aids were unlighted because in the beginning vessels did not transit at night. Initially, the ATON detail worked primarily with the Navy and Marines in I Corps. Freeborn said:

Once we determined needs, we told people how to get aids established or we did it for them. We used tugs or any craft in the harbor. People were more than willing to cooperate because we were helping them. We didn't use sextant angles to set them [buoys]. There weren't a whole lot of harbor charts with accurate landmarks. It wasn't very scientific. We took soundings, found the edge of the channel, and marked it. We'd set up ranges[16] where they were dredging, like Qui Nhon, Tan My, and Cua Viet. We'd tell the Navy, "The only way you're going to get traffic in and out of here is to establish ranges. Somebody with surveying skills is going to have to put a marker at that point and that point." We'd already determined the location, size, and vertical separation. They [the U.S. Navy] would tell the contractors to go put up markers. . . . Anything we did was an improvement over what was there, because there was nothing.[17]

"At first," Freeborn said, "we got materials by begging and bumming. Commanders at ports were grateful for our help and anxious to provide what we needed to improve navigation." Available material, including a supply of old submarine net floats at Cam Rahn Bay, were painted and used for channel buoys. The Fourteenth Coast Guard District started a supply pipeline to get ATON materials to the detail. Without storage facilities or a shop in Saigon, Freeborn relied on Coast Guard field units—WPB divisions and explosive loading detachments—to store supplies that arrived by ship and aircraft. Vehicle and vessel support for ATON projects was provided by the commands being assisted. Demands for ATON planning continued to increase as port projects expanded. On 25 July 1968, the JCS assigned Coast Guard "the task of installing and maintaining maritime aids to navigation in the Republic of Vietnam, subject to reimbursement by Army and Navy as appropriate." A joint Army–Navy–Coast Guard agreement was prepared, defining costs to be reimbursed. Commands used military interdepartmental purchase requests (MIPRs) to transfer funds to pay for buoys, ranges and equipment.[18]

The Coast Guard also used buoy tenders for larger projects, such as setting moorings, offshore buoys, and large channel markers. The ATON detail coordinated tender work during deployments. *Basswood* deployed to Vietnam on 26 October 1967 and established seasonal mooring south of Phu Quoc Island for Market Time support ships. She then worked aids at Vung Tau, Cam Rahn Bay, Qui Nhon, and Danang. Monsoon weather prevented her from servicing aids at Bassac river, Hue (Tan My), and Cua Viet; she departed Vietnam on 27 November 1967. The Coast Guard decided in November 1967 to assign a dedicated 180-foot buoy tender for work in Vietnam. USCGC *Blackhaw* (WLB 390) was given the mission and transferred from Honolulu to Sangley Point, Philippines, to be closer to her operating area. Additional weapons were mounted on *Blackhaw* and her crew was increased to seven officers and sixty-three enlisted men. On 17 March 1968, she arrived on her first of fifteen deployments in Vietnam. By then, 70 U.S.-established aids required tending along the Vietnamese coast. During 30-day deployments, *Blackhaw*'s crew established, repositioned, and maintained buoys, built fixed aids and shore structures, and resupplied lighthouses.[19]

Lt. Eugene E. O'Donnell reported to Vietnam as ATON coordinator in August 1968. He said, "We were taking care of all the aids, including Vietnamese aids. They [the Vietnamese] did nothing. *Cuu Long* never sailed. They had one lighthouse that operated periodically." While O'Donnell was there, the detail built a small ATON storage facility at Cam Rahn Bay. ATON supplies were shipped from the United States to *Blackhaw* in the Philippines for direct delivery to the detail in-country, avoiding the supply system in Vietnam. When *Blackhaw* completed a deployment, she left unused ATON materials at the storage facility before departing. During tender deployments, the detail usually traveled with the ship. O'Donnell said, "We knew the ports, what had been done and what needed to be done. . . . And besides, it was great chow and we got to sea. It was kind of an R&R."[20]

To take care of outages, detail personnel were issued priority 2 travel orders. O'Donnell said, "Most of the time we were able to get on the first available plane heading in whatever direction we were going. We took whatever was available and hopped around until we got to our destination." O'Donnell traveled twenty days a month, going from port to port, inspecting and checking on what needed to be done. On one trip to Qui Nhon, he was in the office of the Army port commander when the colonel received a call from the general commanding the area. O'Donnell said:

> He got burned by the general for not moving more cargo through his port. I told him, "Why don't you try running operations twenty-four hours a day." He said, "I can't do that. I can't get the ships in after dark." I said, "You can if I give you three sets of lighted ranges and some lighted buoys to mark the channel." Qui Nhon was a tough channel with some big turns. The colonel said, "If it will move more cargo for me, do it and I'll fund it." I put in three sets of range lights, moved two lighted buoys, and added another lighted buoy. All his pilots had to do was follow the "yellow brick road." They started moving ammo twenty-four hours a day.[21]

One afternoon in January 1969, O'Donnell got a cryptic call from a Navy officer with MACV special projects, who said, "You've got batteries, right? Do they last a long time?" O'Donnell said, "Hell, they light buoys. They'll stay lit for years." He asked O'Donnell to come to Tan Son Nhut to talk about batteries. When O'Donnell got there, he was briefed about a classified project, code-named "Duffel Bag." The Army was experimenting with deployed sensors. Radio receivers mounted on large tethered barrage balloons picked up signals from the sensors. When a sensor detected activity, its transmission to the balloon was relayed down the tether to a switchboard where it was localized. If the activity was evaluated as hostile, artillery or mortar fire was called in. After successful daylight trials, the system was used at night. Tethered balloons, however, were a hazard to helicopter operations and had to be lighted. The Army's problem was how to keep balloons lit. They already had used all the single-cell lifejacket survival lights the Navy could spare.[22]

O'Donnell and BMC Denny J. Thomas, senior enlisted man on the detail, went to the Army facility near the Cambodian border and looked at the situation; they thought they could help. O'Donnell said, "We got a 12AN10 battery and a whole bunch of half-amp buoy lights. We wired the lights, taped them to the balloon, and ran a wire down [the tether] to the battery. It worked great. Thomas stayed out at the camp a couple nights to make sure there were no problems." When an Army general visited the camp, he was impressed with the arrangement, which included a daylight sensor that turned lights off automatically during the day. He was distressed, however, that his Army R&D people had not been able to come up with a solution. NAVFORV requested additional Coast Guard technical assistance and lighting equipment for similar projects along the Cambodian border in areas called Parrot's Beak and Angel's Wing.[23]

On a visit to Cam Rahn Bay, O'Donnell went with Division 12's commander to Coastal Surveillance Force headquarters, where they called on Capt. Roy F. Hoffman, USN, commander of Market Time (Task Force 115). O'Donnell said, "When we went into his office, he was upset about something. He didn't recognize me and asked, 'Who are you?' I told him I was the Coast Guard buoy guy and he said, 'I wish to hell you could put a string of damned buoys across the DMZ.'" The Navy had had a recent rash of supply vessels missing the Cua Viet river and straying across the DMZ into North Vietnamese waters. O'Donnell said, "We can do that." On 4 March 1969, *Blackhaw* set a string of four lighted buoys out to eight miles offshore, below the DMZ, to warn coastal vessels they were approaching the line.[24]

Aids to the War Effort

An effective system of aids to navigation was important to the war effort. Ports and waterways were the principal means of delivering support for U.S. operations. Buoys and ranges facilitated the movement of troops and logistic support into ports all along the coast; lighted aids enabled traffic to flow both day and night. In I Corps, practically all supplies moved north from Danang by water. Field commanders, recognizing the importance of ATON in ensuring a continuous flow of material, requested more and better aids. In March 1969, the commander at Cua Viet river requested that all unlighted aids be changed to lighted. When aids were damaged or extinguished, commanders were anxious to get outages corrected immediately. They were more than willing to provide material and manpower to make repairs, but they wanted Coast Guard supervision to see that systems were operating and properly positioned.[25]

Aids in Vietnam had four threats: weather, enemy action, collision, and theft. In September 1968, Typhoon Bessie caused heavy damage to buoys and ranges at the Cua Viet river, Tan My, and Vung Tau. A year later, Typhoon Dora hit, knocking out aids all along the coast. In the Cua Viet river, only two of eleven buoys remained on-station. Without buoys and ranges to guide vessels into port, resupply efforts were drastically reduced. The enemy quickly realized the importance of navigation markers to resupply efforts, and sank buoys, destroyed ranges, and shot out lights. O'Donnell said, "Charlie [the Viet Cong] knew what aids were and he knew what they were used for. We lost as many buoys to gunfire as we did to storms. They were old buoys, not filled with foam. After they were hit [by gunfire], they would bounce up and down, eventually taking on enough water to sink." Vessels, particularly tugs and barges, operating in unfamiliar waters, under difficult circumstances, routinely collided with buoys, dragging them off station or sinking them. Channel range markers, structures built on shore, were subject to theft and destruction. It was extremely difficult to prevent batteries and lamps from being stolen from lighted ranges located in remote and sometimes hostile areas. Theft was a serious problem at Tan My, near Hue, where ranges were critical for the movement of shipping.[26]

◆   ◆   ◆

*Aids to navigation detail moves Tan My harbor entrance range
light, located in a Vietnamese cemetery, to mark the shifting
channel, 1970.*

During her first deployment in 1971, *Blackhaw* was tasked with a
special operation to establish a naval gunfire support buoy in the Gulf
of Thailand off the west coast of Ca Mau peninsula, where waters
were shallow and the coast was straight and flat. The shoreline, low
with few trees and no distinctive features, provided a poor radar image.
Navigating—particularly at night—was extremely difficult. A radar-
reflecting buoy was needed to enable naval gunfire support ships to
take position quickly to provide gunfire support for operations ashore.
To position the buoy accurately, *Blackhaw* sent a four-man party onto
the VC-controlled coast. The team surreptitiously set up a radar
reflector so the tender could obtain ranges. After the tender set the
buoy on 27 February 1971 and reconfirmed its position, *Blackhaw*
sailed south to the southernmost island in Vietnam—Paulo Obi. There
the crew packed 35-pound batteries 1,100 feet up a mountain to a light

on top. Next, she went to Bo De river on the eastern tip of the Ca Mau peninsula. The entrance to the river, which led to the Navy's seafloat base at Nam Can, was in an unsecured area. Under cover of the ship's .50-caliber machine guns, the crew repaired the leading light at the mouth of the river.[27]

Blackhaw completed her final Vietnam deployment on 17 May 1971. By then, the Coast Guard was maintaining 175 aids in several waterways and eleven ports. *Blackhaw*'s last mission before departing Vietnam was to tend aids at the port of Qui Nhon. Her message, after completing work in the port, was typical of her missions:

- Found three navaids extinguished due gunfire, two aids extinguished due collision, one aid extinguished due cut battery wires.
- Channel entrance—LB5 relighted and reset on charted position.
- Ammo Channel—LB1, LB3 relighted. Buoy 4 reset on charted position.
- Ammo Wharf Channel—LB1 relighted.
- Bai Tao Lt. (LLNR 23340) relighted.
- Phouc Moi Lt. (LLNR 23330) relighted.
- Entrance range front and rear relighted.
- All Navaids left watching properly.[28]

After her final deployment, *Blackhaw*'s home port was changed to San Francisco. *Basswood,* deploying from Guam, was assigned to take over maintenance of aids in Vietnam as an additional mission. During deployments, *Basswood* made preparations for discontinuing Coast Guard support for ATON. She replaced buoys with shore structures, more easily maintained by Vietnam's Navigation Directorate. Directorate personnel sailed with *Basswood* during deployments for instruction and indoctrination in preparation for U.S. withdrawal.

14

Patrol Boats to the Vietnamese

The disestablishment of COGARDRON [Coast Guard Squadron] ONE upon turnover of the final Wpbs to the Republic of Vietnam marks a significant step in Vietnamization. The Coast Guard performance in Vietnam operations has been characterized by the highest professionalism, traditional with the Coast Guard, and has been recognized by every Navy man, both U.S. and Vietnamese, who have had occasion to work with and receive support from WPBs. The record and reputation achieved by COGARDRON ONE have earned our highest respect.

Adm. John J. Hyland, USN, Commander, Pacific Fleet
25 August 1970

Final Mission

With an orange sun climbing into a cloudless sky, USCGC *Point Marone* (WPB 82331) and USCGC *Point Cypress* (WPB 82326) entered the Co Chien river on 4 August 1970. Ten miles up the muddy river, the cutters moored at a South Vietnamese coastal group base. At 0800, 100 Kit Carson Scouts from Kien Hoa province gathered up their gear and climbed aboard the cutters. The scouts, former Viet Cong guerrillas, were accompanied by Vietnamese Army (ARVN) advisors. The WPBs got under way with fifty scouts aboard each. Winds were slight and waters calm.[1]

Point Marone and *Point Cypress* were engaged in COGARDRON ONE's last mission. Twenty-four of the twenty-six 82-foot cutters

225

deployed to Southeast Asia were sailing under South Vietnamese flags. The last two were scheduled for turnover in eleven days. The cutters kicked up bow wakes when they increased speed and headed southeast toward the river mouth; they turned right, crossed the four-mile-wide river entrance to the south shore, and then slowed. Two miles from the coast, they turned into a canal at 0900; Rach Khau Rau ran southwest from the river into Thanh Phu secret zone. *Point Cypress* launched her 14-foot skimmer and the cutters followed the boat up the waterway. The small force was on a joint U.S.–South Vietnamese Blue Shark raider operation into Viet Cong-controlled territory. Blue Shark was a follow-on to SEA LORDS, which ended 8 May 1970.

The cutters, with full 13-man VNN replacement crews aboard, were in the final phase of turnover. Five Coast Guardsmen, including commanding officers, were still aboard each WPB. Lt. (jg) Joseph F. Angelico, who commanded *Point Marone*, said, "We sailed southwest for two miles to where the canal divided. Then we headed up the west branch where troops would make sweeps along the canal. We nosed onto the bank and they [the Vietnamese troops] went over the bow into the tall grass. The land was flat and dry. If there had been any trees, they were all gone. The area was a free-fire zone."

Troops worked the northern side of the waterway, swinging out in a large semicircle and coming back to the canal a mile further up, where the cutters picked them up and moved to the next location. The canal gradually narrowed from 50 yards wide down to 25 yards wide. Angelico said, "When we waited for the troops we were at modified GQ [general quarters]. The piggyback [combination .50-caliber machine gun and 81mm mortar mount] on the bow was manned along with one .50 [caliber machine gun] on each side." At 1530, while waiting for the scouts to come back from their fourth foray, Lt. (jg) Harry Godfrey, CO of *Point Cypress*, and Angelico decided to make it their last sweep. They did not want to be in the canal after dark. "*Cypress* picked up her skimmer," Angelico said, "and we turned around. I had to put my bow up on the bank, big time, to have enough room to get her around." The cutters were five miles into the narrow canal.

After the WPBs picked up returning scouts, they went to full GQ. On *Point Marone*, the Coast Guard chief engineman manned the bow gun. A VNN second-class engineman (EN2) was on the starboard quarter .50-caliber machine gun and the Coast Guard EN2 manned the one on the port quarter. The Coast Guard cook was on top of the pilothouse with an M60 machine gun and VNN petty officers manned port and starboard waist .50-caliber machine guns. With all guns manned and ready, cutters headed down the canal; *Point Marone* was in the lead. Scouts were above deck, sitting or lying down, resting after making sweeps in the heat of the day. Angelico said, "It was hard to tell if they [the scouts] found anything. There were no U.S. advisors with them. They didn't bring back any prisoners and we didn't hear any shooting."

Marone made it 600 yards down the canal before the afternoon calm was shattered by a tremendous blast. "All I remember is a great big explosion," Angelico said. "It seemed like the whole canal blew up around us." VC guerrillas set off a command-detonated mine at the edge of the narrow canal as the cutter passed. Angelico, who had the con on the bridge, was at the wheel, sitting in the helmsman's chair; The VNN prospective commanding officer (PCO) was with him. The blast went off abeam of the starboard quarter, heaving the cutter to port. The force of the explosion was transmitted along the bottom of the canal and erupted on the port side of the cutter, sending up a plume of water and mud. Concussion on the port side rocked the boat back to starboard, smashing glass out of all bridge windows; glass flew from port to starboard. Angelico said, "It was like we were hit from two directions at the same time. I was thrown to port and then to starboard."

The VNN chief engineman was standing next to the starboard quarter machine-gun mount when the mine went off. His arm was blown off and he was nearly cut in half by shrapnel. The VNN EN2 on the mount was blown back across the deck; the breastplate of the sound-powered phone he was wearing was imbedded in his chest. Both men died instantly. Ten Kit Carson Scouts were wounded; one was hit in the chest with shrapnel. All five Coast Guardsmen were wounded. The EN2 manning the port gun was the most serious; he was hit in the back and legs with shrapnel. The ENC on the bow was struck in the neck by shrapnel and Angelico was hit in the face by flying glass.

Angelico said, "The engines were still running and we had comms. I called *Cypress* and said, 'We're getting the hell out of here.' We didn't take any small-arms fire after the explosion, but I didn't know if there were more mines. I put the throttles down as far as I could push them. We went out of there with all guns blasting on both sides. *Cypress* was right behind us."

Point Grace *and a Navy Swift boat come into the Co Chien river after an incursion into a canal in the Than Phu secret zone.*

Marone ran for ten minutes at maximum speed to clear the area and then slowed to treat casualties and check for damage. She was taking on water through three shrapnel holes in the starboard side of the hull at the waterline. Demolition experts with the explosive ordnance disposal team at Cat Lo determined, from the thickness of shrapnel found in the engineroom, that the mine probably was made from a 5-inch projectile. If the VC had been successful in blowing a hole in the bottom of *Marone,* both cutters would have been trapped in enemy-controlled territory after dark.

The cutters rendezvoused with a medevac helicopter at a clearing where the branch joined the main canal. The scout with the chest wound and the Coast Guard EN2 were evacuated; casualties with lesser wounds were treated aboard the cutter. Several scouts had ruptured or damaged eardrums from the explosion, but Coast Guardsmen who were wearing sound-powered phones did not suffer ear damage.

The blast knocked the watertight door between the mess deck and the forward berthing area off its hinges; lifeline stanchions on the starboard side of the main deck were folded back by the blast. The geyser of water that erupted dumped mud all over the boat; mud was three inches thick on the deck behind the bridge.

Point Cypress escorted *Point Marone* to the base at Cat Lo, concluding Coast Guard Squadron One's Vietnam operations.

Vietnamization

By the close of 1968, support for continuing the war in Vietnam was fading rapidly in the United States. Antiwar sentiment and demonstrations were increasing, and the president and Congress were under pressure to bring American troops home. The Pentagon was ordered to develop plans for turning fighting over to the South Vietnamese and withdrawing forces. In a 2 November 1968 meeting in Saigon, Vice Adm. Elmo R. Zumwalt, Jr., COMNAVFORV, presented a plan to Gen. Creighton W. Abrams, COMUSMACV, for turning over all Navy resources to the South Vietnam Navy by 30 June 1970.

The plan, known as Accelerated Turnover to Vietnamese (ACTOV), called for transfer of operational units first, then support facilities, and, finally, withdrawal of naval advisors. The Navy's plan was based on a gradual replacement of crews; Vietnamese would phase aboard U.S. units and receive on-the-job training from American counterparts. As they completed training, Americans would be transferred ashore. Once an entire crew changed-out, the vessel would became a VNN unit.

Capt. Ralph W. Niesz relieved Capt. John M. Austin as COMCO-GARDACTV on 19 December 1968. Niesz said, "When I got there, there were no specific plans for withdrawing. There was discussion here and there, but it was long-range. It wasn't a big deal until an order came down from General Abrams saying that anything turned over to the Vietnamese would have to be in first-class condition and Vietnamese taking over would have to be properly trained. That's when I decided to come up with a program for turning over WBPs."

Niesz came to Vietnam from the Naval War College at Newport, R.I., where he served as the Coast Guard liaison officer. He was thoroughly familiar with the Navy planning process and sensitive to issues involved in dealing with the South Vietnamese; he had taken advanced courses in intercultural relations while at the war college. "I tasked myself with working up a suitable program," he said, "And briefing Admiral Zumwalt and Commodore Chon [Rear Adm. Tran Van Chon, VNN CNO]. I was familiar with preparing Navy OPLANs [operations plans]."[2]

On 14 January 1969, Niesz presented the Coast Guard plan to COMNAVFORV. The program was similar to the Navy's approach, featuring on-the-job training and gradual replacement of crews. It had an important difference, however—it called for top-down replacement. The Navy plan brought junior Vietnamese enlisted men aboard vessels for training first and worked up through the chain of command with commanding officers reporting aboard last. The Coast Guard plan for WPBs brought prospective Vietnamese commanding officers aboard first and then the next senior man on down the line; nonrated men came aboard last. The top-down approach provided VNN prospective commanding officers the most training and greatest familiarity with cutters. Officers and senior petty officers had an opportunity to observe proper procedures while participating with experienced Coast Guard crews. Zumwalt was enthusiastic about Niesz's plan and ordered it implemented immediately. He directed that cutter turnover should remain under Coast Guard cognizance. On 18 January 1969, Niesz briefed Commodore Chon and his staff about the Coast Guard's turnover plan.[3]

Niesz said top-down and English-speaking were the keys to the plan. He said, "I knew it had to be top-down because of the culture. It was imperative that seniors be the most knowledgeable. They would not be able to accept instruction from their juniors. They would lose face if they appeared to know less. I was very firm on the top-down." When he briefed Zumwalt and Chon, Niesz said, "They were 100 percent behind the program. They couldn't have been more enthusiastic. I dealt directly with them and seldom with their staffs."[4]

The plan consisted of two programs: SCATTOR (Small Craft Assets, Training, and Turnover of Resources) and VECTOR (Vietnamese Engineering Capability, Training of Ratings). SCATTOR trained replacement crews for cutters and VECTOR trained and prepared a Vietnamese repair force to maintain them. Vietnamese engineers assigned to patrol boats first received maintenance and repair training at the VECTOR facility before reporting aboard cutters. More productive initial engineering training was accomplished in the controlled environment of the shore facility rather than aboard an underway cutter, engaged in operations.

Division 13's commander at Cat Lo, Lt. Cdr. Joseph F. Smith, volunteered to conduct the pilot turnover program at his division. He encouraged turnover of 82-footers to Vietnam because he did not agree with the changing mission for WPBs—going from coastal surveillance operations to raids in narrow, inland waterways. Cutters, displacing 80 tons and drawing 6½ feet of water, were too large, too slow, and too thin-skinned to operate in confined waters. Stability and endurance, features that made them ideal coastal patrol vessels, limited their capability in the inshore environment.[5]

First Turnovers

USCGC *Point Garnet* (WPB 82310) and USCGC *Point League* (WPB 82304) were selected for the 15-week pilot turnover program. Until turnover began, cutter crews had limited experience working with Vietnamese Navy personnel. A single Vietnamese liaison petty officer had been assigned to patrolling cutters. Language and cultural differences were important factors, affecting the success of turnovers. Rear Adm. Roger T. Rufe was a Lt. (jg) when he commanded *Point Garnet* in 1969. He said, "We got no special training [for turnover]. They just told us what they had in mind. . . . I worked hard with my crew before the Vietnamese got there to prepare them. I told them, 'These aren't the most squared-away sailors, but we're going to have to work with what we got. And we're going to have to be sensitive to their differences.'" On 3 February 1969, VNN lieutenants reported aboard the two cutters at Cat Lo. Prospective commanding officers immediately relieved cutter executive officers and assumed their duties; relieved Coast Guard officers were transferred to staff assignments ashore. WPBs had a total of thirteen bunks for a crew of eleven; Vietnamese replacements used spare bunks, reporting aboard two at a time. As they were trained, two Coast Guardsmen came ashore and two more Vietnamese reported aboard.[6]

The small size of cutter crews made effective training essential for continued operations. During turnover, WPBs continued to serve as regular components of Market Time operations, boarding and inspecting fishing vessels, providing gunfire support, and conducting SEA

LORDS operations. Everyone aboard had to be able to do his job—manning stations, working on equipment, and standing watches. Joint communications were arranged with VNN and USN coastal surveillance centers so turnover cutters could communicate on both Vietnamese and U.S. radio circuits.

Training progressed rapidly with pilot WPBs achieving full VNN crews—only the Coast Guard commanding officers remained aboard—by 15 April 1969. In evaluating his Vietnamese crew, Rufe said, "Their capabilities were mixed. Lieutenant Sang was articulate and spoke fluent English. He was well-educated and from an upper-class family. He was a reasonably competent seaman and seemed to know what he was doing. Some senior petty officers were good, too. But there were some who weren't so good." Before cutters were turned over, joint operational readiness inspections (ORIs) were conducted to determine if VNN crews were ready to operate independently. Lt. Cdr. Duane P. Gatto, commander, Coast Guard Division 13, reported in his monthly summary, "A joint USCG, USN, and VNN team evaluated each boat as it performed underway general quarters, fire, collision, navigation, abandon ship, and damage-control drills. These drills were conducted entirely by the Vietnamese crew. *Point Garnet* was given an overall evaluation of 'good' while *Point League* was given an overall evaluation of 'very good'. . . . The performance in the ORIs was a concrete demonstration that the Vietnamese Navy has the ability and expertise to properly operate WPBs."[7]

Ceremony

Guests began arriving at the Vietnamese naval base in Saigon at 1430 on 16 May 1969. They took seats on a four-tiered platform facing *Point Garnet* and *Point League;* cutters were moored to a float next to the concrete pier. A canopy of olive drab parachute material covered the seating area. Potted plants in an assortment of containers were spaced along the front of the seating and next to the lectern, which stood on the small speakers' platform. Coast Guardsmen stood at cutter rails at parade rest. Vietnamese Navy crews were mustered on the pier.[8]

Crews, wearing white uniforms, came to attention when Commodore Chon, Admiral Zumwalt, and Captain Niesz arrived at 1500.

The sky was overcast and a stiff breeze was blowing. The ceremony began with Vietnamese training medals being presented to six Division 13 Coast Guardsmen. Niesz made remarks, followed by Chon, and transfer documents were signed. At 1530, the U.S. National Anthem was played and U.S. flags were lowered. Coast Guard crews took the flags and filed down gangways. VNN crews proceeded across the float and onto patrol boats. The Vietnamese National Anthem was played and Republic of Vietnam flags, yellow with horizontal red stripes, snapped in the breeze as they were raised. Patrol boats were renamed *Le Phuc Duc* (HQ 700) and *Le Van Nga* (HQ 701). It was the most significant transfer of naval resources since the beginning of turnover. At the request of the naval advisory group, a Coast Guard liaison officer was assigned to remain with each vessel.[9]

During the final phase of *Point Garnet*'s turnover, Lieutenant Junior Grade Rufe was the only American aboard the cutter for two weeks. In reflecting on the program, he said, "To be honest, I didn't have a great deal of confidence that when we turned it over they were going to be all that effective. From the standpoint of taking the boat to sea and getting it back home again, I had no problem going to sleep at night with them on watch. They were generally good seamen. They weren't as proficient with electronics, but they certainly knew how to navigate. . . . But I just never sensed a strong commitment. There was a kind of *mañana* attitude. Despite some good intentions on the part of the CO, they just weren't going to be very effective." Problems, already apparent with hand-picked crews, became more serious as less-qualified and less-motivated crews were assigned to follow-on cutters.[10]

After completion of the pilot program, SCATTOR continued immediately; the next VNN prospective commanding officer reported aboard USCGC *Point Clear* (WPB 82315) on 27 May 1969. Progress with the VECTOR program was not as rapid; the Vietnamese Navy was slow in assigning engineers to the program. Lack of technical knowledge and language difficulties hindered the maintenance and repair program further. While many Vietnamese could speak some English, few could read English and no manuals or instruction material was printed in Vietnamese. Capabilities and experience of engineers assigned varied widely, running from excellent to very poor.

In keeping with MACV's directive to transfer resources to Vietnam in the best material condition possible, WPBs were scheduled for shipyard availabilities before turnover. Cutters not yet overhauled in Sasebo, Japan, were sent to Singapore. They sailed in pairs from Vietnam to Singapore; four cutters were in the shipyard at a time. When Division 11 was disestablished in the Gulf of Thailand on 5 June 1969, Lt. Cdr. John C. Spence was assigned to Singapore with a small staff to coordinate availabilities.[11]

Initially, fourteen WPBs were scheduled to be turned over to Vietnam. When President Nixon met with South Vietnamese President Nguyen Van Thieu on Midway on 8 June 1969, more resources were provided to South Vietnam. The remaining ten 82-foot cutters and two 311-foot high-endurance cutters were included in the $3 billion "Midway Additive Package."[12]

On 1 July 1969 SCATTOR and VECTOR programs were accelerated with promulgation of a joint turnover letter, signed by COMNAVFORV, CNO VNN, and COMCOGARDACTV. The directive established target reporting dates for all VNN personnel necessary to effect 100 percent turnover of Squadron One. The letter stated the willingness of the Coast Guard to accept Vietnamese of lower rates than billets called for in order to obtain the numbers of personnel needed; crewmen would be trained to fill higher billets.[13]

VNN personnel began reporting to Division 12 in Danang in July 1969 for SCATTOR and VECTOR programs. USCGC *Point Gammon* (WPB 82328) was the first Division 12 WPB in the program and completed training and turnover on 11 November 1969. USCGC *Point Ellis* (WPB 82330), USCGC *Point Hudson* (WPB 82322), and USCGC *Point Slocum* (WPB 82313) completed turnover a month later. Once turned over, Vietnamese patrol boats continued to operate on Market Time patrols. Capt. Thomas G. Volkle, who was a lieutenant commander when he commanded Division 12 in 1969, said, "After we turned boats over, either the [USCG] CO or XO stayed aboard as an advisor." WPBs that had been turned over were controlled by the VNN's surveillance operation at Danang, which paralleled that of the U.S. Navy. Commander CTG 115.1 had a VNN counterpart and commander Coast Guard Division 12 had a counterpart assigned.[14]

When Navy and Coast Guard turnover programs swung into high gear, demand for qualified VNN personnel increased. Niesz said, "After we got five boats fully manned, we had trouble getting people. We got word there was a shortage of senior VNN petty officers who could speak English." By November 1969, 14 WPBs should have been turned over or in the process of being turned over; only nine were because of the shortage of VNN personnel. The program was three months behind the joint turnover letter schedule. U.S. Navy advisors serving with the Vietnamese Navy coordinated the assignment of personnel to both Navy and Coast Guard programs. To improve the flow of people into COGARDRON ONE's programs, Niesz assigned two Coast Guard officers to VNN headquarters to assist with personnel assignments. "That's how I worked around having to go through Navy advisors to get people," he said.[15]

Angelico had the unique opportunity of commanding two cutters during turnovers, first USCGC *Point Jefferson* (WPB 82306) and then *Point Marone.* Of the Vietnamese crews he worked with, he said, "They could operate them [the WPBs] okay, but to them it was a job and not a career. The CO could handle the boat and the engineers could run it. But they didn't run it the way we did. Once boats were turned over, almost all maintenance ceased. They basically ran equipment until it stopped running. They ran the electronics until it just didn't work anymore."[16]

Just as with small organizations everywhere, personalities and capabilities of key individuals influenced the turnover process. VNN personnel came from different backgrounds with varying levels of nautical experience. Lt. (jg) Preston L. Foskey, who commanded USCGC *Point Lomas* (WPB 82321) during turnover, was not impressed with the capabilities of Vietnamese replacing his crew. He said, "There was a general feeling that people who should have been in the [Vietnamese] Navy, weren't. Fishermen and boat operators were generally drafted into the Army because they didn't have any political pull."[17]

AWOL (absence without leave) was a serious problem with VNN crews during turnover. Since four WPBs were in the shipyard at Singapore continuously—two from each division—patrol boats in Vietnam had to run harder to cover all areas; they only had one day in port between patrols to replenish. Angelico said, "When we came in and tied up, we had a hard time keeping them [VNN] aboard to get ammunition, fuel, and food loaded. When we hit the dock they wanted to *di di mou* [go away quickly]."[18]

AWOL was not just a problem with enlisted personnel. Volkle said, "At Danang, it was very common for VNN XOs to go AWOL. Even COs were dragged back in handcuffs. That's when I began to realize this thing [Vietnamization] just wasn't going to work." In 1970, the entire replacement crew aboard USCGC *Point Glover* (WPB 82307)—officers and men—abandoned the cutter for two weeks during Tet holidays. GMCM William R. Wells, II, a chief gunner's mate aboard the cutter at the time, said, "And when they left, they took all the paint with them, too."[19]

Turnover cutters seldom sailed with complete VNN crews aboard; apparently, from lax punishments awarded for AWOL, absences were condoned by Vietnamese officers. Foskey said, "The prospective commanding officer was pretty good about staying. The rest of the crew seemed to go AWOL every other trip. It was an organized thing with them taking turns. They knew who was and wasn't going to show up." Foskey said, "The [Coast Guard] crew didn't have a good attitude toward turnover. Nobody thought they could do the job. They just didn't want to be involved. People didn't feel the Vietnamese could operate the vessel safely. When there were only three of us [USCG] left aboard, I felt threatened. Not by the VN crew themselves, but by their incompetence and uncaring attitude for what we were supposed to be doing."[20]

Motivating Vietnamese to be more aggressive and devote more time to operations was difficult. They had been involved in one war or another most of their lives and saw no end to the fighting. Americans came to Vietnam, stayed for a year, and then went home to a country at peace. For many Americans, duty in Vietnam was an opportunity to enhance their military careers. Despite reasons for Vietnamese behavior, Coast Guard crews resented that they worked harder and took more risks in fighting the war than the South Vietnamese did. They also were distressed when they saw conditions of cutters deteriorate; equipment and machinery they worked long and hard to maintain were abused or neglected.

In November 1969, the U.S. Navy launched a follow-on, expanded turnover program called ACTOV-X, which called for the turnover of an additional 333 craft and further expansion of the VNN by 7,372 men to a ceiling of 37,645 personnel. Turnover training periods for WPBs were reduced to eleven weeks.[21]

Wells first served aboard *Point Glover* during turnover in 1969. When relieved by a VNN gunner's mate, he went aboard *Point Kennedy*, the final Division 12 cutter turned over. He said:

The attitude of Coast Guard crews was pretty good at first. I think every crew was enthusiastic because the word was, "The sooner we get it over

Crews of USCGC Point Kennedy *and USCGC* Point Young *stand at attention as Vietnamese flags are raised over Division 12's last two cutters at Danang, 1970.*

with, the sooner we get home." At first we thought we were doing something pretty good and we really tried. But it just went down hill. The Vietnamese weren't "gung ho" about it. They didn't have the experience or willingness and they saw no end to the war. They were just putting in time. Going to sea for them just meant being away from their families. If the boat didn't work, it meant they didn't have to go out.[22]

While there were different levels of capability among VNN crews, there was little doubt they could satisfactorily operate WPBs—not as well as experienced Coast Guard crews, but well enough to conduct effective patrols. The issue, however, was would they? There appeared to be little inclination for Vietnamese crews to conduct night patrol operations, even though virtually all enemy supply trawlers were detected attempting to reach the coast at night. Once vessels were turned over, VNN crews did little preventive maintenance work;

material failures that kept patrol boats in port were considered fortu-
itous. Vietnamese vessels seldom operated in bad weather; when seas
got rough, they returned to port or sought shelter.

Given circumstances of limited time and personnel lacking experience and motivation, Coast Guard crews did an exceptional job in
turning over fully equipped, functioning cutters with reasonably well-
trained crews. Wells said, "All we did on patrol was prepare them for
the ORI. They could do drills well enough. It was like a mini-GTMO
[USN fleet training center, Guantanamo Bay, Cuba]. When the weather
was good enough, we did drills, boardings, and gunnery shoots with
them day after day." Capabilities of vessels and crews, unfortunately,
were not fully used after turnover.

Division 12 Stood Down

On 16 March 1970, USCGC *Point Kennedy* (WPB 82320) and USCGC
Point Young (WPB 82303) were nested together alongside a float at
Danang. A Buddhist priest in saffron robes walked the decks of the
cutters, chanting and swinging a brass censer; the scent of burning
incense hung heavy in the air. The priest drove evil spirits from the
boats and called for good fortune for new crews. Cutter commanding
officers, mustered with their Coast Guard crews on the float, saluted
when Vietnamese flags were raised over the cutters. Though disillu-
sioned with turnover at this point, commander Division 12 said, "We
know members of the Vietnamese Navy who take our place will continue the outstanding accomplishments of Division 12." The brief ceremony ended at 1140 and Coast Guard Division 12 no longer existed.
Wells said, "Most Coast Guardsmen just walked away without looking
back. It was a new experience—few had ever left a job before it was
finished."[23]

Squadron One Disestablished

Cutter crews worked until the very end, preparing Vietnamese
crews to take over WPBs. Angelico said, "When we got back to Cat Lo
after our last mission, we had to clean up the boat [*Point Marone*] and
get her ready for turnover. We still had to do our ORI. Between the 4th

U.S. flags are hauled down on USCGC Point Cypress *and USCGC* Point Marone *at Cat Lo on 15 August 1970, ending Squadron One's role in Vietnam.*

and the 15th we were really humping it. We had to replace the [VNN] ENC and EN2 who were killed and get their replacements trained." After the action on the Rach Khau Rau canal, which left two of the most popular and capable members of the VNN crew dead, there was a somber mood aboard the cutter. "After a couple of days of practice, I was really worried," Angelico said. "Until the action, there was no question that they would pass the ORI. We had practiced and practiced. They were sharp and had a good attitude. After the incident, nobody's heart was in it. Their minds were somewhere else." The VNN prospective commanding officer had a talk with his crew on the morning of the ORI. Angelico said, "That must have snapped them out of it, because they did great."[24]

After turnover, the Coast Guard continued to provide advisors to the Vietnamese for WPBs. The advisor program was formalized in a

Coast Guard activities Vietnam instruction dated 14 May 1970. The directive established technical assistance groups (TAGs) to "provide assistance to the Vietnamese Navy in the maintenance of former 82' WPBs to the maximum extent possible in order to insure their continued high levels of operation and to continue training of Vietnamese Naval personnel already begun in the SCATTOR/VECTOR programs." Groups were detailed to Navy facilities at Danang, Cam Rahn Bay, Cat Lo, and An Thoi, where they assisted Vietnamese with maintenance of WPBs. Each TAG had an officer in charge and consisted of eight to eleven engineers and technicians and was a sub-unit of COGARDACTV. TAG members who routinely sailed aboard former WPBs as advisors eventually were replaced by U.S. Navy personnel.[25]

In his August 1970 monthly historical summary, commander NAVFORV wrote:

> The two WPBs, *Point Cypress* and *Point Marone,* were the last of the twenty-six 82-foot cutters to be turned over to the VNN [Vietnamese Navy] and with their transfer, at 1100H, 15 August 1970, the history of Coast Guard Squadron One and its remaining division, Coast Guard Division 13, came to an end. Over 3,000 members of the Coast Guard have served in Vietnam since the Coast Guard's participation in Operation Market Time commenced in May 1965.[26]

With the disestablishment of Squadron One, Coast Guard Activities Vietnam also came to an end. To provide continuing administrative support for Coast Guard units and Coast Guardsmen remaining in Vietnam, a new element was created—Senior Coast Guard Officer, Vietnam (SCGOV). His organization was manned by former members of the COGARDACTV staff.

15

Turnover of High-Endurance Cutters

It is requested that JCS authorization be sought for the turnover of two Coast Guard WHECs to the Vietnamese Navy in an effort to further Vietnamize the war. Addition of these two ships to the VNN would provide a more satisfactory all-weather detection and intercept capability in the outer Market Time patrol areas, enhance the Naval Gunfire Support capability of the VNN, and permit the release of additional US military ships and men for other duties.

Vice Adm. Elmo R. Zumwalt, COMNAVFORV
21 June 1969

Fire at Sea

Westerly breezes ruffled muddy coastal waters in the Gulf of Thailand. Light airs did little to relieve the discomfort of Vietnamese Navy and U.S. Coast Guardsmen handling ammunition below deck on the 311-foot USCGC *Yakutat* (WHEC 380). The cutter, anchored 4,350 yards offshore from the Advanced Tactical Support Base (ATSB) at Song Ong Doc, prepared for a naval gunfire support mission on 3 August 1970. Only ten feet of water separated the ship's keel from the muddy bottom. Men of both services, their faces shiny with perspiration, passed 5-inch projectiles and powder casings from the magazine to the upper handling room.[1]

Anchored fore-and-aft, the cutter was stationary, heading toward the ATSB. After dark, she commenced harassment and interdiction (H&I) fire. The cutter's commanding officer, Cdr. Walter F. Bartlett,

241

said, "We fired at the request of the base. They gave us coordinates and the number of rounds. Maybe ten. Or they'd say, 'Give us ten rounds an hour on this position.' We'd go to GQ [general quarters] every hour. . . . Nobody spotted for us. We fired by azimuth. That's why we had to anchor."

Bartlett looked up from his message board toward the radio speaker, when he heard USS *Jennings County* (LST 846) call the base. The LST, anchored 3,000 yards astern of *Yakutat,* reported she had extinguished a fire in her auxiliary engine spaces; no assistance was required. She said her communications, however, would be irregular because the ship lost power as a result of the fire. Bartlett looked at the clock on the bridge; it was 2120.

An hour later, *Jennings County* called *Yakutat* and requested P-250 pumps to remove firefighting water. The cutter's rescue and assistance (R&A) team was called away and five minutes later YAK 2, one of the cutter's 26-foot motor surf boats, departed with a P-250 pump, firefighting gear, and members of the R&A team. Boat No. 1 was right behind her with more gear and the rest of the team. At 2250, *Yakutat*'s damage control assistant (DCA), Lt. (jg) John W. McBride, in charge of the R&A team, called the cutter, using a PRC-59 portable radio. He reported that the fire had reflashed and was out of control. He said, "Without electrical power, she [*Jennings County*] can't handle it. They're running out of foam and OBA [oxygen breathing apparatus] canisters." The LST's commanding officer requested *Yakutat* come alongside to fight the fire.

Bartlett looked aft from the wing of the bridge; he could see the LST's outline under a star-lit sky. "All I saw was smoke coming from *Jennings County,*" he said. "There were flashlights moving around on her decks." *Yakutat* was under way in sixteen minutes. Gunner's mates and gun crew struck below eighty rounds of ready ammunition to the magazine. The engineer officer organized fire parties, made up of Americans and Vietnamese, and readied equipment. BM2 John C. Miller was on deck when the cutter came along the LST's port side. "I remember the oily, black smoke," he said. "It was hectic on deck. Everybody was running around getting ready. I was pulling hoses. It was scary. Our guys went right in to fight the fire."[2]

With heavy smoke billowing out of burning engineering spaces, ten hose teams immediately went onto the LST. Bartlett said, "Vietnamese Navy people were integrated into fire parties with their running mates.

They got right into it and fought the fire. They did very well." With the LST's entire supply of mechanical foam and OBA canisters gone, McBride told Bartlett he was afraid *Yakutat*'s supply of fifty cans of foam and forty OBA canisters wouldn't be enough. The fire raged out of control. Because of smoke, no one could approach the fire without a breathing apparatus. The base at Song Ong Doc put all its foam and canisters aboard a Navy Swift, PCF 102, which got under way to come out to *Yakutat,* but couldn't cross over the bar because of an extremely low tide. The base also requested that additional supplies be helicoptered from Binh Thuy. USS *Duncan* (DD 874) left her station on the gun line 50 miles from Song Ong Doc and headed south at full speed to assist.

Just before midnight, PCF 102 made it over the bar and got critically needed supplies to the cutter. YAK 1 went into Song Ong Doc to wait for supplies from Binh Thuy. Combined Coast Guard, Navy, and Vietnamese fire parties manned fifteen hoses, working from ten fire stations on *Yakutat.* They put foam down escape trunks to blanket the fire and cut off oxygen to the blaze. Hoses cooled bulkheads of adjacent compartments. Diesel oil, flowing from a service tank, continued to fuel the fire. At 0055 on 4 August 1970, the fire was brought under control. All OBA canisters were expended; fire parties could no longer go into smoke-filled spaces. The entire supply of mechanical foam was gone. To control the fire, the auxiliary engine room and diesel generator rooms 1 and 2 were flooded with eight feet of water. At 0102, the fire was out and reflash watches were set; *Duncan* was released before reaching the scene and returned to her gunfire support station.

Yakutat waited for the interior of the LST to cool and used blowers to exhaust smoke before dewatering. Firefighters—USCG, USN, and VNN—blackened by oily smoke cleaned up aboard the cutter. At 0130, *Yakutat*'s cooks served pizza for all hands on the fantail. The cutter's small boat took an injured Navy man to Song Ong Doc for medevac to Binh Thuy; an OBA canister had exploded while he was using it, burning his lungs. Eight other firefighters were treated for smoke inhalation by the cutter's doctor. *Yakutat* rigged emergency lighting aboard the LST and, at 0319, commenced dewatering with two P-250 portable pumps and eductors rigged to the ship's fire main. At 0455, *Yakutat*'s two boats returned from Song Ong Doc with the foam and OBA canisters requested from Binh Thuy.

On the afternoon of 4 August 1970, *Yakutat* got under way, turned around to unmask her main battery, and remoored next to *Jennings County,* port-side-to. The cutter continued dewatering the LST while firing her gunfire support mission. *Yakutat* took the LST's communications guard and provided all services for her crew; *Jennings County* was a dead ship. After the fire, commander naval support activity Saigon sent a message to *Yakutat,* saying, "Your arrival on scene when *Jennings County's* firefighting capabilities were nearly exhausted and your immediate provision of additional foam and water prevented more serious damage and injuries, if not total loss of the ship."[3]

Ships for Vietnam

In late 1969, Vice Admiral Zumwalt coordinated the rapid expansion of the Vietnamese Navy. With U.S. naval forces preparing to withdraw, he recognized the vulnerability of the Vietnamese coast to trawler infiltrations if Market Time's offshore resources were not replaced. Vietnam's Air Force did not have, and would not get, the capability to provide adequate offshore air surveillance. Radar stations were being established along the coast, but long-range ships were still required to protect against infiltrators. Steel-hulled trawlers had proven to be the only significant waterborne infiltration threat during the war. Zumwalt also knew how important naval gunfire support (NGFS) had become in defending coastal facilities and supporting troop operations. U.S. withdrawal would reduce gunfire support resources from seventy guns and rocket launchers, 5-inch or greater, to fourteen 3-inch guns, eight of which had limited capability.[4]

In a 21 June 1969 letter Zumwalt recommended, "COMUSMACV approve the turnover of two Coast Guard WHECs to the VNN," and that "Naval Advisory Group proceed with basic turnover plans by coordinating with the commandant of the Coast Guard and Coast Guard Squadron Three for on-the-job training. Such training to be commenced as early as possible, utilizing on-station Market Time WHECs." He said, "With the approval and implementation of this recommendation, COMNAVFORV can foresee the day when it would become militarily feasible to withdraw all U.S. Navy surface ship support of Market Time." Zumwalt pointed out that cutters had 5-inch guns, capable of indirect fire with effective ranges of seven miles; they would provide the VNN with badly needed NGFS capability.[5]

In 1969, Coast Guard 311-foot *Casco*-class WHECs were being replaced by new-construction 378-foot *Hamilton*-class cutters. Ships scheduled for decommissioning were available for turnover to VNN. *Casco*-class cutters were built for the Navy between 1941 and 1944 as seaplane and torpedo boat tenders. After World War II, the Coast Guard used them for ocean-station vessels (weather, navigation, and search and rescue services for transoceanic flights and voyages). Ships were manned by crews of 13 officers and 137 enlisted men. Powered by four diesel engines, they had twin screws and were capable of making 19 knots. While displacing 2,800 tons, they had relatively shallow drafts of 14 feet.[6]

On 5 September 1969, the chief of naval operations formally requested transfer of two WHECs. Coast Guard Commandant Adm. Willard J. Smith sent a letter to Transportation Secretary John A. Volpe on 6 October 1969 recommending "that you grant approval for the Coast Guard to effect the transfer of two WHECs, specifically CGC *Yakutat* and CGC *Bering Strait* [WHEC 382], to the U.S. Navy for further transfer to the Vietnamese Navy, pending final approval by the Joint Chiefs of Staff." Cutters had to be transferred to the U.S. Navy because the Coast Guard did not have authority to transfer ships directly to a foreign government. Smith pointed out in his letter, "Both cutters are in relatively good material condition and can be provided with minimum disruption to our currently planned operations, since their replacements are already under construction." Secretary Volpe signed the approval block on the letter on 24 October 1969. The Coast Guard planned for a six-month training period for Vietnamese crews before turnover.[7]

Turnover Training

USCGC *Yakutat* (WHEC 380) and USCGC *Bering Strait* (WHEC 382) were scheduled for deployment to Vietnam with Squadron Three when designated for turnover. *Bering Strait*'s deployment was advanced six months so both turnover cutters could deploy together. Cdr. Nguyen Tam, VNN, *Yakutat*'s prospective commanding officer reported aboard the cutter in her home port of New Bedford, Mass., three weeks before she sailed. Bartlett said, "Commander Tam was excellent. He had a lot of experience. He was trained by the French and commanded ships before." Twelve junior VNN petty officers from the Navy's Great Lakes training center also reported aboard the cutter before sailing.

Cdr. Norman C. Venzke from the Coast Guard's military readiness division at headquarters went to New Bedford and briefed *Yakutat*'s crew on turnover plans. Venzke, who had served as senior naval advisor to the Vietnamese fourth coastal zone commander, told the crew what it would be like working with Vietnamese. *Yakutat*'s executive officer and department heads traveled to Washington, D.C., for a four-week Berlitz total-immersion Vietnamese language course. Bartlett said, "There was a lot of interest in the deployment. People were anxious to go. We more or less had a policy that anyone who didn't want to go would be reassigned. We essentially had a volunteer crew." When *Yakutat* reached Hawaii, more Vietnamese came aboard before refresher training began. Bartlett said, "The number thirty sticks in my mind. That included the prospective engineer officer and a couple of *dai uys* [lieutenants]."

The commanding officer of the Honolulu-based *Bering Strait* suffered a back injury just before deployment and had to be replaced. Cdr. Paul D. Henneberry, Fourteenth Coast Guard District comptroller in Honolulu at the time, said, "I was pounding on everybody's door trying to get the [CO Bering Strait] assignment. I had had every job on a 311 [foot cutter], from junior ensign to XO, including assistant engineer officer. I was ready to go." Henneberry got the job and took command of *Bering Strait* the day before she began refresher training at the USN Fleet Training Group (FTG) Pearl Harbor. Cdr. Vu Xuan An and a contingent of thirty officers and enlisted men reported aboard *Bering Strait* at the same time as Henneberry. Henneberry said, "The CO was outstanding. He spoke good English and was a graduate of the French Naval Academy. He was a good sailor." Cutters went through three weeks of training at Pearl Harbor. Naval gunfire support was emphasized during training.[8]

Cutters reached the Philippines on 31 May 1970 and moored at Subic Bay naval station. The following morning, the next group of Vietnamese reported aboard, bringing VNN totals to seven officers and forty-four enlisted men on *Yakutat* and eight officers and forty-four enlisted men on *Bering Strait*. Six days later, cutters steamed out of Subic Bay enroute to Vietnam for their first Market Time patrol. As envisioned by Zumwalt, ships accomplished turnover training while continuing to perform coastal surveillance and gunfire support missions. Methods for accomplishing training were left up to the cutters. Henneberry said, "We got no guidance on training. Each cutter found out what worked for them and did it. It wasn't a bad approach, because nobody had any experience with turnover."[9]

Of the approaches taken by cutters, Bartlett said, "We were pretty much on the same wavelength. We [COs] talked and let each other know what we were doing, but we didn't really coordinate [training]. We didn't try to do things the same way." To accomplish on-the-job training, Bartlett said, "The first thing we did was plug them [the VNN] into the watch quarter and station bill [individual assignments for all shipboard evolutions] with a [CG] running mate. We had two names for one billet. It worked pretty well. The VNN man knew to go wherever his [CG] partner went and do what he did. The men [CG and VNN] got along well. I didn't see any friction."[10]

Squadron Three provided the Vietnamese Navy with operating instructions for machinery and equipment to be translated into Vietnamese. The shipyard at Saigon got allowance lists, damage control books, and docking plans for cutters. After the first week on patrol, *Yakutat* reported, "Completed training of complete VNN boarding team including boat crew. All boardings now carried out by VNNs."[11]

Turnover continued on schedule with the next contingent of twenty-nine Vietnamese reporting aboard cutters during the first week of September 1970. Forty Coast Guardsmen—about a quarter of a cutter's crew—were transferred from each ship to make room for Vietnamese. Eventually, Coast Guard crews were replaced on a one-for-one basis. By 15 September 1970, *Bering Strait* had qualified four VNN officers as underway and inport officers of the deck (OODs). Henneberry commented on OOD training in his monthly summary report, saying:

Our original intent of assigning a Coast Guard officer on the bridge as an observer did not work well. The Vietnamese officers continued to rely on the Coast Guard officer for decisionmaking. Questions and problems on the bridge were referred to the Coast Guard officer rather than the [VNN] OOD. . . . Vietnamese officers now stand watches by themselves. So far the system has worked well. The Vietnamese OODs, three of whom have had previous commands, are now displaying confidence appropriate to their responsibilities.[12]

USCGC Bering Strait is painted gray at Subic Bay, the Philippines, in preparation for turnover to the South Vietnamese Navy.

In his August 1970 report on training progress, Henneberry said that Vietnamese were routinely assigned to watches as quartermaster, boatswain's mate, helmsman, lookout, and messenger. At least one bilingual Vietnamese was assigned to each watch section. In engineering spaces, the 0400 to 0800 and 1600 to 2000 watches were all manned by VNN officers and men. They conducted casualty drills contained in the standard training requirements manual daily. On the bridge, Vietnamese navigation and piloting teams conducted piloting exercises twice a week on patrol and were used for entering and leaving port. All naval gunfire support control stations and about 40 percent of remaining billets were manned by Vietnamese. By September 1970, the VNN gunfire support team on *Bering Strait* had conducted four successful missions.[13]

Cutters regularly engaged in naval gunfire support operations. Because of their draft, they often were called on to support the base at Song Ong Doc, and took station nightly in shallow coastal waters of the Gulf of Thailand to provide "on call" fire. *Yakutat* was firing her fifth consecutive night mission when she went to assist with the fire aboard *Jennings County*. She continued to shoot the next five nights after the fire. *Yakatat* shot her 3,000th round on 1 November 1970, during her twelfth consecutive night of firing.[14]

Coast Guardsmen and Vietnamese Navy crewmen worked, ate, and slept in close quarters. The men—from two very different cultures—got along reasonably well. Miller said, "I don't think there was any difficulty. They were sailors and we were sailors. We had a lot in common. I don't remember any friction in the crew's quarters." Henneberry, who felt that cultural differences influenced the way situations were handled, said, "Americans were more aggressive with a 'get the job done' attitude—fix it, make it work, do it now! Generally, the Vietnamese were more reserved. They waited for someone to tell them to go ahead and do something. They didn't want to be pushy. Being aggressive wasn't part of their nature."[15]

Language differences, a continuing obstacle to training, became even more significant with later drafts of VNN personnel, who had less English-language capability. Inability to communicate reduced effectiveness of Coast Guard trainers and slowed the process; cultural issues also hindered training. When more-senior petty officers reported aboard later in the program, Henneberry said, "Almost without exception, they will not listen to junior, yet more experienced, VNN petty officers. This problem is a cultural one which we must accept and live with. But it is expensive in term of man-hours because we must use our few senior petty officers to train senior VNN petty officers on a man-for-man basis."[16]

As the November 1970 target date for turnover approached, ships were painted gray. More Coast Guardsmen were transferred ashore as Vietnamese took on greater responsibility for operating ships. VNN personnel stood bridge watches and manned engine rooms, guns, and boats. Vietnamese officers took over operations, deck, and engineering departments. Cutters continued to perform all missions, but the level of efficiency declined noticeably as trained Coast Guardsmen rotated ashore. In his November 1970 monthly summary report, Henneberry expressed concerns about diminished capability. He told commander Squadron Three that the state of training and ability of the ship to respond to all requirements was "currently poor." His report concluded:

> Despite the fact that this report does not reflect great optimism, I am nonetheless confident that our VN shipmates are learning and will, by January, be able to operate the ship. It is doubtful that general quarters stations will be manned and ready in three minutes or that a man overboard will be picked up in five minutes. However, I am reasonably sure that the ship will be able to operate at least marginally. The factors of time and experience in operating their own ship will, I am sure, bring remarkable improvements within three to six months.[17]

Transfer

On 3 December 1970, *Yakutat* and *Bering Strait* returned to Subic Bay and CHOPPED (changed operational control) to commander Squadron Three for the final phase of turnover—refresher training. Lt. Jerald B. Rainey, USCG, was assigned temporary additional duty from Fleet Training Group (FTG) Pearl Harbor as training coordinator. A WESTPAC FTG training team, USN advisors from NAVFORV, VNN training command personnel, and twelve Coast Guard officers and crew from each cutter provided training. The two ships, manned by Vietnamese but under command of Coast Guard commanding officers, successfully completed training and passed two-day operational

The South Vietnamese Navy band plays while officers and chief petty officers board Tran Quang Khai, *the former USCGC* Bering Strait, *in Saigon.*

readiness inspections on 20 and 21 December 1970. Bartlett said, "They (the VNN) had no problem operating the ship. They proved that when they went through refresher training at Subic Bay. Commander Tam ran the whole show. In fact, the general feeling on the part of the Vietnamese was that the training period was a little bit long. And I agree with that." Henneberry was pleased with the progress of the Vietnamese. In thinking back about turnover, he said, "I was absolutely confident that they could operate the ship. Maintaining her? That was something else. They ran the ship for the whole last deployment. The EO [USCG engineer officer] was gone by that time and the XO [USCG executive officer] and I were the only deck officers left. They had no problem."[18]

COMCOGARDRON THREE hoisted his flag aboard *Yakutat* on 28 December 1970 and the ships sailed for Saigon. In a turnover ceremony that took place at 1000 on New Year's Day, 1971, *Yakutat* became

Tran Nhat Duat (HQ 3) and *Bering Strait* became *Tran Quang Khai* (HQ 2). The ceremony at the Vietnamese Navy Yard was opened with an invocation by a U.S. Navy chaplain and closed with a benediction by a Buddhist monk. Turnover reduced Coast Guard's commitment to Market Time to two ships. Remaining cutters—newly constructed 378-foot WHECs, USCGC *Rush* (WHEC 723), and USCGC *Morgenthau* (WHEC 722)—were assigned as an offshore reaction group under Coastal Surveillance Force, Vietnam. They operated in areas 8 and 9.[19]

After Bartlett was relieved as commanding officer of *Yakutat*, he reported to COGARDRON THREE for duty as chief staff officer. He represented the squadron at a June 1971 meeting in Saigon, convened by NAVFORV to discuss the possibility of transferring more WHECs to Vietnam. While in Saigon, Bartlett had the opportunity to go aboard *Tran Quang Khai* (HQ 2), former *Bering Strait,* which had just returned from patrol. After his visit, he said, "Ship and crew presented smart appearance. State of cleanliness and preservation was excellent. All machinery and equipment was reported operating with exception of the evaporator, which was awaiting parts, and the surface-search radar, which had been down for four days, awaiting parts."[20]

Additional Turnovers

In June 1971, the Navy inquired informally about the availability of two more Coast Guard 311-foot WHECs for turnover to the Vietnamese Navy. The transfer of two additional cutters would conclude Coast Guard participation in Operation Market Time. In a 29 June 1971 message to the commandant, the CNO said, "In the event the decision is made to turnover WHECs, it is envisioned that progressive on-station comanning will commence in October 1972. CNO VNN has indicated willingness to use cadres from current (VNN) WHECs to facilitate process."[21]

USCGC *Cook Inlet* (WHEC 384) arrived at Subic Bay on 8 July 1971 for regular deployment with Squadron Three; turnover plans had not been finalized. She sailed on her first routine Market Time patrol a week later. USCGC *Castle Rock* (WHEC 383) reached the Philippines on 17 July 1971 and reported for duty with COGARDRON THREE. With arrival of the two cutters, *Morgenthau* and *Rush* completed deployments and headed for home.

On 26 August 1971, the Navy formally requested transfer of two WHECs to the VNN. The acting commandant, Vice Adm. T. R. Sargent, wrote in a 22 September 1971 letter to the transportation secretary:

> Plan to provide *Cook Inlet* and *Castle Rock* currently with Squadron Three. Vessels are excess to Coast Guard needs and are being replaced by new construction.
>
> Anticipate turnover [will be] completed by 31 December 1971, terminating Coast Guard Squadron Three activity.
>
> Recommend approval for Coast Guard to effect transfer to [U.S.] Navy for further transfer to Vietnamese Navy, pending final approval by Joint Chiefs of Staff.

Secretary Volpe approved the transfer on 28 September 1971. COMCOGARDRON THREE wrote in his monthly summary, "The month of September began the squadron's last major scheduled project, the Vietnamization of cutters *Castle Rock* and *Cook Inlet*."[22]

Lt. Cdr. Edmond G. Case joined *Castle Rock* while she was in the shipyard in Singapore in September 1971, relieving the executive officer. He said, "Turnover hadn't started when I got there. We were a regular Coast Guard crew on a regular Squadron Three deployment. . . . The ship was in good shape and all machinery was in good working order."[23]

Cook Inlet took aboard her first contingent of VNN personnel—eight officers and forty-four enlisted men—at Vung Tau on 4 October 1971. *Castle Rock* received fifty-five Vietnamese at Vung Tau on 10 October 1971 and sailed the next day for Subic Bay to commence turnover training. Cutters used the same on-the job training (OJT) approach as the first turnover cutters. Case said, "It was pretty much an experiment because we didn't have a text to go by. I let the word out, 'You'll go home when your running mate is trained.' It was a real motivator. I got reports the troops were working very hard at training." In general, Coast Guardsmen involved in turnover of WHECs were impressed with the capability of Vietnamese crews. Case said, "We learned a lot of respect for the Vietnamese. At first, the crew had negative attitudes about them. They hadn't had any contact with Vietnamese during the first months there."[24]

The second contingents of Vietnamese boarded at Vung Tau—*Castle Rock* took aboard fifty-four on 15 November 1971 and *Cook Inlet* received fifty-three and a USN advisory team on 21 November 1971.

Paul M. Duffin, a yeoman aboard *Cook Inlet* during turnover, said, "I was assigned a running mate. Someone to work in the ship's office with me. For the most part it was OJT. I thought it worked out pretty good. Language was a problem. I had very limited Vietnamese and he knew little English, but we could still communicate. I enjoyed working with my counterpart in terms of being exposed to someone from a different culture. It was a challenge and an accomplishment for both of us." Off duty, Duffin said the two crews stayed to themselves. "We just kind of hung around with our own people. It just worked out that way. Our languages and customs were different. Everybody got along in the crew's quarters. There was no trouble whatsoever. There were no arguments. I think we respected one another."[25]

For shipboard evolutions, Coast Guard organization was duplicated with VNN counterparts. Duffin was the captain's sound-powered-telephone talker on the bridge for gunfire support missions. His running mate was the talker for the VNN prospective commanding officer. They communicated on separate, but parallel, circuits to fire control and the mount. Duffin said, "I trained my counterpart to do the same job I did. He relayed the same information in Vietnamese. They appeared to be capable. Whether they would be able to sail the ship after we left, I didn't know."[26]

Cook Inlet made the Coast Guard's last Market Time patrol in early December 1971; she fired gunfire support missions in areas 7 and 9. With COMCOGARDRON THREE embarked in *Cook Inlet*, the squadron's last two cutters departed Subic Bay on 12 December 1971, arriving at Saigon on 15 December 1971 and mooring alongside pier B at VNN headquarters. The last contingents of fifty Vietnamese sailors reported aboard on 17 December 1971. In preparation for turnover, cutters were transferred to commander, U.S. Naval Forces Vietnam, using a single standard form DD 1149, "Requisition and Invoice/Shipping Document." The ubiquitous document, dated 16 December 1971, transferred "2 Each, WHEC Class Coast Guard Cutters," from commander USCG Squadron Three to commander, USN Forces Vietnam. The ships were decommissioned and delivered to Vietnam in a ceremony on 21 December 1971, and renamed *Tran Binh Trong* (HQ 5) and *Tran Quoc Toan* (HQ 6). Rear Adm. Robert S. Salzer, COMNAVFORV, represented the United States and Rear Adm. Tran Van Chon, CNO VNN, represented Vietnam. The certificate of delivery cited the "Terms and conditions of the Pentalateral Agreement of 1950" as authority for the transfer.[27]

The Coast Guard was able to reduce turnover training to less than three months, because experienced VNN personnel from *Yakutat* and *Bering Strait* were used to man the ships. Refresher training for Vietnam's newest ships, *Tran Binh Trong* and *Tran Quoc Toan*, was Squadron Three's final mission. Ships arrived at Subic Bay naval station to begin training on 4 January 1972. Training was conducted by a team made up of USN fleet training group personnel from Yokosuka, Japan, and Pearl Harbor, Hawaii; VNN personnel from the newly established Vietnamese naval training group; and Coast Guardsmen from Squadron Three. An advisory detachment from *Cook Inlet* and *Castle Rock*, consisting of the XO, an officer, and ten senior petty officers from each ship, flew to Subic Bay to assist with training. Ships satisfactorily completed training and operational readiness inspections on 18 January 1972. When it was over, Case said, "There was no question in my mind that they were fully capable of operating the ship. There were some really good sailors in the bunch. The CO was very, very good. He didn't put up with any nonsense. JOs [junior officers] were great and the POs [petty officers] were great. They were ready to go."[28]

Capt. Richard E. Hoover disestablished Coast Guard Squadron Three on 31 January 1972. Thirty-two cutters and 4,500 officers and men served with the squadron from 1967 to 1972.[29]

Postturnover

There was little doubt Vietnamese crews were qualified to operate cutters or that ships were operationally ready when turned over. Unfortunately, two pervasive factors quickly degraded the capability of the ships and crews: Organizational culture, and inadequate logistic support. Once turned over, vessels operated in the same fashion as other VNN fleet command ships. They no longer conducted aggressive patrols, instead they spent too much time anchored or in port. Eventually, equipment failed due to lack of maintenance and spare parts.

For the VNN to have been a more significant factor in defending Vietnam, the overall culture of the organization would have had to change. The United States initially attempted to upgrade VNN orga-

Three additional high-endurance cutters, USCGC McCulloch, *USCGC* Absecon, *and USCGC* Chincoteague, *sail from the east coast of the United States enroute to Guam for transfer to the South Vietnamese Navy.*

nizational capabilities during the advisor phase of the conflict. Primary emphasis shifted, however, to hardware; more and more vessels and equipment were provided. Little effort was devoted to developing and strengthening the Vietnamese Navy as an effective organization. The entire VNN structure needed to be revamped with better training, a promotion system based on merit, and improvements in pay and benefits. Core problems, however, often were complicated by cultural considerations. Organizational improvements proved to be too daunting and success too uncertain for U.S. commanders to invest a great deal of effort. One-year tours of duty were too brief to provide continuity for instituting systemic changes.

Once U.S. naval involvement advanced from advising to implementing, focus shifted away from efforts to get the VNN to carry out operations; U.S. commanders, frustrated by the lack of Vietnamese aggressiveness, resorted to using U.S. resources and personnel. The majority of Vietnamese, weary of prolonged conflict, were more than willing to abdicate the active role to eager Americans. When the decision was made to withdraw, it was too late; time was insufficient to strengthen Vietnamese organization and attitudes. Rapid expansion overwhelmed the VNN. Manpower doubled to provide crews for turnedover vessels. The Vietnamese Navy received more equipment than they could effectively use and personnel were promoted to positions beyond their capability. They had neither the trained personnel to man the equipment, nor the logistic infrastructure to maintain it. And, unfortunately, they relied too heavily on continuing U.S. support. Case, who commanded the first Coast Guard WPB to reach Vietnam in 1965 and served as executive officer on the last Market Time WHEC turned over to the Vietnamese, said, "My worst memories of Vietnam are thoughts of what happened to those people [VNN] when we left. When we pulled the plug on Vietnam. They never thought we would desert them."[30]

Final Transfer

In response to a third and final U.S. Navy request for 311-foot WHECs for turnover to Vietnam in 1972, the Coast Guard formed Squadron Two (COGARDRON TWO) on 10 March 1972. Cutters USCGC *Chincoteague* (WHEC 375) and USCGC *McCulloch* (WHEC 386) were ordered to Little Creek, Va., to join USCGC *Absecon* (WHEC 374). Capt. Herbert M. Hartlove was relieved of command of *Absecon* and designated squadron commander. Cutters, sailing with reduced crews, rounded Cape Henry on the morning of 22 March 1972 and turned south along the Virginia coast, heading for the Panama Canal. Their final destination was Guam.[31]

At 1030 on the morning of 9 May 1972, Hartlove transferred cutters to the U.S. Navy for further transfer to the VNN in a ceremony at Apra Harbor, Guam. The next day, 250 Coast Guardsmen flew back to the United States; thirty-five officers and men stayed with the cutters for an additional ten days after transfer. *Chincoteague* and *McCulloch* were turned over to Vietnam on 21 June 1972 and *Absecon* was turned over on 15 July 1972.[32]

16

The Coast Guard Withdraws

Paris, France—The Vietnam cease-fire agreement was signed here today in eerie silence without a word or gesture to express the world's relief that the years of war were officially ending.

Flora Lewis, New York Times
27 January 1973

Jackal 33

Air Force Capt. Robert D. Sponeybarger was at the controls of his F-111 on the night of 22 December 1972. The aircraft from the 429th Tactical Fighter Wing out of Tahkli, Thailand, was on a mission over Hanoi, North Vietnam. A warning light flashed on in the cockpit, signaling a right-engine shutdown. He reported his situation and position to an EC-121 airborne early warning aircraft and he and his weapon system officer (WSO) ejected into the darkness at 2143.

Reconnaissance aircraft, supporting B-52 Strato Fortress linebacker strikes the next afternoon, picked up signals from the downed airmen. The men, call signs Jackal 33 Alpha and Jackal 33 Bravo, were ten miles apart. The Aero Rescue and Recovery Squadron (ARRS) operations center at Nakhon Phanom, Thailand, was alerted at 1610 on 23 December 1972; plans were immediately made for a night rescue attempt. The mission was canceled, however, because of poor weather in the objective area and uncertain locations for the men. The pilot and his WSO were told to move to high ground and come up on their radios whenever they heard a jet fly over.[1]

Weather finally broke on 27 December 1972 and rescue crews from 40th ARRS were scrambled; rotors were engaged and chocks pulled. Two camouflaged Super Jolly Green Giant HH-53C helicopters—Jolly

258

Green 66 and 73—lifted off at 0925. After crossing into Laos, helicopters headed north with scattered clouds overhead and lush jungle below. Coast Guard Lt. Robert E. Long was at the controls of one of the huge helicopters. A-7 Corsair II close-support aircraft called Sandies took off from Korat Royal Thai Air Force Base and flew north to support the rescue mission. Flying at 160 knots, helicopters reached their holding position in Laos, southwest of Hanoi, at 1145 and refueled from King 21, a C-130P Hercules tanker; the airborne mission coordinator was aboard the C-130. F-4 Phantom weather reconnaissance aircraft reported conditions in the objective area as marginal.

The rescue attempt was coordinated to occur under cover of a B-52 linebacker strike. At 1427, two Sandies went into the objective area to confirm the airmen's position and suppress ground fire. Four more Sandies escorted rescue helos to the scene. Two additional helicopters, Jolly Green 32 and 52, were held in reserve in Laos with two Sandies for cover.

Jackal 33B's position was fixed; he was located in the Karst area, 17 miles southeast of Hanoi. Jackal 33A's whereabouts were unknown; nothing had been heard from him for two days. An A-7 smoke flight put down a protective screen over the Black river valley to cover the approach of helicopters. Long said, "I was high bird. I should have been low bird, the one that goes in [for the pickup], but they just changed the policy. They made alert pilots flip a coin to see who would be low bird. The other helicopter won."

Low bird went down the river between two smoke screens. The downed aviator popped a red smoke just on the other side of a gentle ridge. Low bird banked into the area of the smoke and began taking ground fire. It went into a hover 30 feet above the pilot, who was hiding on a ledge in tall elephant grass, a third of the way down the ridge. A crewman lowered the jungle penetrator to the ground and the man tried to get to it. He had trouble maintaining his balance under the downwash from the rotor blades; he fell down the slope and couldn't get back to the penetrator. The helicopter began taking heavy fire from all sides. Rounds came through the cockpit windshield and the copilot hunched over in his seat. Blood splattered the inside windshield and lube oil from ruptured lines streaked the outside. "The North Vietnamese were waiting," Long said. "They opened up on him with automatic weapons. [Capt.] Miguel Pereira [copilot] was hit. His elbow was shattered. They managed to get out of there, but the aircraft was shot up pretty good and losing fuel. We lost comms with the downed pilot and everything kind of went to pieces."

Long said, "I told King Bird to come north, because the other Jolly is going to need fuel. I said, 'He's going down unless you get him some fuel.' I told them it was safe in the area." The damaged helo lost air pressure and could not get its refueling probe extended; attempts to refuel with the probe in were unsuccessful.

The helicopters, escorted by Sandies, managed to make it into Laos. Long went ahead and found a place where the damaged helo, fuel draining from its tanks, could put down. He said, "I remember seeing a place on top of a hill. I went into a hover and checked out the spot. It was clear. I went back and told him, 'Follow me in.' They [low bird] took some more hits as they came in over a village. He plopped it down and I went in next to him. I had to land on the side of the hill and punched out my radar dome." Long's helicopter picked up the six crewmen, including the wounded copilot, and took off. Long said, "It was getting dark as we flew out. I was concerned about Miguel going into shock. He was in bad shape."

A backup Jolly Green landed to salvage gear from the downed helo and sanitize it. The crew removed electronic gear and miniguns. When they began taking fire from surrounding trees, they cleared the area. A-7 Sandies came in and destroyed the abandoned helicopter with bombs at 1731. When Long landed at Udorn at 1845, an ambulance was waiting to take Pereira to the hospital. Long returned to Nakhon Phanom after flying his helicopter for ten hours, including four in-flight refuelings.

Drawdown

After Coast Guard Activities Vietnam (CGACTV) was disestablished 15 August 1970, Senior Coast Guard Officer Vietnam (SCGOV) provided continuing support for Coast Guard activities remaining in Vietnam. Working out of offices at Naval Forces Vietnam (NAVFORV), the small staff provided administrative support for personnel serving with the Army, Air Force, and the U.S. Embassy, and at Coast Guard LORAN stations in Vietnam. Aids to navigation specialists on the SCGOV staff continued to support U.S.-maintained aids, schedule Coast Guard buoy tender deployments, and act as advisors to the Vietnamese Bureau of

Navigation. In April 1972, SCGOV was assigned an additional duty on the commander Naval Forces Vietnam staff—special assistant for Coast Guard matters.

Port Security and Explosive Loading

The Vietnamese Army began assuming the port security mission from the U.S. Army in August 1971. Responsibility for security at the last ammunition port the Coast Guard was responsible for, Cogido, was transferred to the Vietnamese in September 1971. In 1972, enemy attacks on explosive facilities were on the increase. Several ammunition depots were sapped and ammunition barges from Cat Lai were fired on. Of one incident, SCGOV wrote in his March 1972 monthly summary, "A B-40 rocket hit a barge loaded with 105mm ammunition. The resulting blast was monumental."[2]

In April 1972, U.S. military withdrawal and turnover of operations to the Vietnamese accelerated. MACV ordered in-country Coast Guard strength reduced to a total of eighty-seven personnel. The Port Security and Waterways Detail (PS&WD)—in the process of turning over explosive-loading duties to the Vietnamese Army—was directed to reduce to thirteen men by 1 July 1972. After that date, the PS&WD organization consisted of an officer in charge at Long Binh, and explosive loading detachment (ELD) advisors at Danang (an officer and three petty officers), Cam Rahn Bay (an officer and three petty officers), Qui Nhon (two petty officers), Cat Lai (an officer and two petty officers), and Vung Tau (two petty officers.)[3]

Lt. Cdr. Homer A. Purdy arrived in Vietnam to take over as officer in charge of PS&WD on 14 June 1972. Viet Cong sappers welcomed Purdy by blowing up the Army petroleum, oil, and lubricants dump by the river at USARV's Long Binh headquarters; he awoke the night he arrived to see flames lighting up the sky. Two days later, sappers hit a barge at Vung Tau. "Then it slowed down," Purdy said. "When they started talking peace [in Paris], our problems pretty much went away. There were fewer and fewer incidents."[4]

While Purdy continued to serve as USARV's port security advisor, he was more and more involved with coordinating transfer of explosive loading duties to the ARVN ordnance command (OCO); he worked closely with the ARVN colonel in command. "With Colonel Viet's cooperation," Purdy said, "We were able to get CG 108 [the Coast Guard explosives handling manual] translated into Vietnamese. That was probably the biggest plus in the whole process. Lots of Vietnamese could speak English, but few could read it." To consolidate the Coast Guard's diminishing resources, Purdy moved into SCGOV's offices in Saigon in August 1972.[5]

In taking over from the Coast Guard, Vietnamese Army personnel had little difficulty with technical aspects of explosive loading operations. They had gained a great deal of experience working with Coast Guard ELDs. OCO was a stable organization—once personnel were assigned to explosive loading at a port, they were seldom reassigned. But confronting masters and officers on U.S. ammunition ships was a more serious problem for Vietnamese. Purdy said, "Because of their small stature and reluctance to assert themselves, they [the Vietnamese] were frequently beaten down verbally by American merchant mariners." The problem became critical as Vietnamese took over operations at more and more ports. After a few incidents, during which U.S. masters refused to follow directions from ARVN OCO supervisors and went so far as to have them removed from their ships, PS&WD's officer in charge took action. He prepared letters to be given to uncooperative masters, stating that Vietnamese were assuming responsibility for explosive off-loading and failure to comply with their safety instructions would be reported to the Coast Guard captain of the port in the United States who issued the master's license. Purdy said, "It was sort of blackmail, but it worked. It was amazing how quickly masters came into line."

Lt. Jay A. Creech, officer in charge of ELD 1 and Lt. Gilbert Aguilar, officer in charge of ELD 4, conducted explosive-loading courses for ARVN personnel at Cat Lai and Danang. ELD 1 supervised three-week courses taught by Vietnamese at Cat Lai, and ELD 4 personnel taught two-week courses at Danang. Purdy said, "They [the South Vietnamese] needed leadership training more than technical training. They needed encouragement to look an American master in the eye and say, 'Captain, you have to do this.'" To bolster Vietnamese authority, a combination USCG and ARVN explosive-loading emblem was designed and issued to Vietnamese who successfully completed courses. It displayed an ARVN (OCO) bomb symbol in the middle of a Coast Guard shield and was marked "USCG" and "ARVN." The field of the patch was half red and white, the colors of the Coast Guard ensign, and half red and yellow, the colors of Vietnam's flag. It indicated to merchant mariners that Vietnamese wearing it were Coast Guard trained. While the emblem achieved its intended purpose, Purdy said, "I got hell later, because I didn't go through [U.S. Army] heraldry to get the design approved. But we did what we had to do to get the job done."[6]

Turnover of explosive-loading operations began in May 1972 and by November 1972, ELDs were disestablished. Remaining Coast Guard ELD personnel were reassigned from being shift supervisors to advisors and instructors for the Vietnamese. On 30 January 1973, PS&WD—the Coast Guard's last operating unit in Vietnam—was disestablished at an Army awards ceremony in Saigon. During their service in Vietnam, ELDs of the PS&WD handled more than 11 million tons of explosives and munitions. The mission was accomplished "without loss or damage to cargo, equipment or vessel attributable to improper handling procedures or violation of safety practices." PS&WD and its ELDs received three Army Meritorious Unit Commendations. Individual awards for units—which never exceeded a strength of thirty-five personnel—included the Legion of Merit, Silver Star Medal, forty Bronze Star Medals, eighty Army Commendation Medals, and numerous other U.S. and Vietnamese awards. For its size, it was one of the most decorated units in Coast Guard history.[7]

To provide continuity for explosive-handling operations after withdrawal of ELDs, the Coast Guard commandant and the commander of the Pacific area approved PS&WD's recommendation that ARVN OCO officers be permitted to attend explosive loading supervisor courses at the Coast Guard port security station, Concord, Calif. The commanding officer, PSS Concord, was designated as ARVN OCO's point of contact for technical information.

On Sunday, 28 January 1973, Purdy settled back into his seat aboard the crowded Pan Am 747 and closed his eyes; he was the only Coast Guardsman aboard the flight. The airliner lumbered to the end of the main runway at Tan Son Nhut airport and turned. The pilot increased thrust on the jet's engines and let up on the brakes; the plane surged forward. When the wheels lifted off the runway, a cheer went up from the passengers. Purdy had mixed emotions; he was elated to be going home, but frustrated as well. He said, "I felt we didn't accomplish the job we were sent there to do. We went there to help the Vietnamese.

Then we signed a cease-fire and pulled out. We backed out on a commitment. I understand what happened, but I don't think we did as well as we could or should have."[8]

Aids to Navigation

In February 1970, the Joint Chiefs of Staff and the commandant of the Coast Guard agreed on a program for transferring maintenance of aids to navigation; the Vietnamese were to take over when capable of assuming the responsibility. COGARDACTV completed a study on the Vietnamization of the aids to navigation system (VANS), which MACV concurred with on 12 June 1970. The plan called for replacing buoys with more easily maintained concrete structures. On 20 October 1970, the U.S. Navy's officer in charge of construction for the Republic of Vietnam was given notice to proceed with construction of twenty-nine aids to navigation structures.[9]

Responsibility for aids was transferred to Vietnam's Directorate of Navigation (DON) on 13 December 1970 by a joint COMUSMACV/SCGOV/GVN agreement. The agreement called for a Coast Guard buoy tender to deploy to Vietnam to maintain aids until the DON was ready to take over. By July 1971, little was accomplished on the Navy construction program and Vietnamization was not progressing; the Coast Guard continued to maintain virtually all Vietnamese aids. The commander, Fourteenth Coast Guard District, who provided the buoy tender for Vietnam, protested the lack of progress on Vietnamization of aids to navigation. The Coast Guard said it could no longer assign a buoy tender dedicated to maintaining Vietnamese aids. USCGC *Blackhaw* (WLB 390) was reassigned from Sangley Point, Philippines, to San Francisco in July 1971. USCGC *Basswood* (WLB 388), homeported in Guam, was assigned—as an additional duty—to deploy to Vietnam to service aids, as needed.[10]

Basswood arrived in Vietnam on her first deployment on 19 October 1971. She took observers from the Vietnamese lighthouse service aboard the ship at Vung Tau for indoctrination. The tender began discontinuing aids and replacing buoys with more easily maintained shore aids. *Basswood* returned for a second deployment in January 1972, servicing more aids and discontinuing others, in preparation for a Vietnamese takeover. Aids at Cam Rahn Bay and Vung Tau were turned

USCGC Blackhaw*'s crew works with South Vietnamese trainees in preparation for turnover of the aids to navigation mission.*

over to the Vietnamese lighthouse service on 17 January 1972. The tender then sailed to Qui Nhon to service aids for turnover. By February 1972, the VANS program was determined to be a failure; of the twenty-nine planned structures only twelve were completed. Fixed structures, constructed to be accessible for servicing, also were accessible for pilfering, vandalism, and sabotage. Two of the structures, built by the Navy at a cost of $36,000 each, were destroyed by sabotage within a month of completion.

The futility of attempting to maintain a sophisticated aids to navigation system in Vietnam after withdrawal became apparent. Representatives of SCGOV, MACV, MSCOV, NAVFORV, and MMD, meeting in Saigon to address the problem, agreed that buoy tender support would not be required after *Basswood's* March-April 1972 deployment. They determined that no further aids support would be required at Cua Viet, Tan My, Chu Lai, and the Bo De river. While aids were still required at Vung Tau/Soi Rap/Cau Tieu for access to Saigon and New-port, Vietnam's Directorate of Navigation could maintain them. If future aids were required at Cam Rahn Bay, the directorate would take care of them, as well. Shore aids established at Danang were considered adequate for navigation. Aids at Qui Nhon were changed to unlighted buoys and structures; the Directorate of Navigation took responsibility for maintaining them. Aids were no longer maintained on the Bassac river, so mariners had to rely on local knowledge for navigation.[11]

Basswood made her final deployment to Vietnam on 24 March 1972. At the end of the deployment, SCGOV reported in a 3 May 1972 message:

> Serviced Navaids in Danang, Qui Nhon, Cam Rahn Bay, and Vung Tau in addition to resupplying Vietnamese lighthouses from Con Son to Danang. All areas left in best condition possible. All unused Navaid equipment delivered to Vietnamese lighthouse service in Saigon for use by them in maintaining Navaids.[12]

After the tender departed, the ATON detail at SCGOV in Saigon had the entire responsibility for attempting to hold together Vietnam's navigation system. Lt. Bill Lawrence took over as SCGOV's ATON coordinator in July 1972. He worked closely with the Vietnamese and deployed aboard their tender, *Cuu Long*, to advise them on buoy operations. When the cease-fire was signed on 27 January 1973, SCGOV sent a letter to the director of the navigation directorate giving him a point of contact at Coast Guard headquarters in Washington, D.C., for technical assistance. The letter stated that in-country Coast Guard advisory support for aids to navigation had ended.[13]

Rescue Pilots

The last two Coast Guard aviators reported for duty with the 37th ARRS at Danang in July 1972. Lt. Robert E. Long arrived on 12 July 1972 and Lt. Jack K. Stice reported a week later. Long said, "The first thing I noticed when I got off the aircraft was that everyone was armed. All of a sudden it came to me. This is for real!"[14]

In 1972, Super Jolly Green Giant helicopters of the 37th ARRS supported bombing missions against North Vietnam. Long said, "We worked with Air Force planes, mostly F-4s flying out of Danang, and

Navy planes coming off carriers. Later, President Nixon sent a lot of B-52s in. We would go up into the Gulf of Tonkin and orbit offshore, ready to go in if somebody went down." Improvements in electronic counter-measure equipment, tactics, and target selection resulted in fewer downed planes. Long said, "There wasn't much rescue activity at all. I expected more." Coast Guard aviators were impressed by the professionalism of the aero rescue and recovery squadron. Long said, "Everybody was focused. They wanted to get home alive, but they knew they had a job to do. One thing we never discussed was why we were in Vietnam or whether we should be. Some people didn't want to be there, but they were. They accepted it."[15]

When Long and Stice arrived at Danang, they heard talk of phasing back. The Army already was making preparations to pull out and the squadron had concerns about security of the airbase, since rocket attacks from the area around the base were becoming more common. Long said, "The VC harassed us. They'd launch in a few [rockets] and hit runways and aprons. They left holes about six feet in diameter and 3-feet deep. They did hit a helicopter once, but no one was in it." Air Force A-1E Skyraiders, which flew close support for Jolly Green Giant missions, were turned over to the Vietnamese Air Force (VNAF). While markings on aircraft were changed to VNAF, they were still flown by USAF pilots for close-support during ARRS rescue missions.

At 1000 on 30 November 1972, HH-53C helicopters of 37th ARRS lifted off the runway at Danang Airbase for the last time. The sky was clear with a brilliant sun overhead. Helicopters formed up and headed south before turning west for Thailand. The squadron was transferred to the U.S. Air Force facility at Royal Thai AFB, Nakhon Phanom, and was integrated into the 40th ARRS. Maintenance crews departed earlier with the squadron's personal gear, spare parts, and heavy equipment aboard C-130s. Remaining squadron equipment and supplies were transported by helicopter. The helicopter Long flew to Thailand had an additional passenger for the transit; he carried a nine-foot, eighty-pound python, the mascot of the pararescue specialists (PJs). When he was ordered to climb to 13,000 feet to refuel, Long was afraid the temperature would be too cold for the snake, had the mascot survived the flight.

ARRS helicopters continued to fly rescue missions from Thailand in support of air strikes on North Vietnam. Instead of orbiting over Tonkin gulf, helos were held over Laos, ready to go in to pick up downed pilots. Long said, "We had several missions on the back side of Laos and into the west side of North Vietnam, by Hanoi. We went as far north as we could and orbited." When an aircraft went down in the People's Republic of China, Long was sent to pick up the pilot. He said, "We were excited about the mission. They had him [the downed pilot] pinpointed 60 miles inside China. But before we could get there, they lost contact with him and we were recalled."

Life was easier for men of the ARRS at Nakhon Phanom; facilities were better and the base was more secure. Rescue missions, however, were just as harrowing. Jolly Green Giant crews knew the North Vietnamese let downed pilots remain free so they could ambush aircraft that came to rescue them. Long said, "We realized we were going to be set up, but we felt we had good cover [support aircraft]. A-1s gave us very close support—right next to us. A-7s had better electronics and could carry more weaponry, but they couldn't give the close support that slow-moving A-1s could. And they couldn't stay with you very long."

Coast Guard Explosive Loading Detachment 4 provided Stice and Long with a vehicle for their use in Danang. Vehicles were more readily available because U.S. units were withdrawing. When the 37th ARRS transferred to Thailand, ELD 4 gave Coast Guard pilots a Jeep to take with them. By using creative paperwork, Stice and Long managed to get the Jeep shipped aboard an Air Force C-130 to Nakhon Phanom with the rest of the squadron's gear. The Jeep, of questionable origin, was later used by the Air Force for spare parts.

Long extended his tour an extra week so both Coast Guard aviators could depart the squadron together. The men departed Nakhon Phanom on 14 July 1973; they were the last Coast Guard aviators to fly rescue missions over Vietnam.[16]

LORAN Stations

Lt. Ray Riutta was waiting at the airstrip at Phu Bai when the C-130 carrying his Coast Guard Academy classmate landed. Lt. Dennis R. Erlandson had orders to relieve Riutta as commanding officer of Tan My LORAN station. Erlandson tossed his gear into a waiting HU-1E Iroquois helicopter and the men climbed aboard for the short flight to Tan My. Erlandson looked through the open side door, past the gunner, at the jungle passing below. He said, "When we got to the

[LORAN] station, I was amazed at the size of it. It was a lot larger than imagined. It was a fortified compound."[17]

An Army air cavalry company—Fox of the Fourth—was the nearest U.S. military unit remaining in the area. They were based on Tan My island, a mile offshore. While the LORAN station was capable of defending itself against sappers and guerrilla raids, it could not withstand a concerted enemy attack. Erlandson said, "We weren't there to be the Alamo. If things started to really heat up, we were to be evacuated by Fox of the Fourth. As long as they were there, I felt we had a safety valve."[18]

Logistic support for the LORAN station became an increasing problem as U.S. forces withdrew. Erlandson said, "Toward the end, our main concern was loss of support. Communications became more difficult and we were concerned about food and water. We were stretched for basic necessities." Needed supplies were difficult to obtain through normal Army channels. Pilferable materials, items that would sell on the black market, never made it through to the station. When perimeter lighting became unreliable because of deterioration, the entire system had to be rewired; lights were critical for security. To ensure that required supplies got to the station, the Coast Guard flew a dedicated C-130 logistics flight from Air Station Barbers Point, Hawaii, to Phu Bai, Vietnam. In addition to lighting supplies, the log flight carried unique electronics parts and other difficult-to-obtain items. Before flying the final leg into Vietnam, the flight stopped in Guam and loaded up with fresh vegetables and fruit, and commissary supplies.

To get supplies from Phu Bai—the closest field where a C-130 could land—to the station, trucks had to be sent overland. The one remaining road to the airfield passed through unsecured territory. The LORAN station crew put together a convoy, using vehicles accumulated from departing military units. Erlandson said, "We had a semi tractor, a couple of deuce-and-a-halfs [2½-ton trucks], four ¾-tons [trucks], and five Jeeps. The Air Force had one of the Jeeps rigged with machine guns. We knew we had to pass through closed-in jungle areas. We had air reconnaissance, but they [NVA and VC] could attack out of the jungle at any place." The convoy plan called for no stopping, with any vehicle that broke down to be abandoned. The twelve-vehicle convoy drove the seventeen miles to Phu Bai, loaded up, and returned over the same route, without incident. It was the only time Erlandson ever traveled the road.

When plans were made for withdrawing from Vietnam, U.S. commanders recognized the continuing need for the precise navigation information provided by Tight Reign LORAN stations; positioning data would still be needed for air operations. To continue operations at the two LORAN stations in Vietnam after a cease-fire, commander Southeast Asia Section (SEASEC) began investigating the use of civilian contractors. Lt. Cdr. Phillip J. Kies, chief of the electronics division at SEASEC, said, "I put together a proposal in early 1972, and we went out for competitive bids. There were a lot of contractors already doing service-type work in South Vietnam. The proposal covered everything: housekeeping, food service, electronics, electrical power, and security." Contractors were interested in making proposals, but had difficulty finding experienced electronics technicians to operate and maintain LORAN transmitters and timers. Kies said, "We kind of worked hand-and-glove with contractors. We gave them a list of former Coast Guard technicians who had LORAN experience. When it was evident they still weren't going to get enough technicians, the Fourteenth [Coast Guard] District, with headquarters concurrence, granted ETs [on LORAN stations] up to six-month early-outs [from enlistments] if they signed one-year contracts with contractors." Eighty percent of technicians for the stations were former Coast Guardsmen from Tight Reign or other Pacific LORAN stations; they retired, if eligible, or were given early discharges.[19]

Erlandson said, "At Tan My, Senior Chief [Winfield G.] Pierce [ETCS] and two others [USCG] stayed. They brought in three more [former USCG ETs] from Thailand. Third-country nationals were brought in to operate the rest of the station. Koreans were the mechanics. Stations had about twenty people to operate them, plus security." Since access to Con Son Island was tightly controlled by the Vietnamese government, it was difficult to hire third-country nationals. Except for the electronics technicians, Vietnamese operated the station at Con Son.[20]

Turnover of the two stations to Federal Electronics Corp. occurred over a two-week period in January 1973; Coast Guardsmen rotated out as they were replaced. Erlandson said, "The turnover for engineers was pretty fast. They came in and took over in a few days. By then we had finally gotten new generators. The [American] civilian in charge didn't have a technical background, but he had operated contract stations before." During turnover, there was no interruption to the signal and no noticeable change in operation of the chain. Operations were essentially unchanged with the three stations in Thailand manned by Coast Guard crews and the two stations in Vietnam with civilian crews. The Coast Guard continued to provide technical and logistic support for all stations.[21]

Operating Plan Change Orders (OPCO) were issued on 22 January 1973, disestablishing Con Son and Tan My LORAN stations as Coast Guard–manned units. A Coast Guard logistic support detail was established at Sattahip, Thailand, the same day to provide logistic support for the two stations in Vietnam. Coast Guardsmen from SEASEC also visited stations to provide technical support.[22]

An Army CH 47 Chinook helicopter, on a regular run from Hue to Phu Bai, approached the helo pad at Tan My on 25 January 1973; it was almost noon. The last three Coast Guardsmen from Tan My LORAN station waited at the pad with their gear, oblivious to the falling rain. They turned their backs when the helo went into a hover over the pad, its twin rotors whipping puddled rain into spray. They handed their gear to a crewman and boarded through the side door. The helicopter lifted off, circled the tower, and headed south for Phu Bai. Erlandson said, "I was thankful everybody [in the crew] left in one piece. We took some chances, doing humanitarian work. We drove injured villagers to the hospital at Hue in the middle of the night. We knew the road wasn't secure at night, but people's lives were at stake. Typically, it was a lantern or a stove that exploded, badly burning people—usually children. Or a sick child that had to get to the hospital." Erlandson took a last look at the station through the partially lowered rear ramp before the helicopter changed course.[23]

Merchant Marine Detail

Cdr. Dorwin W. Newman got his first look at Saigon from the front seat of a Jeep on his way into the city from Tan Son Nhut airport. YNC William A. Price maneuvered through thickening traffic near the U.S. Embassy; motor scooters, pedicabs, and bicycles merged with trucks, taxicabs, and military vehicles clogging the street. Price was administrative assistant to the officer in charge, Coast Guard Merchant Marine Detail (MMD), Saigon. The third member of the detail, a lieutenant, had departed Vietnam three days earlier without relief. Newman, assigned to relieve Capt. Walter B. Alvey as officer in charge, took over on 9 June 1972. The MMD was attached to the consulate section and had its office in the embassy compound. Newman said, "The [consular] section was separate because we handled the public. It was less secure than the rest of the Embassy."[24]

In October 1972, the Coast Guard made preparations to turn over its functions and remove all personnel in conjunction with the overall military withdrawal. U.S. merchant shipping, however, would still be needed to support Vietnam's war effort. Newman said, "I requested to stay in-country, because I thought there was still a job for me to do. Even Ambassador [Ellsworth] Bunker wanted me to stay." On 30 October 1972, Newman sent a letter to COMNAVFORV to assure him that the Coast Guard Merchant Marine Detail—Newman and his administrative assistant—would be under the umbrella of the U.S. Embassy. In his letter, Newman described the Detail's continuing functions as:

- Examination of merchant vessels in order to determine that they are in substantial compliance with their certificate of inspection and . . . examination of official log books
- Investigation of marine casualties and accidents, including deaths and injuries of persons on merchant vessels of the United States
- Investigations of violations of law, negligence, misconduct, unskillfulness, incompetence, or misbehavior of merchant vessel personnel
- Enforcement of vessel inspections, navigation, and seamen's laws in general.[25]

Newman concluded his letter by saying that, based on the MMD's mission, authority, and functions, it was not part of the military establishment nor under the Department of Defense and should not be included as military support personnel. He said, "The ambassador wanted me to continue [with my job]. He didn't think I should be counted as one of the military." On 7 February 1973, four days before SCGOV was disestablished, the MMD was transferred from SCGOV to SEASEC for administrative control; it remained under the embassy for operational control.[26]

Closing the Door

On 10 February 1973, the three remaining Coast Guardsmen from SCGOV—Lt. Cdr. William T. Leahy, Lt. Jay A. Creech, and senior chief machinery technician Stephen H. Petersen—made preparations to leave Vietnam. Creech said, "We had three Jeeps left. One had a trailer. We took what was left of the equipment and supplies out of the office and loaded it into the trailer. After we turned in all our weapons to the Navy security group—and we had a lot—we drove out to Colonel Viet's OCO [ARVN Ordnance Command] compound. We left two Jeeps and the trailer full of gear with him."[27]

The next morning the men, who were billeted separately, met back at the office; they wore khaki uniforms instead of greens. They made a final check of the offices and picked up three boxes of files for delivery to SEASEC. Typewriters were still on the desks. "When we shut that door and pad-locked it," Creech said, "It was like we're turning the whole thing over. It was just us, turning out the lights and leaving. And no one really cared that we'd never be back. It was a somber time. We knew we hadn't won." When Creech made a final check of desk drawers, he found a .45-caliber automatic. "There was no time to turn it in," he said, "So I handed it to the Vietnamese guard at the door as I left the building."[28]

The three men drove to Tan Son Nhut airport with the file boxes and their bags. After checking in for their flight, they parked the Jeep in a secluded spot. Creech said, "We used black spray-paint to cover over the ID number and Coast Guard markings. We just left the Jeep with the keys in it. There were so few Americans left, there was no one to give it to." The Thai Airways Boeing 727 took off for Bangkok at 1230. SCGOV's final monthly report of operations said, "Senior Coast Guard Officer Vietnam disestablished this date as per Commandant's message 051557Z February 1973. All personnel attached to SCGOV departed country."[29]

Cease-Fire

Newman said, "I didn't notice any difference in Saigon after the cease-fire and withdrawal of [U.S.] forces. It was business as usual. There was no feeling of anxiety. My mission didn't really change.

274 The Coast Guard at War

Things did become more difficult for us in doing our job. It wasn't as easy to get around in-country." Newman frequently had to drive his Jeep 50 miles overland to Vung Tau to meet arriving ships. He said, "Sometimes the road was secure and sometimes it wasn't." In April 1973, the State Department sent a cable to the Coast Guard, saying it would fund Newman's billet; the message, with a copy to the Embassy, was transmitted in the clear. Reference to Newman in the transmissqon raised questions about his continued presence in Vietnam: Should he be counted in the limited number of U.S. military personnel allowed to remain in-country? Newman said, "The message blew the whole thing. After that, the ambassador said, 'I can't do anything. You'll have to go.'"[30]

Newman went through the MMD's files, sending important documents and classified material to SEASEC in Bangkok; the rest he shredded. He said, "A new consular officer had just taken over. I left him all my material [manuals and publications] and briefed him as well as I could [on merchant marine matters]. I left notes on the kinds of incidents to expect. He wasn't going to handle any misconducts or do any investigating, but he would sign off on ship's logs." On 2 May 1973, commander Southeast Asia section sent a brief message to the commandant reporting that "IAW [in accordance with] OFCO [Operating Facility Change Order] 123-73 of 23 April 1973, MMD Saigon, RVN, disestablished 1 May 1973."[31]

Newman returned the Marine sentry's salute and the black sedan pulled away from the embassy compound. The Vietnamese driver merged into traffic—swelled by refugees flocking to the city—and headed for Tan Son Nhut airport. At the airport, Newman checked his two bags and boarded an Air Vietnam Boeing 707; his khaki uniform stood out among the mostly civilian passengers going to Bangkok. At 1430 on 5 May 1973, the last Coast Guardsman assigned to Vietnam departed.

17

The End

Saigon, South Vietnam—President Duong Van Minh announced today the unconditional surrender of the Saigon Government and its military forces to the Viet Cong.

Columns of South Vietnamese troops pulled out of their defensive positions in the capital and marched to central points to turn in their weapons.

New York Times
30 April 1975

Lt. Thad W. Allen heard a knock and looked up from his desk on 29 April 1975. Chief Radio Electrician Chris W. Percival, the station's executive officer (XO), stood at the open door. "The signal building just called, Skipper. The watch says you'll be interested in RATT [radio teletype] traffic between Con Son [LORAN station, Vietnam] and Bangkok [Coast Guard Southeast Asia Section, Thailand]." Allen drained his coffee mug, took his cap from a hook by the door, and headed out into the mid-day heat. His XO was right behind him.[1]

Their heavy boots kicked up dust as they walked down the slight hill to the signal/power building at Coast Guard LORAN station Lampang, Thailand; it was the dry season. Despite temperatures in the 90's, everyone on the station always wore long pants and heavy boots to protect themselves against poisonous snakes. Vipers, asps, and cobras were a concern, but the deadly banded krait was the greatest danger.

They entered the building—relieved to be back in air-conditioning—and turned left down the corridor to the small communications center. When they entered the room, the electronics technician on watch was standing at the old model 40 Teletype. "Something's going on at Con Son," he said and moved aside to let them read the traffic. The informal communications read:

Bangkok, this is Con Son. There is a chopper on the station. They say
we are supposed to be evacuated, now. Request instructions. Should we
leave or wait for Navy evacuation?

Southeast Asia Section replied:

This is Bangkok. Stand by one minute. We are getting Mr. Carter now.

Lt. Cdr. David A. Carter, chief of the electronics division at SEASEC,
had been planning the removal of equipment and evacuation of personnel from Con Son ever since Tan My LORAN station was abandoned on 19 March 1975. The evacuation could not be done, however,
until the last minute; the signal was still critical for navigation. Some
of Lampang's crew filtered into the signal building to find out what
was happening at their sister station. In Bangkok, Carter and a radioman crowded into the cubicle housing SEASEC's teletype machine.

Con Son this is Bangkok. Mr. Carter here. Understand you have a chopper on the station, correct?
    This is Con Son. Roger. It is an Air America chopper. It is a local Air
America shuttle to the ship.
    This is Bangkok. You are authorized to go off-air when necessary. Get
what you can recover in the way of cesiums [time standards]. What
equipment you cannot recover, I want you to destroy. If Air America
wishes to use the site, you are authorized to turn it over to them. Otherwise, try to destroy the generators by running them without oil. If you
have the time. As soon as you are safely aboard, please send immediate
message to this office with information copy to COMUSMAG Nakhon
Phanom, Thailand.
    This is Con Son. Request to know if you have a programmed plane
or helicopter for us. No plane can land any more on this airfield. The
chopper here cannot take out any equipment with it.
    This is Bangkok. We have been working on a C-130 to make one trip.
But we have no firm word yet. Please reconfirm that strip is unusable
for fixed-wing aircraft. Also, if you can't take the cesiums, then you are
directed to smash them.
    This is Con Son. Airstrip packed with inoperative VNAF [Vietnam
Air Force] planes. If you want the equipment, send us a larger chopper.
We must know within one hour. The Air America chopper will leave at
that time.
    This is Bangkok. We will get back to you ASAP [as soon as possible].
Please stand by.
    This is Con Son. Roger. We'll try.

As word of the impending evacuation of Con Son spread at Lampang, the rest of the crew gathered near the Teletype. Allen said, "People just couldn't believe it was happening. All the press we had access to was much more optimistic."

> Sattahip, Lampang, Udorn, this is Bangkok. I am assuming net control at this time. Repeat, COMSEASEC is now net control. No traffic, repeat no traffic, will be passed without my say so. Circuit silence at this time, 0412Z.
>
> Bangkok this is Con Son. The situation here is as follows: If the 7th Fleet will take refugees off the island now, we can remove crashed and inoperative VNAF aircraft from the runway and a C-130 can land to evacuate us and the equipment. Must know if refugees will leave also. What is the plan with the 7th Fleet? Must know in one hour because [Air America] chopper will leave and not come back. Please advise, ASAP.
>
> This is Bangkok. Roger. There is a C-130 enroute, but I don't know of any plans to evacuate refugees. Advise if they, plus your crew, will fit on the C-130.
>
> This is Con Son. Negative. There are over 1,000 refugees and more coming. C-130 cannot land at this time because of aircraft on runway.

VNAF planes fleeing from Saigon continued to crash-land on the station's airstrip.

> This is Bangkok. Roger. I am checking on a larger chopper and will advise soonest. In the meantime, do not miss the last Air America chopper.
>
> This is Con Son. Roger. Big chopper is best way. Let us know within 40 minutes.
>
> This is Bangkok. Roger. Time is now minute 21. I will try to get to you by minute 45 to be on the safe side.
>
> Bangkok this is Con Son. Roger. Will stand by.

Paul C. McCurry, a senior chief electronic technician at SEASEC, said, "Things were happening so fast, we didn't have time to write down messages before we sent them. People were on phones trying to get information and arrange for aircraft."[2]

> This is Con Son. There is a possibility that a C-130 might be able to land, but there is still one crashed plane on the runway.
>
> This is Bangkok. What is your estimate of the mood of the refugees? What will happen if only one plane should land.

This is Con Son. The military situation here is stable, so far.

This is Bangkok. I feel a C-130 is a gamble. We will cancel the plane and work on a large chopper.

This is Con Son. Roger. Get back to us in 30 minutes so we will know.

Lampang's crew waited in the signal building, clustered in small groups. They talked in lowered tones as they waited to hear what was going to happen to Con Son's crew. Allen said, "We were saying, 'This can't be real.' It was so peaceful and calm where we were. It was surreal. It wasn't really happening."

The situation in Vietnam deteriorated so rapidly, it was questionable whether a later helicopter could safely get into and out of Con Son. McCurry said, "The feeling was, 'Don't bother trying to get help from any other source. There was no guarantee that we could. It was time to get those guys off.'"

A little more than a month earlier, COMSEASEC received an unexpected telephone call on the afternoon of 18 March 1975. The caller, from the defense attache office (DAO) at the American Embassy in Saigon, said, "Hey, how do you guys intend to evacuate Tan My?" He reported conditions in the area were rapidly deteriorating and developing into an evacuation and abandonment scenario. Until that moment, SEASEC was unaware of the gravity of the situation. Three members of the staff had visited Tan My nine days earlier; the situation appeared normal. Capt. Edward A. Hemstreet, chief of SEASEC's civil engineering division, was a lieutenant commander at the time. He said, "We were at Tan My on 9 March 1975. They told us the situation was as stable as it had been in a long time. The threat level was low." McCurry, a member of the inspection team, said, "We went up to Hue to look around and take some pictures. We drove back to Tan My that evening." On 13 March 1975, the North Vietnamese captured Ban Me Thuot, capital of Dar Lac province, in the central highlands; South Vietnamese forces withdrew from Pleiku and Kontum. A precipitous rout followed.[3]

Twenty-one hours after the phone call, Tan My was off-air and in the final phase of evacuation. Hemstreet said, "Everything at Tan My was abandoned. It was signed over to the ARVN commander. The crew oversped the generators and smashed electronic equipment before leaving."[4]

At 1239 on 29 April 1975, COM SEASEC decided it was time to evacuate:

Con Son this is Bangkok.
   For Harry Miller
   From COMSEASEC
   Destroy equipment. Evacuate via Air America chopper. When safely evacuated, advise COMSEASEC your location, names of personnel, and equipment salvaged, if any.

Con Son's crew was obviously ready to depart. They replied:

This is Con Son. Roger that. We will be going off-air in five minutes and will destroy equipment. Will try to keep communications until the end.
   This is Bangkok. Roger.
   Udorn this is Bangkok. Do not blink Yankee [Con Son] when they go off. Just forget about them and worry about master [Sattahip] and Xray [Lampang]. Do not blink.

Con Son LORAN station ceased transmission and signal SH-3 Yankee went off-air at 1246 on 29 April 1975, concluding the Coast Guard's role in Vietnam.

Notes

Chapter 1. Arms from the Sea

1. "Floating Island," 36, 37; and "Eighty Tons of Vietcong Arms Captured," 2.
2. Schreadley, *Rivers to the Sea*, 80–81.
3. Defense Department, *Evidence*, 1, 10 (pamphlet).
4. Ibid., 9.
5. Marolda and Fitzgerald, *From Military Assistance to Combat*, 104.
6. Ibid., 169.
7. Ibid., 172.
8. Ibid., 173, 176.
9. Ibid., 177.
10. Ibid., 228, 231, 239, 240, 306.
11. Schreadley, *Rivers to the Sea*, 82, 83.
12. Marolda and Fitzgerald, *From Military Assistance to Combat*, 519.
13. Ibid., 514, 515.
14. Smith, *Reminiscences of Admiral Willard J. Smith*.
15. Nitze, letter to Fowler, 16 April 1965.
16. McNamara, "Memorandum," 29 April 1965.

Chapter 2. Squadron One Deploys

1. Webber, interview.
2. Cass, interview.
3. Hodgman, "Market Time," 40; and CINCPACFLT, "Provision of U.S. Coast Guard Boats," message 252231Z.
4. Cass, interview.
5. CINCPACFLT, "Provision of U.S. Coast Guard Boats," message 252231Z.
6. Navy and Coast Guard agreement signed 2 July and 8 July 1965; and Hodgman, interview.
7. CINCPACFLT, "Provision of U.S. Coast Guard Boats," message 252231Z.
8. Walden, interview.
9. Ibid.
10. Mense, interview.
11. "Coast Guard Squadron One Information Bulletin," 28 August 1965.
12. Ibid.
13. Ibid.
14. Personal experience of the author.

15. Webber, interview.
16. NAVADGRUV, "Coast Guard Activities Vietnam, Operations, June-August 1965."
17. Ibid.
18. COGARDRON ONE, "Squadron Organization; Recommendations Concerning," letter, 23 June 1965.
19. NAVADGRUV, "Coast Guard Activities Vietnam, Operations, June-August 1965."
20. Uithol, personal journal, 16 July 1965.

Chapter 3. Division 12 on Patrol

1. Sources for narrative account of 11 August 1966 attack on USCGC *Point Welcome* (WPB 82329): Bell, interview; USCGC *Point Caution*, "Summary of Events, 11 August 1966," letter, 12 August 1966; and NAVFORV, monthly historical summary, August 1966.
2. On 21 August 1966, Gen. William C. Westmoreland, COMMACV, restricted the conditions under which U.S. aircraft were permitted to fire on small vessels to "prevent the recurrence" of the attack on *Point Welcome*.
3. Knapp, interview.
4. COMCOGARDIV 12, diary, 20 July 1965.
5. Cece, interview.
6. Knapp, interview.
7. COMCOGARDIV 12, diary, 4 August 1965; and Knapp, interview.
8. Knapp, interview.
9. COMCOGARDIV 12, diary, 10 August 1965.
10. Knapp, interview.
11. COMCOGARDIV 12, memorandum, 10 March 1965.
12. CHNAVADGRUV, OPORDER CTF-115 201.YR.
13. COMCOGARDIV 12, diary, 8 June 1966.
14. Saunders, interview; and COMCOGARDIV 12, diary, 10–16 July 1967.
15. Saunders, interview; and Carr, interview.
16. COMNAVFORV, message 192356Z.
17. Cece, interview; and Saunders, interview.
18. COMCOGARDIV 12, diary, 24 July 1965; and Cece, interview.
19. Lehr, interview.
20. Sources for narrative account of 10 March 1968 ammunition fire: Carr, interview; COMCOGARDIV 12, diary, 10 March 1968; Coast Guard, *Commandant's Bulletin*, 5 April 1968; Defense Department, "Lieutenant (jg) Carr—Narrative"; and USCGC *Point Arden*, "Damage incurred on 10 March 1968; report of," letter, 13 March 1968.
21. Tugman, interview.

22. Ibid.
23. CTG 76.4, message 140626Z.
24. Coast Guard Headquarters, Military Readiness Division, memorandum serial 09973.
25. Volkle, interview.

Chapter 4. Market Time in the Gulf of Thailand

1. Sources for narrative account *Point Glover* and *Point Marone* actions: Nelson, interview; "Coast Guard Squadron One Information Bulletin," 3 December 1965; "Coast Patrol in Viet Nam Far From Jersey Routine"; NAVADGRU, "Coast Guard Activities Vietnam, Operations, September-October 1965"; Coast Guard Division 11, "List of Events, Deployment to 31 December 1965"; and Hodgman, "Market Time," 55, 56.
2. NAVADGRU, "Coast Guard Activities Vietnam, Operations, September-October 1965."
3. COGARDRON ONE, diary, 29 July 1965.
4. COMCOGARDRON ONE, message 300200Z.
5. COMCOGARDRON ONE, message 020400Z; and COGARDRON ONE, diary, 1 August 1965.
6. Hodgman, "Market Time," 48.
7. Causey, interview.
8. Author's experience while in command of USCGC *Point Comfort* (WPB 82317).
9. Lehr, interview.
10. Nelson and Currier, "Operation of Coast Guard Patrol Boats in Southeast Asia," 407, 408; and Hayes, interview.
11. Hodgman, "Market Time," 48, 49.
12. Sources for narrative account of amphibious raid: Author's experience in command of USCGC *Point Comfort* (WPB 82317); and Lt. Alexander R. Larzelere, "Statement of Facts and Circumstances Surrounding the Striking of an Underwater Object by USCG *Point Comfort* on 27 September 1965."
13. Larzelere, "Viet Nam," 90–99.
14. Hayes, interview.
15. Causey, interview.
16. Larzelere, "Patrol Boat Activity," 1–3.
17. Ibid., 3.
18. Angel, "Evaluation of Coast Guard Fire," letter, (undated).
19. Venzke, interview.
20. Sources for narrative account of 10 May 1966 trawler engagement: Mosher, interview; NAVFORV, press release, 15 August 1966; Schreadley,

Rivers to the Sea, 94–96; and NAVFORV, "Trawler Caught in Infiltration Attempt by Market Time Units," press release, 11 May 1966.

21. Hodgman, "Market Time," 64.
22. Hayes, interview.
23. Venzke, interview.
24. Schreadley, *Rivers to the Sea*, 148–50.

Chapter 5. Patrolling the Delta

1. Sources for narrative account of 20 June 1966 trawler engagement: Ulmer, interview; Ulmer, "Account of events on 20 June 1966, Republic of Vietnam"; Coast Guard, *Commandant's Bulletin*, 22 June 1966; Sheehan, "Sea Watch"; and COMNAVFORV, public information release no. 46–66, (undated).
2. Ulmer, debriefing report, 24 June 1966; and Thomson, debriefing report, 24 June 1966.
3. CINCPAC, message 021810Z; and U.S. Defense Department, Military Assistance Command Vietnam, Naval Advisory Group, Historical Review, September 1965.
4. Thomson, interview.
5. Gilbert, interview.
6. Lehr, interview; and COMCOGARDIV 13, diary, 10, 12 December 1965.
7. Lehr, interview.
8. Ibid.
9. COMCOGARDIV 13, letter, 24 January 1966.
10. COMCOGARDIV 13, diary, 22, 23 February 1966; and "Coast Guard Squadron One Information Bulletin," 25 March 1966.
11. Gilbert, interview; and William J. Miller, interview.
12. Thomson, interview.
13. William J. Miller, interview.
14. Ibid.
15. Mumford, "Jackstay."
16. Ibid.; and COGRADRON ONE, diary, 7 March 1966.
17. Hickey, interview.
18. Ibid.
19. Mumford, "Jackstay," 79.
20. USCGC *Point Partridge*, "*Point Partridge* Junk Incident of 19 April," letter, 21 April 1966.
21. COGRADRON ONE, diary, 12–18 December 1966.
22. COMCOGARDIV 13, diary, 11–17 September 1967.
23. Sources for narrative account of 22 January 1969 rescue: Underwood, interview; COGARDIV 13, monthly summary report, January 1969; and

Coast Guard, "California Coast Guardsman Awarded Silver Star Medal," news release, 2 August 1969.

24. Busavage, interview.
25. Smith, interview; and COMCOGARDACTV, "Remarks at Division 13 Change of Command," 31 May 1969.
26. Underwood, interview.
27. Busavage, interview.
28. Smith, interview.
29. Ibid.

Chapter 6. Command in the Gulf

1. Sources for narrative account of 10 May 1969 Duong Keo river action: Spence, interview; CTE 194.5.4.9, "Spot Report," message 052040Z; and NAVFORV, monthly historical summary, May 1969.
2. Cdr. Paul A. Yost, USCG, received a Silver Star Medal for heroism during the operation.
3. Cutler, *Brown Water*, 308, 309; and Schreadley, *Rivers to the Sea*, 219.
4. Hayes, interview.
5. Hodgman, "Market Time," 58, 59; and Yost, interview.
6. Sources for narrative account of sinking and salvage of PCF 4: Uithol, interview; COGARDIV 11, diary, 14, 15, 18 February 1966; and Hodgman, "Market Time," 62, 64.
7. "In Memoriam, Crew Members Swift Boat 4," program (undated); and author's memories of service attended while in command of USCGC *Point Banks* (WPB 82327).
8. COGARDIV 11, diary, 18 February 1966.
9. Hodgman, "Market Time," 57.
10. Ibid., 47.
11. Ibid., 58.
12. Venzke, interviews; and Hayes, interview.
13. Yost, interview.
14. Sources for narrative account of 6 April 1966 Operation Roundup: VNN, 4th coastal zone, "Operation Order," 4 April 1966; and author's personal experience.
15. COGARDIV 11, diary, 15 December 1965.
16. Venzke, interviews.
17. Ibid.; and Hayes, interview.
18. Ibid.
19. Lonsdale, interviews. Before the end of the war, Dang Cao Thang became an admiral and was in charge of the VNN's riverine forces. His family escaped Vietnam a week before the communists took over. Thang

made it down the Mekong river the day before the takeover and boarded a U.S. Navy destroyer to escape. He was reunited with his family with Lonsdale's help after he reached the United States. Thang and his family lived with the Lonsdales for six months until they could make a new start. Thang is now a successful international banker.

20. Lonsdale, interviews.
21. Venzke, interviews.
22. Lonsdale, interviews.
23. Ibid.
24. Ibid.
25. Yost, interview.
26. Ibid.; and Lonsdale, interviews.
27. Yost, interview; NAVFORV, monthly historical summary, June 1969; and NAVFORV, monthly historical summary, July 1969.

Chapter 7. The Coast Guard Role Expands

1. Sources for narrative account of action on 9 March 1966: Hickey, interview; Naval Advisory Group, news release, 16 March 1966; USCGC *Point White*, "Situation Report One and Final, Junk Sinking," message 092015Z; and COMCOGARDRON ONE, letter, 14 March 1966.
2. COMCOGARDRON ONE, "Coast Guard Matters," letter, 9 September 1965.
3. Joint Chiefs of Staff, "Attachment," message 152103Z.
4. COGARDRON ONE, diary, 15 January 1966; and Bauman, interview.
5. Hanson, interview; MACV, "Port Security," message 041003Z; and COGARDRON ONE, "Port Security," message 120618Z.
6. Kaplan, "The Coast Guard's Other War"; and Naval Advisory Group, monthly historical review, October 1965.
7. Ibid.
8. CINCPAC, "Coast Guard Explosive Handling Teams," message 202237Z; and COGARDRON ONE, diary, 19, 21 March 1966.
9. COGARDRON ONE, diary, 19 April 1966.
10. Ibid., 25 April 1966; and Coast Guard Advisor to MSTS, Saigon, diary, 3 December 1966.
11. Ibid.
12. Navy, MSTS Far East Area, "U.S. Coast Guard Hearing Officer," letter, 31 August 1966.
13. Kaplan, "The Coast Guard's Other War," 5; and Kendall, "U.S. Merchant Shipping and Vietnam."
14. NAVFORV, "Coastal Surveillance Force," letter, 28 September 1966.
15. COGARDRON ONE, diary, 25 July 1966.

16. Ibid., 2 November 1966.
17. Ibid., 31 October 1966–4 November 1966.
18. Coast Guard Commandant, "Establish Coast Guard Activities Vietnam," Operation Change Order No. 75-67.
19. Hathaway, interview.
20. Ibid.
21. Ibid.
22. Ibid.

Chapter 8. Squadron Three

1. Sources for narrative account of trawler action 17–22 November 1970: Durfey, interview; and USCGC *Rush*, "Action Report Infiltration Trawler SL-3-70."
2. Chief of Naval Operations, "Additional Coast Guard Cutters," memorandum, 8 March 1967.
3. SECNAV, "Additional High Endurance Cutters for Assignment with U.S. Naval Forces in South Vietnam," memorandum, 10 March 1967.
4. Coast Guard Commandant, "WHEC Deployment," message 102226Z.
5. Scherer, interview.
6. Morse, "Underway Replenishment," 289; and COGARDRON THREE, *Squadron Three*, 14.
7. COGARDRON THREE, *Squadron Three*, 3, 4.
8. Ibid., 4.
9. Scherer, interview.
10. Beiter, "Life with Squadron Three," 13, 14, 15.
11. Coast Guard, "Enemy Infiltrators," 2.
12. COMCOGARDIV 12, "Trawler 29 B-2," letter, 8 March 1968.
13. Coast Guard, "Enemy Infiltrators," 2.
14. Bauman, interview.
15. COMCOGARDIV 12, "After-action Report"; and Coast Guard, "Enemy Infiltrators," 3.
16. Bauman, interview.
17. COMCOGARDIV 12, "After-action Report."
18. Lynch, interview.
19. COMNAVFORV, message 101114Z.
20. COMCOGARDRON THREE, "Lessons Learned."
21. COMCOGARDRON THREE, "NGFS Incident," 25 May 1970.
22. Beiter, "Life with Squadron Three," 16, 17.
23. Morse, "Underway Replenishment," 289.
24. COGARDRON THREE, *Squadron Three*, 7.
25. Durfey, interview.

26. COGARDRON THREE, *Squadron Three*, 9.

27. USCGC *Rush*, "Vietnam Cruise Book," 57.

28. COGARDRON THREE, *Squadron Three*, 16.

29. Durfey, interview.

Chapter 9. With the Jolly Green Giants

1. Sources for narrative account of rescue on 2 July 1968: Eagan, interview; Eagan, "Statement Concerning Talley"; and COGARDACTV, "Coast Guard Aviators," press release, 18 October 1968.

2. When Joel Talley returned to the United States after his tour of duty in Vietnam, Jack Modica got in touch with him. The two men became close friends. Modica is godparent to Talley's two sons.

3. Crowe, interview.

4. Defense Department and Treasury Department, "Memorandum of Agreement between Air Force and Coast Guard."

5. Chief of Naval Operations, "Game Warden Patrol Operations," message 152108Z; and Coast Guard Commandant, "Game Warden Patrol Operations," message 162055Z.

6. Frischmann, interview.

7. Ibid.

8. COGARDACTV, "Personnel Casualty Report," message 130536Z.

9. Loomis, interview.

10. Crowe, interview.

11. Loomis, interview.

12. Taylor, *Jane's All the World's Aircraft*, 451, 452.

13. Eagan, interview.

14. Crowe, interview.

15. Loomis, interview.

16. Crowe, interview.

17. Crowe, letter to Moreau, 27 April 1973.

18. Sturm, "Miracle Mission," 43–47.

Chapter 10. Explosive Loading Detachments

1. Sources for narrative accounts of attacks on 14 and 18 February 1968: Berry, interview; Coast Guard, "Yered Interview"; COGARDACTV, "Report of Activity During Period 11–18 February 1968," letter, 21 February 1968; and COGARDACTV, monthly summary report, February 1968.

2. NAVADGRU, monthly historical summary, August 1965.

3. MACV, "Port Security Saigon Harbor," message 041003Z.

4. Matilla, interview.

5. Matilla, interview; and Kaplan, "The Coast Guard's Other War," 3.
6. Matilla, interview; and PS&WD, diary, 7–13 November 1966.
7. NAVADGRU, monthly historical summary, November 1965.
8. MACV, "Coast Guard Explosive Handling Teams," message 170837Z; and CINCPAC, "Coast Guard Explosive Handling Teams," message 202237Z.
9. O'Keefe, interview.
10. Ibid.; and Willis, interview.
11. Ibid.
12. O'Keefe, interview.
13. COGARDRON ONE, diary, 3–9 October 1966.
14. O'Keefe, interview.
15. Ibid.
16. Ibid.
17. O'Keefe, interview; and COGARDRON ONE, diary, 1–10 July 1966.
18. O'Keefe, interview; and COGARDRON ONE, diary, 3–9 October 1966.
19. Willis, interview; and COGARDRON ONE, diary, 1–7 August 1966.
20. Willis, interview.
21. COGARDRON ONE, diary, 1–10 July 1966; and Willis, interview.
22. Ibid.
23. Willis, interview.
24. Ibid.
25. PS&WD, diary, 27 February–5 March 1967; and COGARDACTV, diary, 1–8 July 1967.
26. Berry, interview.
27. Ibid.
28. Ibid.
29. Kinkade, interview.
30. Law Enforcement Division, "Item for *Commandant's Bulletin*," memorandum, 27 March 1969.
31. First Logistical Command, "U.S. Coast Guard Port Security and Waterways Detail Mission Statement."
32. Schneider, interview.
33. Ibid.
34. PS&WD, diary, 30 January–5 February 1967; and Commander Western Area, "Explosive Loading Detachments," letter, 13 June 1967.
35. PS&WD, diary, 23–29 October 1967.
36. Ibid.
37. COGARDACTV, monthly summary report, March 1968.
38. SS *Longview Victory*, "Master's Storage Evaluation Report, Voyage Commencing 22 March 1967"; and SS *North Platte Victory*, "Master's Voyage Report," 21 May 1967.

39. COGARDACTV, diary, 3–9 April 1967; and NAVSUPPACT Danang, "Coast Guard Explosive Cargo Inspection," message 311013Z.
40. COGARDACTV, monthly summary report, July 1968.

Chapter 11. Shipping and Port Security

1. Sources for narrative account of 20 December 1966 sea trials: Oliver, interview; Oliver, "Coast Guard Shipping Advisory Unit Vietnam," 2–12; and shipping advisor, diary, 19–25 December 1966.
2. Oliver, interview.
3. Oliver, "Coast Guard Shipping Advisory Unit Vietnam," 1.
4. Kendall, "U.S. Merchant Shipping and Vietnam," 146; and Oliver, "Coast Guard Shipping Advisory Unit Vietnam," 2.
5. Oliver, "Coast Guard Shipping Advisory Unit Vietnam," 3, 4.
6. Oliver, "Coast Guard Shipping Advisory Unit Vietnam," 5.
7. Ibid.
8. Shipping advisor, diary, 5 December 1966; and Kendall, "U.S. Merchant Shipping and Vietnam," 142.
9. Shipping advisor, diary, 5 December 1966.
10. Shipping advisor, diary, 19–25 December 1966; and Kaplan, "The Coast Guard's Other War," 7.
11. Consular section Saigon, "UCMJ—Application to Seamen," memorandum, 6 December 1966; and Kaplan, "The Coast Guard's Other War," 7.
12. Kendall, "U.S. Merchant Shipping and Vietnam," 142, 143.
13. Oliver, "Coast Guard Shipping Advisory Unit Vietnam," 6.
14. Ibid., 7.
15. Ibid., 8, 9; Kaplan, "The Coast Guard's Other War," 6; and Oliver, interview.
16. Oliver, interview.
17. Ibid.
18. Coast Guard Activities Vietnam, monthly summary report, December 1969; and senior Coast Guard officer Vietnam, monthly summary report, December 1970.
19. MACV, "Coast Guard Port Security Team," message 201310Z.
20. Hertica, interview.
21. Ibid.
22. Ibid.; and PS&WD, diary, 15–23 October 1966.
23. First Logistical Command, "Mission Statement," (undated).
24. First Logistical Command, "General Order 6417"; Law Enforcement Division, "Item for *Commandant's Bulletin*: Port Safety/Security in Vietnam," memorandum, 27 March 1969; and PS&WD, diary, 15–23 October 1966.

25. Hertica, interview.
26. PS&WD, diary, 15–23 October 1966.
27. Ibid.
28. Hertica, interview; and PS&WD, diary, 28 November–4 December 1967.
29. PS&WD, diary, 21–27 November 1966.
30. Hertica, interview.
31. Ibid.
32. Ibid.
33. PS&WD, "Security Recommendations for Newport," letter, 29 October 1966.
34. PS&WD, diary, 27 February–5 March, 27 March–2 April, 10–16, 17–23 July, and 31 July–6 August 1967.
35. PS&WD, diary, 27 February–5 March 1967; Law Enforcement Division, "Item for *Commandant's Bulletin*: Port Safety/Security in Vietnam," memorandum, 27 March 1969; and Hertica, interview.
36. Hertica, interview.
37. Schneider, interview.
38. Ibid.
39. Ibid.
40. COGARDACTV, monthly summary report, December 1968.
41. Ibid.
42. COGARDACTV, monthly summary report, April 1969; "Fighting Boats," 312; and Schneider, interview.
43. Schneider, interview.
44. Ibid.
45. Ibid.

Chapter 12. Operation Tight Reign

1. Sources for narrative account of events of 15–17 January 1966 in Bangkok: Sargent, interview; Herbert, interview; and Crowell, interviews.
2. Sargent, interview.
3. Brock, interview.
4. Ibid.; and U.S. Coast Guard Historian file, "Operation Tight Reign," undated summary.
5. Sargent, interview.
6. Ibid.; "Operation Tight Reign Complete Success"; and Brock, interview.
7. "Operation Tight Reign Complete Success."
8. Tight Reign Construction Detachment, "Proposed Article for *Commandant's Bulletin*," letter, 2 May 1966.
9. Herbert, interview.
10. Crowell, interviews; and "Operation Tight Reign Complete Success."

11. Judd, "Tight Reign Happenings," 350; Sargent, interview; and Judd, "The LORAN Station on Con Son Island Was One of Many U.S. Coast Guard Contributions to the Vietnam War," 10, 58, 59.
12. Sargent, "Opinions and Commentary," 3.
13. Tight Reign Construction Detachment, "Proposed Article for *Commandant's Bulletin,*" letter, 2 May 1966.
14. Crowell, interviews; and Brock, interview.
15. Crowell, interviews.
16. USCG Construction Detachment, "Tight Reign I Resident Engineer; designation of," letter, 28 March 1966.
17. "Operation Tight Reign Complete Success."
18. Ibid.; Brock, interview; and LORAN Station Con Son, "General Information Book," IV-2.
19. Tight Reign Construction Detachment, "Proposed Article for *Commandant's Bulletin*"; Brock, interview; and Crowell, photographs.
20. Ibid.
21. Sargent, interview.
22. Brock, interview.
23. Ibid.; Crowell, interview; and "Operation Tight Reign Complete Success."
24. Ibid.; and Sargent, interview.
25. Brock, interview.
26. Ibid.; and Judd, "Tight Reign Happenings," 352.
27. Crowell, interview.
28. Judd, "Tight Reign Happenings," 349, 351.
29. "Operation Tight Reign," undated summary.
30. Judd, "Tight Reign Happenings," 346.
31. Brock, interview; and Sargent, interview.
32. CINCPAC, "SEASIA LORAN C," message 010231Z.
33. Ibid.
34. Beran, "Project Combat Aid," 21, 22.
35. Ibid.; Roland, interview; and Moreau, "The Coast Guard in the Central and Western Pacific," 292.
36. Riutta, interview.
37. Ibid.
38. Ibid.
39. Karnow, *Vietnam: A History,* 640.
40. Riutta, interview.
41. Ibid.; and Roland, interview.

Chapter 13. Aids to Navigation

1. Sources for narrative account of events of 25–28 March 1966: Young, interviews; and USCGC *Planetree*, "Vietnam Cruise Report."
2. COGARDRON ONE, diary, 26 April 1966; and Linnon, "Aids to Navigation in Vietnam," 99, 100.
3. COGARDRON ONE, diary, 5 May and 1–10 July 1966.
4. Young, interviews.
5. Ibid.
6. USCGC *Planetree*, "Vietnam Cruise Report."
7. COGARDRON ONE, diary, 12–18 December 1966.
8. Aids to Navigation Detail, diary, 19 December 1966.
9. Ibid., 7 January 1967.
10. Ibid., 27 December 1966.
11. COGARDACTV, diary, 6–12 March and 27 March–4 April 1967.
12. Aids to Navigation Detail, diary, 10–16 and 17–23 July 1967.
13. Ibid., 7–13 August 1967.
14. COGARDACTV, monthly summary report, November 1967; and Freeborn, interview.
15. Freeborn, interview.
16. A range consisted of two markers, lighted or unlighted, some distance apart. When a ship was on the axis of the channel, the markers appeared to be in line, one over the other. By steering to keep the markers in line, the ship remained within the confines of the channel.
17. Freeborn, interview.
18. Joint Chiefs of Staff, "Maritime Aids to Navigation in the Republic of Vietnam," message 261931Z.
19. Fourteenth Coast Guard District, "National Defense Transportation Association Award Nomination," letter, 12 May 1971.
20. O'Donnell, interview.
21. Ibid.
22. Ibid.
23. COGARDACTV, monthly summary report, January 1969; and COGARDACTV, monthly summary report, February 1969.
24. O'Donnell, interview; and COGARDACTV, monthly summary report, March 1969.
25. COGARDACTV, monthly summary report, March 1969; and Aids to Navigation Detail, diary, 17–23 July 1967.
26. O'Donnell, interview; and COGARDACTV, monthly summary report, September 1969.
27. USCGC *Blackhaw*, "News release (draft)," 1971.
28. USCGC *Blackhaw*, "Qui Nhon Navaids," message 101135Z.

Chapter 14. Patrol Boats to the Vietnamese

1. Sources for narrative account of 4 August 1970 event: Angelico, interview; COGARDIV 13, monthly summary report, August 1970; and NAVFORV, monthly historical summary, August 1970.
2. Niesz, interview.
3. COGARDACTV, monthly summary report, January 1969.
4. Niesz, interview.
5. Smith, interview.
6. Rufe, interview.
7. COGARDIV 13, diary, April 1969; Rufe, interview; and COGARDIV 13, monthly summary report, May 1969.
8. Republic of Vietnam Navy, "Ceremony for the Transfer of USCGC *Point Garnet*"; and Niesz, interview.
9. Ibid.
10. Rufe, interview.
11. Ibid.; and COGARDIV 13, diary, January 1969.
12. Navy Grant Aid Branch, "Improvement and Modernization of Vietnam Armed Forces," memorandum for the record, OP-421, 15 July 1969.
13. COGARDACTV, monthly summary report, July 1969.
14. Volkle, interview.
15. Niesz, interview.
16. Angelico, interview.
17. Foskey, interview.
18. Angelico, interview.
19. Volkle, interview; Wells, "'Vietnamization' Sounded Good," 70; and Wells, interview.
20. Foskey, interview.
21. Schreadley, *Rivers to the Sea*, 344, 345.
22. Wells, interview.
23. Wells, "'Vietnamization' Sounded Good," 8.
24. Angelico, interview.
25. COGARDACTV, "Instruction 4950.1—WPB Advisors."
26. NAVFORV, monthly historical summary, August 1970.

Chapter 15. Turnover of High-Endurance Cutters

1. Sources for narrative account of 3–4 August 1970 events: Bartlett, interview; USCGC *Yakutat*, monthly summary report, September 1970; and USS *Jennings County*, "Fire in Engineering Spaces," message 031730Z.
2. John C. Miller, Jr., interview.

3. NAVSUPPACT Saigon, "Fire Aboard *Jennings County*," message 080402Z.
4. NAVFORV, "Request for Turnover of Two Coast Guard WHECs," letter, 21 June 1969.
5. Ibid.
6. Rowe and Morison, *The Ships and Aircraft of the U.S. Fleet*, 214.
7. USCG commandant, "ACTION—Turnover of Two High-Endurance Cutters to the Vietnamese Navy," letter, 22 September 1971.
8. Henneberry, interview.
9. Ibid.
10. Bartlett, interview.
11. USCGC *Yakutat*, monthly summary report, 6 July 1970.
12. USCGC *Bering Strait*, monthly summary report, 15 September 1970.
13. Ibid.
14. USCGC *Yakutat*, "Administrative Remarks, Page 7—John C. Miller, Jr.," 28 August–9 November 1970.
15. Miller, interview; and Henneberry, interview.
16. USCGC *Bering Strait*, monthly summary report, 14 November 1970.
17. Ibid.
18. Bartlett, interview; and Henneberry, interview.
19. Republic of Vietnam Navy, "Turnover Ceremony," 1 January 1971.
20. COGARDRON THREE, "Monthly Summary," June 1971.
21. Chief of Naval Operations, "Turnover of Two Additional WHECs to VNN," message 292044Z.
22. USCG commandant, "ACTION—Turnover of Two High-Endurance Cutters to the Vietnamese Navy," letter, 22 September 1971; and COGARDRON THREE, monthly summary report, September 1971.
23. Case, interview.
24. Ibid.; and COGARDRON THREE, monthly summary report, November 1971.
25. USCGC *Cook Inlet*, monthly summary report, December 1971; and Duffin, interview.
26. Duffin, interview.
27. COGARDRON THREE, "Requisition and Invoice/Shipping Document," 16 December 1971; and VNN, "Certificate of Delivery," 21 December 1971.
28. Case, interview.
29. COGARDRON THREE, *Squadron Three*, 10.
30. Case, interview.
31. Fifth Coast Guard District, "Coast Guard Squadron Two," message 091419Z.
32. PACFLT, "WHEC Transfer," message 250328Z.

Chapter 16. The Coast Guard Withdraws

1. Sources for narrative account of 27 December 1972 mission: Long, interview; 40th ARRS Rescue Coordination Center, "Rescue Progress Reports 1 through 12 and Rescue Suspending Report," 24 December 1972–7 January 1973; and 40th ARRS Rescue Coordination Center, "Mission 40–133," report, 27 December 1972.
2. SCGOV, monthly summary report, March 1972.
3. SCGOV, monthly summary report, April 1972.
4. Purdy, interview.
5. Ibid.
6. Ibid.
7. Creech, interviews; and SCGOV, "Last Coast Guard Operating Unit in Vietnam Disestablished," news release, 31 January 1972.
8. Purdy, interview.
9. Joint Chiefs of Staff Memorandum, MJCS-58-70, 10 February 1970; and MACV, "Vietnamization of Aids to Navigation System (VANS) Staff Study," letter, 12 June 1970.
10. Fourteenth Coast Guard District, "Termination of USCG ATON Operations in Republic of Vietnam," message 040055Z.
11. SCGOV, "Coast Guard ATON Operations in Vietnam," message 011430Z.
12. SCGOV, "USCGC Basswood Departs Vietnam," message 031033Z.
13. SCGOV, monthly summary report, 1 January–11 February 1973.
14. Long, interview.
15. Ibid.
16. Lt. David F. Cooper, USCG, and Lt. Michael F. McCormack, USCG, reported to 40th ARRS in November 1973 for duty, but the ARRS did not fly any missions over Vietnam during the officers' tours.
17. Erlandson, interview.
18. Ibid.
19. Kies, interview.
20. Erlandson, interview.
21. Ibid.
22. Coast Guard, "Operating Plan Change Order (OPCO) No. 61–73," 22 January 1973; and Coast Guard, "Operating Facility Change Order (OFCO) No. 62–73," 22 January 1973.
23. Erlandson, interview.
24. SCGOV, monthly summary report, June 1972; and Newman, interview.
25. Coast Guard MMD, Saigon, "Merchant Marine Detail," letter, 30 October 1972.
26. Ibid.; and Newman, interview.
27. Creech, interviews.

28. Ibid.
29. Ibid.; and SCGOV, monthly summary report, 1 January–11 February 1973.
30. Newman, interview.
31. Ibid.; and SEASEC, Bangkok, message 0020250Z.

Chapter 17. The End

1. Sources for narrative account of evacuation of Con Son LORAN station: Allen, interview; and SEASEC, "The End of an Era of U.S. Coast Guard Operations," transcript (undated).
2. McCurry, interview.
3. Ibid.; and Hemstreet, interview.
4. Ibid.

Glossary of Abbreviations and Terms

ACTOV—Accelerated turnover to the Vietnamese
Adm.—Admiral (0-10)
AKL—Cargo ship, light
AMVER—Automated merchant vessel reporting system
AOG—Tanker, gasoline
AP—Air police
APC—Armored personnel carrier
APL—Barracks craft (non-self propelled)
ARG—Amphibious ready group
ARL—Repair ship, landing craft
ARRS—U.S. Air Force Aero Rescue and Recovery Squadron
ARVN—Army of Vietnam
ATLS—Air transportable LORAN system
ATON—Aid to navigation
ATSB—Advanced tactical support base
AWOL—Absent without leave
BEQ—Bachelor enlisted quarters
Blink—Intermittent signal when LORAN system is out of tolerance
BM—Boatswain's mate
BMCM—Master chief boatswain's mate
BMOW—Boatswain's mate of the watch
BOQ—Bachelor officers quarters
Capt.—Captain (0-6)
CASREP—Casualty report (equipment)
Cdr.—Commander (0-5)
CG—Coastal group or commanding general
CGUSARV—Commanding general, U.S. Army Vietnam
CHNAVADVGRU—Chief naval advisory group
CHOP—Change operational control
CIC—Combat information center
CIDG—Civilian irregular defense group, Vietnam
CINC—Commander in chief
CINCPAC—Commander in chief Pacific

CINCPACFLT—Commander in chief Pacific fleet
CNO—Chief of naval operations
CO—Commanding officer
COGARDACTV—Coast Guard activities Vietnam
COGARDIV—Coast Guard division
COGARDRON—Coast Guard squadron
COMCRUDESREP—Commander cruiser-destroyer group, Seventh Fleet, representative
COMNAVFORV—Commander naval forces Vietnam
COMNAVSUPPACT—Commander naval support activity
COMPHIBPAC—Commander amphibious forces Pacific
COMSEVENTHFLT—Commander Seventh Fleet
COMUSMACV—Commander U.S. military assistance command Vietnam
COMWESTAREA—Commander U.S. Coast Guard western area
CPO—Chief petty officer
CSC—Coastal surveillance center
CTE—Commander task element
CTF—Commander task force
CTG—Commander task group
CTU—Commander task unit
Cutter—U.S. Coast Guard ship or boat
CWO—Commissioned warrant officer
CZ—Coastal zone
DAO—Defense attache office
DCA—Damage control assistant
DD—Destroyer
DE—Destroyer escort
DER—Radar picket escort ship
DG—Dangerous cargoman
DMZ—Demilitarized Zone
DOD—Department of Defense
DON—Vietnamese directorate of navigation, Vietnam
DR—U.S. Army disposition report
DRT—Dead reckoning tracer
DRV—Democratic Republic of Vietnam (North Vietnam)
ECM—Electronics countermeasures
ELD—Explosive loading detachment, Coast Guard
EN—Engineman

ENS—Ensign (0-1)

EO—Engineer officer

EOD—Explosive ordnance disposal

ET—Electronic technician

ETC—Chief electronic technician

ETCS—Senior chief electronic technician

1st Log—U.S. Army 1st Logistical Command

FM—Frequency modulated

FTG—Fleet training group

FTJ—Failure to join (merchant service AWOL)

GM—Gunner's mate

GMCM—Master chief gunner's mate

GQ—General quarters

GTMO—Guantanamo Bay, Cuba

GVN—Government of Vietnam (South Vietnam)

HE—High explosive

HF—High frequency

H&I—Harassment and interdiction

ID—Identification

JCS—Joint Chiefs of Staff

Junk Force—Vietnamese Navy coastal groups

KCS—Kit Carson scout

KIA—Killed in action

LARC—Lighter, amphibious, resupply cargo

LCM—Landing craft, mechanized

LCU—Landing craft, utility

LCVP—Landing craft, vehicle, personnel

LDNN—Lien Doc Nguoi Nhia (Vietnamese Navy SEALs)

LLNR—Light list number

LOP—Line of position

LORAN—Long range aid to navigation

LSD—Landing ship, dock

LSIL—Landing ship, infantry, large

LSM—Landing ship, medium

LSSL—Landing support ship, large

LST—Landing ship, tank

Lt.—Lieutenant (0-3)

Lt. Cdr.—Lieutenant commander (0-4)

Lt. (jg)—Lieutenant (junior grade) (0-2)

LZ—Landing zone
MAAG—Military assistance and advisory group
MACTHAI—Military assistance command Thailand
MACV—Military assistance command Vietnam
MAF—Marine amphibious force
MAP—Military assistance program
MAR AD-V—Maritime administration, Vietnam
Market Time—Coastal surveillance and interdiction operation
MEDCAP—Medical civic action program
MIPR—Military interdepartmental purchase request
MKCS—Senior chief machinery technician
MMD—Merchant Marine detail
MP—Military Police
MSC—Minesweeper, coastal
MSF—Mobile strike force
MSO—Minesweeper, ocean
MSTS—Military sea transportation service
MSTSFE—Military sea transportation service, Far East
NAVADVGRP—Naval advisory group
NAVFORV—Naval forces Vietnam
NAVSUPPACT—Naval support activity
NCO—Noncommissioned officer
NGF—Naval gunfire
NGFS—Naval gunfire support
NGLO—Naval gunfire liaison officer
NILO—Naval intelligence liaison officer
NSAD—Naval support activity detachment
NVA—North Vietnamese Army
NVN—North Vietnam
OBA—Oxygen breathing apparatus
OCO—Army ordnance command, Vietnam
OFCO—Operating facility change order
OICC—U.S. Navy officer in charge of construction
OINC—Officer in charge
OJT—On the job training
OOD—Officer of the deck
OPCO—Operating plan change order
OPLAN—Operation plan
OPNAV—Office of the chief of naval operations

ORI—Operational readiness inspection
OTC—Officer in tactical command
PBR—Patrol boat, river
PC—Submarine chaser
PCE—Patrol craft escort
PCF—Patrol craft, fast
PCO—Prospective commanding officer
PEO—Prospective engineer officer
PG—Gunboat
PGM—Gunboat, motor
PJ—U.S. Air Force pararescue specialist
PO—Petty officer
POL—Petroleum, oil, lubricants
POW—Prisoner of war
PS&WD—Port Security and Waterways Detail, Coast Guard
PSYOPS—Psychological operations
PT—Torpedo boat, motor
PTF—Patrol boat, fast
QMOW—Quartermaster of the watch
R&A—Rescue and assistance
RAG—River assault group
RATT—Radio teletype
Rear Adm.—Rear admiral (0-7)
RF/PF—Regional force/provisional force, Vietnam
RPG—Rocket propelled grenade
R&R—Rest and recreation
RSSZ—Rung Sat Special Zone
RVN—Republic of Vietnam (South Vietnam)
RVNAF—Republic of Vietnam Armed Forces
SAC—Strategic air command
Sandy—Close support aircraft
SAR—Search and rescue
SCATTOR—Small craft assets, training and turnover of resources
SCGOV—Senior Coast Guard officer Vietnam
SEA LORDS—Southeast Asia lake, ocean, river, and delta strategy
SEAL—Sea, air, and land (U.S. Navy special forces)
SEASEC—Coast Guard southeast Asia section
SECDEF—Secretary of defense
SERE—Survival, escape, resistance, and evasion

SITREP—Situation report
SLF—Marines special landing force
SN—Seaman
SS—Subsistence specialist
STR—Standard training requirement
SVN—South Vietnam
Swift—U.S. Navy patrol craft, fast
TAD—Temporary additional duty
TAG—Technical assistance group
Tight Reign—Coast Guard southeast Asia LORAN chain
UCMJ—Uniform Code of Military Justice
UDT—Underwater demolition team
UNREP—Underway replenishment
USA—U.S. Army
USAF—U.S. Air Force
USAID—U.S. Agency for International Development
USARV—U.S. Army, Vietnam
USCG—U.S. Coast Guard
USCGC—U.S. Coast Guard cutter
USMC—U.S. Marine Corps
USN—U.S. Navy
USS—United States ship
VANS—Vietnamization of aids to navigation system
VC—Viet Cong
VECTOR—Vietnamese engineering capability, training of ratings
VHF—Very high frequency
Vice Adm.—Vice Admiral (0-9)
VNAF—Vietnamese Air Force
VNMC—Vietnamese Marine Corps
VNN—Vietnamese Navy
VOA—Voice of America
WAK—U.S. Coast Guard cargo ship
WHEC—U.S. Coast Guard high endurance cutter
WLB—U.S. Coast Guard buoy tender, seagoing
WMEC—U.S. Coast Guard medium endurance cutter
WP—White phosphorus
WPB—U.S. Coast Guard patrol boat

WSO—Air Force weapons systems officer
XO—Executive officer
YFHB—Storage barge, large
YNC—Chief yeoman
YR—Floating workshop (non-self propelled)

Bibliography

Books

Barrett, David M. *Uncertain Warriors: Lyndon Johnson and His Vietnam Advisors.* Lawrence, Kans.: University Press of Kansas, 1993.

Bender, Chester R. *The Reminiscences of Admiral Chester R. Bender, USCG, Ret.* Annapolis, Md.: U.S. Naval Institute, 1979.

Bowman, John S., ed. *The World Almanac of the Vietnam War.* New York: Bison Books, 1985.

Chinnery, Philip. *Vietnam: The Helicopter War.* Annapolis, Md.: Naval Institute Press, 1991.

Croizat, Victor. *The Brown Water Navy: The River and Coastal War in Indo China and Vietnam, 1948–1972.* Dorset, United Kingdom: Blandford Press, 1984.

Cutler, Thomas J. *Brown Water, Black Berets: Coastal and Riverine Warfare in Vietnam.* Annapolis, Md.: Naval Institute Press, 1988.

Gregory, Barry. *Vietnam Coastal and Riverine Forces Handbook.* Northamptonshire, United Kingdom: Patrick Stephens, 1988.

Gurney, Gene. *The United States Coast Guard: A Pictorial History.* New York: Crown Publishers, 1973.

Hooper, Edwin B., et al. *U.S. Navy and the Vietnam Conflict.* Vol. I, *Setting of the Stage.* Washington, D.C.: U.S. Government Printing Office, 1987.

Johnson, Lyndon B. *The Vantage Point: Perspectives of the Presidency, 1963–1969.* New York: Holt, Rinehart, and Winston, 1971.

Johnson, Robert Erwin. *Guardians of the Sea: A History of the U.S. Coast Guard, 1915 to the Present.* Annapolis, Md.: Naval Institute Press, 1987.

Kaplan, Hyman R., and James F. Hunt. *This Is the Coast Guard.* Cambridge, Md.: Cornell Maritime Press, 1972.

Karnow, Stanley. *Vietnam: A History.* New York: Viking Press, 1983.

Marolda, Edward J., and Oscar P. Fitzgerald. *The United States Navy and the Vietnam Conflict.* Vol. 2, *From Military Assistance to Combat, 1959–1965.* Washington, D.C.: Navy Historical Center, 1986.

Marolda, Edward J., and G. Wesley Price III. *A Short History of the United States Navy and the Southeast Asia Conflict, 1950–1975.* Washington, D.C.: Navy Historical Center, 1984.

McNamara, Robert S. *The Essence of Security: Reflections in the Office.* New York: Harper and Row, 1968.

Mersky, Peter B., and Norman Polmar. *The Naval Air War in Vietnam*. Annapolis, Md.: Nautical and Aviation Publishing Co., 1981.

Mesko, Jim. *Riverine: A Pictorial History of the Brown Water War in Vietnam*. Carrollton, Tex.: Squadron/Signal Publications, 1985.

Momyer, William W. *Airpower in Three Wars*. Washington, D.C.: Department of the Air Force, 1978.

Olson, James S., ed. *Dictionary of the Vietnam War*. New York: Greenwood Press, 1988.

Riverine Warfare, the U.S. Navy Operations on Inland Waterways. Washington, D.C.: Navy Historical Center, Navy Department, 1969.

Roland, Edwin J. *The Reminiscences of Admiral Edwin J. Roland, USCG, Ret*. Annapolis, Md.: U.S. Naval Institute, 1977.

Rowe, John S., and Samuel L. Morison. *The Ships and Aircraft of the U.S. Fleet*. Annapolis, Md.: Naval Institute Press, 1972.

Scheina, Robert L. *U.S. Coast Guard Cutters and Craft, 1946–1990*. Annapolis, Md.: Naval Institute Press, 1990.

Schreadley, R. L. *From the Rivers to the Sea: The U.S. Navy in Vietnam*. Annapolis, Md.: Naval Institute Press, 1993.

Sharp, U.S.G. *Strategy for Defeat: Vietnam in Retrospect*. San Rafael, Calif.: Presidio Press, 1978.

Sheehan, Neil. *The Arnheiter Affair*. New York: Dell Publishing Co., 1973.

_____. *A Bright Shining Lie: John Paul Vann and America on Vietnam*. New York: Random House, 1988.

Smith, Willard J. *Reminiscences of Admiral Willard J. Smith, USCG, Ret*. Annapolis, Md.: U.S. Naval Institute, 1978.

Taylor, John W. R., ed. *Jane's All the World's Aircraft*. New York: McGraw-Hill, 1971.

Tilford, Earl H., Jr. *Search and Rescue in Southeast Asia*. Washington, D.C.: Office of Air Force History, 1980.

Uhlig, Frank, Jr., ed. *Vietnam: The Naval Story*. Annapolis, Md.: Naval Institute Press, 1986.

Waterhouse, Charles. *Vietnam War Sketches From the Air, Land and Sea*. Tokyo: Charles E. Tuttle Co., 1970.

Zumwalt, Elmo R., Jr. *On Watch: A Memoir*. New York: New York Times Book Co., 1976.

Articles

Baldwin, Hanson W. "Spitkits in Tropic Seas." *Shipmate*, August-September 1966, 8–12.

Beiter, Richard H. "Life With Squadron Three." *U.S. Coast Guard Academy Alumni Association Bulletin*, November-December 1968, 13–19.

Beran, A. Bruce. "Project Combat Aid." *Coast Guard Engineering Digest*, January-March 1971, 20–23.

"Captured Trawler an Arsenal." *Our Navy*, September 1967, 30.

"Coast Guard Squadron One Information Bulletin." *Commandant's Bulletin*, 28 August 1965.

"Coast Guard Squadron One Information Bulletin." *Commandant's Bulletin*, 3 December 1965.

"Coast Guard Squadron One Information Bulletin." *Commandant's Bulletin*, 25 March 1966.

"Coast Guard Squadron One." *Navy*, August 1965, 14–16.

"Coast Patrol in Viet Nam Far From Jersey Routine." *Commandant's Bulletin*, 11 March 1966.

Ebersole, J. F. "Skimmer Ops." U.S. Naval Institute *Proceedings*, July 1974, 41–46.

"Eighty Tons of Vietcong Arms From Hanoi Captured on Beach." *The New York Times*, 21 February 1965, 2.

"Fighting Boats of the U.S." *Naval Review*, 1968, 296–329.

"First Sinking." *Our Navy*, April 1966, 32.

"Floating Island." *Newsweek*, 8 March 1965, 36–37.

Gammell, Clark M. "Naval and Maritime Events, 1 July 1966–30 June 1967." *Naval Review*, 1968, 239–72.

Gonzales, Arturo F., Jr. "Battling Bloodhounds of the South China Sea." *Saga*, February 1968, 8–11, 74–76, 78.

Harris, William R. "Market Time Mother Ship." U.S. Naval Institute *Proceedings*, December 1966, 148–51.

Hodgman, James A. "Market Time in the Gulf of Thailand." *Naval Review*, 1968, 36–67.

Judd, Ralph W. "The LORAN Station on Con Son Island Was One of Many U.S. Coast Guard Contributions to the Vietnam War." *Vietnam*, April 1990, 10, 58, 59.

_____. "Tight Reign Happenings." *U.S. Coast Guard Academy Alumni Association Bulletin*, November-December 1967, 346–59.

Kaplan, Hyman R. "The Coast Guard's Other War in Vietnam." *Defense Transportation Journal*, July-August 1968, 22–27.

_____. "Coast Guard Played Vital Role in Vietnam War." *Navy: The Magazine of Seapower*, November 1970, 31–34.

_____. "Coast Guard in Vietnam." *The World Wars Officer Review*, September-October 1967, 8–13.

Kendall, Lane C. "U.S. Merchant Shipping and Vietnam." *Naval Review*, 1968, 129–47.

King, Herbert T. "Naval Logistic Support, Qui Nhon to Phu Quoc." *Naval Review*, 1969, 84–111.

Larzelere, Alexander R. "Viet Nam—A Day on Patrol." *USCG Academy Alumni Association Bulletin*, March-April 1967, 90–99.

Linnon, John L. "Aids to Navigation in Vietnam." U.S. Naval Institute *Proceedings*, December 1970, 99–100.

Lonsdale, Adrian L. "Fourth Coastal Zone, Vietnam." *U.S. Coast Guard Academy Alumni Association Bulletin*, November-December 1968, 20–24.

Miller, Richard T. "Fighting Boats of the United States." *Naval Review*, 1968, 297–329.

Moore, Thomas L. "Duty: Coastal Surveillance." *All Hands*, September 1965, 20–22.

Moreau, James W. "The Coast Guard in the Central and Western Pacific." *Naval Review*, May 1973, 286–95.

Moredock, W. J. "The DER in Market Time." U.S. Naval Institute *Proceedings*, February 1967, 136–38.

Morse, Richard M. "Underway Replenishment." *U.S. Coast Guard Academy Alumni Association Bulletin*, September-October 1967, 288–92.

Mumford, Robert E., Jr. "Jackstay: New Dimensions in Amphibious Warfare." *Naval Review*, 1968, 68–87.

Nelson, Robert T., and Douglas G. Currier. "Operation of Coast Guard Patrol Boats in Southeast Asia." *Naval Engineers Journal*, June 1966, 403–8.

Oliver, Edward F. "Coast Guard Shipping Advisory Unit Vietnam." *U.S. Coast Guard Academy Alumni Association Bulletin*, November-December 1968, 2–12.

_____. "The Largest Maritime Police Beat in the World." U.S. Naval Institute *Proceedings*, April 1970, 120–22.

"Operation Tight Reign Complete Success." *Commandant's Bulletin*, 6 January 1967.

Polmar, Norman. "The Sea and River War in Vietnam." *Navy*, July 1966, 236–37, 241.

Powell, David L. "The Last and Forgotten 100." *U.S. Coast Guard Academy Alumni Association Bulletin*, March-April 1972, 49–53.

Sargent, Thomas R., III. "Opinions and Commentary." *U.S. Coast Guard Academy Alumni Association Bulletin*, October 1994, 3.

Scheina, Robert L. "Coast Guard at War." *Commandant's Bulletin*, 13 February 1987, 14–39.

Schreadley, R. L. "The Naval War in Vietnam, 1950–1970." *Naval Review*, 1971, 180–209.

Sheehan, Neil. "Sea Watch for Foe Off Vietnam Long and Tedious." *The New York Times*, 12 July 1966.

Simmons, Edwin H. "Marine Corps Operations in Vietnam, 1965–1966." *Naval Review*, 1968, 3–35.

Sturm, Ted R. "Miracle Mission." *Airman*, August 1973, 43–47.
"The U.S. Public Health Service in South Vietnam." *The World Wars Officers Review*, September-October 1967, 14–17.
"U.S.-Vietnam Anti-Smuggling Patrol." *Navy*, August 1965, 22–25.
Wells, William R., III. "'Vietnamization' Sounded Good, But Turning Over U.S. Coast Guard Cutters Was Not an Easy Task." *Vietnam*, February 1994, 8, 67–70.
Whitehead, B. S., and Edward F. Oliver. "A Chain of Ships." U.S. Naval Institute *Proceedings*, November 1969, 92–107.

Public Documents

Principal sources for public documents and official records were: Vietnam collection at the U.S. Coast Guard historian, Washington, D.C.; and U.S. Navy Historical Center archives, Washington, D.C., filed under "Non-Navy—Coast Guard, CGACTV OPS and RON 3."

United States

Defense Department

Air Force. 40th ARRS Rescue Coordination Center, Royal Thai Air Force Base, Nakhon Phanom. "Mission 40–133, Summary of SAR Actions," 27 December 1972.
Air Force. 40th ARRS Rescue Coordination Center, Royal Thai Air Force Base, Nakhon Phanom. "Rescue Progress Reports 1 through 12 and Rescue Suspending Report," 24 December 1972–7 January 1973.
Air Force. "Memorandum of Agreement Between United States Air Force and United States Coast Guard Concerning an Exchange of Rescue and Recovery Officers." Signed by Adm. Willard J. Smith, USCG, on 14 March 1967, and by Gen. John P. McConnell, USAF, on 31 March 1967.
Air Force. Military Airlift Command. Gen. Howell M. Estes, Jr., letter to Adm. Willard J. Smith, Coast Guard commandant, 24 February 1969.
Armed Forces Information and Education. *The Evidence at Vung Ro Bay*. Pamphlet No. DoD GEN-16. Washington, D.C.: U.S. Government Printing Office, 1965.
Commander in Chief Pacific. "Coast Guard Explosive Handling Teams." Message 202237Z, 20 February 1966.
Commander in Chief Pacific. "SEASIA LORAN C." Message 010231Z, 1 November 1966.
Commander in Chief Pacific. "WHEC Transfer." Message 250328Z, 24 April 1972.

Joint Chiefs of Staff. "Attachment of Coast Guard Officer to MACV Staff." Message 152103Z, 15 December 1965.

Joint Chiefs of Staff. "Maritime Aids to Navigation in the Republic of Vietnam." Message 261931Z, 26 July 1968.

Military Assistance Command. Army Vietnam. First Logistical Command. "General Order 6417," 18 November 1966.

Military Assistance Command Vietnam. Army Vietnam. First Logistical Command. "Port Security and Waterways Detail Mission Statement," (undated).

Military Assistance Command Vietnam. Army Vietnam. First Logistical Command. "U.S. Coast Guard Port Security and Waterways Detail." Disposition Report, 28 November 1966.

Military Assistance Command Vietnam. Army Vietnam. Special Forces Detachment A-421. "Evaluation of Coast Guard Fire." Letter, (undated).

Military Assistance Command Vietnam. "Coast Guard Explosive Handling Teams." Message 170837Z, 17 February 1966.

Military Assistance Command Vietnam. "Coast Guard Port Security Team." Message 201310Z, 20 July 1966.

Military Assistance Command Vietnam. Naval Advisory Group. "Coast Guard Activities Vietnam, Operations, June-October 1965."

Military Assistance Command Vietnam. Naval Advisory Group. Coast Guard Squadron One. "Coast Guard Matters." Letter, 9 September 1965.

Military Assistance Command Vietnam. Naval Advisory Group. Coast Guard Squadron One. Division 11. "List of Events, Deployment to 31 December 1965," (undated).

Military Assistance Command Vietnam. Naval Advisory Group. Coast Guard Squadron One. Division 12. "Lt. Cdr. Knapp memo to Capt. Shepherd (NAG N-3)," 10 March 1966.

Military Assistance Command Vietnam. Naval Advisory Group. Coast Guard Squadron One. Division 13. USCGC *Point Partridge* (WPB 82305). "*Point Partridge* Junk Incident of 19 April." Letter, 21 April 1966.

Military Assistance Command Vietnam. Naval Advisory Group. Coast Guard Squadron One. Division 13. USCGC *Point White* (WPB 82308). "Situation Report One and Final, Junk Sinking." Message 092015Z, 9 March 1966.

Military Assistance Command Vietnam. Naval Advisory Group. Coast Guard Squadron One. "Letter to Commander, Western Area, regarding the action of the *Point White* in the sinking of a Viet Cong junk with 16 Viet Cong on board in Soi Rap River in March 1966," 14 March 1966.

Military Assistance Command Vietnam. Naval Advisory Group. Coast Guard Squadron One Liaison Officer. "Port Security." Message 120618Z, 12 August 1965.

Military Assistance Command Vietnam. Naval Advisory Group. Coast Guard Squadron One. "Squadron One Diaries," July 1965-March 1966.

Military Assistance Command Vietnam. Naval Advisory Group. Coast Guard Squadron One. "Squadron Organization; Recommendations Concerning." Letter, 23 June 1965.

Military Assistance Command Vietnam. Naval Advisory Group. "In Memoriam, Crew Members Swift Boat 4, PCF Division 101, U.S. Navy, Republic of Vietnam." Memorial Service Program. An Thoi, Vietnam, 14 February 1966.

Military Assistance Command Vietnam. Naval Advisory Group. "Monthly Historical Summaries," July 1965-March 1966.

Military Assistance Command Vietnam. Naval Advisory Group/Naval Forces Vietnam. Coast Guard Squadron One. Division 11. "Division 11 Diaries," July 1965-May 1969.

Military Assistance Command Vietnam. Naval Advisory Group/Naval Forces Vietnam. Coast Guard Squadron One. Division 12. "Division 12 Diaries," July 1965-March 1970.

Military Assistance Command Vietnam. Naval Advisory Group/Naval Forces Vietnam. Coast Guard Squadron One. Division 13. "Division 13 Diaries," December 1965-April 1969.

Military Assistance Command Vietnam. Naval Advisory Group. Operations Order CTF-115 201.YR.

Military Assistance Command Vietnam. Naval Forces Vietnam. "Coastal Surveillance Force." Letter, 28 September 1966.

Military Assistance Command Vietnam. Naval Forces Vietnam. Press Release No. 78–66, 15 August 1966.

Military Assistance Command Vietnam. Naval Forces Vietnam. Coast Guard Activities. "Instruction 4950.1—WPB Advisors," 14 May 1970.

Military Assistance Command Vietnam. Naval Forces Vietnam. Coast Guard Activities. Merchant Marine Detail Saigon. "Merchant Marine Detail, Saigon, Authority for; Mission of." Letter, 30 October 1972.

Military Assistance Command Vietnam. Naval Forces Vietnam. Coast Guard Activities. "Personnel Casualty Report." Message 130536Z, 13 June 1968.

Military Assistance Command Vietnam. Naval Forces Vietnam. Coast Guard Activities. "Remarks at Division 13 Change of Command," 31 May 1969.

Military Assistance Command Vietnam. Naval Forces Vietnam. Coast Guard Activities. "Report of Activity During Period 11–18 February 1968." Letter, 21 February 1968.

Military Assistance Command Vietnam. Naval Forces Vietnam. Coast Guard Activities. "U.S. Coast Guard Aviators Serving With Air Force in South Vietnam." Coast Guard press release, 18 October 1968.

Military Assistance Command Vietnam. Naval Forces Vietnam. Coast Guard Activities Vietnam. Aids to Navigation Detail. "Aids to Navigation Detail Diaries," December 1966-January 1973.

Military Assistance Command Vietnam. Naval Forces Vietnam. Coast Guard Activities Vietnam. Merchant Marine Detail. "Merchant Marine Detail Diaries," July 1968-April 1973.

Military Assistance Command Vietnam. Naval Forces Vietnam. Coast Guard Activities Vietnam. Port Security and Waterways Detail. "Port Security and Waterways Detail Diaries," October 1966-January 1973.

Military Assistance Command Vietnam. Naval Forces Vietnam. Coast Guard Activities Vietnam. Shipping Advisor. "Shipping Advisor Diaries," December 1966-June 1968.

Military Assistance Command Vietnam. Naval Forces Vietnam. Coast Guard Activities Vietnam and Squadron One. "Monthly Summary Reports," January 1967-August 1970.

Military Assistance Command Vietnam. Naval Forces Vietnam. Coast Guard Squadron One. "Debriefing Report of Lt. (jg) B. F. Thomson III, Commanding Officer, USCGC *Point Slocum*, Covering 20D2 (Trawler) Incident of 20 June 1966," 24 June 1966.

Military Assistance Command Vietnam. Naval Forces Vietnam. Coast Guard Squadron One. "Debriefing Report of Lt. (jg) Stephen T. Ulmer, Commanding Officer, USCGC *Point League*, Covering 20D2 (Trawler) Incident of 20 June 1966," 24 June 1966.

Military Assistance Command Vietnam. Naval Forces Vietnam. Coast Guard Squadron One. Division 12. "Trawler 29 B-2; combat operation after-action report; inner blockade unit." Letter, 8 March 1968.

Military Assistance Command Vietnam. Naval Forces Vietnam. Coast Guard Squadron One. Division 12. USCGC *Point Caution* (WPB 82301). "Summary of Events, 11 August 1966." Letter, 12 August 1966.

Military Assistance Command Vietnam. Naval Forces Vietnam. Coast Guard Squadron One. Division 13. "Monthly Summary Reports," May 1969-August 1970.

Military Assistance Command Vietnam. Naval Forces Vietnam. Coast Guard Squadron One. "Lieutenant (jg) Carr—Narrative of Cua Viet LST Ramp Ammo Fire," (undated).

Military Assistance Command Vietnam. Naval Forces Vietnam. Coast Guard Squadron One. Lt. Alexander R. Larzelere. "Market Time—August 1965: A Resumé of Coast Guard Patrol Boat Activity," 16 September 1965.

Military Assistance Command Vietnam. Naval Forces Vietnam. Coast Guard Squadron One. Port Security and Waterways Detail. "Security Recommendations for Newport." Letter, 29 October 1966.

Military Assistance Command Vietnam. Naval Forces Vietnam. Coast Guard Squadron One. "Squadron One Diaries," April-December 1966.

Military Assistance Command Vietnam. Naval Forces Vietnam. Coast Guard Squadron One. USCGC *Point Arden* (WPB 82309). "Damage incurred by *Point Arden* on 10 March 1968; report of." Letter, 13 March 1968.

Military Assistance Command Vietnam. Naval Forces Vietnam. "Monthly Historical Summaries," April 1966-August 1970.

Military Assistance Command Vietnam. Naval Forces Vietnam. Naval Support Activity Saigon. "Fire Aboard *Jennings County.*" Message 080402Z, 8 August 1970.

Military Assistance Command Vietnam. Naval Forces Vietnam. "Request for Turnover of Two Coast Guard WHECs to the Vietnamese Navy." Letter, 21 June 1969.

Military Assistance Command Vietnam. Naval Forces Vietnam. Senior Coast Guard Officer Vietnam. "Coast Guard ATON Operations in Vietnam." Message 011430Z, 1 March 1972.

Military Assistance Command Vietnam. Naval Forces Vietnam. Senior Coast Guard Officer Vietnam. "Last Coast Guard Operating Unit in Vietnam Disestablished." Coast Guard news release, 31 January 1972.

Military Assistance Command Vietnam. Naval Forces Vietnam. Senior Coast Guard Officer Vietnam. "Monthly Summary Reports," September 1970-February 1973.

Military Assistance Command Vietnam. Naval Forces Vietnam. Senior Coast Guard Officer Vietnam. "USCGC *Basswood* Departs Vietnam." Message 031033Z, 3 May 1972.

Military Assistance Command Vietnam. Naval Forces Vietnam. Support Activity, Danang. "Coast Guard Explosive Cargo Inspection and Advisory Team." Message 311013Z, 31 August 1967.

Military Assistance Command Vietnam. Naval Forces Vietnam. Task Element 194.5.4.9. "Market Time Spot Report." Message 052040Z, 5 May 1969.

Military Assistance Command Vietnam. Naval Forces Vietnam. "Trawler Caught in Infiltration Attempt by Market Time Units." Press release no. 30–66, 11 May 1966.

Military Assistance Command Vietnam. Naval Forces Vietnam. USS *Jennings County* (LST 846). "Fire in Engineering Spaces." Message 031730Z, 3 August 1970.

Military Assistance Command Vietnam. "Port Security Saigon Harbor." Message 041003Z, 4 August 1965.

Military Assistance Command Vietnam. "Vietnamization of Aids to Navigation System (VANS) Staff Study." Letter, 12 June 1970.

Navy. Chief of Naval Operations. "Additional Coast Guard Cutters for Assignment with U.S. Naval Forces in South Vietnam." Memorandum for the Secretary of the Navy, 8 March 1967.

Navy. Chief of Naval Operations. "Game Warden Patrol Operations." Message 152108Z, 15 May 1967.

Navy. Chief of Naval Operations. "Turnover of Two Additional WHECs to VNN." Message 292044Z, 29 June 1971.

Navy. Commander in Chief Pacific Fleet. "Provision of U.S. Coast Guard Boats." Message 252231Z, 25 April 1965.

Navy. Military Sea Transportation Service, Far East Area. "U.S. Coast Guard Hearing Officer, Request for Assignment of." Letter, 31 August 1966.

Navy. Secretary. "Additional High Endurance Cutters for Assignment with U.S. Naval Forces in South Vietnam." Memorandum for the Secretary of Defense, 10 March 1967.

Navy. Secretary. Paul H. Nitze, letter to Treasury Secretary Henry H. Fowler, 16 April 1965.

Navy and Treasury Departments. "Agreement Between the Department of the Navy and the United States Coast Guard." Signed by Navy, 2 July 1965, and by Coast Guard, 8 July 1965.

Secretary Robert S. McNamara. Memorandum for the President, 29 April 1965. Jointly signed by Treasury Secretary Henry H. Fowler. Letter initialed by President Lyndon B. Johnson, 29 April 1965.

State Department

Saigon Embassy. Consular Section. "UCMJ—Application to Seamen." Memorandum, 6 December 1966.

Treasury Department

Coast Guard. "Coast Guard Squadron Three Units Help Destroy Enemy Infiltrators." *Coast Guard Feature*, press release no. 23–68, 14 March 1968.

Coast Guard. Commandant. "Establish Coast Guard Activities Vietnam." Operation Change Order No. 75-67, 11 January 1967.

Coast Guard. Commandant. "WHEC Deployment to South Vietnam Market Time Forces." Message 102226Z, March 1967.

Coast Guard. Construction Detachment. "Proposed Article for *Commandant's Bulletin* (Project Tight Reign)." Letter, 2 May 1966.

Coast Guard. Construction Detachment. "Tight Reign I Resident Engineer; designation of." Letter, 28 March 1966.

Coast Guard. Fourteenth District. USCGC *Planetree* (WLB 307). "Vietnam Cruise Report," 21 July 1966.

Coast Guard. Historian. "Operation Tight Reign." Summary, (undated).

Coast Guard. Liaison to the Chief of Naval Operations. "Deployment of Five Coast Guard HECs to Market Time Operations." Memorandum for the Record, 22 March 1967.

Transportation Department

Coast Guard. "California Coast Guardsman Awarded Silver Star Medal." Coast Guard news release no. VN 96–69, 2 August 1969.

Coast Guard. Commandant. "ACTION—Turnover of Two High-Endurance Cutters to the Vietnamese Navy." Letter, 22 September 1971.

Coast Guard. Commandant. "Game Warden Patrol Operations." Message 162055Z, 16 May 1967.

Coast Guard. Commandant. Office of Operations. Law Enforcement Division. "Item for *Commandant's Bulletin*." Memorandum, 27 March 1969.

Coast Guard. Fifth District. "Coast Guard Squadron Two." Message 091419Z, 9 March 1972.

Coast Guard. Fourteenth District. "National Defense Transportation Association Award Nomination." Letter, 12 May 1971.

Coast Guard. Fourteenth District. "Termination of USCG ATON Operations in Republic of Vietnam." Message 040055Z, 3 March 1972.

Coast Guard. "Operating Facility Change Order (OFCO) No. 62–73," 22 January 1973.

Coast Guard. "Operating Plan Change Order (OPCO) No. 61–73," 22 January 1973.

Coast Guard. Southeast Asia Section. "The End of an Era of U.S. Coast Guard Operations." Teletype transcript, (undated).

Coast Guard. Southeast Asia Section. LORAN station Con Son. "General Information Book," August 1971.

Coast Guard. Squadron Three. "Lessons Learned by Squadron Three Cutters," 1 April 1969.

Coast Guard. Squadron Three. "Monthly Summary Report of War Operations," May 1967-January 1972.

Coast Guard. Squadron Three. "NGFS Incident in Song Ong Doc Area on 18 May 1970; investigation of," 25 May 1970.

Coast Guard. Squadron Three. USCGC *Bering Strait* (WHEC 382). "Monthly Summary Reports of War Operations," June-December 1970.

Coast Guard. Squadron Three. USCGC *Cook Inlet* (WHEC 384). "Monthly Summary Reports of War Operations," September-December 1971.

Coast Guard. Squadron Three. USCGC *Rush* (WHEC 723). "Action Report Infiltration Trawler SL-3–70, Infiltration Attempt, 17–22 November 1970," 1 December 1970.

Coast Guard. Squadron Three. USCGC *Rush* (WHEC 723). "Vietnam Cruise Book," 1971.

Coast Guard. Squadron Three. USCGC *Yakutat* (WHEC 380). "Administrative Remarks, Page 7—John C. Miller, Jr.," 28 August-9 November 1970.

Coast Guard. Squadron Three. USCGC *Yakutat* (WHEC 380). "Monthly Summary Reports of War Operations," June-December 1970.

Coast Guard. Squadron Three. *U.S. Coast Guard Squadron Three.* Subic Bay, Philippines: USCG Squadron Three, 1972.

Coast Guard. *United States Coast Guard Annotated Bibliography.* Washington, D.C.: U.S. Department of Transportation, 1982.

Coast Guard. USCGC *Blackhaw* (WLB 390). "News release (draft)," 1971.

Coast Guard. USCGC *Blackhaw* (WLB 390). "Qui Nhon Navaids." Message 101135Z, 10 May 1971.

Coast Guard. Western Area. "Explosive Loading Detachments for Vietnam; requirements for." Letter, 13 June 1967.

Coast Guard. "Yered Interview." *Coast Guard Feature,* release no. VN7-68-1, 25 March 1968.

Kaplan, Hyman R. *Coast Guard in Vietnam.* Washington, D.C.: U.S. Coast Guard Public Information Division, 1971.

Scotti, Paul W. "Fact Sheet, the U.S. Coast Guard in Vietnam—Chronology, Units, and Statistics," 1985.

Tulich, Eugene N. *The United States Coast Guard in Southeast Asia During the Vietnam Conflict.* Washington, D.C.: U.S. Coast Guard Public Affairs Division, 1986.

Republic of Vietnam

Navy. "Ceremony for the Transfer of USCGC *Point Garnet* and USCGC *Point League* to the Vietnamese Navy," 16 May 1969.

Navy. Fourth Coastal Zone. "Operation Order," 4 April 1966.

Navy. "Turnover Ceremony Program," 1 January 1971. USCGC *Yakutat* (WHEC 380) and USCGC *Bering Strait* (WHEC 382) transferred to the Vietnamese navy.

Unpublished Material

Crowe, Joseph L. Letter to Adm. J. W. Moreau, USCG, concerning duty with 37th ARRS, 27 April 1973.

Eagan, Lance A. "Statement Concerning the Conspicuous Gallantry of A1C Joel E. Talley, USAF, in North Vietnam on 2 July 1968."

SS *Longview Victory.* "Master's Storage Evaluation Report, Voyage Commencing 22 March 1967," 23 April 1967.

SS *North Platte Victory.* "Master's Voyage Report," 21 May 1967.

Uithol, Jon C. "*Point Clear,* Captain's Journal." Personal File, 1965.

Ulmer, Steven T. "Account of events on 20 June 1966, Republic of Vietnam," 4 April 1983.

Author's Tape-recorded Interviews

Allen, Capt. Thad W., USCG, 1 August 1995. Commanding officer Coast Guard LORAN station, Lampang, Thailand, 1974–75.

Angelico, Cdr. Joseph F., USCG (Ret.), 5 April 1995. Commanding officer USCGC *Point Jefferson* (WPB 82304) and *Point Marone* (WPB 82331), 1969–70.

Bartlett, Capt. Walter F., USCG (Ret.), 3 May 1995. Commanding officer USCGC *Yakutat* (WHEC 380), 1969–70, and chief staff officer, Squadron Three, 1971.

Bauman, Rear Adm. Richard A., USCG (Ret.), 18 July 1994. Commander Coast Guard Division 12 and chief staff officer Squadron One, 1967–68.

Bell, Capt. Ross, USCG (Ret.), 8 June 1993. Executive officer USCGC *Point Welcome* (WPB 82329), 1966.

Berry, Master Chief Boatswain's Mate J. William, USCG (Ret.), 9 August 1994. Explosive loading detachment 1, 1967–68.

Brock, Cdr. Harold R., USCG (Ret.), 18 January 1995. Operation Tight Reign planning group and commander, USCG construction detachment, 1965–66.

Busavage, Capt. John G., USCG (Ret.), 3 February 1994. Commanding officer USCGC *Point Comfort* (WPB 82317) and Division 13 operations officer and chief staff officer, 1968–69.

Carr, William C., 23 December 1993. Commanding officer USCGC *Point Arden* (WPB 82309), 1967–68.

Case, Capt. Edmond G., USCG (Ret.), 8 May 1995. Executive officer USCGC *Castle Rock* (WHEC 383), 1971, and commanding officer USCGC *Point Arden* (WPB 82309), 1965–66.

Cass, Capt. William F., USCG (Ret.), 19 April 1993. Assistant chief of operations for roles and missions, Coast Guard headquarters, 1965.

Causey, CWO (W-2) George T., USCG (Ret.), 10 February 1994. Chief engineman aboard USCGC *Point Young* (WPB 82303) and Squadron One engineer officer, 1965–66.

Cece, Capt. John M., USCGR (Ret.), 21 December 1993. Commanding officer USCGC *Point Orient* (WPB 82319), 1965, and Division 12 chief staff officer, 1966.

Creech, Capt. Jay A., USCG, 5 July 1991 and 13 July 1995. Watch officer, USCGC *Mendota* (WHEC 69), 1969. Officer in charge explosive loading detachment 1 and advisor to ARVN ordnance command office, 1972–73.

Crowe, Capt. Joseph L., USCG (Ret.), March 8, 1993. Aviator 37th ARRS, 1971–72.

Crowell, Capt. Everett L., USCG (Ret.), 19 January and 2 February 1995. Operation Tight Reign working group, Tight Reign I resident engineer at Lampang and contracting officer's representative, 1965-66.

Duffin, Paul M., 12 May 1995. Third-class yeoman aboard USCGC *Cook Inlet* (WHEC 384), 1969-70.

Durfey, Rear Adm. Robert W., USCG (Ret.), 29 March 1992. Commanding officer, USCGC *Rush* (WHEC 723), 1970-71.

Eagan, Capt. Lance A., USCG (Ret.), 28 July 1993. Aviator 37th ARRS, 1968-69.

Erlandson, Cdr. Dennis R., USCG (Ret.), 6 June 1995. Commanding officer USCG LORAN station, Tan My, Vietnam, 1972-73.

Foskey, Preston L., 5 April 1995. Commanding officer USCGC *Point Lomas* (WPB 82321), 1969-70.

Freeborn, Capt. David H., USCG (Ret.), 20 February 1995. Aids to navigation coordinator, Coast Guard Activities Vietnam, 1967-68.

Frischmann, Cdr. Thomas F., USCG (Ret.), 11 March 1993. Aviator 31st ARRS 1968-70.

Gilbert, Rear Adm. Marshall E., USCG (Ret.), 1 February 1994. Division 13 operations officer and chief staff officer, Division 11 operations officer and spare boat commanding officer, 1965-66.

Hanson, Capt. Harlan D., USCG (Ret.), 11 May 1994. Chief staff officer, Division 12, commanding officer USCGC *Point Orient* (WPB 82319), and Coast Guard liaison officer to naval advisory group, Saigon, 1965-66.

Hathaway, Capt. Charles B., USCG (Ret.), 6 June 1994. Chief staff officer, Coast Guard Activities Vietnam and Squadron One, 1967-68.

Hayes, Adm. John B., USCG (Ret.), 15 November 1993. Commander Division 11, commander Gulf of Thailand surveillance group, and senior naval advisor to the 4th coastal zone commander, 1966-67.

Hemstreet, Capt. Edward A., USCG (Ret.), 24 July 1995. Chief civil engineering division, Coast Guard Southeast Asia section, Bangkok, Thailand, 1974-75.

Henneberry, Capt. Paul D., USCG (Ret.), 9 May 1995. Commanding officer USCGC *Bering Strait* (WHEC 382), 1970.

Herbert, CWO (W-3) Baker W., USCG (Ret.), 29 October 1994. Contracting officer, certifying officer, and agent cashier for Operation Tight Reign, 1966.

Hertica, Capt. Raymond C., USCG (Ret.), 1 September 1994. Officer in charge port security and waterways detail, 1966-67.

Hickey, Capt. Eugene J., Jr., USCG (Ret.), 12 February 1994. Commanding officer USCGC *Point Welcome* (WPB 82329), commanding officer USCGC *Point White* (WPB 82308), and chief staff officer Division 13, 1965-66.

Hodgman, Capt. James A., USCG (Ret.), 19 April 1993. Commander Division 11, commander Gulf of Thailand surveillance group, and senior naval advisor to the 4th coastal zone commander, 1965-66.

Kies, Capt. Phillip J., USCG (Ret.), 19 June 1995. Chief electronics division, Southeast Asia section, Bangkok, Thailand, 1971–73.

Kinkade, Chief Boatswain's Mate Ronald W., USCG (Ret.), 25 July 1994. Explosive loading detachment 1, 1968–69.

Knapp, Rear Adm. Richard J., USCG (Ret.), 23 November 1993. Commander Division 12, 1965–66.

Lehr, Capt. William E., USCG (Ret.), 1 July 1993. Engineer officer Squadron One, commander Division 13, and chief staff officer and repair officer Squadron One, 1965–66.

Long, Cdr. Robert E., USCG (Ret.), 7 June 1995. Aviator 37th and 40th ARRS, 1972–73.

Lonsdale, Capt. Adrian L., USCG (Ret.), 31 July 1993 and 10 May 1994. Commander Gulf of Thailand surveillance group and senior naval advisor to the 4th coastal zone commander, 1968–69.

Loomis, Lt. Cdr. James M., USCG (Ret.), 11 March 1993. Aviator 37th ARRS, 1969–70.

Lynch, Capt. Herbert J., USCG (Ret.), 28 March 1993. Commanding officer, USCGC *Winona* (WHEC 650), 1968.

Matilla, Capt. Risto A., USCG (Ret.), 6 July 1994. Naval advisory group, port security survey, 1965–66.

McCurry, Master Chief Electronics Technician Paul C., USCG (Ret.), 28 July 1995. Southeast Asia section, Bangkok, Thailand, 1966–69 and 1974–75.

Mense, Cdr. Louis H., USCG (Ret.), 23 April 1993. Chief enlisted assignment branch, enlisted personnel division, office of personnel, USCG headquarters, 1965.

Miller, John C., Jr., 10 May 1995. Second-class boatswain's mate USCGC *Yakutat* (WHEC 380), 1969–70.

Miller, Master Chief Boatswain's Mate William J., USCG (Ret.), 2 February 1994. Second-class boatswain's mate USCGC *Point Partridge* (WPB 82305) and USCGC *Point Slocum* (WPB 82313), 1967–68.

Mosher, Lt. Cdr. Charles B., USCG (Ret.), 12 October 1993. Commanding officer USCGC *Point Grey* (WPB 82324), 1966–67.

Nelson, Vice Adm. Robert T., USCG, 9 October 1993. Commanding officer USCGC *Point Glover* (WPB 82307), 1965–66.

Newman, Cdr. Dorwin W., USCG (Ret.), 8 June 1995. Officer in charge, USCG merchant marine detail Saigon, Vietnam, 1972–73.

Niesz, Capt. Ralph W., USCG (Ret.), 11 April 1995. Commander Coast Guard Activities Vietnam and commander Squadron One, 1968–69.

O'Donnell, Capt. Eugene E., USCG (Ret.), 14 February 1995. Aids to navigation coordinator, Coast Guard Activities Vietnam, 1968–69.

O'Keefe, Cdr. Edward G., USCG (Ret.), 27 July 1994. Officer in charge explosive loading detachment 1, Nha Be, 1966–67.

Oliver, Capt. Edward F., USCG (Ret.), 20 September 1994. Coast Guard shipping advisor, 1966-67.

Purdy, Capt. Homer A., USCG (Ret.), 5 June 1995. Officer in charge Coast Guard port security and waterways detail, 1972-73.

Riutta, Rear Adm. Ernest R., USCG, 10 February 1995. Commanding officer, USCG LORAN station, Tan My, 1971-72.

Roland, Capt. William F., USCG (Ret.), 5 February 1995. Executive officer, USCG Southeast Asia section, 1966-68. Project officer, air transportable LORAN system (ATLS), 1968.

Rufe, Rear Adm. Roger T., USCG, 12 April 1995. Commanding officer USCGC *Point Garnet* (WPB 82310), 1968-69.

Sargent, Vice Adm. Thomas R., III, USCG (Ret.), 28 October 1994. Civil engineering division LORAN program coordinator and project officer, Operation Tight Reign, 1965-66.

Saunders, Rear Adm. Norman T., USCG, 14 December 1993. Commanding officer USCGC *Point Orient* (WPB 82319), 1967-68.

Scherer, Capt. Norman L., USCG (Ret.), 27 March 1993. Commanding officer, USCGC *Gresham* (WHEC 387), 1967-68.

Schneider, Cdr. Emanuel, USCG (Ret.), 5 July 1994. Officer in charge, port security and waterways detail, 1968-69.

Smith, Capt. Joseph F., USCG (Ret.), 7 July 1993. Commander Division 13, 1968-69.

Spence, Capt. John C., USCG (Ret.), 7 June 1993. Commander Division 11, 1968-69.

Thomson, Capt. Barham F., USCG (Ret.), 31 January 1994. Commanding officer USCGC *Point Slocum* (WPB 82313), 1966.

Tugman, Master Chief Boatswain's Mate William A., USCG (Ret.), 9 February 1994. Chief boatswain's mate, USCGC *Point Arden* (WPB 82309), 1968.

Uithol, Capt. Jon C., USCG (Ret.), 12 April 1994. Commanding officer USCGC *Point Clear* (WPB 82315), 1965-66.

Ulmer, Rev. Stephen T., 3 June 1993. Commanding officer USCGC *Point League* (WPB 82304), Division 13, executive officer USCGC *Point Gammon*, operations officer Division 12, 1965-66.

Underwood, Capt. Gerald L., USCG (Ret.), 22 February 1994. Commanding officer USCGC *Point Banks* (WPB 82327), 1968-69.

Venzke, Rear Adm. Norman C., USCG (Ret.), 31 July and 10 November 1993. Commander Gulf of Thailand surveillance group, commander Division 11, and senior naval advisor to the 4th coastal zone commander, 1967-68.

Volkle, Capt. Thomas G., USCG (Ret.), 8 June 1993. Commander Division 12, 1969-70.

Walden, Capt. Stanley J., USCG (Ret.), 22 April 1993. Officer assignment branch, USCG headquarters, 1965, and chief staff officer, Coast Guard Activities Vietnam, 1969–70.

Webber, WO (W-1) Bernard C., USCG (Ret.), 23 April 1993. Senior chief boatswain's mate, USCGC *Point Banks* (WPB 82327) and staff Division 12, 1965–66.

Wells, Master Chief Gunner's Mate William R., III, USCG (Ret.), 10 April 1995. First-class gunner's mate, USCGC *Point Dume* (WPB 82325), USCGC *Point Glover* (WPB 82307), and USCGC *Point Kennedy* (WPB 82320), 1969–70.

Willis, Capt. Gerald T., USCG, 2 August 1994. Officer in charge explosive loading detachment 2, Cam Rahn Bay, 1966–67.

Yost, Adm. Paul A., USCG (Ret.), 11 May 1994. Commander Gulf of Thailand surveillance group, senior naval advisor to the 4th coastal zone commander, commanding officer Sea Float, and commander task group 115.3, 1969–70.

Young, Capt. Glenn F., USCG (Ret.), 16 February and 9 March 1995. Commanding officer USCGC *Planetree* (WLB 307), 1965–66.

Index

Abrams, Creighton W., 229
Absecon (WHEC 374), 257
Accelerated Turnover to Vietnamese, 229
Advanced Tactical Support Base, 133, 241
Advisor, Fourth Coastal Zone
  coastal groups, 98
  Coastal Surveillance Center, 97, 98,
    102
  construction program, 97
  cultural differences, 99, 100, 102
  dangers, 99
  move ashore to An Thoi, 102
  personnel turnover, 98
  program objectives, 99, 100
Advisors, U.S. Navy, 5
Aerospace Rescue and Recovery Service
  Coast Guard–Air Force exchange
    program, 140-43
  need for rescue pilots, 140, 141
Aerospace Rescue and Recovery
  Squadron
  airborne rescue package, 142
  behind enemy lines recovery of
    strike pilots, 141, 145
  40th ARRS: Coast Guard pilots
    assigned, 267, 268; Detachment 1,
    clandestine operations, 146; "lima
    sites," 146; mission, 146; opera-
    tions center, 258; professionalism,
    267; training, 142
  rescue package, 147
  Royal Thai Air Force base, 241
  survival schools, 142
  tempo of operations, 244, 245
  31st ARRS, 143
  39th ARRS, 143
  37th ARRS: aircraft, 145; Coast
    Guard vehicle support, 268; duties,
    145, 147; facilities, 144; in-country
    orientation, 143, 144; organization,
    144, 145; personnel complement,
    145; rocket attacks at Danang, 267;

  tempo of operations, 147, 148, 267;
    transferred to Thailand, 267, 268
  training, 236, 237
  transition pilots, 146, 147
  volunteers, 236
Agana, Guam, 217
Aguilar, Gilbert, 262
Aids to navigation
  additional aids, 211
  advisors, 214-16
  aids to navigation coordinator, 217,
    218
  aids to navigation detail, 214, 215,
    218, 219
  aids to navigation study, 216
  aids to navigation team, 118, 120
  buoy tenders: buoys along DMZ, 221;
    deployments, 213, 214, 216, 217,
    219, 220, 223, 224; establishing and
    servicing aids, 217, 220-24; naval
    gunfire support buoy project, 223;
    replacing buoys with structures,
    224; setting tanker mooring
    assemblies, 209-11, 213, 214; sup-
    plies for ATON detail, 219; tender
    dedicated for Vietnam work, 219
  Coast Guard tasking, 209, 211, 212
  COMNAVFORV Aids to Navigation
    Advisor, 216, 218
  importance, 222
  increasing need, 211
  joint Army–Navy–Coast Guard Aids
    to Navigation agreement, 219
  military interdepartmental purchase
    request (MIPR), 219
  supplies, 212, 219, 220
  special projects, 220-23
  threats to aids, 222
Air America, 276, 277, 279
Airborne Mission Coordinator, 148
Aircraft, Air Force
  A-1E Skyraider, 138, 144, 148, 267

About the Author

Alex Larzelere served on seven USCG cutters, commanding five, and was the first Coast Guard Aide to the president (Nixon). He is a graduate of the USCG Academy, the National War College, and a Distinguished Graduate of the Naval War College. He holds a master's degree in International Affairs from George Washington University, and wrote *The 1980 Cuban Boatlift: Castro's Ploy—America's Dilemma* (NDU Press, 1988) while a research fellow at the National Defense University.

The **Naval Institute Press** is the book-publishing arm of the U.S. Naval Institute, a private, nonprofit, membership society for sea service professionals and others who share an interest in naval and maritime affairs. Established in 1873 at the U.S. Naval Academy in Annapolis, Maryland, where its offices remain today, the Naval Institute has members worldwide.

Members of the Naval Institute support the education programs of the society and receive the influential monthly magazine *Proceedings* and discounts on fine nautical prints and on ship and aircraft photos. They also have access to the transcripts of the Institute's Oral History Program and get discounted admission to any of the Institute-sponsored seminars offered around the country.

The Naval Institute also publishes *Naval History* magazine. This colorful bimonthly is filled with entertaining and thought-provoking articles, first-person reminiscences, and dramatic art and photography. Members receive a discount on *Naval History* subscriptions.

The Naval Institute's book-publishing program, begun in 1898 with basic guides to naval practices, has broadened its scope in recent years to include books of more general interest. Now the Naval Institute Press publishes about 100 titles each year, ranging from how-to books on boating and navigation to battle histories, biographies, ship and aircraft guides, and novels. Institute members receive discounts of 20 to 50 percent on the Press's nearly 600 books in print.

Full-time students are eligible for special half-price membership rates. Life memberships are also available.

For a free catalog describing Naval Institute Press books currently available, and for further information about subscribing to *Naval History* magazine or about joining the U.S. Naval Institute, please write to:

Membership Department
U.S. Naval Institute
118 Maryland Avenue
Annapolis, MD 21402-5035
Telephone: (800) 233-8764
Fax: (410) 269-7940
Web address: www.usni.org